Adver

APRIL	MAY	JUNE	JULY	AUGUST	SEPTEMBER

Ruined Lands of Oaxaca, Southern Mexico

Descending the main pyramid at Yaxhá, Guatemala

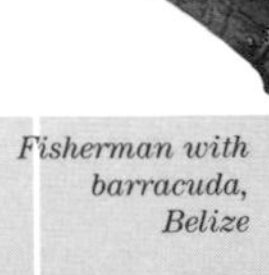

Fisherman with barracuda, Belize

Treasure Islands, Northern Coast

The Historic Río San Juan, Southern Nicaragua

*A keel-billed toucan (*Ramphastos sulfuratus)

Northern Exposure, Northern Costa Rica

Where Wild Things Go, Pacific Coast

Jungle Paddlers, Central Cordillera

Trail of the Turtle Catchers, Caribbean Coast

A Nicoyan Odyssey, Pacific Coast

ADVENTURE TRAVELLERS

CENTRAL AMERICA

Produced by AA Publishing

Coloured maps produced by the Cartographic Department,
The Automobile Association
Black and white maps produced by Advanced Illustration,
Congleton, Cheshire
A CIP catalogue record for this book is available from
the British Library
ISBN 0-7495-2319-0

The contents of this publication are believed correct at the time of printing. Nevertheless, the publishers cannot be held responsible for any errors or omissions or for changes in the details given in this guide or for the consequences of any reliance on the information provided by the same. Assessments of sights, accommodation, restaurants and so forth are based upon the authors' own experience and, therefore, descriptions given in this guide necessarily contain an element of subjective opinion which may not reflect the publisher's opinion or dictate a reader's own experience on another occasion.

We have tried to ensure accuracy in this guide, but things do change and we would be grateful if readers would advise us of any inaccuracies they may encounter.

The areas covered in this guide can be subject to political, economic, and climatic upheaval, readers should consult tour operators, embassies and consulates, airlines, e.t.c. for current requirements and advice before travelling. The publishers and authors cannot accept responsibility for any loss, injury, or inconvenience, however caused.

Published by AA Publishing, a trading name of Automobile Association Developments Limited, whose registered office is Norfolk House, Priestley Road, Basingstoke, Hampshire RG24 9NY.
Registered number 1878835.

Visit our website at www.theaa.co.uk

Colour separation by Chroma Graphics, Singapore
Printed and bound in Hong Kong by Dai Nippon

PREVIOUS PAGE: The easy route to the Mexican town of Satevo!
INSET: Canoeing on the Río Quehueche, Guatemala

CONTENTS

INTRODUCTION

A region of extremes, where old and new worlds collide, Central America appears as just a narrow strip of land between two massive continents, and yet is one of the most fascinating regions of the world. With landscape ranging from arid desert to dense teeming jungle: from violent erupting volcanoes to beautiful tropical beaches, there is every form of natural beauty here. The human experiences too are marked by extremes; dire poverty sits beside great wealth, modern industry beside jungle-covered ruins. Although Central America has a large and growing population and Mexico has the largest capital in the world, the region also has vast empty landscapes perfect for hikers, cavers, climbers, and horseback-riders. Raging rivers and coral bays are perfect for rafters, canoeists, scuba-divers, and sailors, while the 30,000 species of plant, 1,000 bird species and 450 mammal species make perfect surroundings for naturalists. Inhabited from at least 2000 B.C., flourishing civilizations have left their mark everywhere; the ruins of the great Mayan culture rise mysteriously from the deepest jungle—many still virtually inaccessible and some still awaiting discovery—and the lovely colonial towns, built by Spanish invaders, still provide welcome shade and hospitality in their plazas and cantinas. This, the most friendly of regions, is ideally suited to the more adventurous traveller.

RIGHT The tumbling cascades of Agua Azul, southern Mexico
ABOVE Inside Venado Cave, La Fortuna, Costa Rica

About the Authors

Fiona Dunlop

Fiona Dunlop's taste for the tropics, for ancient cultures and for developing countries has been tested to the full while writing travel books on Indonesia, Singapore and Malaysia, Vietnam, India, Costa Rica and Mexico. Before her immersion in this peripatetic lifestyle, she spent 15 years in Paris where she worked in, and wrote about, the arts for numerous art and interior design magazines. Now based in London, she continues to cover contemporary design between her travels. Her articles have appeared in the *Observer*, the *Sunday Times*, *The Times*, *Elle Decoration*, and *Homes & Gardens* amongst others.

Jane Egginton

Jane Egginton is a travel writer and researcher who writes magazine features as well as guide books. Jane has written for many publishers including

Reader's Digest and Thomas Cook, and was a winner in the *Observer* Young Travel Writer of the Year Award. Jane has travelled extensively throughout Britain, Asia, Australasia and the Americas, both for work and for pleasure. Central and South America remain favourite destinations both for their beautiful, varied landscapes and for the adventures and activities they offer. She is currently writing a guide book to Mexico.

Carl Pendle

Carl Pendle studied photography and creative writing whilst at university in America. After graduating, he returned home to England, first working as a newspaper photographer and then as a copywriter for an advertising agency. He's been a freelance travel writer and photographer since 1991 and has

recently become a member of the British Guild of Travel Writers. During his assignment in Central America, he braved hurricane Mitch in a single-engined plane in Nicaragua, so swimming with sharks in Belize was no problem. Carl's work has also appeared in *GQ*, *Active*, *Maxim*, *Washington Post* and the *Independent*.

Steve Watkins

Photographer and writer Steve Watkins specialises in covering adventure travel, extreme sports and cultural issues, especially if it involves his favourite destinations—

Latin America and Australia, where he lived for four years. His work has featured in numerous magazines, newspapers, books and corporate brochures, including *Wanderlust*, *Traveller*, *Travellers Handbook*, *No Limits World*, *Global Adventure*, *Mountain Biking UK*, and various BBC publications, and his photographs have been widely exhibited, including at London's Barbican gallery. He has recently finished writing *Adventure Sports Europe*, to be published by Queensgate Publishing in spring 2000. He is now based in South Wales.

How to Use this Book

The book is divided into three distinct sections:

SECTION 1 — PAGES 6–17

This comprises the introductory material and some general practical advice to guide you on your travels. We have included an introduction to the writing team. Our authors come from all walks of life and cover a wide age range. What they do have in common, though, is a spirit of adventure and a wealth of travel experience.

The map on pages 10–11 shows the areas covered, and is colour-coded to highlight the regional divides. The 25 adventures are numbered for reference; the contents page will guide you straight to the relevant page numbers.

Pages 12–13 and 16–17 offer practical advice from experienced travellers, complementing information given later.

The seasonal calendar on pages 14–15 gives a guide to the optimum time to visit the areas covered in the adventures. However, there are many factors affecting when you might like to go, and greater details of climate patterns and their effect on activities are given at the end of each chapter. When arranging your trip always seek advice about the conditions you are likely to encounter from a tour operator or country tourist information office.

SECTION 2 — PAGES 18–256

The main section of the book contains 25 adventures, chosen to give you a taste of a wide range of activities in a variety of places—some familiar, others not. The first page of each adventure carries a practical information box that gives you an idea of what to expect, plus a grade, numbered according to the relative difficulty of the activity or the level of skill required.

Going it Alone—Each adventure ends with a page of dedicated practical advice for planning that specific adventure yourself. This information should be used in conjunction with the "Blue Pages" at the end of the book (see below).

Any prices mentioned in the book are given in US$ and were the approximate prices current at the time of the trip. Due to variations in inflation and exchange rates these are only meant as guidelines to give an idea of comparative cost.

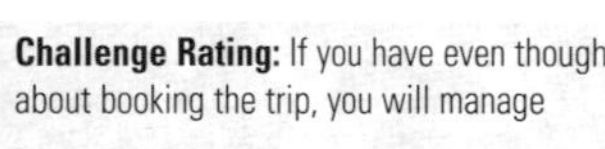

Challenge Rating: If you have even thought about booking the trip, you will manage

Not too difficult but you may need some basic skills

You will need to be fit, with lots of stamina and may need specialist qualifications

You need to be fit and determined—not for the faint-hearted*

This is for the serious adventurer—physically and mentally challenging!*

**Sometimes only part of the trip is very hard and there may be an easier option*

Comfort rating: Indicates the degree of hardship you can expect, where 1 is comfortable and 3 is uncomfortable. This category not only covers accommodation, but also factors such as climate and other conditions that may affect your journey.

Specialist equipment: Advice on any equipment needed for the journey, covering specialist items like diving gear, and also clothing and photographic gear.

SECTION 3 — PAGES 257–320

"Blue Pages"—*Contacts* and *A–Z of Activities*—begin with selected contacts specific to the 25 main adventures. Here you'll find names referred to in the main stories, including tour operators, with addresses and contact numbers.

The A–Z lists a wide range of the best activities available in the region, with general information and full contact details of the outfits and organizations able to help you plan your journey. Finally, the book ends with a comprehensive index and gazetteer.

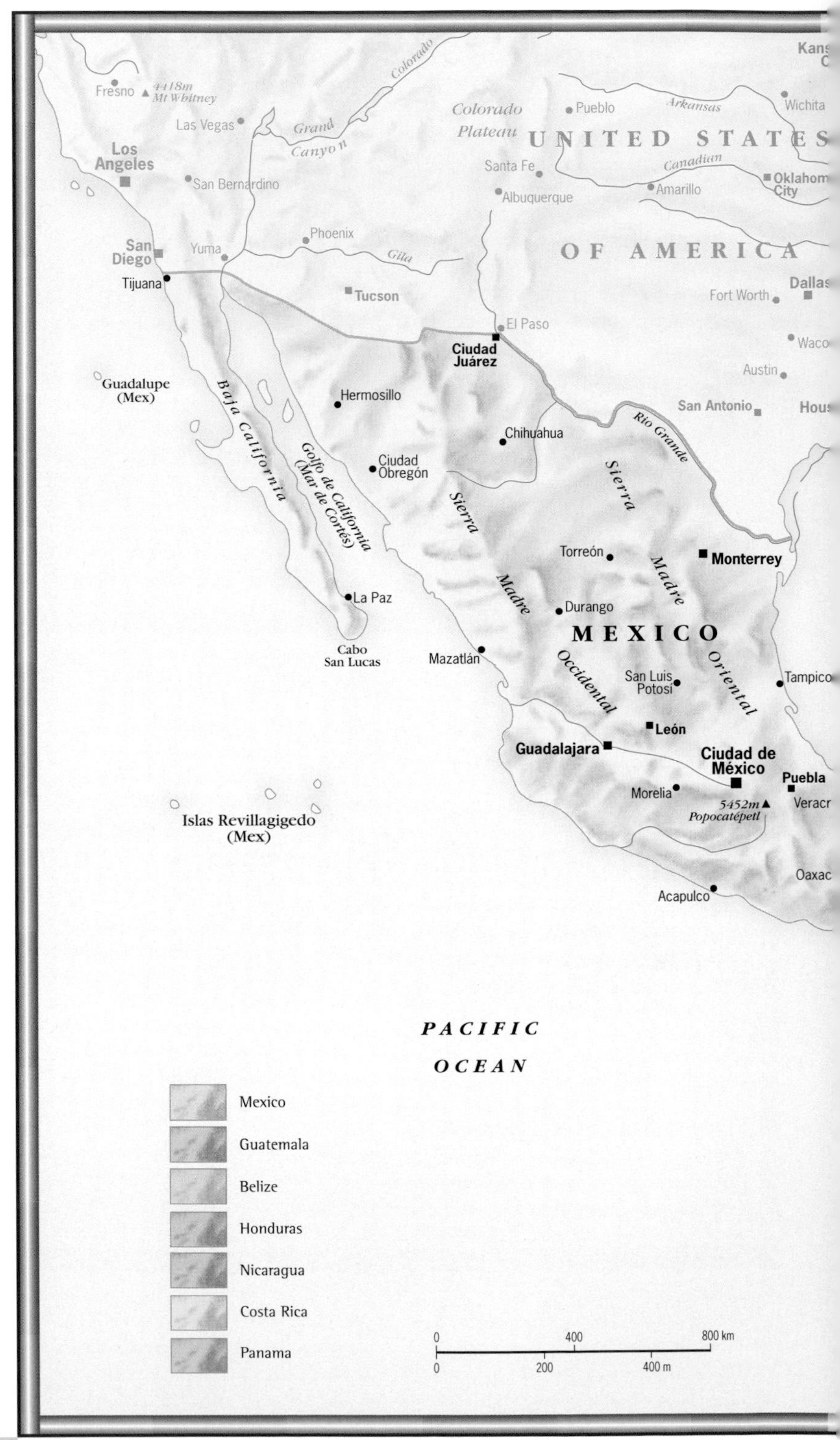
Fresno
4418m
Mt Whitney
Las Vegas
Los Angeles
San Bernardino
Colorado
Grand Canyon
Colorado Plateau
Pueblo
Arkansas
Wichita
UNITED STATES
Santa Fe
Canadian
Amarillo
Oklahoma City
Albuquerque
Phoenix
San Diego
Yuma
Gila
OF AMERICA
Tijuana
Tucson
Fort Worth
Dallas
El Paso
Ciudad Juárez
Waco
Austin
Guadalupe (Mex)
Baja California
Hermosillo
San Antonio
Chihuahua
Rio Grande
Golfo de California (Mar de Cortés)
Ciudad Obregón
Sierra
Sierra
Torreón
Monterrey
Madre
Madre
La Paz
Durango
MEXICO
Cabo San Lucas
Mazatlán
Occidental
Oriental
San Luis Potosí
Tampico
León
Guadalajara
Ciudad de México
Puebla
Morelia
5452m
Popocatépetl
Islas Revillagigedo (Mex)
Acapulco
PACIFIC OCEAN
Mexico
Guatemala
Belize
Honduras
Nicaragua
Costa Rica
Panama
0
400
800 km
0
200
400 m

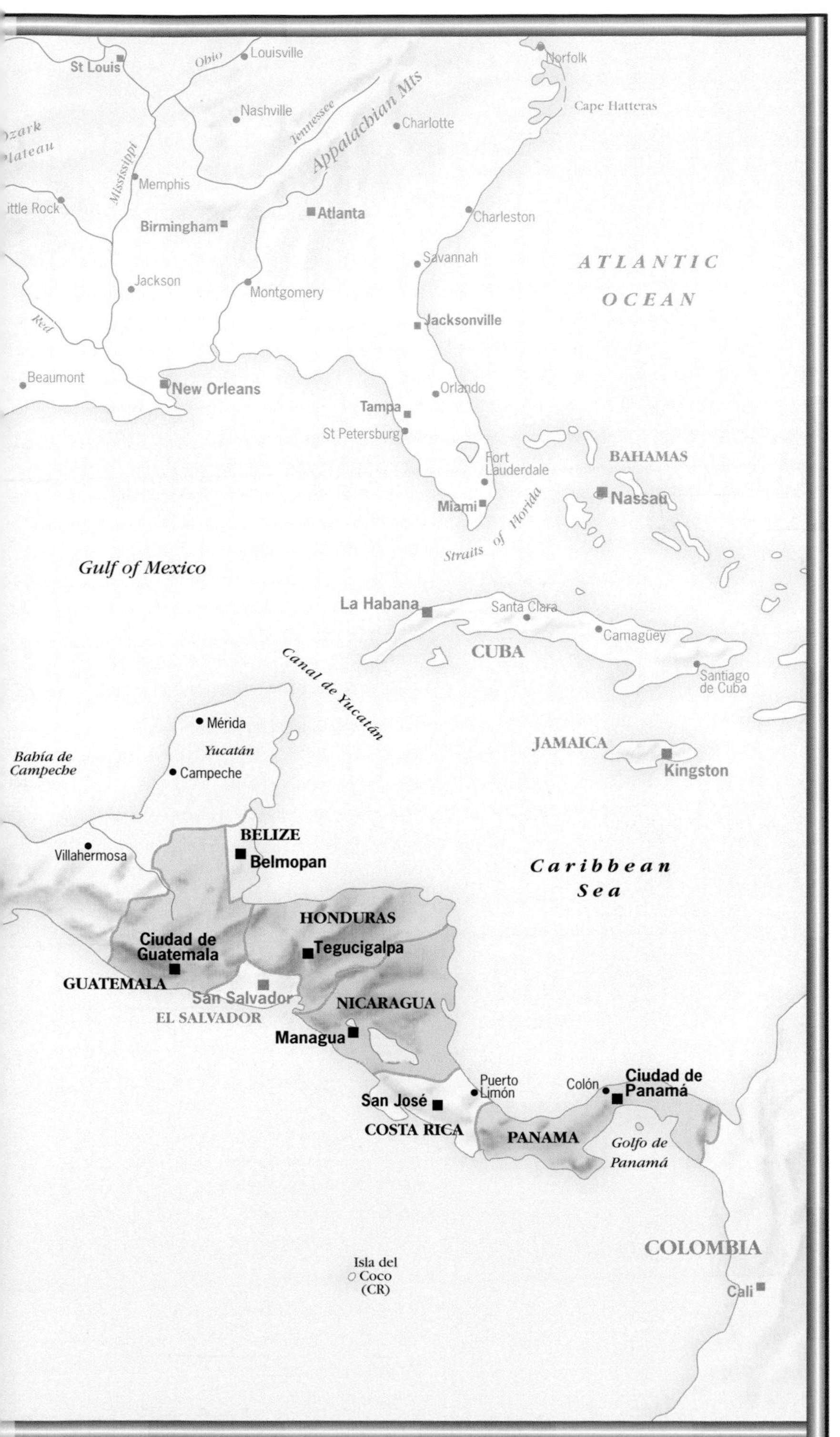

St Louis
Louisville
Ohio
Norfolk
Nashville
Tennessee
Appalachian Mts
Charlotte
Cape Hatteras
Ozark Plateau
Mississippi
Memphis
Little Rock
Atlanta
Birmingham
Charleston
Savannah
ATLANTIC OCEAN
Jackson
Montgomery
Red
Jacksonville
Beaumont
New Orleans
Orlando
Tampa
St Petersburg
Fort Lauderdale
BAHAMAS
Nassau
Miami
Straits of Florida
Gulf of Mexico
La Habana
Santa Clara
Camagüey
CUBA
Santiago de Cuba
Canal de Yucatán
Mérida
Yucatán
Bahía de Campeche
Campeche
JAMAICA
Kingston
BELIZE
Belmopan
Villahermosa
Caribbean Sea
HONDURAS
Ciudad de Guatemala
Tegucigalpa
GUATEMALA
San Salvador
EL SALVADOR
NICARAGUA
Managua
Puerto Limón
Colón
Ciudad de Panamá
San José
COSTA RICA
PANAMA
Golfo de Panamá
COLOMBIA
Isla del Coco (CR)
Cali

Practical Matters

Preparation

To get the best out of your adventure holiday it's worth taking time to plan carefully. Research the areas you are interested in and use the "Blue Pages" to help you find a suitable tour operator. Think about when you will be travelling and what type of activities will be involved. Make sure your chosen tour operator knows the region well and can offer advice and alternative arrangements in case of unforeseen circumstances.

LANGUAGE AND CUSTOMS

Many of the languages spoken in the countries and regions covered will be unfamiliar to visitors. Where there are many local languages or the area is remote, it may prove difficult to communicate. However, there is often a widely used language in any area (such as English or Spanish) of which many locals will have some knowledge. It is generally appreciated if visitors attempt a few words or phrases and a phrase book or mini-dictionary will be useful. Try to learn something of the local customs and etiquette to minimize the risk of causing offence through inappropriate gestures, body language, or dress.

Most Common Local Languages

Belize: English, Spanish
Costa Rica: Spanish, English
Honduras: Spanish, English
Guatemala: Spanish, Mayan Indian (a number of languages and numerous dialects)
Nicaragua: Spanish
Mexico: Spanish, Náhuatl, Maya, Zapotec
Panama: Spanish, English

Travel Documents

Make sure you have a full, valid passport and that it is valid for much longer than your stay. Check with the embassy or consulate of the countries you might be visiting about visa requirements. These can vary enormously and can change rapidly. If you intend travelling across borders, make sure you have all the relevant documents. Before you go, check the political situation for potential problems, (see below) especially in disputed areas, and try to find out local information before you travel to remoter areas.

Contacts:

U.S. State Department
Website: travel.state.gov/travel_warnings.html
Travel warnings and consular information.

Foreign and Commonwealth Office, UK
Tel: 020 727 01500
Website: www.fco.gov.uk
Travellers' advice line for information about potential political risks around the world.

Health Matters

Many of the countries covered here are developing areas with relatively basic medical facilities. Check with your doctor or travel clinic and allow plenty of time for any necessary vaccinations. Record your vaccinations on an International Health Certificate and carry it with you.

Contacts:

World Health Organization
Website: www.who.ch/
For the latest information on health matters around the world.

U.S. Centers for Disease Control
Tel: (888) 232-3228; faxback: (888) 232-3229
Website: www.cdc.gov
Telephone and fax hotlines offering the latest health information and advice on vaccinations.

LOCAL CURRENCIES

Belize:	**Belize dollar consisting of 100 cents**
Costa Rica:	**Colón (pl colones) = 100 céntimos**
Guatemala:	**Quetzal = 100 centavos**
Honduras :	**Lempira = 100 centavos**
Nicaragua:	**Córdoba = 100 centavos**
Mexico:	**Nuevo Peso = 100 centavos**
Panama:	**Balboa = 100 centésimo and $U.S. dollars**

Currency

The safest way to carry currency is by traveller's cheques, preferably in US$, which are readily accepted in most places. Local currencies rates can fluctuate. Carry your money concealed in a money belt and avoid carrying all your valuables and money in the same place.

Please note: Any prices given in this book are in US$ and were the approximate prices current at the time of the trip. Due to variations in inflation and exchange rates these are only guidelines.

Insurance

Always make sure you have comprehensive travel and medical insurance before you travel. Check the policy carefully and make sure those arranging the insurance are aware you will be taking part in "dangerous" activities.

Most standard insurances do not cover you for "dangerous" activities such as scuba diving, rock climbing, canoeing e.t.c.—the very type of activities you may wish to tackle.

At The Border

Local import/export laws vary and you should seek the advice of consuls, border officials or carriers to ensure you are not contravening them. If buying souvenirs, bear in mind that there are universally strict laws against importing items made from some animals, obscene material, offensive weapons and narcotics. Some countries require additional documentation for prescription drugs and in others, alcohol is strictly controlled. Never take risks and always pack your own luggage.

TIME DIFFERENCES

	London, noon = 0 hours (Greenwich Mean Time)	New York Noon local time	San Franicisco Noon local time
Belize	-6 hours	-1 hour	+2 hours
Costa Rica	-6 hours	-1 hour	+2 hours
Honduras	-6 hours	-1 hour	+2 hours
Guatemala	-6 hours	-1 hour	+2 hours
Nicaragua	-6 hours	-1 hour	+2 hours
Mexico	-6 hours	-1 hour	+2 hours
except for northwest states	–7 hours)	-2 hours	+1 hour
(Baja California Norte	-8 hours)	-3 hours	0 hours
Panama	-5 hours	0 hours	+3 hours

No account has been taken of daylight saving time

When to Go

OCTOBER | NOVEMBER | DECEMBER | JANUARY | FEBRUARY | MARCH

MEXICO

Into the Desert, Baja California

The Railway in the Wilds, Northern Mexico

Sea and Sierra, Pacific Coast

Rafting in Veracruz, Central Mexico

Art in the Jungle, Southern Mexico

GUATEMALA

Between the Volcanoes, The Highlands

Mayan Heritage, The Lowlands

Cruising Around Río Dulce, The Caribbean Coast

A Great Green Macaw (Ara ambigua)

BELIZE

Waterworld, Caribbean Coast

Stuck on the South, Southern Belize

Under the Spell of the Maya, Western Belize

HONDURAS

Escape to the Wild Side, Northern Honduras

A Life in Ruins, Northwestern Honduras

Rivers of Time, Eastern Honduras

NICARAGUA

Utopia in the Forest, North-Central Highlands

Into the Volcano, Lago de Nicaragua

COSTA RICA

Crossing a stream near Corvacado, Costa Rica

PANAMA

Where Oceans Meet, Central Panama

Adventure Planner

APRIL	MAY	JUNE	JULY	AUGUST	SEPTEMBER

Ruined Lands of Oaxaca, Southern Mexico

Descending the main pyramid at Yaxhá, Guatemala

Fisherman with barracuda, Belize

Treasure Islands, Northern Coast

The Historic Río San Juan, Southern Nicaragua

*A keel-billed toucan (*Ramphastos sulfuratus)

Northern Exposure, Northern Costa Rica

Where Wild Things Go, Pacific Coast

Jungle Paddlers, Central Cordillera

Trail of the Turtle Catchers, Caribbean Coast

A Nicoyan Odyssey, Pacific Coast

Travelling Safe

What To Do Before You Go

Confirm in advance of departure as many flights or voyages, and as much accommodation, as possible.

If you have only a limited time available, arrange your "adventures" in advance—some destinations restrict the number of visitors allowed in a particular period. A planned and packaged itinerary, though perhaps more expensive, may prove a wise investment.

- Photocopy all important documents and carry them separately from the originals. Keep a copy at home.
- Do not pack essential items in your suitcase—carry them in hand luggage.
- Give a copy of your itinerary and any contact numbers you have to friends or relatives.
- Research thoroughly the places you are visiting to ensure that you are adequately aware of the conditions that await you.
- Choose the right seasons.
  In some countries election times are best avoided, while public holidays may make travelling difficult.
- Check whether you need a visa.
- Check with a doctor about vaccinations or prophylactics necessary for the area you are visiting, and obtain an International Health Certificate with your vaccinations recorded on it.
- Purchase travel insurance, ensuring it covers your proposed activities—most standard insurances do not include adventure activities.

THE FOLLOWING WILL MAKE ANY TRAVELLING EXPERIENCE MORE COMFORTABLE:

- A torch/flashlight and spare batteries.
- A first aid kit to include rehydration tablets and insect repellent. Effective suncream/block. Diarrhoea treatment, antihistamines, aspirin.
- Water bottle
- Waterproof bag for valuable items
- An umbrella
- Passport and spare passport photographs
- A supply of books to read and/or short-wave radio
- A folding walking stick for mountain descents

What To Take

A soft bag is much better than a hard-frame suitcase. Make sure you have a way of securing the bag, such as a lock or a strap. Pack fewer clothes than you think you will need, and more photographic film. If you do not want to be bothered with washing clothes, laundry services can be cheaply and easily obtained in most of the places featured in this book. It is always better to take film than to have to buy it locally. A spare camera battery is also recommended.

Take the RIGHT clothes. It may be sweltering on the coast, but if you are climbing a mountain, it will be very cold at the top. Shorts may be fine on the beach but not in a church. Footwear is especially important if you are tackling a number of contrasting adventures, for example sandals or sneakers for island hopping but boots for trekking. And don't forget your bathing suit.

Money

Take US$ travellers cheques and a separate supply of American dollar bills. Don't forget to take note of the numbers. Most major credit cards are widely accepted (although some countries favour one over another), but this cannot be relied on in remoter areas.

What To Avoid

Check whether you need anti-malaria tablets as most of Central America is not malarial. However, to avoid being bitten by mosquitoes in the first place, cover all exposed flesh in a good insect repellent.

Avoid offending local sensibilities, whatever your own opinions. Liberal views and open debate may be acceptable at home, but in some countries discussion of religion and politics can be touchy subjects and possibly illegal.

If you are planning to go scuba-diving, or take part in some other instructor-led activity, don't automatically go for the cheapest options unless you are very experienced and competent to judge. A reputable operator may cost more to use, but it may save your life.

Avoid taking things for granted. Local people often presume you know about local conditions or else trivialise or exaggerate possible dangers or irritations, so don't be embarrassed to ask questions.

It is best to be careful about what you eat and drink. Water anywhere may be contaminated so always drink bottled water and avoid ice in drinks, no matter how hot it is. Eat only cooked food and, remember, washing food is only helpful if the water used is pure.

Drugs

Do not, under any circumstance, be tempted by offers of drugs—traffickers can face the death penalty. Do not ever carry anything for anyone else, no matter how apparently innocent the request.

PERSONAL SAFETY

Theft

Take only what you really need when out and about—leave as much as possible in a safe at your accommodation. In countries where mugging is a real threat, it is as well to carry a little cash to give away if necessary. Unfortunately, those countries where street theft is a problem, may expect you to carry ID—make a reduced copy of your passport, include a proper passport photograph and enclose the whole thing in a plastic wallet.

Beggars, Sellers and Confidence Tricksters

Difficult though it may be, think twice before you give money to beggars. Sometimes it is a ploy—before long you are surrounded by a sleeve tugging crowd, from among which one member leaps out and snatches your bag or camera. Persistent sellers are a nuisance. If you can avoid looking them in the eye and learn the local words for "no thank you", you will find them less troublesome. As for confidence tricksters, do not be taken in by flattery and be deeply suspicious of bargains.

Violence

As a foreigner, you are unlikely to be affected by violent crime. In cities, ask locally if there are areas that are best avoided.

Travelling Alone

The two main things for individuals are to let people know where you are travelling and to carry an absolute minimum of luggage—there will be no one else to watch over it.

Women

It is a tiresome truism that Western women travelling alone may be considered of easy virtue, if only because in some countries women rarely venture anywhere alone. Ignore, with as much dignity as possible, the unwelcome attentions that may come your way. Dress with consideration for local customs (especially completely covering arms and legs when visiting churches or in remote areas). Note that although most toiletries will be available in major towns, they may not be elsewhere.

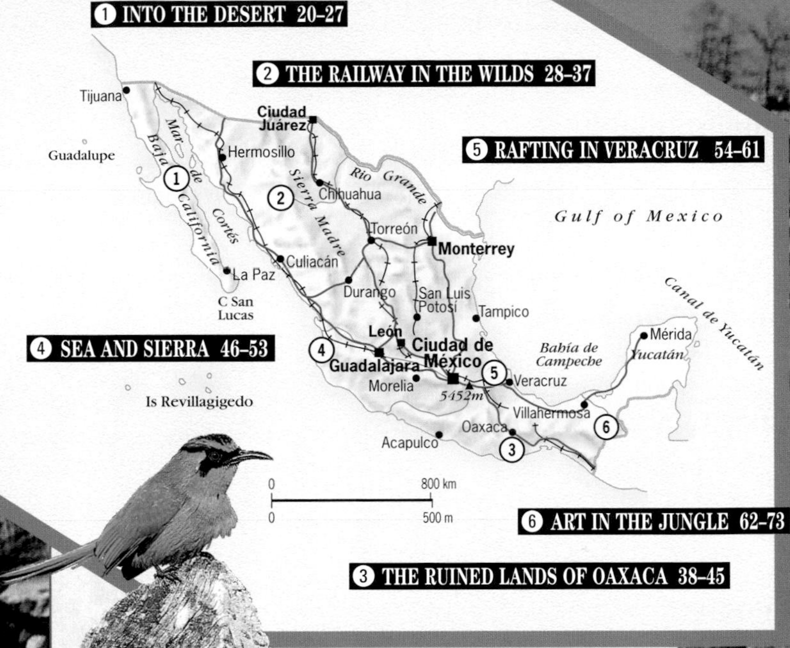

MEXICO

Mexico's vast and immensely varied terrain harbours a bewitching range of cultures, land, and people. Covering an area a quarter the size of the United States, it wavers between the Old and New Worlds, between southern poverty and northern prosperity, between rain forest and desert, and between run-down *cantinas* and state-of-the-art bars. However, it is also a country in constant flux. The globalization of trade has seen the growth of middle-class prosperity, together with an awakening consciousness that extends to environmental issues, and this has consequent spin-offs for adventure tourism. Mexico is perfectly positioned for this fast-developing industry, its empty landscapes just begging for trekkers, mountain bikers, and horse riders, and a succession of seas and gulfs seducing snorkellers, scuba-divers, and yachtsmen. Altogether there are an estimated 30,000 species of flowering plants, 1,000 species of birds, and about 450 species of mammals—enough to keep any nature lover happy from the southern jungles of Chiapas to the arid canyons of Baja California.

Stunning rock formations surround the town of Cusarárare, Mexico; ABOVE A Turquoise-browed Motmot

Into the Desert

by Fiona Dunlop

Baja, the finger of land that points south from California, is a strikingly beautiful, uninhabited region where marine wildlife and desert vegetation thrive side by side. A good way to enter its desert spirit is to trek down a canyon on muleback.

Extending 1,700km (1,100 miles) from north to south, Baja California is far longer than Italy, yet its population numbers barely a million. Lapped to the east by the Mar de Cortés (Gulf of California) and to the west by the Pacific Ocean, this arid peninsula encapsulates the extremes of unadulterated desert landscapes. Marine life around the unspoiled islands of the gulf (many of which are nature reserves) is also exceptional, making Baja northern Mexico's best site for diving and snorkelling, with sea-kayaking following close behind. And, every winter, whale-watching becomes an obsession when the lagoons of Baja California's Pacific coast receive their annual visitation from the grey whales (*Eschrichtius robustus*).

The southern half of the peninsula, the state of Baja California Sur (BCS), is the more picturesque and less Americanized part, although its tip, Los Cabos, is fast developing into a condo-land and warm-weather escape for North Americans. In total contrast is an area in the very centre of the peninsula, just below the dividing line between north and south Baja: the Sierra de San Francisco. These remote canyons and mountains in the Desierto de Vizcaíno are now being targeted by archaeologists and historians, for it is here that Mexico's greatest concentration of rock-paintings is found, exceptional both in terms of abundance and in quality. I have long been lured by desert topography and flora, and was also intrigued by the as yet unexploited nature of this area. It was not until 1996 that these rare paintings were made accessible to the public, and even then to only a very few. The reason for this is simple: to get to them you have just one option, and that is a mule—not a horse, nor a four-wheel drive, only a mule.

Heat, dust, a saddle-sore mule ride, and some rough scrambling over rocky terrain are the less comfortable aspects, although they are all within the capabilities of anyone of average fitness. A knowledge of Spanish is useful to facilitate communication with your guide.

You spend two nights sleeping in a tent, with no washing facilities available. There are adequate budget and mid-range hotels in San Ignacio.

Good walking shoes or boots are required.

The Long Approach

For anyone arriving from mainland Mexico, the obvious starting point for exploring Baja California Sur is **La Paz**, as it has a well-served international airport in addition to a regular car-ferry service to Topolobampo. In this relatively prosperous state capital English is widely spoken, people are friendly, and duty-free shops abound. Sunsets are an added bonus since, thanks to the curve of the Mogote peninsula, La Paz actually faces west despite being on the east coast. It may lack the history and quaintness of most Mexican towns, but the breezy, palm-lined *malecón* (promenade) and generous bay more than compensate.

With a day to fill and a beckoning deep blue bay before me, I thought I would do some sea-kayaking. However, this was not to be, as the winds from the north were judged too strong that day. Still searching, I found my way to the local anthropological museum (Museo Antropológico de Baja California Sur), which I was told had a good display on Baja's rock-paintings. Here I was foiled once again, this time by a museum workers' strike. In desperation, I whiled away a couple of hours drinking coffee and surfing the Net at a local cyber café.

The following day, as the little 20-seater prop plane finally winged its way northwards from La Paz in a cloudless sky, I was transfixed by the land below me. We hugged the coastline of the gulf all the way, so were treated to an endless expanse of rugged desert to the west and a succession of rocky islands strewn over the turquoise gulf to the east. The clear light made it easy to identify Isla Espiritu Santo, a favourite with sea lions and sea-kayakers, which can be reached from La Paz in a few hours. Inland, the craggy sierra took on a pinkish tone, its ripples, fissures, and strata creating natural sculptures on a gigantic scale. A few tracks were visible, along with dry riverbeds, endless beaches, and more rocky outcrops—but otherwise *nada*! I wondered where Baja's ten inhabitants per sq km (26 per square mile) actually lived. Then, as we approached Loreto, the magnificent Sierra de la Giganta rose to the west, while off the coastline the white sails of yachts anchored in the bays of tiny islands became visible. Flying straight in to the runway from over the sea, the plane touched down to applause from my fellow passengers, a group of young Japanese tourists who constituted a rarity in what is essentially gringo land.

BAJA GEOLOGY

About 25 million years ago the San Andreas Fault set into motion the split that separated Baja from the mainland to create the Gulf of California. Mountain formation increased, and volcanic activity led to the creation of the Sierra de San Francisco and the Sierra de la Giganta. This seismic past is still evident in the Volcán Las Tres Virgenes and Volcán Azufre, which tower 1,920m (6,300 feet) and 1,650m (5,400 feet) respectively beside Highway 1 between San Ignacio and Santa Rosalía. Geothermic energy is now being harnessed by forcing water through these volcanoes to create steam that is then used to drive turbines.

HIGHWAY 1

As my guide, Enrique, spirited me away through the sierra in his four-wheel drive, I began looking at cacti, then stopped this pointless activity. I realized that there were literally millions of *cardones* (*Pachycereus pringlei*), an endemic Baja species of cactus whose form is the stuff of advertising executives the world over. Highway 1 continued to snake its way north, rounding the endlessly beautiful contours and headlands of Bahía Concepción on its way, and eventually heading to Tijuana and the U.S. border. Gazing at the stunning offshore arrangement of rocky islands and deep metallic azure, I wondered how the Sierra

VAGARIES OF HISTORY

The history of La Paz has been far from smooth ever since Hernán Cortés failed to establish a settlement here in 1535. There followed a string of vicious conflicts with Baja's indigenous Pericue, Cochimi, and Guaicura, as well as droughts, famines, epidemics, and pirates, before La Paz finally became the capital of Baja, in 1830. It displaced Loreto, which had been founded by Jesuit missionaries much earlier, in 1697. In 1853, the infamous William Walker tried to install an official state of slavery, and in 1940 a mysterious disease wiped out local oyster-beds. Despite these hardships, today La Paz is one of Mexico's most prosperous towns.

ABOVE The muleback trail to the floor of Santa Teresa Canyon takes about two hours to complete, and drops 700m (2,300 feet) in altitude
LEFT Shortening stirrups in readiness for the descent down the near-vertical slope

de San Francisco would compare, as this was truly magnificent. But the huge, indented bay has also been discovered, attested to by beaches south of Mulegé that are lined with campervans (RVs), beach shacks, and even in places overlooked by embryonic real-estate developments.

Yet emptiness wins hands down, for this is Baja with vast, deserted landscapes that are only occasionally interrupted by the efforts of man. A further 60km (37 miles) beyond the palm groves of Mulegé is the rusting copper-mine machinery of **El Boleo**, right beside the highway in Santa Rosalía. The fortune of this curious little town was made in the 1880s by a French mining company. As a

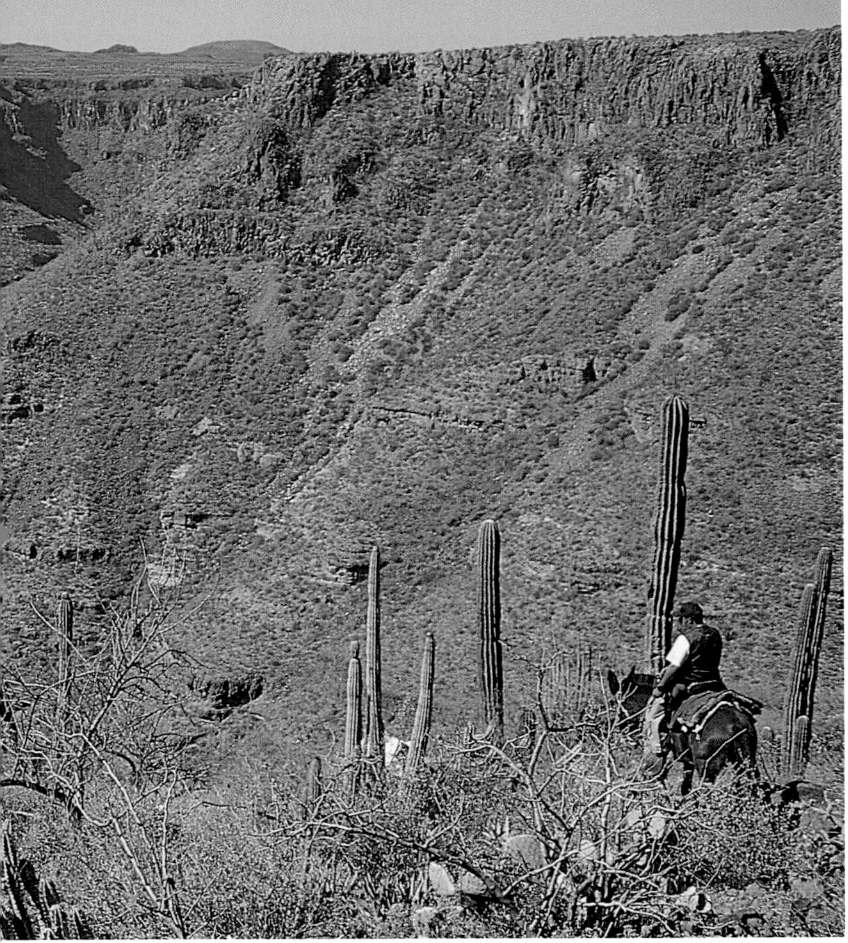

result, it has a unique character (more Caribbean than French, as many guide-books describe it) and visual harmony in its colourful one- and two-storey frame houses. Not least, its prefabricated, iron-plated church has been attributed to none other than Gustave Eiffel, of Paris's Eiffel Tower fame, although it has recently been established that it was actually the work of one of his collaborators. At Santa Rosalía we stocked up on fresh bread rolls at the renowned Boleo bakery on the main street, then headed out and onwards.

The jumping-off point for the Sierra de San Francisco is the tiny town of **San Ignacio**, another oasis in the desert due to the huge and prolific date plantation it inherited from its missionary founders. This comes together with a lovely Dominican church (1786), which replaced the first adobe version built by the Jesuits in 1728. Next door is a small museum and, in a damp vault below, the INAH (Instituto Nacional de Arqueología Historia) office. Here, permits are issued for visiting **Santa Teresa Canyon**, where most of the rock-paintings are concentrated. I was now legal, and ready to go.

Down the canyon

The next day, as my obstinate mule stumbled down the sheer face of the canyon and my cap was whisked away by a particularly aggressive thorn tree, this preliminary paperwork seemed to belong to another planet. We had left so-called civilization and were now entering

DESERT AND CANYON CACTI

Baja is known for its 120 species of cactus, which range from miniature spiked cushions to the most common, namely the organ-pipe cactus (*Lemaireocereus thurberi*). At lower levels, the Desierto de Vizcaíno is virtually monopolized by the *cardón*, the traditionally shaped cactus which can tower to a height of over 20m (65 feet). As the elevation increases, so enters the cirio, or bojum tree (*Idria columnaris*), whose slender, sprouting trunk seems to dance over the slopes; some even bend over completely to resemble elongated ostrich necks in the sand. The bojum is specific to the area between El Rosario and San Ignacio, and is one of Baja's 70 unique cactus species. Back in the canyon, you will see several varieties of squat barrel cactus (*Ferocactus* spp.), the multi-branched candelabra (*Myrtillo cactus conchal*), chain-link cholla (*Opuntia cholla*), the whiskered "old man" cactus (*Lophocereus schottii*), and endless prickly pear cacti (*Opuntia* spp.).

what felt like unexplored territory: eagles, cacti, and rattlesnakes (apparently) were our only companions. This sense of adventure had, in fact, started the moment we left Highway 1. Our early morning drive along a dirt road that curled 37km (23 miles) up into the sierra was visually extraordinary. After traversing the cool, thick cloud that blanketed millions of sentinel-like cardons in the valley, the road climbed above the cloud to emerge finally onto a hot, dusty plateau where the sun shone mercilessly. And then came the tiny community of San Francisco, its rickety tin-roofed shacks and ruddy-cheeked goatherds a far cry from the sophistication of La Paz.

Metaphorically speaking, we had already come a long way, but this was just the beginning. In front of me rode Manuel, a one-eyed local cattle rancher who was in charge of our four loaded donkeys; I followed behind them astride my male mule, while bringing up the rear was Enrique, the organizer of this expedition, on his distinctly more alert and responsive female mule. It didn't take me long to learn to yodle the refrain "*Macho-o-o-o*!" (as in macho, or male) while urging my nameless mount into action (these beasts of burden receive no baptismal friendship from the ranchers here). "*Burro*!" (Donkey!) yelled Manuel, the moment one of his protégés decided to follow its own nose and trot in a spirited manner off the trail, its load of cutlery and cooking pots rattling lyrically with its bell.

The mule's revenge

Riding a mule was a far easier task than I had imagined, despite bouts of frustration at its slowness. Having experienced the unpredictability of horses over the years, I was pleasantly surprised at how docile this creature was and at how comfortably I was seated. The well-worn leather saddle had a front stump that proved invaluable for clinging to during the steeper, rockier, downhill stretches, while deep leather-covered stirrups protected my feet from attack by passing vegetation. Local leatherwork also extends to ankle boots worn by all the hundred or so inhabitants of the tiny community of San Francisco de la Sierra; Manuel's were made by his son, and the corrugated rubber-tyre soles seemed ideal for this slippery, stony trail.

At times it was difficult to even see where the trail led: switchbacks abounded, as did rocks, cacti, and diverse desert vegetation stuggling for rootholds on what was an almost vertical slope. On a few occasions we had to dismount when the trail was too rough for our mules to carry us or when Manuel needed to shorten or lengthen our stirrups. And the mule's revenge definitely exists, for just when I was settling into the comforting rhythm of Manuel's clicking noises and enjoying the dramatic scenery and clear, hot air, my mount stopped dead, his nose up against the canyon wall. "*Macho-o-o-o-o!*" I bellowed, again and again. Nothing. I tugged the reins, kicked him in his ribs—still nothing. Finally, my Anglo-Saxon sensibilities capitulated and I adopted a thin branch that from then on served as ultra-effective stimulation for my stubborn mount.

Wild things

From the rim of the canyon (almost an hour's ride from our starting point) to its floor is a difference in altitude of 700m (2,300 feet), altogether making a sheer descent that took about two hours to accomplish. At the bottom, temperatures became palpably warmer, although they were to dive again at night, and the vegetation was transformed. A lone farm nurtured orange and olive trees as well as crimson oleander (*Nerium oleander*), but this was nothing compared to the beauty of our campsite clearing. Here, in a narrow, rocky arroyo between the high walls, was a magnificent grove of shaggy California fan palms (*Washington filifera*) and lofty palma palmia (*Erythea brandegeei*), an elegant, endemic fan-palm. At night, their 30-m (100-foot) forms (calculated by my Baja companions in terms of pick-up truck length) were silhouetted against a dazzling starry sky. Crickets and cicadas set up their nocturnal symphony, and the donkeys nosed around for food in the distance, their bells clonking melodically.

Later, from the safety of my tent, I heard the rustling of nocturnal creatures that remained faceless but were probably desert mice. Loud snoring came from a more obvious source—both my companions were just a few yards away. I listened in vain for the howl of the coyote, common enough in Baja but strangely absent here. And first thing in the morning, I was at last able to indulge in that legendary gesture of shaking my shoes out for scorpions; in this canyon it went together with keeping a lookout for rattlesnakes and black widow spiders (*Latrodectus mactans*), which although rare do exist here. So far, so good.

Back in time

The two branches of Santa Teresa Canyon contain seven rock-paintings in all, but the most graphic are Las Flechas and the most spectacular La Pintada. Seeing prehistoric rock-paintings such as these in a wild and remote context is a truly moving experience, and is the crowning glory of a long trip that includes a bumpy, extremely dusty drive followed by an arduous descent on muleback into the canyon, and a night in a tent listening for potential desert attacks. And then, after a further hour spent scrambling over huge boulders, wading through streams, and climbing up rocky hillsides, you at last stand in awe in front of these sublime images from the past, the numerous human figures, arms raised to

WATCHING THE WHALES

Between January and March, San Ignacio becomes the centre for organizing whale-watching tours, some of which set up camp beside the Laguna San Ignacio itself, 72km (45 miles) to the west. This is the mating and calving season for the grey whales, which make their 8,000-km (5,000-mile) trip to Baja from the cool waters off Alaska every year. Three companies run daily shuttles out to the lagoon, where trained and registered guides take out enthusiasts in *pangas* (dinghies). The whales are extraordinarily affectionate, and actually come right up to the boats to be patted and stroked. These gentle giants, weighing 20–40 tonnes (44,000–88,000 pounds), also home in on Laguna Ojo de Liebre (Scammon's Lagoon) near Guerrero Negro, and Bahía Magdalena, reached from Puerto San Carlos to the south. Whale-watching trips are offered from all three locations.

ABOVE The huge overhang of the Cueva La Pintada is covered with prehistoric paintings of flora and fauna
LEFT One of the figures in the Cueva de Las Flechas is pierced by dozens of arrows

ROCK-PAINTING HISTORY

Baja's rock-paintings are mainly located between Mulegé to the east and Guerrero Negro to the west. In all, some 700 sites have been registered, leading in December 1993 to the Sierra de San Francisco being designated a World Heritage Site by UNESCO. For some years the paintings were declared off limits while archaeologists carried out their investigations. Carbon-14 dating has so far revealed 38 different dates from *c.* 2350 B.C. to A.D. 1480, while the Cueva del Ratón (on the access dirt road) has shown dates of up to A.D. 1650. When Jesuit missionaries were first shown these paintings by local Cochimi Indians in the 18th century, the latter claimed they had been painted by "giants from the north." Little is certain, however, other than their creators were hunter-gatherers.

the heavens, surrounded by countless depictions of desert fauna.

Time seems to stand still as you pick out the forms of hares, squirrels, mountain goats, antelopes (identified as American pronghorns), pumas, birds, turtles, and even a whale (although this is disputed). One figure, in the **Cueva de Las Flechas**, is traversed by dozens of arrows, others have six fingers or headdresses denoting their role as shamans, while nearly all are larger than life. Black, red ochre, yellow, and touches of mauve are the only colours used, all obtained from natural pigments, but there is a surprising intricacy in the interlocking drawings and even conceptual moments. The latter is exemplified by a figure painted around a protruding bump in the rock, thought to represent a pregnant woman. Curiously, these murals are not inside caves (the Spanish word *cueva* means cave) but are actually painted high up on the canyon rockface, sheltered by overhangs. Most striking of all is the **Cueva La Pintada** as its groups of figures and fauna extend some 150m (500 feet) beneath a gently curving overhang. Stand down below by the river and gaze upwards for a fantastic general vista that encompasses all aspects of this spectacular place. It is well worth the mule ride.

GOING IT ALONE

Internal Travel

Baja California is an easy destination for west coast Americans, who can drive across the border at Tijuana (Highway 1) or Mexicali (Highway 5). There are also numerous flights from Los Angeles and other North American cities to La Paz and Los Cabos. Car ferries operate between Topolobampo in Sinaloa state and La Paz, and between Guaymas and Santa Rosalía. Aeromexico operates the 40-minute flight between La Paz and Loreto. Alternatively, there are several long-distance buses a day between Santa Rosalía/Loreto and La Paz; these take a lot longer than the plane (about 7–8 hours) but cost less than a tenth of the price and are perfectly comfortable. Aeromexico and Aerocalifornia both operate domestic flights from Mexico City to La Paz, but the latter airline is best avoided as delays and cancellations are common. Car rental is available at the airport in La Paz.

Some caves are quite difficult to reach and not for every tourist!

When to Go

Baja California has an enviably warm, sunny climate peppered with flash floods, but during the summer months (June–September) temperatures can become uncomfortably high, hitting 40°C (over 100°F). The whale season (January–March) is a good time to visit, but this is also the coldest, driest period when desert temperatures can fluctuate by 25°, descending to 0°C (32°F) at night. March to May, when the desert is blooming, is ideal for desert tours, as is September to November. Winter rains include the poetically named *equipatas* (horses' hooves), downfalls that sometimes last two to three days, while summer and early autumn see occasional tropical storms. Ocean-related activities such as snorkelling, diving, and sea-kayaking are best undertaken between October and May.

Planning

There aren't many tour agencies that organize mule treks, so such a trip needs to be booked well in advance. If you are visiting the region during the whale-watching season, also make sure you book your accommodation in advance as what little there is becomes much in demand. It is quite possible to undertake the trip independently if you bear in mind the following:

- ❑ You need your own transport to reach San Francisco.
- ❑ You need to take drinking water, food, camping gear, and a first-aid kit.
- ❑ It is obligatory to organize your INAH permit at San Ignacio, then to register at San Francisco, where a local guide, donkeys, and mules will be allocated.
- ❑ A good command of Spanish is necessary to communicate with the local guide.
- ❑ Strict rules and regulations for the canyon include no alcohol or donkey droppings near the rock-paintings!

Travellers' Tip

- ❑ Baja California offers an endless choice of outdoor activities, and this factor, together with its vast distances, means that there is really no need to take in any other Mexican region on a single trip. Instead, it is enough to combine time spent on the coast with a tour of the desert.

What to Take

- ❑ Take a minimal amount of clothes in a small, sturdy bag that can stand being bashed around on a donkey's back. Pack a pullover for the cool evenings, and if you visit during January–February you will also need warm trousers and socks.
- ❑ The bottom of the canyon sees sunshine only during the middle part of the day, but on the way down and up you will need sunblock and a hat or cap.
- ❑ Good walking shoes are essential.

Health

Ensure your typhoid, polio, and tetanus inoculations are up to date. On the canyon trip you are a long way from the nearest hospital, so check that your guide has a comprehensive emergency first-aid kit that includes the relevant antivenoms.

The Railway in the Wilds

by Fiona Dunlop

The dramatic and grandiose mountains and canyons of the Sierra Tarahumara are one of Mexico's greatest natural wonders. Their staggering scale offers the perfect backdrop for hiking, mountain biking, and horse riding—or simply enjoying one of the world's great train journeys. I made the town of Creel my base for walking and bus tours of the area, and saved the spectacular Creel–El Fuerte railway journey until last.

Mention the Copper Canyon and the first thought that usually comes to mind is the Chihuahua–Pacífico Railway. In the 1960s this celebrated engineering feat finally opened up what was formerly a high-altitude wilderness where only the Tarahumara (or Rarámuri, their own name) dared to tread. And tread they did, or rather sprint, so creating the legend of a unique ability for endurance and long-distance running. These are the only indigenous people in Mexico to have preserved this once common characteristic, thanks mostly to their geographical isolation and a rugged environment of climatic extremes. You may not be able to match this physical prowess, but you can certainly hike to breathtaking waterfalls or follow the Tarahumaras' annual migration by rattling down by bus to the subtropical oasis of Batopilas.

This is not a luxurious trip, but travelling is relatively easy along the main well-trodden route. Hikes can range from straightforward to very difficult.

★ There are no sleeping berths on the train, so all Copper Canyon accommodation is in hotels along the route, which range from basic to luxury (Batopilas, for example, has one luxury hotel and several that are very simple). Power cuts are common, as is the case throughout Mexico.

Good walking shoes are essential if you intend to go hiking.

ESSENTIAL BUYS

In Creel you'll find yourself gravitating towards the main square adjoining the railway station, as this is where essentials such as the bank and the Mission shop are located. The latter is the place to buy topographical maps of the region for long hikes, as well as Tarahumara arts and crafts. Other shops sell similar wares (minus the maps), but the difference is that the profits of the Mission shop go towards essential medical care for the Tarahumaras at their 60-bed hospital. Also unmissable here is a small ethnographic museum that gives good background information.

Creel's cowboys

Creel and Divisadero are the most popular bases in the immense Sierra Tarahumara. I chose to start off at the lumber town of **Creel**, which I reached by bus from Chihuahua. It lies at one of the highest points along the railway (2,400m, or 7,900 feet) on a plateau where pine forests alternate with huge stacks of sculptural boulders. This strikingly beautiful scenery recurs throughout the sierra, but Creel's infrastructure makes it all the more accessible—it has several hotels and is the start point for tours to Batopilas. It's a dusty, windy town whose pioneering soul is emphasized by local cowboys striding along the main street or rattling

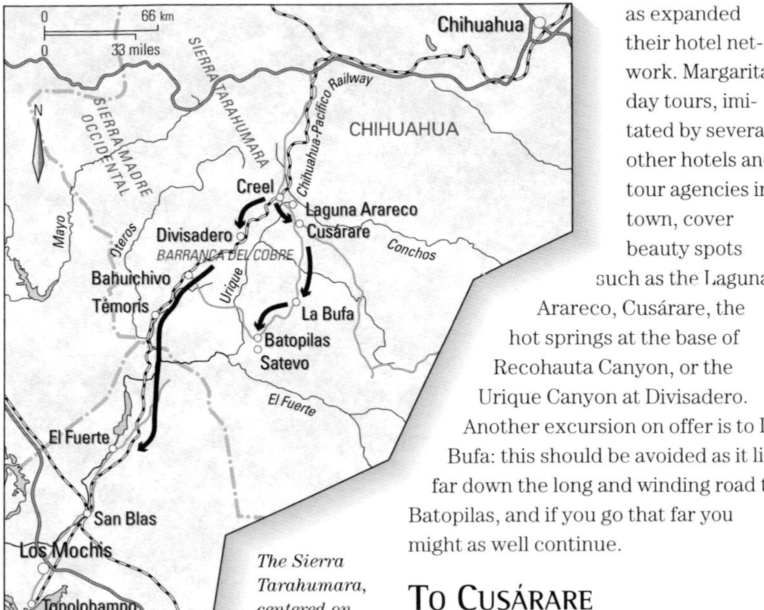

The Sierra Tarahumara, centered on Creel.

down it in four-wheel drives, and by the whistling and shunting of cargo trains echoing across the valley. Directions are generally given in relation to the railway tracks that run parallel to the single main street, along which all hotels and restaurants are located. Here, too, you will see impoverished though brilliantly clad Tarahumaras clustered in doorways, as this is the administrative and provisions centre for a vast area.

Creel's best-known institution in travellers' terms is Casa Margarita, a ramshackle guest-house next to one of the churches on the main square. This was the first to cater for the rare foreign traveller who came this way 20 years ago. Since then, the voluble lady owner and her sons have successfully monopolized the backpacking brigade, as well as expanded their hotel network. Margarita's day tours, imitated by several other hotels and tour agencies in town, cover beauty spots such as the Laguna Arareco, Cusárare, the hot springs at the base of Recohauta Canyon, or the Urique Canyon at Divisadero. Another excursion on offer is to La Bufa: this should be avoided as it lies far down the long and winding road to Batopilas, and if you go that far you might as well continue.

To Cusárare

One cool November morning, after kicking my heels with the *paseo* boys awaiting other potential customers for Divisadero, I finally gave up and entered the mayhem of Margarita's. At least 20 people were crowded into the noisy kitchen, where coffee was being ladled out and a lone man attempted to cope with a tour list. Divisadero was not one of the options on offer at Margarita's, so I chose to join an imminently departing day trip to Cusárare instead, and retired to wait outside. Soon, ten of us were bouncing along in a minibus heading 20km (12 miles) south out of Creel, stopping for an obligatory photo-opportunity at the "Elephant Rock" and briefly at the beautiful **Laguna Arareco** before turning off down a dirt road through the pine forest. By this time, spirits in the bus were high and conversations in full flow between the American, English, and

DAY-TOUR ORGANIZATION

All day tours, whether Margarita's or the official tours (*paseos*) that are run from a hut on the square, leave only if they have enough passengers, so you are at the mercy of majority tastes. If your group is large enough or if you have a generous budget, you can charter a car yourself: the local tour cars are called *suburbans* and take up to 12 passengers.

ABOVE Tarahumara children rarely get any opportunity for schooling
BELOW In addition to weavings and woodcarvings, Tarahumara crafts include pine-needle baskets
RIGHT You can walk around Laguna Arareco, which lies south of Creel on the road to Cusárare

Dutch travellers, whose ages ranged from mid-20s to 50s. Some were reaching the end of a long journey that had started in South America, while others had just crossed the border from the United States to commence their holiday, so discussions were intense.

At an isolated *tienda* (shop) we gathered our provisions for the hike to the **Cusárare waterfall** and set off behind our guide, a timid Tarahumara girl swathed in a bright orange blanket. Communication remained limited as her Spanish did not go very far and nor did that of her young brother, who trotted along behind, a state of affairs indicative of the official neglect that rules in this region. The easy 3-km (1.8-mile) walk to the waterfall followed a gently undulating trail beside an often dry riverbed. Clear air, crystalline light, shady, fragrant pine trees, and smooth boulders were the main features, while dramatically formed rockfaces gave shape to the riverbed. After passing some Tarahumara children who had optimistically laid out weavings and pine baskets for sale, we came to the spectacular flat

"roof" of the waterfall. This magical spot allowed us to rest while a few intrepid souls actually picked their way across stones over the watery top of the 30-m (100-foot) cascades.

A couple of hours later, we were back in our bus heading for the village of **Cusárare** itself. This lies off the main road across open grassland studded with more of the region's landmark rock formations. At the centre of the village, surrounded by a few dilapidated houses, stands the Jesuit **church of Los Santos Cinco Señores de Cusárare**, built in 1744 and extensively restored in 1972. What is remarkable about it are its interior friezes of geometric patterns in red-ochre pigment: these recall the designs of Paquimé pottery found in Casas Grandes, Mexico's northernmost archaeological site.

Here we were confronted with the strangely silent, non-aggressive nature of the Tarahumara. In the walled church courtyard groups of Tarahumara women and children were gathered, while inside the church dozens more huddled down one side of the nave. We finally understood why they were there when we saw a glass-topped coffin in front of the altar. Obviously, a respected figure of the community had just died and we were

THE TARAHUMARA, OR RARÁMURI

An estimated 50,000 Tarahumara live in the southwestern corner of the state of Chihuahua. Their bleak and rugged homeland covers about 35,000sq km (13,500 square miles), where climatic extremes force them to descend the canyons with their sheep and goats every winter. Long-isolated, reserved, disdainful of "civilization," and in close touch with their beautiful land, they are said to have strong telepathic powers. Their greatest belief is respect for the individual, to which are linked their conviction in man's control over time and an intense spirituality. High illiteracy and child mortality rates remain common, and in the last few years many have suffered from near famines.

imposing on their grieving ceremony, but not one Tarahumara had made a movement or gesture to dissuade us. This same passive attitude recurred on our return to Creel when our driver led us to visit a Tarahumara cave-dwelling. Feeling uncomfortably like voyeurs, we peered into the smoke-blackened kitchen, then sat on a stone ledge beneath the rock overhang outside. Beside us hung some rags—the family's laundry. But before us unfolded yet another idyllic plateau studded with cornfields, cattle, and the odd log cabin with smoking chimney. To me it seemed clear that for now the Tarahumaras' salvation had to come from the power and beauty of this environment, because it wasn't coming from anywhere else.

Batopilas

I had long yearned to visit **Batopilas**—since reading about the extravagant American mining magnate Alexander Shepherd, who in 1880 took his family deep down to the subtropical floor of a canyon together with the essentials of life: a piano and a pool table. In those days it took five days on muleback to reach Batopilas along a tortuous track from Creel. Today, in a bone-shaking local bus that throws in generous food stops, it takes seven or eight hours, or with more sophisticated tourist cars or a chartered *suburban* it can take under five hours. The 140-km (87-mile), partly dirt road, passes some of the Sierra Tarahumara's most spectacular sights, from La Bufa to the Doble Herradura (Double Horseshoe), while the altitude descends radically from 2,400m to 500m (7,900 feet to 1,640 feet) above sea-level. Vegetation follows the climatic change as fir and pine forests give way to yuccas, cacti, aloes, and pepper trees, and then, at Batopilas itself, to a grande finale of mango trees, citrus trees, and splashes of crimson bougainvillaea.

It is an extraordinary adventure, however much comfort you choose to do it in, purely because of the wild, untouched beauty of the landscapes coupled with the apparent isolation of your destination, eight hours or so away. A journey into the unknown? On the bus that left from Creel, just over half my fellow passengers were also foreigners, joined by Tarahumaras and cowboy-hatted locals who continued to pile in until eventually they filled the aisle. As the fast-maturing vehicle lurched around tighter and tighter corners with more curling switchbacks visible below, the inevitable happened—some passengers were carsick. Solidarity reigned, however, and window seats were donated to the needy. We finally reached **La Bufa**, the nickname for either of two things: a craggy rock in the apex of the valley that, to some, resembles a conquistador's helmet; or the noise made by the wind around this same outcrop. The imagination reels. This spectacular canyon is also the site of one of Batopilas' mines, and this has produced what resembles a manmade pyramid but is in fact a gigantic mound of solidified mine-tailings.

From here onwards three of us chose to ride high on the roof of the bus, squashed between backpacks and bundles, and clutching metal bars that had rusted loose from the luggage rack. Above us soared sheer, eroded rockfaces, their strata cut horizontally as if with a knife, below were hair-raising drops into nothingness, and in the distance rose curious mushroom-shaped stacks; the 360-degree panorama beneath the deep azure sky was awesome. As the road descended 2,000m (6,560 feet) in altitude, the air heated up and we three on the roof became painfully aware of the effects of low-hanging branches. And then we spotted an eagle perched on an organ-pipe cactus—but without a snake in its mouth (this was, historically, the sign that led the Aztecs to build their capital in the Valley of Mexico, and is today featured on the national flag). Our own fate was soon to come.

Illusions

Just before the final swing across the bridge into Batopilas, we were overtaken by a convoy of smart *suburbans* with upholstered rooftop seats and seatbelts. This was the first sign that we intrepid adventurers were not to be alone at Batopilas. At the main plaza everyone disappeared smartly in search of accommodation, something that turned out to be extremely sparse owing to the alternate-day bus timetable and the presence of several tour groups. But without phones, how could you know? I ended up walking a mile back to the village entrance, where at last I found a hotel with a room left. First thing the following day, after the 5am bus had vacated some hotel space, I changed to a more central location. This was Monse's, a ramshackle place with a Tarahumara arts store at the front and a vague garden at the back full of sacks of concrete and general building debris.

This was the final confirmation that my romantic image of Batopilas was a long way fromthe reality. Yes, the ruins of the silver-magnate's adobe mansion do stand in graphic splendour across the river, their crumbling bougainvillaea-shrouded walls enclosing the long-abandoned swimming pool. Yes, the climate is subtropical. Yes, the surroundings are delightful, from the background rushing of the river to the cobbled streets, whitewashed houses, and dazzling blue sky above the cacti-studded sierra. Yes, I was far from civilization—the nightly power cuts underlined this. But what I had not expected were the large numbers of tourists, above all those staying at a $250 per night restored hacienda in the middle of town, nor the groups monopolizing other hotels and restaurants alike. The sad truth is that Batopilas, with a population of about 600, is a victim of its uniqueness and popularity. Guest-house owners make little effort at cleanliness or comfort, knowing they have a ready market when the next bus rolls in. And while these mestizo inhabitants prosper, further up the canyon Tarahumaras are living at subsistence level. This said, the trip to Batopilas

HIDDEN RICHES

Batopilas' prosperity does not come just from the tourist trade. High up in the sierra are vast, illegal fields of poppies cultivated by local entrepreneurs. This accounts for the high military presence in the area, and in Batopilas itself. Searches of vehicles on the road to Creel reveal little, as most of the drugs are flown out by light aircraft at night. Another source of income lies in the gold and silver deposits of the area, which today are attracting both Japanese and Canadian mining interests 50 years after the silver mines closed down completely and a century after the town's heyday, when it was one of the richest in Mexico.

remains a fantastic experience and one that I in no way regret.

A MISSION STROLL

Along the Río Batopilas 8km (5 miles) due south of town lies the mission of **Satevo**, offering a perfectly distanced morning walk that can include a swim in the emerald-green river. Mules, cattle, goats, turkey vultures, and kingfishers are your companions, rushing water the inimitable soundtrack, and organ-pipe cacti and pepper trees the main vegetation. Take enough food and water as there is none at Satevo, and aim to return to Batopilas when the track is in the shade (after about 1pm). There is a suspended bridge near the mission, and you can also wade across the boulder-strewn river at certain points, so it is possible to combine the easy dirt road with some wilder stetches along the opposite bank.

I joined up with two other hikers who were equally intrigued by this remote church, which still raises questions as to its original function. It is dedicated to San Pedro Claver (1580–1654), a Jesuit missionary who was canonized in 1888 and who is the patron saint of the Tarahumaras, but the question remains why such an elaborate church was built in this isolated spot. Even today, the multi-domed red-brick construction is flanked by a mere handful of houses, all

ABOVE The 17th-century Satevo mission, dedicated to Jesuit San Pedro Claver
OPPOSITE The 8-km (5-mile) route to Satevo from Batopilas crosses the river by way of a suspended bridge
BELOW Entering one of the many tunnels along the Chihuahua–Pacífico Railway

recently built. At the first house on your left as you arrive on the dirt road you can pick up the key to the church. The señora here also sells beers, officially unavailable in Batopilas itself (though if you ask around discreetly, you will not go thirsty). Inside the recently restored church you can see a few of the original wall-paintings between the fresh whitewash and a remarkably dense ultramarine over the altar section, but it is the exterior that holds more architectural interest.

The Great Railway Journey

Back in Creel, my last step in this adventure was to board the Chihuahua–Pacífico train and head for the Pacific. Punctually at 11:30am, I heard its whistle and in rolled the smart turquoise *primera especial* (first-class service) with only three carriages to cope with a vast crowd of waiting passengers. All managed to squeeze in, along with several heavily armed soldiers whose presence was a reaction to an incident two days earlier when 100 tourists were robbed and one actually shot dead by bandits. This was proof that the Sierra Tarahumara does not resemble the Wild West in topographical fashion alone—cowboys are alive and well, and still ride off into the sunset. And then off we rolled to start one of the world's most scenic railway journeys.

This marvel of railroad engineering is the only land connection covering the 700km (430 miles) between the Pacific coast and the city of Chihuahua. It was initiated at the beginning of the 20th century by American mining companies under the name Kansas City, Mexico and Orient Railroad, but it was the Mexican government that finally completed the most complex section in 1961. A total of 86 tunnels were blasted through solid rock, and 39 bridges and endless breathtaking loops were built around mountains. The longest tunnel measures over 1km (3,300 feet), while the highest bridge soars at 120m (393 feet). Among the diverse contributors to this remarkable construction were President Adolfo López Mateos, the entrepreneur Enrique Creel, Ulysses Grant, the dictator President Porfirio Díaz, the revolutionary Pancho Villa, Benjamin Johnson, and, of course, the Tarahumaras, who constituted much of the labour force.

The railway soon lived up to its reputation as we circled around the incredible twist of El Lazo (The Loop), and then, over an hour later, pulled into the station at the town of **Divisadero**. Here, dozens of Tarahumara women and children crouched on the platform, some selling handicrafts, others tacos or drinks, as this is where the train makes a 15-minute stop. This allows time for passengers to get down and walk to a stunning viewpoint overlooking the Río Urique, which snakes through the Barranca del Cobre (Copper Canyon) about 1,760m (5,770 feet) below.

From Divisadero, the next 85-km (53-mile) stretch to the village of Témoris is the most spectacular of the railway, where increasingly dramatic canyons are spanned by bridges and linked by tunnels. This inspired a general rush among passengers for seats with the best views from the left side of the train, as well as a certain amount of elbowing at the open windows between the carriages.

Then, as the light gradually faded and night fell, I chatted with the man sitting next to me, a middle-aged Mexican who had been travelling 24 hours non-stop from Monterrey. We shared our limited provisions and dozed until, around 9pm, the train clattered into **El Fuerte**. This small, 16th-century town was my chosen terminus—anything to avoid the hellhole of Los Mochis, at the end of the line, where I had the misfortune to stay a few years previously. Off I tumbled, into the dark night and onto the familiar broken springs of a *colectivo* taxi. I had returned to Earth.

GOING IT ALONE

Internal Travel

The termini for embarking on the Chihuahua–Pacífico (Copper Canyon) Railway are Los Mochis, on the Pacific coast (together with Topolobampo, its port), and the city of Chihuahua. The railway terminus you choose will depend on your starting point. Train tickets can be bought at the stations or on board.

The *primera especial* (first-class) passenger train leaves both Los Mochis and Chihuahua at 6am, taking over 13 hours between the two termini. You can stop off anywhere along the line (aside from Creel, Divisadero, and El Fuerte, accommodation is available at Basaseachi, Posada, Bahuichivo and nearby Cerocahui, and Guachochi) then reboard the train another day with the same ticket. The second-class train (*mixto*) that should follow 2 hours later is often seriously delayed and, as a result, you will miss half the views as night falls.

There is a good road covering the 246km (153 miles) between Chihuahua and Creel, soon to extend to Divisadero, which Estrella Blanca buses cover in about 4 hours. These run every 2 hours 6am–6pm. The Batopilas bus from Creel leaves on Tuesday, Thursday, and Saturday at 7am, returning Monday, Wednesday, and Friday at 5am.

When to Go

With such extremes of altitude, the Sierra Tarahumara presents a wide range of climates. At altitudes of over 1,800m (5,900 feet; Creel and Divisadero), the climate varies from temperate to cold. In winter there is rain and snow, and temperatures fall below freezing point, sometimes descending to -23°C (-9°F). Summer temperatures average 20°C (68°F) and during this period the arid landscapes are freshened by frequent showers. In contrast, at the bottom of the canyons (Batopilas, for example) winter temperatures average a mere 17°C (63°F), shooting up in summer to 35°C (95°F) and occasionally over 40°C (104°F). This is when heavy rains fill the riverbeds and replenish waterfalls. A good time to visit is during the halfway seasons of April/May and October/November.

Easter needs to be booked well in advance, as this is when the Tarahumara enact their most extraordinary processions and ceremonies, the best of which can be seen at Arareco, Cusárare, and Norogachi. Nocturnal festivities make Batopilas a trying place to sleep during this time.

Note There used to be a time difference of 1 hour between the coast and Chihuahua, but this is no longer the case.

Planning

Most activities can be arranged on the spot, although you may want to reserve mountain bikes in advance during the high seasons (Christmas and Easter) as off-road biking is a very popular local activity. For those who want their comforts assured, numerous American tour agencies cover this area, although there are fewer in Mexico itself.

Travellers' Tip

- There is a Banco Serfín on Creel's main square that changes dollar travellers' cheques and has an ATM for Visa and Mastercard. There are no money-changing facilities in Batopilas.

What to Take

- Good hiking boots are essential.
- Warm clothes for the evenings.
- Power cuts are frequent in Batopilas, so take a torch (they can also be bought locally).
- First-aid kit.

Health

Ensure that your typhoid, polio, and tetanus inoculations are up to date. As there are no hospitals for many miles (the nearest is at Chihuahua), take a comprehensive first-aid kit.

SAFETY

Although the Mexican government is making efforts to ensure the protection of tourists travelling on the Chihuahua–Pacífico Railway, it is recommended that anyone planning on undertaking the tour checks in advance with the U.K. Foreign Office or U.S. State Department Travel Advisories for up-to-date information on the situation.

Ruined Lands of Oaxaca

by Steve Watkins

The gorgeous Oaxaca Valley was home to some of Mexico's first civilizations. I took a fascinating driving tour to three important and very different pre-Hispanic sites at Monte Albán, Yagul, and Mitla, and then exchanged my car for a horse to ride into the rugged Sierra Madre mountains.

Oaxaca (pronounced "wa-HAH-ka") is one of Mexico's biggest states and has the largest indigenous population in the country: over a third of its 3 million inhabitants have a pre-Columbian ancestry. It is situated to the south of Mexico City, and marks the point where the western and eastern chains of the Sierra Madre mountains mould into one to become the single southern chain, the Sierra Madre del Sur (this chain then continues into South America to become the Andes). Oaxaca is a rugged state of high peaks, hundreds of deep, steep valleys, and the wide, flat Oaxaca Valley, home to the main city, also called Oaxaca. This fractured geography caused towns and villages in the area to grow in physical isolation from one another, and led to the development of uniquely diverse and rich pre-Columbian cultures. At least 16 distinct languages (including Zapotec and Mixtec) were spoken in the region, and their continued survival reflects the lack of modern development in the state, now one of Mexico's poorest.

A recently built toll route from the country's capital to the city of Oaxaca has cut the bus journey time by half to five hours. Along the way, the road twists and turns, climbs and plunges through dramatic, virtually unpopulated, dry mountain scenery where cactus-covered deserts conjure up images of old Hollywood Westerns. As I dropped out of the range onto the wide flatlands of the main Oaxaca Valley I felt a real sense of arrival, and **Oaxaca City**, its wide cobbled streets lined with brightly coloured colonial houses and ornate public buildings, did not disappoint as a destination. Although the city is a growing industrial centre, strict building regulations have helped retain its old charm, the result being that it has become a major tourist destination. Anyone interested in art, handicrafts, architecture, museums, and historic churches could spend a whole week exploring the city alone.

For those with less time or other priorities, like myself, there are a couple of places that should not be missed. The refurbished **Santo Domingo church**, five blocks north of the main plaza, is an outstanding example of how extravagant the Spanish could be with the free-flowing gold of colonial times. The high wall behind the main altar is completely covered in gold leaf, while the underside of the entrance roof is elaborately decorated with the family tree of the Dominican order. Next door to the church, in a converted stone monastery,

Open to all fitness levels. This adventure is mainly about culture and history, and is not physically strenuous. It is also suitable for families.

Accommodation can be found to suit all budget ranges, from backpacker to deluxe.

No special equipment is needed.

The Spanish dome-roofed church at Mitla, viewed here from the site's Temple of the Columns, was built over the top of a Mixtec building

OAXACA'S BLACK POTTERY

If you wander through the markets of Oaxaca you are bound to notice the proliferation of shiny black pottery. These wares have been made in the village of San Bartolo Coyotepec, just 8km (5 miles) south of Oaxaca City, for centuries, but it was the accidental discovery of a new technique that brought the shine to the village. The renowned potter Doña Rosa Real became a local legend when she found that the black pottery could be polished. Unfortunately, Doña Rosa died in 1980 but her techniques survive in her large workshop. Rather than using a wheel, the potters utilize two concave clay plates, one upturned on the other, to throw the pots, a method dating back to well before the Spanish conquest in 1521. The whole process takes about 25 days due to the slow drying technique and the polishing, which is done with quartz stones. As sturdy as they look, the pots cannot hold water and so are mainly used for decoration or storage. The workshop can be visited on a half-day trip from Oaxaca City.

is the impressive **Museo del Estado** (**Regional Museum of Oaxaca**). Within its labyrinthine rooms are well-presented displays of ornate pre-Hispanic jewellery created from gold, jade, obsidian, and other precious materials, as well as many other artefacts found in the region, including at nearby Monte Albán.

AN ISLAND CAPITAL

The fertile Oaxaca Valley area was originally populated around 10,000 years ago by nomadic hunter-gatherers. By 850 B.C., over 80 villages had developed, and over the next few hundred years they began to organize themselves into culturally and politically distinct regions. This regionalization of power resulted in the growth of urban centres, the first of which was **Monte Albán** (later the Zapotec capital), on top of an "island" hill just 9km (5½ miles) from present-day Oaxaca City. To get there, I hired a Volkswagen Beetle and invited Tim and Colleen, travellers from the United States, to join me on the 20-minute drive up the switchback road to the ruins. On the indistinct footpath that leads up a scruffy slope towards the main plaza, we stopped to admire a bronze relief of Mexican archaeologist Alfonso Caso. In 1931, he began the major excavation project that was to uncover many of the site's secrets.

Entering the Great Plaza, through a narrow gap between two stone walls, was a revelation. Without notice, a vast, flat, grassy area surrounded by immense stone platforms and stairways opened up before us. It was like walking into an old wooden hut and finding a marble hallway. When Monte Albán began to establish its reputation as a major trading centre around 500 B.C. there were probably just a few villages built on the slopes of the hill. As it grew and the hill became the focus of political and religious activity, the Zapotec rulers oversaw a project to flatten the hilltop (no mean feat as it covers 20 hectares, or 50 acres) in order to build larger ceremonial buildings.

Several factors probably played a part in the Monte Albán site development. After climbing the steep, oversized steps to the top of the immense North Platform, we took in the 360-degree view of the valley below, the same view that made it easy for the Zapotecs to defend themselves against rival groups. Food was another important consideration. The Oaxaca Valley was very fertile and could grow enough food to support around 17,000 people. Crucially, the population of Monte Albán at the peak of its power reached 25,000 and possibly overstretched available food supplies, eventually contributing to the centre's rapid demise around A.D. 750.

Wall of the Dancers

By A.D. 500, trade was booming in Mesoamerica, a region that stretched from the Aztec lands to the north of Mexico all the way down to the Mayan territories in Honduras. Monte Albán was right at the centre of the region, and on market days the Great Plaza would have been bustling with large numbers of traders. Pottery from across the region has been found in the great Aztec capital of Tenochtitlán, site of modern-day Mexico City, while jade, found in some of the tombs at Monte Albán, was probably acquired from the Maya.

As we wandered around the plaza's western edge, we came across perhaps the most fascinating artefacts at the ruins. The wall of Los Danzantes (the dancers) is a rather curious, almost gruesome collection of human reliefs carved on large stone tablets. They depict male figures, either Olmec (the first major pre-Hispanic civilization, which developed on Mexico's south-central coast) or Negroid, in various contorted positions, hence the "dancers" name tag. Some appear to have had their stomachs or genital organs cut open. So far researchers have failed to come up with a convincing explanation for the figures, but several hypotheses have been put forward. It is possible that they represent captured prisoners who were mutilated as part of a sacrificial ceremony, though it is hard to imagine so much artistic effort being expended on the enemy, dead or alive. Another theory is that Monte Albán was a medical research centre where deformed subjects were experimented on, though little supporting evidence has been found at the site for this theory. Whatever the truth behind the carvings, they are compelling.

The southern end of the site is dominated by the tallest platform, which used to have a temple at its summit and was probably used for religious ceremonies. The structure's wide, low shape and its construction of large stone blocks was designed to make it earthquake-proof. Most of the limestone, sandstone, and conglomerate used to build Monte Albán was quarried from the local hills and then fashioned into blocks using stone tools. About halfway up the plaza we found a sunken tunnel entrance, and couldn't resist crawling into the confined passageway with our headtorches on. It was just possible to squeeze our way along, until we reached a tiny ventilation hole, after which the tunnel was sealed off. A whole network of tunnels crisscrosses the plaza, linking all the main structures. The purpose of these tunnels remains unknown, but they may have been part of a defence system. Back at the northeastern corner, we climbed onto a smaller platform and gazed down at the site's ballcourt. After a brief visit to the small but impressive museum, where one of the burial tombs

A Game for Winners

Many Central American pre-Hispanic sites, including Monte Albán and Yagul, have an I-shaped ballcourt. This was the stadium where lives were won and lost in the Mesoamericans' equivalent of football. The rules of the game are not really known, but it is thought that just a few players made up a team. They used a rubber ball that could be hit only with the feet, hips, or elbows, and was allowed to bounce only once between touches. The sloping sides of the court, today covered in tiny steps, would have been topped off with white plaster to give a smooth surface off which the ball could rebound. In some ballcourts in the region (although not at Monte Albán) there are stone rings at either end, which probably acted as goalposts. It is thought that only high-ranking people played the game and that losers were sacrificed—a sobering thought for modern football players! A similar game, called *pelota Mixteca*, is still played in the region today.

has been re-created, we jumped back into the Beetle and free-wheeled all the way back to Oaxaca.

MOUNTAIN TREK

To get a different perspective on the region, we took a 15-minute taxi journey out to the San Felipe Riding Club, owned by Doug French, a friendly and knowledgeable expat American, and spent the afternoon horseriding in the **Sierra Madre mountains**. Constantino, our guide, made sure that the horses we chose suited our abilities. The trail dropped down from the riding centre and crossed over a small river before climbing to the forested slopes. All Latin Americans train their horses to be controlled with only one hand; the relaxed position allows the rider greater movement in the saddle for checking out the scenery. Behind us, we could see back down the valley to the city, and it felt refreshing to be leaving the polluted air behind for a while. Constantino allowed us to gallop whenever we wanted, which was probably too often for the horses. At the highest point on the trek, we stopped and looked across at the dominant hills of Monte Albán. From there, the horses knew they were on their way home and picked up the pace themselves.

Back at base, Doug treated us to some sample glasses of his own mescal brew, a potent liquor that was first brewed by the local Indians after the Spanish introduced distilling techniques in the 1800s (see box on page 44). Armed with limes and salt, we downed the shooters with style before snacking on another local delicacy, fried and salted grasshoppers.

ANCIENT CITY-STATES

After Monte Albán and other urban centres were abandoned around A.D. 750, a different, more controlled form of social organization developed in the region, which lasted until the Spanish conquest. The new city-states not only served as cultural, trading, and political centres, but also exercised and enforced controlling policies on all the communities within their territory. Two prime examples of these new centres, Yagul and Mitla, lie off Route 190, the Pan-American Highway, which heads south out of Oaxaca.

Lydia and Ben, first-time travellers from Germany, joined the three of us in the now very full Beetle for the trip. Driving in Mexico is a fun and absorbing activity, though not recommended for those with high blood pressure. Getting out of Oaxaca is perhaps the biggest challenge: both southbound lanes often have three or four cars across them, buses stop and start without warning, and traffic lights seem to attract all of the region's colour-blind drivers. Utilizing my self-named driving style of "relaxed aggression" I made it out onto the open highway and prepared to negotiate the obstacle course of large trucks, huge potholes, and seriously dangerous *topes*. Found around villages and towns, *topes*

ABOVE The view over the plazas of Yagul from the nearby hilltop fortress
RIGHT The Los Danzantes (dancers) wall at Monte Albán portrays male figures in contorted positions
LEFT The Tlacolula Vallley spreads out beyond this curious ruin at Yagul

are speed bumps (often unmarked) that can rip your car's wheels off if you don't spot them in time.

CHANGE OF LIFESTYLE

After an action-packed 29km (18 miles), we turned off to the left for the short drive up to **Yagul**. The site's location reflects the changed priorities of the new phase: the city-states were built on lower ground rather than hilltops, preferably near a water source and fertile alluvial plains. For defence, simple fortified structures were constructed on hilltops near the main site where inhabitants could retreat to during attacks. Yagul's location is so breathtakingly beautiful and its buildings so neatly arranged that it could have been used as a showcase to tempt community leaders into buying into the new lifestyle.

Parts of Yagul were built during the Zapotec heyday, but most of the structures seen today are from the Mixtec city-state era, from A.D. 750 onwards. The main area is built on three different levels, and we started by exploring the lowest. The Patio of the Triple Tomb is a small, square plaza, surrounded by low platforms, with an altar placed in the middle and a rather bizarre stone frog sculpture on the eastern side. It was built during the Monte Albán I period (around 600 B.C.) but was developed and used right through to the Monte Albán V period in A.D. 950. Below the altar, steps led us down into the dark, cramped tomb, one of the oldest structures at the site. The burial chambers had all been looted by the time archaeologists got to them in the 1950s, but they retain frescoed door lintels and traces of the original red-ochre paint. The new era also saw a reduction in the number of large public building projects—perhaps as a symbolic rejection of the powerful élite that ruled at Monte Albán—but Yagul's ballcourt obviously escaped such regulation. Built on the second level, it is the second biggest (after the one at Chichén Itzá in the Yucatán Peninsula) and perhaps the best preserved in Mesoamerica. It still features the round, stone platform halfway down the field on which the ball may have been bounced to restart the game. The trail to the ballcourt, surrounded by cactus plants, also leads to the final level of the main area and to the impressive maze of rooms dubbed the "Palace of the Six Patios." This was where Yagul's rulers lived.

Yagul was an important centre in the

THE MAKING OF MESCAL

Mescal is a potent liquor made in Oaxaca state from the agave cactus plant. The agave plants have to grow for at least eight years (preferably ten) before they are picked. The cores are then baked in a pit and ground down into a mash, which is put into a water-filled barrel. Heated bronze tanks, placed under a load of earth, are used to distil the mash. The resulting condensation is the finished, smoky tasting product. The worms that live in the agave plant are added to mescal for those who fancy a (slightly hallucinogenic) snack after finishing the bottle.

Oaxaca Valley, and although defence was seemingly less of an issue than at Monte Albán, attacks were still common. At Yagul, a small fortress was built high on the hill behind the main site. We climbed the steep, rocky path to reach its main wall and were treated to an outstanding aerial view of the ruins and the sweeping Tlacolula Valley beyond. Whilst the ruins are not on the same grand scale as those at Monte Albán, they are aesthetically very pleasing and certainly worth a stop on the way to the more popular ruins at **Mitla**, some 30km (19 miles) further along Highway 190.

A SUBTLE SPANISH CONQUEST

Evidence found in rock caves to the north of Mitla shows that this area was one of the very first places in the region to be inhabited, dating back to thousands of years before Christ. The town area saw every phase of civilization development until it became a major centre during the city-state era after A.D. 750. The construction techniques used have thrown archaeologists into confusion over who actually lived here. It was very much a Zapotec region both before and after the Mixtecs moved in, but the structures are almost purely of Mixtec design. However, the oddest structure stands outside the main entrance in one of three courtyards known as the Church group. The structure in question is a dome-roofed church built by the Spanish over the top of the southernmost courtyard using stones from the original Mixtec building. This aided the Spaniards' religious conversion policy by showing clearly that their religion was more powerful than the old one and also, by using the Mixtec stones, demonstrated that it was an integrated development rather than a distinct change.

In the Group of Columns lie the best-preserved palaces. Bright red-ochre stucco still adorns the façades of low platforms that surround a stone plaza. At the top of the broad stairway leading to the intricately decorated Temple of the Columns, we passed through one of three large doorways into the Column Room. Here, six monolithic stone pillars still stand strong but no longer have a roof to support. Their tapered shapes are perfectly smooth, an amazing achievement considering that the builders had only stone tools. From the columns, we had to duck to get through the long, dark, twisting passageway that leads to the Patio of the Grecas, named after the tiny geometric block designs that line many of the walls at Mitla. No significance other than decoration has ever been attributed to them, but they must hold importance as they are contained in some of the codices (fabric panel "books") that survived the systematic Spanish destruction of indigenous historical records. This is just one of many mysteries still to be solved in the Oaxaca Valley.

Exploring the old ruins, with their palaces and plazas, fortresses and artwork, was an absolute thrill and gave us a unique insight into the civilizations that were at one time dominant in the region but today remain in the shadow of the Aztecs and the Maya. Perhaps with the passage of time and a little more study these sites will gain their rightful recognition as being important centres of two of the great civilizations of Mexico.

GOING IT ALONE

Internal Travel

Getting to Oaxaca City from Mexico City is cheap and quick on the numerous buses run by ADO and Cristóbal Colón. There is a daily train that makes the journey, too, but it is very slow and prone to opportunistic robberies, and although it travels through very scenic country the majority of the journey takes place at night.

When to Go

During the rainy season (June–October) Oaxaca experiences regular afternoon showers, with bright weather the rest of the day. From December to April temperatures rocket and the sun beats down mercilessly. One of the best months to visit is November, when there are few tourists yet enough sunshine. Get to Monte Albán early in the morning as the light is beautiful then, temperatures are cooler, and the tour buses don't arrive until about ten o'clock.

Planning

There are frequent bus services to all the main sites, and they can all be reached and visited as day trips from Oaxaca City. Both Yagul and Mitla can be visited in a single, albeit long, day as they both lie off Highway 190. Ask the bus driver to stop at the Yagul junction, from where it is a 15-minute walk up to the site. All the major car-hire companies, including Avis, Hertz, and Budget, have offices in Oaxaca City. Ring around before booking as there are often special offers. The horse riding can be booked with the San Felipe Riding Club; the price includes taxi rides from and to your hotel.

Travellers' Tips

- If you hire a car, check it thoroughly for any damage before you leave the office and make sure that any dents are indicated on the appropriate sheet. If the petrol tank is full when you pick the car up, make sure you return it in the same state, as the hire firm will charge perhaps three times as much for the fuel.
- Be extremely careful when driving over *topes* (speed bumps) as they are potentially damaging even at a crawl and many are not signed or painted. *Vibradores* are rumble strips of corrugated bitumen found around towns. They, too, must be taken slowly.
- Never leave any items in view within the car. Things that may not seem precious to you may be tempting enough for someone to risk breaking in.
- Buses stop anywhere along the road if you hold your arm out, but sometimes fly straight past if they are full.

What to Take

- Water bottle.
- Sunglasses.
- Sunblock.
- Torch for exploring tombs.
- Strong walking shoes.

Health

Precautions against malaria should be taken; consult your doctor for up-to-date advice. Temperatures can soar in the Oaxaca Valley during the day, so take plenty of water to the ruins. Make sure it is sterilsed or boiled. Be sure to wear a sun hat and sunblock, which you should re-apply during the day.

MORE OAXACA VALLEY RUINS

- **Cerro de la Campana (Huijazoo)** Situated to the northwest of Oaxaca City. The ruins are set on a number of impressive ridges. There is a ballcourt, along with wonderful artwork in Tomb 5, but the site has been only partially excavated.
- **Dainzu** Just to the west of Lambityeco (see below). Has a well-preserved tomb featuring lintels with jaguar carvings, as well as several large platforms.
- **Lambityeco** A small site just off Highway 190 before Yagul. It features impressive temple façades adorned with beautiful stone masks.
- **San José Mogote** Just to the north of Oaxaca City. This was one of the most important centres during the village stage of development in the valley. Some of the residential areas have been excavated.

Sea and Sierra

by Fiona Dunlop

Puerto Vallarta is arguably Mexico's most attractive beach resort as it artfully combines the magnificent Pacific with jungle-clad sierra, cultural history, crafts, and endless activities. Few people go away disappointed from this hedonistic hub.

Once just a sleepy little fishing village, Puerto Vallarta kicked off in Hollywood style in 1963 when John Huston filmed his *Night of the Iguana* in Mismaloya with stars Ava Gardner and Richard Burton. In the backgound was an enamoured Elizabeth Taylor, whose off-screen romance with Burton, picturesquely set in the steep cobbled streets of Old Vallarta , brought fame and rapid fortune to this Pacific resort.

Today, much of the population of over 100,000 is dependent on tourism. Yet although part glitzy and rife with happy-hour bars and high-rise hotels, Vallarta has a spirit of its own, from the ever-fuming buses that thunder through the narrow downtown streets to roadside juice and taco stalls, time-share sharks, or the real thing either swimming in the bay or on sale at the fish market. Here, too, enticing shops display the innovative best of Jalisco's artisan skills, which include the psychedelic works of the Huichol Indians. And then there is the lush green jungle rising above the southern end of the Bahía de Banderas, Mexico's largest bay (25km, or 16 miles, long), allegedly the world's second largest and certainly one of its deepest (it plummets to 1,865m, or 6,120 feet). Beaches beckon, as do the blue ocean depths.

Most beach activities here are aimed at people with little or no experience, so they are not strenuous. All-day hikes, bike rides, or horse rides in the sierra can be harder work.

Puerto Vallarta's hotels span the entire range, from basic rooms in the old town to luxurious establishments at Marina Vallarta and on the southern beaches. Self-catering apartments are a popular alternative, especially with families.

No equipment other than good walking shoes and binoculars is needed.

Vallarta lay-out

The scale can be confusing as hotels are scattered along 15km (9 miles) of shore. In the north are the all-in resorts of **Nuevo Vallarta**, a development that actually lies in the state of Nayarit. **Marina Vallarta**, just south of the airport, is where some of Vallarta's plushest accommodation and yachts lie, while the scenic bays of the southern stretch, from Playa Conchas Chinas to Mismaloya, are home to several luxury hotels. Halfway up the bay lies **Vallarta** itself, divided into two main areas north and south of the pretty Río Cuale, both of which have a wide selection of hotels to suit most budgets. This is my personal favourite as its more authentic Mexican scale and atmosphere leave you free to explore on foot and to pick and choose bars and restaurants—before walking to the beach.

No one should miss out on **Playa de los Muertos**, with its fun-loving weekend crowds that gravitate between sea and beachside restaurants, some of which date from Vallarta's nascent days of tourism in the 1950s. This area is also where official vendors dressed in obligatory white sell anything and everything from model cars to woven blankets, jewellery, wind chimes, and huge baskets, and consequently become the plague of the sunbathers. Above them, para-sailers

The marina at Puerto Vallarta, once a sleepy fishing village, is now filled with luxury boats, and surrounded by new hotels for the flourishing tourist trade

VALLARTA TRANSPORT

The international airport is most people's point of entry to Puerto Vallarta, and is often their first experience of unnecessary cost. Avoid taking the exorbitantly priced individual airport taxis; instead, stick to the *colectivos*, which ferry several passengers together to their various hotels. Those on a low budget with little baggage can simply walk out onto the highway and catch a bus marked *Centro*: this goes past Marina Vallarta on the way to Old Vallarta. On departure, take a bus marked *Aeropuerto* or use a regular urban taxi. After years of enduring rip-offs, tourists can now enjoy fixed rates for taxis around Vallarta, while buses cost only a few pesos.

are drawn through the air for 15 minutes of adrenalin-rush, while in front water-skiers and jet-skiers monopolize the waves. Peace is not something you will find on this beach.

Even if you have experienced Vallarta before, enjoyed the restaurants, done the shopping, and revelled in the nightlife, there is always more. On my third trip I wanted to dig deeper, explore further afield, and see some of the natural riches claimed by its inhabitants. Whales were definitely not on the agenda, as I was there out of season, but dolphins were, as were the vast colonies of resident fish and birds that paradoxically live on the fringe of this sophisticated resort.

MATINAL FEATHERS

Birds first, I thought, in the interests of tanning gently (the sun in these parts is fierce). The birding appointment was fixed at 6:45am at a tour agency in the old town. Setting off from my hotel along the dark backstreets of Playa de los Muertos (meaning beach of the dead, and so named due to the dirty deeds of 16th-century pirates), I felt very much part of Vallarta. There is an intimacy about dawn streets the world over that is shared between the few humans up and about, and this was no exception. Some recalcitrant clubbers staggered home, oblivious to anyone else, far brighter workmen set about repairing a *palapa* (palm-thatched) roof with freshly cut palm-fronds, a moustachioed man in immaculate white overalls and apron squeezed carrot, grapefruit, and orange juice at his roadside stall, several cocks crowed purposefully, and the church bells emphatically struck 6:30am.

At the tour office I discovered that, due to last-minute cancellations, there were only two of us. All the better, exclaimed the other bird-watcher, a Canadian-British woman whose bubbly enthusiasm was to continue unabated for the next five hours. We were soon heading north out of town in a huge Chevrolet four-wheel drive steered by our guide Kimberley, a cheerful American biologist who turned out to have a highly trained eye for winged creatures. As we sped along Vallarta's palm-lined coastal freeway, which to any European looks distinctly American, the sun was rising at our backs over the sierra. And that is another of Vallarta's peculiarities: sunsets are spectacular as the glowing orb sinks into the Pacific horizon, but sunrises are non-existent owing to the mountainous sierra. As we turned off past some dilapidated, semi-industrial structures, the background was becoming increasingly rural. Then, after neatly accomplishing a suicidal turn across the main road, Kimberley bumped down a dirt road and finally pulled up beside a large field. Binoculars were whipped out and focused, and absorbed cries of delight soon followed. This spot, edged by palm trees and shrubs, turned out to be an ornithological heaven.

Into our respective lenses came groove-billed anis (*Crotophaga sulcirostris*), yellow-winged caciques (Cacicus cela), northern jacanas (*Jacana spinosa*), egrets, flycatchers, and gnatcatchers, as well as a purple gallinule (*Gallinula martinica*), multi-coloured despite its name. They just kept on appearing and, even to my untrained eye, seemed to be parading for us from tree branches, shrubs, and electricity cables. It was hard to keep up, though Kimberley did her best to explain the intricate markings of different species during breeding or as juveniles, while I peered through her sharply focused telescope. The odd bicycle or truck rolled past, sending up clouds of dust in true Mexican style, and groups of farmers or workers strolled by on foot. One old man with a wide, toothy smile was invited by Kimberley to look through her scope. Like us he was transfixed and, before eventually pursuing his morning route, shook hands all round. As he strode off, an elegant quail (*Coturnix coturnix*) strutted across the track in front of him.

Water-birds

Our next stop was a few miles further on, past banana groves, mango trees, and tangled mangroves edging the Río Ameca. *En route*, as we crawled along the dirt road, we had a field-day spotting iguanas in all shapes and sizes, two of them sunning themselves on a huge termites' nest in the fork of a tree while others draped themselves over a rusting fence. Sacklike nests of the golden oriole (*Oriolus oriolus*) were suspended from one tree, calabash from another, and we drove through the generous shade of several gigantic Guanacaste trees (*Enterolobium cyclocarpum*). Cattle grazed in the distance, black vultures (*Coragyps atratus*) circled overhead, butterflies fluttered past; the scene was idyllically and unexpectedly bucolic. The riverside vantage point introduced some new water-birds—white ibis (*Eudocimus albus*), belted kingfishers (*Megaceryle alcyon*), royal terns (*Thalasseus maximus*)—as well as repeats on some of the species sighted inland, plus a perfectly posed American kestrel (*Falco sparverius*). From here, it was a short walk to the estuary, the Boca de Tomate, where fishermen using handheld nets brought in catches for the seafood restaurants that were setting up for the day on the sand. The pelican numbers multiplied, while in the distance the towering modern hotels of Marina Vallarta and Nueva Vallarta were silhouetted against the moody Sierra Madre, a clear reminder of the urban sophistication we had temporarily left behind.

By now we had been birding for well over three hours, and despite continuing chirrups of delight from my companions, it was time to move to our last lookout. This turned out to be a peaceful café-restaurant sited beside a large lagoon blanketed in water hyacinths. As great, snowy, and cattle egrets (*Egretta alba*, *E. thula*, and *Bubulcus ibis*) watched us from a tree, we totted up the morning's total: 46 species spotted. With averages of around 30 in this coastal area, ours had been an excellent innings.

Pacific plunge

The Bahía de Banderas is vast: from a boat in the centre of the bay, you can only just see the northern headland of Punta de Mita and the southern cape, both fuzzily outlined in the heat-haze. Punta de Mita is in fact part of a volcanic formation whose shallow underwater

BIRDING OPTIONS

Vallarta's alternative birding destination, the sierra, has fewer numbers of species but specializes in the more exotic, such as macaws, parrots, hummingbirds, and parakeets. Further north, the waterways of La Tovara around San Blas are another good place to spot the 300 or so species known to inhabit the region. Avoid taking a day trip there from Vallarta, however, as this leaves too little time on the spot, but instead opt for an overnight trip (these can be arranged through a tour agency).

shelf joins up with a tiny group of islands, the **Islas Marietas**. The islands are much favoured by scuba-divers for their vertiginous drop-offs, a total contrast to the shadowy depths at the southern end of the bay.

The rocky outcrops of the Marietas are also natural havens for water-birds as well as for unadulterated underwater life, the result being that they have become candidates for national marine sanctuary status, decades after Jacques Cousteau gave them his approval. For me, these islands seemed a natural follow-up to my inland bird-watching forays, and the ideal place for taking the Pacific plunge in a setting somewhat wilder than the congested waters off the Playa de los Muertos.

The snorkelling and dolphin-watching group I joined was led by Oscar Frey, an oceanologist and obsessive researcher into local whale activity, and the owner of an adventure travel agency. At 9am sharp, 12 of us piled into a canopied motorboat at Marina Vallarta: two guides, two crew, and eight tourists. With us came the snorkelling gear and several lunchboxes—it didn't look as if we would starve. About an hour later we were anchoring at the first island for our baptismal snorkel of the day. I couldn't wait, and leapt into the welcoming waves to be instantly surrounded by an underwater serenade of technicoloured fish. Angel-fish, damselfish, and butterflyfish (*Chaetodon auriga*) were the easiest to identify, but other species that were new to me darted in and out of the rocky crevices. A sharply pointed trumpet fish (*Aulostomus maculatus*) sailed by, looking ready to skewer the next cherubfish that crossed its path, while a sergeant-major (*Abudefduf marginatus*) looked appropriately in control. When I dived deeper, I could see lobsters, starfish, and sea urchins clinging to the bottom. Coral is scarce here, in part due to the warming and consequent bleaching effect of El Niño; at present, red sea squirts, polyps, and some fan coral deeper down are the only representatives.

In the middle of this aquatic paradise, I

LEFT The waters around the Islas Marietas, at the northern end of the Bahía de Banderas, teem with shoals of technicoloured fish
BELOW The film set for John Huston's Night of the Iguana *at Misamaloya, 10km (6 miles) south of Puerto Vallarta, has been turned into an iguana park*

heard the all-too-familiar sound of boat engines. Our departure was to be precipitated by the arrival of a large cruise boat containing at least 60 people and with a bright yellow "happy hour" banner flapping on its side; the habits of Vallarta's *malecón* (promenade) had closed in on us even out here. As the new arrivals flopped into the water, we climbed the ladder back onto our little boat and the captain accelerated away. Cruising close to the shore, he gave us a wonderful close-up of colonies of magnificent frigatebirds (*Fregata magnificens*) wheeling above the island, nosediving pelicans, and blue-footed and brown boobies (*Sula nebouxii* and *S. lucogaster*) with their black juveniles lined up on the clifftop, seemingly saluting our departure.

Dolphin search

We circled around the outer islands searching in vain for dolphins. None appeared, so we anchored in a small bay off the most far-flung island, where this time we held on to our monopoly long enough to demolish a copious cold lunch on board between further bouts of aquatic indulgence. Here we could snorkel up to a small beach that was backed by towering cliffs or swim through the choppy waves of a natural rock archway to inner caves. Not everyone was a water-lover, and one woman opted to spend most of the trip sunbathing in the boat while her husband snorkelled happily below. Another suffered from seasickness, and so was treated to her lunch on the island beach, specially ferried in a floating lunchbox by a swimming guide. That's what I call service!

Later in the afternoon, as we chugged back across the bay feeling well scorched by the sun, the dolphins did, finally, appear. The captain had continued to scan the water, so it was he who saw them first, and he immediately steered the boat towards their undulating forms. Using his hydrophone (an underwater microphone wired up to a small loudspeaker), Oscar was able to interpret the underwater gurglings of dolphins communicating and feeding, and estimated there were probably about 100 or so in small groups around the bay. A few turned on a dance for us, leaping vertically in and out of the waves as our boat zigzagged back and forth between them, while some of my companions snapped away wildly with their cameras. Even if their photos subsequently showed only blurred waves, we had lived the experience of the dolphins' welcome to the Bahía de Banderas.

WHALES AND DOLPHINS

The Bahía de Banderas is a favourite breeding ground and seasonal habitat for several species of whales and dolphins. The friendly spotted dolphins are visible all year round, but other species generally appear from November to April and often into May. Rarest are the sperm whales (*Physeter macrocephalus*), but killer and false killer whales (*Orcinius orca* and *Pseudorca crassidens*) can be seen, as can Bryde's whale (*Balaenoptera edeni*) and, most commonly, the humpback whale (*Megaptera novaeangliae*). Bottlenosed dolphins (*Tursiops truncatus*) and spinner dolphins are also frequent visitors.

Natural therapies

Mexico is big on alternative medicines and treatments, possibly a logical progression from the deeply rooted rituals of the ancient Mesoamericans and confirmation of man's intimate relation with nature. Some rituals are being revived, or have never even died out, one of these being the *temazcal*, or Aztec steam-bath. This you can indulge in at Puerto Vallarta's recently opened therapy centre, **Terra Noble**, a spectacularly sited and designed organic structure that offers massages and body treatments as well as pottery and painting for larger groups. By chance, I was in Vallarta during the full moon, traditionally a time for spiritual renewal and considered perfect for a *temazcal*. At Terra Noble sessions are organized separately for male and female groups, and do not just stop at the physical side of things. Thus I found myself howling, chanting, drinking sage tea, and sweating profusely in the company of 11 Vallarta women.

This cathartic experience takes place inside an igloo-like stucture that symbolizes the maternal womb. At its centre is a hole in the ground, into which are shovelled glowing hot stones; a few cups of water thrown over these high-temperature rocks produces a steam that beats any hammam (Turkish bath) I've been in. Seated in a circle around the edge, we followed the lead of Gracia de la Luz, who for that evening had taken charge of our souls in a forcefully didactic fashion. Between each "act" (for we went through a highly theatrical ritual, successively honouring all the elements, albeit in total darkness), Gracia doused each of us in cold water. Relief. But the heat mounted again, and two hours later I emerged drenched, physically drained, and, I hoped, spiritually purified. The next day I returned for more punishment, this time in the form of a massage.

Terra Noble's various structures are laid out on a landscaped hillside with stunning views over the bay. The adobe massage rooms are open-fronted, so if you book your massage for late afternoon as I did, you are in for a surprise. When you first lie down, you see the high-rise-lined bay and freeway; by the time you turn over, halfway through your massage, night will have fallen to produce the glittering stage-set of nocturnal Vallarta. Several types of massages are available, as well as salt or clay treatments, and Terra Noble's masseuses take into consideration your current physical form. It's an idea to save this experience for the end of your trip, after you have stretched your body to the limit with watersports, horse riding, hiking, or biking. Only then will you feel ready to descend the hillside to plunge back into Old Vallarta and indulge in the resort's other big draw, its traditionally excellent gastronomy.

GOING IT ALONE

Internal Travel

Getting to Puerto Vallarta is easy as the airport receives international flights (including charters) from North America and Europe, as well as a regular schedule of domestic flights from Mexico City, Guadalajara, Los Cabos, Monterrey, and Mazatlán. First-class long-distance buses come to Vallarta from Guadalajara, Tijuana, Mazatlán, Ciudad Juárez, Monterrey, Aguascalientes, León, Manzanillo, Querétaro, Colima, Barra de Navidad, and Mexico City. Car or jeep hire is widely available in Vallarta.

When to Go

June to September are the hottest and least pleasant months in Puerto Vallarta, when the rainy season combines with average temperatures of 29°C (84°F) to make it uncomfortably humid. The best (and high) season doubles up with the whale season from December to April, so follow the cetaceans' example by heading for the Bahía de Banderas to enjoy average temperatures of 23–26°C (73–79°F), albeit lower in January to March. It is essential to book hotels in advance at this time as occupancy rates are high.

Planning

Most tourists come to Vallarta on an all-inclusive holiday, but this is by no means essential as English is widely spoken and locals are very used to helping foreigners. In the high season it is advisable to book your hotel in advance, at least for the first few nights, but the rest of your stay can be left entirely open. Most adventure activities are geared to half- or full days and can be booked the previous day, with the exception of specialist actvities such as bird-watching, which are dependent on rounding up enough enthusiasts. Puerto Vallarta's activities do not come cheap, so make sure you know your budget before you sign up.

You can easily combine a stay at Puerto Vallarta with a few days in Guadalajara, Mexico's second-largest and culturally very active city. Alternatively, hire a car and explore the beautiful coastline to the south, or play it safe and take a flight to Los Cabos in Baja California.

What to Take

- ❑ Binoculars for bird-watching.
- ❑ Good-quality sunglasses to shield the glare.
- ❑ Cotton cap or wide-brimmed hat for sea-kayaking or any other boat trip.
- ❑ High-factor sunblock.
- ❑ A T-shirt if you plan to snorkel for long periods.

Health

In health terms, this is a place to relax as Puerto Vallarta's food is hygienically prepared and its tap-water standards exceptionally high.

OTHER ACTIVITIES IN THE AREA

Puerto Vallarta offers a myriad of watersports. Jet-skiing, para-sailing, and kayaking are ubiquitous on the town beaches, while sea-kayaking is another popular activity, and is often organized at picturesque Punta de Mita, also a surfers' paradise. Sailing cruises and fishing charters are a less strenuous way of seeing the bay. Vallarta's offshore depths offer great scuba-diving opportunities both for beginners and more advanced divers. Near the southern tip of the bay is Chimo, where two spectacular underwater formations are best explored by certified divers. Beginners can learn at the beautiful beaches of Majahuita and Quimixto, while both snorkellers and advanced divers can enjoy the national marine park of Los Arcos. In the northern part of the bay, beyond the Islas Marietas, lies El Morro, a series of pinnacles where jacks, rays, and yellowtails lurk in numerous caves and tunnels. Whales also visit this site, whose wonders are reserved for certified divers.

Landlubbers have the choice between several riding stables that lead treks up into the sierra. All-terrain vehicles (ATVs) are an alternative way to explore the back roads, though not the most ecologically correct. More silent and demanding more energy are mountain bikes, which are perfectly adapted to the sierra terrain.

Rafting in Veracruz

by Fiona Dunlop

Diverse scenery, balmy microclimates, historical reminders, and its proximity to Mexico City (it's only a three-hour drive away) make the state of Veracruz a natural playground for the country's capitalinos *(capital-dwellers). Whitewater rafting is the number one activity here, and can easily be combined with cultural forays.*

Most people think of Veracruz in terms of the steamy tropical port itself, but this is just the beginning—and it certainly was the beginning for Hernán Cortés, who landed just north of Veracruz on April 21, 1519. From here he marched west through the misty heights of the Sierra Madre Oriental to conquer Moctezuma's lake capital of Tenochtitlán, no doubt fording a few rivers on the way. Rushing torrents are one of the natural highlights of Veracruz, and are now targeted by a string of whitewater-rafting companies, the helmeted conquistadors of today. Add to this several important archaeological sites, the excellent coffee that grows in the hills, and the fresh seafood that lands on coastal plates, and you have an enticing destination.

Never having tried whitewater rafting, I was keen to experience what is touted as a fantastic adrenalin-rush, though not without a fair amount of trepidation. With an agency in Mexico City, I worked out a four-day itinerary that would not only take me to the best rafting sites in Veracruz but also whisk me through a diversity of landscapes to several major historical sites. And as a bonus I would spend a night in the resort of Veracruz itself—how could I pass up on such an excellent offer?

The very essence of whitewater rafting is that it is a challenge. Apart from energetic paddling, it is quite usual to take a tumble in the river, and you should be aware that accidents do happen.

★★ The base camp is reasonably comfortable but you may have to share a tent (they sleep four) as well as the washing facilities. At night, torchlight is the rule. Fellow rafters can be noisy.

All equipment is provided by the rafting company. You need a swimming costume, shorts, a T-shirt, and, preferably, waterproof sandals. If you are doing more than one expedition, take a change of this clothing as it is slow to dry.

The base camp

Nearly five hours after leaving Mexico City, we arrived at our first destination,

the rafting base camp near **Jalcomulco**. As Alejandro, my young guide, driver, and alter ego, swung his car into the car park, a recycled U.S. schoolbus was disgorging at least 30 bedraggled people. When I realized that this was the morning rafting expedition returning for lunch, I looked at them more closely. They seemed perfectly normal, covered both sexes and all ages from teens to 50s, and appeared to have all their limbs intact. Some were even laughing as they disappeared into the shade of the mango trees, so perhaps I would survive the afternoon after all.

The base camp accommodates over 100 people, most of whom come at weekends by car from the capital. There was a handful of foreigners (Japanese and Canadians), but otherwise this was a truly Mexican assembly. Somehow, it felt like a scouts' camp, with its volleyball court, open-air pool tables, and alleys of tents raised on platforms and acting as a backdrop to a sporty looking crowd striding around in shorts. At the far end were the communal washing facilities, which turned out to be surprisingly well designed and maintained. Another surprise was the food, which was fresh, varied, and flavoursome—not easy to accomplish on such a scale. And then, much to my post-prandial pleasure, there were those typically Mexican

LEFT The Río Pescados features Class III and IV rapids
BELOW Preparing the dinghies and donning life jackets and safety helmets at Jalcomulco prior to entering the Río Pescados

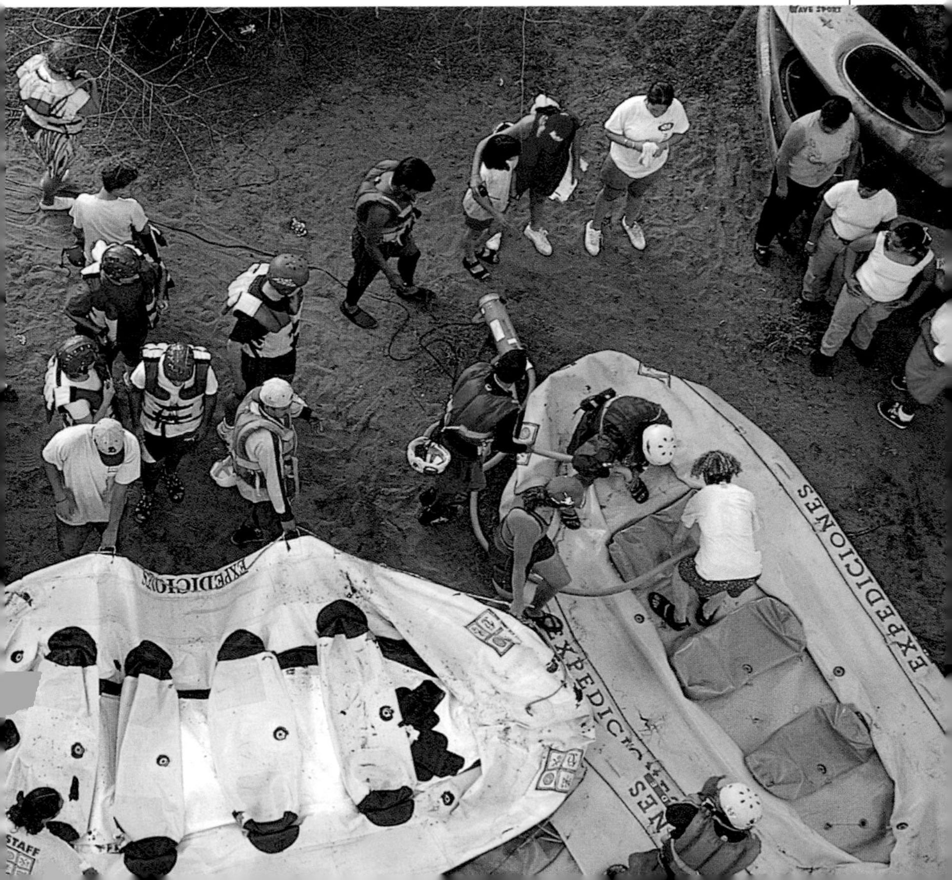

appendages, namely hammocks.

Alejandro finally roused me from my siesta and steered me towards the shaky old bus that was to transport the afternoon group to the river. Clutching life jackets and helmets, we rattled away past donkeys and fields of sugarcane to Jalcomulco, no doubt a sleepy, deserted little village during the week but now, on a Saturday afternoon, bustling with rafters and kayakers with their voluminous gear. On and under the bridge were groups from at least four rafting companies, each one colour-coded by its rafts and life jackets. The Río Pescados and its extension, the Río Antigua, are the state's most varied Class III and IV rivers, and at this time of year monopolize much of the rafting.

By now the sun that had been blazing earlier was fading, but we had reached an important moment—the technique itself. There followed general instructions, an outline of the orders that would be used, and an explanation of what to do if you fell out and how to avoid injury. The supremely calm Alejandro, an experienced rafter, tried to boost my fast-diminishing spirits with repeated utterings of "*No preocupate*" (Don't worry), but my morale was not helped by the threatening mood of darkening skies. After a rafting guide had been allotted to steer each dinghy (for six or eight people) we underwent a series of warm-up exercises, something that not all rafting companies indulge in. However, in view of the plummeting temperatures I wasn't against the idea.

RAFTABLE RIVERS IN VERACRUZ

Rivers are classified for rafting from the easiest, Class I, to the most difficult, Class V. Veracruz offers the following:

- **Barranca Grande** Class IV and V. For experienced rafters. Features 12km (7½ miles) through canyons. Navigable October–December.
- **Río Actopán** Class II and III. Ideal for families. Very beautiful scenery of fruit trees and waterfalls for 12km (7½ miles). Navigable January–May.
- **Río Antigua** Class III and IV. A 24-km (15-mile) stretch with continuous rapids and high waves. Navigable from June–November.
- **Río Filobobos** Class II and III. Stunning landscapes include the Encanto waterfall and archaelogical sites. Said to be Mexico's best, and 58km (35 miles) long. June–September.
- **Río Pescados** Class III and IV. Sixty sets of rapids over a distance of 18km (11 miles). Navigable all year round.

THE DINGHY MASTER

The moment of truth finally came as we clambered into our rubber dinghies, paddle in hand, and sat on the edge with our feet tucked into the crack. My rafting guide, Emilio, a fine-limbed, tattooed Mexican who also spoke some English, turned out to be one of the best, not only in technical terms but also in maintaining a stream of witty communication that allayed most of my fears. The guide's role is in fact fundamental, for it is he who shouts instructions from his vantage point at the rear, telling us when to paddle on the right or on the left, when to paddle backwards, when to stop paddling altogether, or when to slip off the edge and crouch inside the dinghy. We were mere slaves fulfilling his orders, but at the same time fulfilling ourselves. It is not surprising to learn that whitewater rafting is being used increasingly in corporate incentive training programmes. Bonding happens without even trying, the proof being that at the end of three hours my five co-rafters raised their paddles in honour of *Inglaterra*.

With Emilio in charge, we crash through the first set of rapids. In retrospect, these were the worst, as his orders became lost in our confusion and beginners' shock. However, from then on we feel like experts, paddling smoothly and energetically when we are told to, then stopping to let the rapids swing the boat through the currents. Each time the adrenalin flow pumps hard, and each time we feel triumphant. Behind us, the Japanese contingent does equally well, but we often have to wait for the other two dinghies, which are having more difficulty. And all the way we are accompanied by our personal kayaking lifesaver, a Quebécois with very limited Spanish who appears to be truly dedicated to his role. Luckily, we don't have to test his abilities, but it is reassuring to know he is skimming along behind us.

About three hours later we are all shivering. The sun has long since retreated and drizzle from the heavens joins the sprays of water from the river. Normally it takes over four hours to cover 18km (11 miles), but Emilio decides that we have had enough. We power through our last set of rapids as usual, congratulating ourselves with enthusiasm. Wading from the dinghy we climb onto terra firma, still trembling from the cold, to be greeted with crates of Corona beer—more appropriate for a sun-soaked expedition than for this damp, chilly moment. By this time the rain is falling steadily and, as a result, once we are safely and wetly inside the old bus its wheels churn pointlessly in the mud. Conflicting advice and manual pushing follows, until at last the bus rolls forwards to deliver us to very welcome hot showers back at the camp. Those in the know head for the ultimate heat treatment: the *temazcal*, or Aztec steam-bath.

Later that evening, more self-congratulation follows as we watch a video of the high points of our expedition, filmed by a particularly multi-talented kayaker. This takes place in the open-sided bar, but while the tequila flows the rain continues to pour down outside. Although most people here arrived with ready-made groups of friends or their families, communication is easy and there is a relaxed atmosphere in which even the shy Japanese participate. A live rock concert inspires some dancing, then most tired rafters start drifting off by torchlight to their tents and oblivion.

On the Road Again

Alejandro had arranged an early start for us the next day, as we were heading north past the university town of Xalapa to the Río Filobobos, about two hours' drive away. Filobobos would, according to my mentor, give me equally exciting rafting with the added bonus of some spectacular landscapes, including the Encanto waterfall, where I could swim. Our agenda was to meet up with a different rafting company in the town of Tlapacoyán at 9am. So, before anyone else was even thinking of emerging from behind their insect screens, we were already on the road, driving past banana palms, tropical forest, and brilliant orange flame-trees to the higher elevations around Xalapa. As we twisted upwards, mists shrouded the coffee bushes, cattle, and prickly pear cacti, an effect of the proximity of the glowering

XALAPA MUSEUM

Veracruz is exceptionally rich in the ancient cultures of the Gulf. Not only did this state nurture the Olmecs, the mother of all Mesoamerican cultures, but also the Totonacs (known as Classic Veracruz) and the northern Huastecs. The best place to learn about them is the Museo de Antropologia (Anthropological Museum) on Avenida Xalapa in Xalapa itself. This beautifully designed museum (1986), second only to that in Mexico City in terms of scale and quality, displays its collection in a series of sunlit patios and terraced marble halls. There are several examples of the Olmecs' giant basalt heads, a stunning series of "smiling" clay figures, votive *hachas* (axes), and countless superb pieces of pottery.

The remote city of Cantona, located in the foothills of the Sierra Madre, was abandoned in the early 11th century

Cofre de Perote, Mexico's fifth-highest mountain at 4,250m (14,000 feet). From bananas to pine forests, the astoundingly varied ecosystems also extended to bleak stretches of heath peppered with giant yucca trees.

The only town of any importance we went through was **Teziutlán**, located on a severely potholed road despite recent prosperity brought by newly founded *maquiladores* (tax-free assembly plants that re-export to the United States). Bumps aside, this place seemed akin to paradise. The pretty town lies in a stunningly lush, wild valley overlooked by rocky outcrops, with waterfalls gushing onto the road and mists rolling around the summits. From here onwards the road descended to the fertile valley and market town of **Tlapacoyán**, where bamboo stands, hillsides of poinsettia (*Euphorbia pulcherrima*), and vast orange groves indicated yet another microclimate.

To go or not to go

Twelve aspiring rafters stood looking despairingly at the churning brown waters of the Río Filobobos as the rafting organizers and guides conferred to one side. The rafting was not looking promising owing to the previous night's torrential rain, which had left dangerously high water-levels. Two other rafting companies had already cancelled their expeditions on the Filobobos, while ours still procrastinated. Alejandro, ever the optimist, assured me that it would be that much more of an adventure, but I was decidedly less convinced. Finally, our expert leaders announced that the expedition would run but that any inexperienced rafters (such as myself) should be aware that it would be extremely tough from start to finish, about twice as difficult as my previous day's experience.

Before any whitewater-rafting trip, rafters sign a disclaimer form stating that there are no reprisals in the case of accident or death. These abstract words now returned to me…I thought long and hard, decided I wanted to live, and announced my withdrawal. Luckily for my ego I was not the only one, and soon four of us were squashed into a VW Beetle and bouncing back to Tlapacoyán. Alejandro was the only one to be disappointed, but I heard later that the rafters who did participate spent most of their morning saving another dinghy that had capsized and become caught in the rocks.

Coastal discoveries

From Xalapa, we headed southeast to the balmier air of **Veracruz**, the quintessential tropical port. Here, the atmosphere was transformed as we entered a 1940s and 1950s timewarp that harked back to the golden age of this resort. An evening spent beneath the palm trees at the Plaza de Armas provides one of Mexico's greatest live entertainments as at nightfall it takes on a carnival atmosphere. Armies of vendors are out in force, persuasively offering cigars, model galleons, seashell

jewellery, hammocks, or just chewing-gum; acrobats, fire-eaters, and mime artists perform; and the eternal marimba band alternates with guitar-strumming *mariachis*. If you're lucky, there may be a dance performance in the town hall beside the church. As the night advances bemused tourists and locals alike take to the tables of the bars that line the square. It is an inspiring experience. But when I left my hotel the following morning, the square was virtually empty. Had it all been a wonderful illusion?

The next target on my Veracruzian journey of discovery was **La Antigua**, originally named Villa Rica de la Vera Cruz, which lies about 30km (18 miles) north along the coast. This is the very spot where Hernán Cortés set up his first settlement on Mexican soil, in 1519, then left eight soldiers in residence before marching on Tenochtitlán, the Aztec capital. As we cruised into this picturesque little village, we were accosted by local boys offering themselves as guides. Alejandro adopted one of them, who proceeded to mouth an expressionless monologue about Cortés. This took place in the evocative ruins of the conquistadors' Andaluz-style villa, constructed of local stone, brick, coral, and volcanic rock from the Cofre de Perote. Hefty, tentacular roots draped over the walls underline the fact that nearly five centuries have slipped by since it was built. A short walk away stands a simple whitewashed chapel, the **Ermita del Rosario** (1523), whose courtyard design represents the 14 stations of the cross. From here it is not far to the river, that same Río Antigua of rafting fame, which here trickles gently by.

Ruins of the Past

Across the Río Antigua, 20km (12 miles) further north, lies the Totonac site of **Zempoala**, whose burnished white lime-coating, reflected in the sun, once seemed to the conquistadors to be of silver. As Alejandro steered around lazily ambling dogs and sped past coconut palms and fields of sugarcane, I mused on the community that had so facilitated Cortés' advance. Without help from the Zempoalans, the story of his conquest would have been very different. But who were they and what happened to them?

A mustachioed local Totonac loitering at the ticket-booth became our guide. He may not have had lip-rings but his purple jeans were adorned with a huge bunch of keys, his neck jangled with silver chains, and his fingers were covered with rings. A cowboy hat, boots, and Ray Bans completed this original style, doing full justice to his ancestors. Overflowing with fascinating facts and gesticulating wildly for emphasis, he described how the pacifist Totonacs had built this city (whose name means twenty water sources; the remains of aqueducts have, in fact, been found) in A.D. 1027, using shells, coral, cacti, and rounded stones from the river.

A boundary wall with gates at each of the four cardinal points encloses the peaceful, ceremonial 7.5-hectare (18½-acre) complex. There are five pyramids, including the Sun Temple where human sacrifices were once made, a custom that was imported from the Aztecs in the late 15th century when Zempoala fell under their sway. Another structure, circular and crenellated, demonstrates unusual acoustic properties linked to astronomy, for the Totonacs, like other Mesoamerican societies, were adept in their understanding of the heavens.

As we took our leave, our Totonac friend recounted the end of Zempoala.

THE ZEMPOALANS

"The men had great holes in their lower lips in which some carried stone disks spotted with blue, and others thin sheets of gold. They also had great holes in their ears, in which they had inserted disks of stone or gold and they were very different in their dress and speech from the Mexicans who had been staying with us."

This description of Zempoalan messengers meeting Cortés was written in 1568 by Bernal Díaz, a Spanish army captain.

Soon after the arrival of Cortés, the deadly smallpox virus decimated the population: some 30,000 people died and only eight families survived. By 1600 Zempoala was completely abandoned. This tragic destiny was shared by countless indigenous societies who came into contact with the Spaniards, although others disintegrated as a direct result of rival fiefdoms. A prime example of this is **Cantona**, a huge archaeological site and one of the most remote in central Mexico. This was the last stop on our tour, and one that nearly finished us off. As Cantona only opened to the public in 1996, after three years of restoration, it does not yet figure on maps and, as this is Mexico, we are talking about access via long, dusty dirt roads that are only occasionally used by horses or pick-up trucks. So there we were, with nothing but stones and cacti on the horizon, the sun high in the sky, and Alejandro bent double under the car trying to diagnose a suspicious rattle. Mexico City was still three hours away, and so was the plane that I aimed to catch that afternoon. And we hadn't even reached Cantona.

Finally we did, and it was well worth it. This isolated site of the Late Classic period (A.D. 600–1000) nestles almost invisibly in the stark foothills of the Sierra Madre, just over the state border in Puebla. Its strategic position between Mexico's central plateau and the Gulf coast led to spectacular expansion, and at its zenith Cantona's 80,000 inhabitants lived in an area covering 13sq km (5 square miles), their prosperity closely linked to the obsidian trade. However, in the early 11th century more bellicose cultures gained the upper hand and Cantona's population dispersed. Today, this is all reflected in the extensive ruins of ballcourts, terraced hillside dwellings, pyramids, patios, and long, walled streets called *calzadas*. Very few visitors make the trip out to this arid, isolated corner, so cacti, maguey, and yuccas are likely to be your only companions—along with the rattlesnakes. There are plenty of these, so watch your step, but the reward is great.

GOING IT ALONE

Internal Travel

The only way of covering this adventure is by renting a car. This can be done from Mexico City or, easier still, from Veracruz. To get to Veracruz from Mexico City you should take a long-distance ADO bus from the Tapo Terminal (Oriente; Metro stop San Lázaro). The trip takes about 4 hours via Puebla and Córdoba. Demand is high in summer, so book your ticket in advance. A quieter alternative base is Xalapa, also accessible by long-distance ADO bus (5 hours from Mexico City; 2 hours from Veracruz).

There is an extensive network of domestic flights to Veracruz from all over the country, arriving at the airport of Las Bajadas, 12km (7½ miles) from the centre. Continental Airlines operates direct flights from Houston, Texas.

Those in search of nostalgia should settle into the old second-class train that takes some 11 hours from the capital to Veracruz via Córdoba.

When to Go

The rafting season varies according to the river you choose (see box on page 56), so it can be a year-round sport. Temperatures are higher in the summer and rains more frequent, but this brings good water-levels to the rivers. The microclimates of the state of Veracruz are particularly apparent around the 4,250-m (14,000-foot) Cofre de Perote near Xalapa and the 5,610-m (18,500-foot) Pico de Orizaba to the south. Swirling mists, rain, and poor visibility are almost permanent features of the roads in their vicinity, but the skies clear further on. Nearer the coast, the climate is almost Caribbean, with hot, humid conditions.

Planning

It is a good idea to contact a rafting company in advance to see when it is scheduling long-weekend packages. You can stay at their base camps in Jalcomulco, or alternatively just drop in for a half-day rafting expedition, though this will also need to be booked. If there are six of you in a group, you can fill a dinghy yourselves. For real whitewater fanatics, there are three-day packages at very reasonable rates, although you have to arrange your own transport.

The minimum requirements for rafting are that you weigh over 35kg (77 pounds) and are in good health.

Travellers' Tips

- Accommodation in Veracruz is at a premium in summer (roughly June–September), when it is advisable to book a hotel in advance. Xalapa is less frequented, although it has some excellent, reasonably priced hotels. If you are intent on trying out the attractions of Río Filobobos (rated by many as the best in Mexico), there is a good hotel in the nearby town of Tlapacoyan (see Contacts).
- If you are covering this adventure by car, it is well worth investing in a Guía Roji road map. Make sure you have enough Spanish to ask and understand basic road directions, and always check on them twice—you can waste a lot of time by taking the wrong mountain road. To drive to Cantona, watch out for the sign on Highway 140 (Puebla–Xalapa), about 20km (12 miles) southwest of the town of Perote. From the turn-off, drive along a dirt road to Tepeyahualco, and from here start asking directions; the site is another 22km (14 miles) further on.

Rafters' Tips

- Do not apply suntan lotion to your forehead as it will run into your eyes, nor to the backs of your legs as you will slip off the sides of the rubber dinghy.
- Pack all valuables into one of the dry bags supplied. Normal plastic bags do not keep things dry in whitewater conditions.

What to Take

- Swimming costume, shorts, T-shirt, and waterproofs sandals for rafting.
- Waterproof camera.
- Layers of clothing for the changing altitudes along the route.
- Torch.
- Compass if you are driving yourself.

Health

Make sure your typhoid, tetanus, and polio inoculations are up to date. Vaccination against Hepatitis A is recommended though not essential. Veracruz is not a malarial region.

Art in the Jungle

by Fiona Dunlop

Mexico's border with Guatemala is partly defined by the Río Usumacinta, the longest river in the Mayan world, which runs along the edge of the Selva Lacandón biosphere reserve. On the Usumacinta's banks in the troubled state of Chiapas are the complementary archaeological sites of Bonampak and Yaxchilán: visiting them is one of Mexico's great adventures.

Several years ago, I was fascinated to hear about the brilliantly coloured Mayan frescoes of Bonampak and the nearby ruins of Yaxchilán, once ruled by the evocative-sounding Bird Jaguar king. Both sites lie close to the mighty Usumacinta river on the edge of the Selva Lacandón (Lacandón Jungle), a biosphere reserve inhabited by the last of the rapidly disappearing Lacandón Maya. This area has also hit the headlines on numerous occasions since 1994, when the Zapatistas, an insurgent group supporting the rights of Chiapas' indigenous peoples, staged an armed uprising in several highland towns. As a result, this troubled Mexican state has seen so many conflicts between paramilitary groups, the Mexican Army, and Mayan peasants that military checkpoints are now part of the landscape—along with bandits. All these factors (wild nature, ancient culture, ethnic interest, and potential danger) drew me to Palenque, the launch pad for this remote corner of Mexico.

The jungle trek to Bonampak is strenuous and demands a good level of fitness, as does the hike to the summit pyramid of Yaxchilán.

★★ Sleeping in tents, cool, damp nights, and rudimentary washing facilities are the bottom line here, although better accommodation is available for groups at Frontera Corozal.

Good walking boots or shoes are essential.

PALENQUE

The modern town of **Palenque**, located 6.5km (4 miles) from the great Mayan site of the same name, lies in the humid, jungle-clad foothills of the Chiapas highlands. It is a firm favourite on the Mayan trail, so much of local life revolves around

INSET: Lacandón Maya, Palenque
BELOW: Palenque's Palace, topped with a pagoda-like tower, was the residence of the great ruler Lord Pakal
RIGHT: Boarding a boat on the Río Usumacinta at Frontera Corozal

EARLY IMAGES OF PALENQUE

The first publicized images of Palenque were those of Frederick Catherwood, an English illustrator who accompanied the American adventurer, John Lloyd Stephens, on his first Central American foray, in 1837. Four years later, Stephens' two-volume work, *Incidents of Travel in Central America, Chiapas and Yucatan*, was published, its detailed illustrations including 35 of Palenque. It is still in print today and makes for fascinating reading. About ten years earlier, romanticized engravings of Palenque were also made by the Austrian Baron Waldeck, an eccentric former pirate who eventually left Mexico after he was accused of smuggling Mayan treasures to Europe.

tourism, and souvenir shops and travel agencies abound. Highland women in colourful Mayan costumes squat on the pavement, often with a baby snoozing happily in a back-sling, surrounded by piles of embroidered shirts, belts, bracelets, or tiny clay animal sculptures. It is easy to visit the ruins from town as *colectivos* run there directly every 15 minutes, but less easy to avoid the crowds. I decided to go after lunch when there is a slight lull, mainly due to the languid heat and humidity, which leave most people in a state of suspended animation.

Although it covers a total area of 6sq km (2 square miles), Palenque is a beautiful, strangely intimate archaeological site, much enhanced by the liana-draped jungle, streams, pools, and waterfalls of its surroundings. After clambering around several structures, all built of a grey stone that was once painted in bright pinks and greens, I tackled the impressive Temple of Inscriptions. This stepped, 25-m (80-foot) pyramid, Palenque's highest, contains the tomb of Lord Pakal, the great ruler who masterminded Palenque's seventh-century zenith. If you have a problem with vertiginous Mayan steps, walk round the back, where you will find an easy access path from the hillside to the top of the pyramid.

Pakal's vault was only discovered in 1948 by an observant Mexican archaeologist. His curiosity was rewarded with what was an astonishing find: below ground level, at the base of a steep, corbel-vaulted staircase inside the pyramid, lay the bodies of eight guards surrounding the remains of Lord Pakal himself. The latter, dressed in ceremonial finery and jade ornaments, lay in a magnificent sarcophagus. When, in my turn, I reached the bottom of this silent, airless staircase I found myself completely alone—a rarity in such a popular tourist destination. There were no skeletons or treasures as these had been whisked away to Mexico City long ago, but the exquisite bas-reliefs of the sarcophagus were sufficient reward. Outside, the bas-reliefs are echoed by the superb stucco sculptures on the façade of Palenque's Palace, which stands opposite and forms the central structure of the site. This was once Pakal's residence, and is unmistakable for its unique pagoda-type tower and interconnecting courtyards.

ON THE ROAD

With this foretaste of Mayan decorative prowess, I had no qualms about rising at 5am to await the tourist bus that was to take me to Bonampak and Yaxchilán. After rolling through the streets of a deserted town to pick up three other tourists from their respective hotels, we spent what seemed like an inordinate amount of time at the petrol station on the outskirts of town—time enough, however, for us ravenous passengers to make a dive for the impromptu coffee and *tamale* stands. It was only later that I understood that this was where police escorts are arranged. Finally, after having our passports inspected at the first of four military checkpoints, we truly set off.

Our first destination was Frontera Corozal on the Río Usumacinta, the end of a 172-km (109-mile) road that was paved only in 1997, a decade after it was built by Pemex, the Mexican oil company. The road's existence was partly in response to the growing violence on the Guatemalan side of the border and military incursions into Mexico from that country. For the first 50km (30 miles) it runs through a string of tiny villages, each one liberally sprinkled with the ubiquitous *topes* (speed bumps), the bane of every driver in Central America. Behind stretches jungle, or rather notions of it, for it is mainly a desolate sight of deforested horizons, yet another sad reminder that today barely a third of the original 15,000-sq-km (5,750-square-mile) Selva Lacandón remains. Shorn

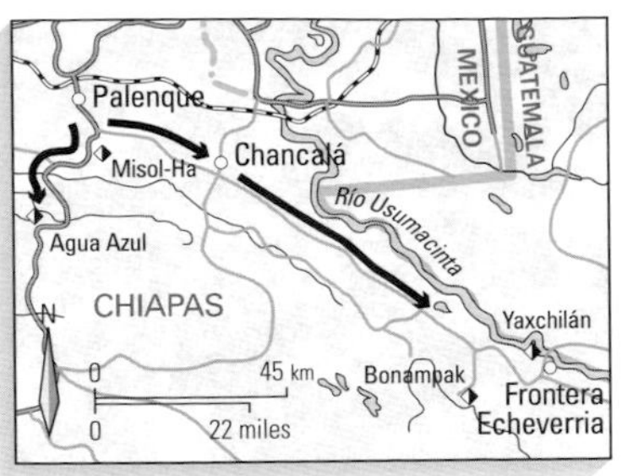

From Palenque to Bompak and Yaxchilán along the Río Usumacinta

hillsides, the combined victim of logging companies, slash and burn farming, and forest fires, stand side by side with isolated stands of original tropical forest, forlorn stumps, or tangled regrowth. This apocalyptic image recurred along our entire journey to Yaxchilán, and at this stage was only slightly alleviated by the sight of the morning mists rolling through the valleys across the treetops.

Our police escort started after we stopped for a copious breakfast at Chancala. From here onwards settlements disappeared, the landscape became wilder, and there was still no light—only a permanent mist. Luckily for us, there were no *banditos*, just the silent flashing lights of our motorized protectors. About two hours later we reached a campsite restaurant at the crossroads in Lacanja, where a suprising mix and match of tourists took place to allow the different travel agencies involved to save on excessive vehicles. Some visitors continued straight to the border and onwards to Flores and the nearby site of Tikal in Guatemala (see page 84), others set off on the hike to Bonampak, while seven tourists joined me in a minivan bound for Yaxchilán. Some 45 minutes later, after we had passed a serious-looking military encampment lined with rows of amphibian vehicles followed by yet another checkpoint, our newly formed group of Dutch, Mexican, French, and American adventurers found itself at Frontera Corozal (also known as Echeverría).

THE LACANDÓN

Calling themselves Hach Winik (meaning the true people), the 400 or so remaining Lacandón live in a total area of 6,140sq km (2,371 square miles). This was where they once hunted and farmed freely and alone, their culture inextricably bound to the rain forest. In the 1940s they were forcibly resettled into three communities and, more recently, they have had to share their land with relocated Chol and Tzeltal farmers from the highlands. The work of evangelical missionaries was obviously much helped by the Lacandóns' grouping in communities and today you may hear them singing Baptist hymns translated into their language, although some traditional worship does endure.

Yaxchilán

Snaking its way to the Gulf of Mexico through Chiapas from its source in the mountains of Guatemala, and at this point creating a natural international frontier, the Río Usumacinta was once the Mayas' greatest trade route. Cacao from Tabasco, jade from Guatemala, and salt from the Yucatán peninsula were all carried along this river some 1,300 years ago, when the waterway would have been alive with small canoes. Today, however, nothing moved on the placid water except our long wooden motorboat and the occasional egret and kingfisher. Frontera Corozal, once a flourishing river port, now seemed semi-abandoned and its inhabitants not to be trusted, judging by our driver's insistence that we take all our bags with us. Yet once we were settled under the thatched canopy of our boat and motoring the 20km (12 miles) downriver to Yaxchilán, a peace descended. The notion of our remoteness hit all seven of us, and our earlier chat and general swapping of travellers' tales came to a halt. It really felt like we were venturing into the unknown.

The magnificently isolated though once strategic site of **Yaxchilán** dates from the Classic period (A.D. 250–900), a contemporary of both Palenque and Tikal, and reached its zenith under the great king Escudo Jaguar, around

A.D. 700. A total of 120 structures nestle in dense jungle that slopes uphill from the riverbank to the highest point, crowned by Structure 41, but only about 40 per cent have been excavated so far. This magical site is rife with fantastic sculptural details, whether perfectly preserved limestone lintels, towering stelae, or hieroglyphs on walls. However, if you

RIGHT The roofcomb crowning the top of Yaxchilán's impressive Palace of Hachakyum (Structure 33) is reached via a 70-m (230-foot) staircase
ABOVE Welcome shade on our boat
BELOW Structure 41 sits at the summit of the ruins cascading down the riverbank

look closely you will notice that the theme is very often macabre: warfare and ritual self-mutilation were an integral part of Mayan life.

As we crossed the impressive 900-m (3,000-foot) long main plaza, we were greeted by the familiar crashing sounds of a family of spider monkeys (*Ateles geoffroyi*) high up in a mahogany tree. What was unusual in this case was that the monkeys were happily sharing the branches with a toucan—a rare sign of communal jungle life. From this vast plaza, your eyes are inevitably drawn upwards to Yaxchilán's architectural showpiece, Structure 33, which shows off its elaborate roofcomb at the top of a steep 70-m (230-foot) staircase. (The roofcomb is a wall along the roof's centre-line, the purpose of which was to raise the appearance of a structure.) After conquering the ascent and then exploring the interior of this remarkable building, we continued along a slippery trail through the jungle, ever upwards, finally reaching the elevated setting of Structure 41. And just as the hardier souls among us climbed up some perilously loose stones to the summit of this final pyramid, the howler monkeys (*Alouatta palliata*) started their unearthly chorus, a fitting accompaniment to the sweeping views north towards Guatemala.

By then, everyone was duly impressed but also duly exhausted; our next stop was a very civilized albeit late lunch prepared in a riverside hut by the site guardian's wife. Due to river currents, the return boat trip took considerably longer than the 45 minutes of our arrival, but by this time, with the sun descending scenically behind the trees, the relaxed pace was exactly what I needed.

Bonampak

I was shown a tiny little woman standing shyly to one side of the rickety campsite restaurant and was told that this was Paola, the Lacandón guide who would accompany me the 9km (5½ miles) through the jungle to the site of Bonampak. I had noticed her about an hour earlier when I emerged from my tent into the cool early morning mist; she had high Mayan cheekbones and long, black, centrally parted hair atop a tiny body dressed in a loose floral tunic that was typically Lacandón. So now, again in mix and match fashion, I bade farewell to the two Italians who had also spent the night at the camp and were waiting to head on to Guatemala with the next van-load from Palenque. A third Italian from Verona, who looked as if he had stepped straight off the set of Romeo and Juliet, was courageously venturing further into the biosphere, armed with a tent. Once again, it was a parting of ways.

Small and fragile she may have looked, but Paola was swift—and observant. By the time we left the dirt road to plunge into the jungle, I was suitably impressed not only by her energetic pace but also by her affability. I had been warned by my Yaxchilán companions and by my Italian acquaintances that their respective guides to Bonampak had remained virtually wordless for the

ETERNAL WORSHIP

What is extraordinary about Yaxchilán is that, contrary to other abandoned Mayan sites, it is still visited by Lacandón Mayas for ceremonial purposes. Evidence of this lies inside Structure 33, the Palace of Hachakyum (Our True Lord), the Lacandón solar deity. Here, a headless sculpted torso stands next to a copal incense burner that relatively recently has left its mark on the smoke-blackened walls. The torso represents Bird Jaguar IV, son of Escudo Jaguar and Yaxchilán's last ruler, who was later deified. The Lacandóns believe that if ever the head is restored to this torso, it signifies the end of the world.

entire trek, their role theoretically being limited to showing the way. But it seemed I had struck lucky in the rota that allocated guides to visitors, for Paola imparted endless tips about the jungle, its flora, and its fauna, as well as responding confidently to my questions about her children, husband, and their way of life. Occasionally, caught by my enthusiasm and her speed, I would trip over a root and fall headfirst into the mud, but I never hurt myself: Paola's gentle voice would warn me just in time not to stretch out to grasp the nearest trunk, which just happened to be clothed in evil-looking spines.

Although the jungle was not primary growth it had an impressive range of tropical hardwoods. We climbed over the huge buttress trunks of the ramon, or breadnut, tree (*Brosimum alicastrum*), passed in front of mahogany trees (*Swietenia mahagoni*), ceibas (*Ceiba pentandra*), marmalade trees (*Lucuma mammosum*), fan-palms (used locally for thatching), and tangled lianas and vines. Butterflies were everywhere, and at one point a luminous-blue morpho (*Morpho peleides*) fluttered in front of me. Finally, after resuming our trek along the dazzling white dirt road, we reached Bonampak.

Like Yaxchilán, **Bonampak** (meaning painted walls) was still being used ceremonially by the Lacandón when archaeologists "discovered" it in 1946. Although founded around A.D. 200, its high point came in the early seventh century during the reign of Chaan Muan I. Later still, in A.D. 746, Bonampak and Yaxchilán allied to defeat Lacanja, and under Chaan Muan II (776–92) the famed stelae (pillars) and Temple of Paintings were accomplished. By A.D. 800 the site was abandoned. A short distance from the entrance you come to a vast grassy plaza that ends in steps rising to the chambers of paintings. Before this, in the centre of the plaza, rises an astonishing 6-m (20-foot) stele, one of the tallest in the Mayan world, inscribed with the faces of corn gods and an earth monster. On the steps, another stele is delicately carved with images of the Mayan gods. But it is Structure 1, home to Bonampak's unique frescoes, that is far and away the star.

Three adjoining rooms in Structure 1 together reveal 150sq m (1,615 square feet) of vivid paintings that were executed using thick coats of lime and powdered stone plaster mixed with mineral and vegetal pigments. In the first corbel-vaulted chamber you see bands of friezes in turquoise, red ochre, yellow, umber, and green depicting the presentation of Chaan Muan II's heir. Ceremonial garb and formal poses rule. In contrast, in the second chamber, the far more active images show battle scenes, captives, and torture, while in the third, unfinished chamber is depicted the presentation and sacrifice of prisoners. There are some gruesome details of decapitation or fingernails being removed, but altogether this breathtaking visual panorama (depicting 108 hieroglyphic texts, 270 figures, and 30 godlike images) gives us a fantastic insight into the bloodthirsty Mayan world. Although much of the paint has flaked away and faded over the centuries, astute Mexican restoration has revived some areas and colours.

After we had staggered back to the campsite and been revived by a late lunch, I felt ready to follow Paola to her home in Lacanja to see the local waterfall. The 3km (2 miles) of asphalted road were easy, but the sun was still strong and my muscles had definitely been overworked. My spirits wavered. Suddenly, around the corner came a barefoot Lacandón, perfectly attired in his long white tunic, his black hair cut with an inimitable fringe above a deeply lined face. He was closely followed by a young

OVERLEAF More than 500 waterfalls tumble over the rocks at Agua Azul, said to be one of southern Mexico's most beautiful natural wonders. You can cool off with a refreshing swim in some of the pools here

LOCAL MAYA DRESS

In contrast to the soberly clad Lacandón, the Tzotzil and Tzeltal Maya of highland Chiapas have retained a remarkable diversity of dress. It is in Palenque and, above all, in San Cristóbal de las Casas that you will see the greatest variety. Over the centuries, the plumed headdresses and loincloths of the men depicted in Bonampak's frescoes and Palenque's bas-reliefs have evolved into hats hung with coloured ribbons or pom-poms, and baggy shorts or trousers, while rabbit fur has been replaced by woven sheep's wool. Women, meanwhile, remain faithful to brilliantly woven *huipiles* (tunics) and *enredos* (wrap-around skirts belted with a waist sash), often set off by elaborate ribbons plaited into their hair. Continuity comes in the patterns. Dreams and mythology are woven into complex cloth designs that may represent the sun, a feathered serpent, or a jaguar penis; a dazzling palette of magenta, crimson, yellow, orange, and blue outlines geometric patterns of chevrons, triangles, zigzags, squares, and rhombuses. The rhombus actually represents the Mayan universe, its four sides denoting the limits of time and space, while smaller rhombuses in each corner symbolize the four cardinal points.

boy in similar attire. In the last few days I had gained the impression that the Lacandón had been absorbed into more mainstream Mexican society and that their identity had consequently been lost, so were these ghosts? This man, despite not responding to my "*Buenas tardes*" greeting (thereby either confirming his ghostliness or his healthy ignorance of Spanish) seemed proof that some customs do survive.

WATER, WATER EVERYWHERE

Although the soak at Lacanja waterfall was well worth the exertion, it was far surpassed in splendour by the last outing I made from Palenque. The tumbling cascades of **Agua Azul** (meaning blue water) are said to be one of southern Mexico's greatest natural wonders, so it was impossible to pass up on an excursion. Day trips to Agua Azul abound, and it was easy to buy a ticket at the last minute. As usual, the transport was a minivan shared with a motley group of tourists whose origins ranged from Ireland to Quebec. After a short stop on the way to admire the 25-m (80-foot) cascades of **Misol-Ha**, the van zigzagged up the mountainous 62km (38-mile) road, giving us sweeping views over the river valley and villages below.

Agua Azul itself may lie in a protected nature reserve, but this hasn't stopped the local tradespeople from coming, nor the local swimmers. For, uphill from the car park along a path that meanders parallel to the thundering cascades, are dozens of souvenir stands and family restaurants, while in the calm pools below the first waterfall hordes of locals escape the heat by plunging into the cool depths. Altogether, over 500 falls froth and roar over huge limestone rocks, their path laid out by the meeting of the rivers Yaxha (also known as the Agua Azul) and Shumulha. The best time to visit if you plan on taking a dip is during the dry season as the currents can be dangerous when the water is high. Although the pools by the car park are the safest for swimming, one of the most scenic, relaxing places is a canyon about 40 minutes' walk away. For a real bird's-eye view of the entire area, hop into the five-seater Cessna that operates from here for a 15-minute tour. Even better, try out the microlight that also offers aerial excursions. And if you really want a close encounter with the rapids, take to a raft—the afternoon will disappear in a haze of white water and adrenalin that is far removed from the gentle canoes of the Mayan past.

GOING IT ALONE

Internal Travel

Palenque's tiny airport receives direct flights from Cancún, Mérida, Oaxaca, and Tuxtla Gutiérrez, and from Flores in Guatemala.

Many people opt to reach Palenque from Villahermosa, a 2-hour bus journey, which has a more extensive and frequent flight timetable. Long-distance buses also connect Palenque with San Cristóbal de las Casas, Chiapas' fascinating highland town.

When to Go

Palenque is best visited between December and February, when it is dry and not too hot. Temperatures rise considerably in March–April, and the rainy season sets in from May/June until October/November, which makes for exceptionally wet and difficult jungle treks. As always, remember that the dry season also corresponds to the high season and so hotel reservations are essential, above all from mid-December to mid-January.

Planning

No advance planning is needed for the Yaxchilán/ Bonampak trip as there are daily departures. Avoid the one-day trips as these pack both sites into a very long and exhausting day; you will also miss out on the jungle trek to Bonampak.

There are two campsites at Lacanja, one at the crossroads and the other beyond Lacanja village; the former is marginally more comfortable. Escudo Jaguar, a group of attractively sited, rustic "eco" cabins at Frontera Corozal, can be booked by small groups.

Prices vary considerably between Palenque's travel agents, though some do offer better services, so check to see where you will be staying and what exactly is included in the tour price. Make sure that the outline of your trip is written in full on your ticket, as the numerous options available can lead to confusion, and without your itinerary in writing you have no argument.

It is possible, though not advisable, to do this trip on your own. Hiring a motorboat at Frontera Corozal to go to Yaxchilán will work out prohibitively expensive unless there are at least four of you. Infrequent public buses cover the Palenque–Frontera route.

Travellers' Tips

- ❑ There are no shops at Lacanja, so stock up on film, snacks, and the like in Palenque.
- ❑ The Lacandón make and sell seed necklaces, crude clay figures, and woodcarvings, so there is no shortage of souvenirs.
- ❑ Be generous with your tips.

What to Take

- ❑ Good walking shoes or boots for the jungle trails.
- ❑ Insect repellent.
- ❑ Suncream.
- ❑ Light cotton clothes (long-sleeved shirts and trousers), plus a pullover or jacket for the cool evenings.
- ❑ Rain poncho if you visit during the rainy season.
- ❑ Water bottle.
- ❑ Toiletries and towel.
- ❑ Swimsuit for Agua Azul.

Health

This is a malarial region during the rainy season, although there are few mosquitoes in the dry season (December–April). Remember to take the appropriate medication, starting two weeks before you arrive in the region and continuing at least six weeks after you leave. Also ensure that your typhoid, tetanus, and polio vaccinations are up to date.

WARNING!

This is Chiapas, so nothing and no one is safe. Agua Azul has a history of attacks in the less frequented areas further along the path away from the centre of activity. Before heading up there, check at the tourist office near the entrance to see what the security situation is or, best of all, hire a local guide to act as bodyguard. Also be aware that swimming in some of the pools at Agua Azul is very dangerous, and that several people have drowned over the years. Be sure to pay attention to the warning notices posted at the site.

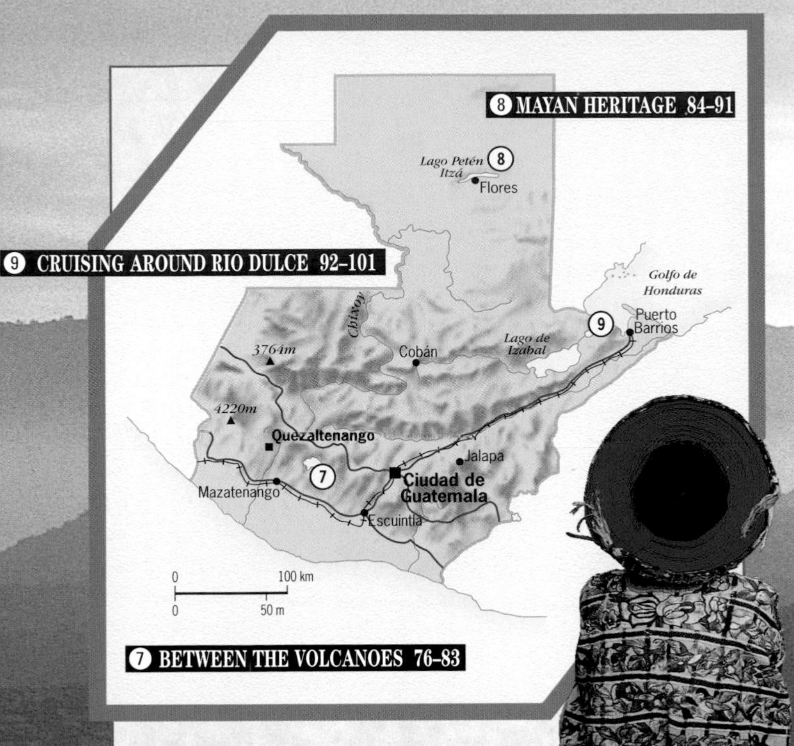

GUATEMALA

Guatemala is strategically situated at the northern end of the Central American isthmus, with Mexico to the north, the Pacific Ocean to the west, the Caribbean Sea and Belize to the east, and Honduras and El Salvador to the south. It is a land of immense topographical contrasts, from towering volcanoes and high plateaux to tropical plains, valleys, lowland jungle, swamp, and beaches. The *altiplano* (highlands) to the west is home to the majority of Guatemala's indigenous people, numbering roughly two-thirds of the total population of 10 million, who lend fantastic cultural interest to this region. Their extraordinary flair for crafts has been heavily commercialized at Antigua, Guatemala's old capital, and at the Lago de Atitlán, both of which make excellent bases none the less. In contrast, on the Caribbean coast, around the Río Dulce, you will encounter a far more laid-back sector: the Garifunas, or black Caribs. Last but by no means least comes Guatemala's ancient Mayan past, visible in endless evocative archaeological sites that lie scattered throughout the dense jungle of the Petén.

The view from Volcán San Pedro over the mist-shrouded Lago de Atitlán, Guatemala
INSET: The traditional women's cinta *headdress, commonly seen in Santiago Atitlán, is created from a coiled red belt*

Between the Volcanoes

by Fiona Dunlop

Far up in Guatemala's highlands lies the stunning volcanic lake of Atitlán. Numerous activities on offer in the region include horse riding, volcano climbing, windsurfing, scuba-diving, para-gliding, kayaking, or simply exploring the timeless Mayan villages along the lake's shores.

It took 11 million years for the **Lago de Atitlán** to develop into the vast, breathtakingly beautiful lake seen today, 116km (72 miles) due east of Guatemala City at an altitude of 1,562m (5,123 feet). From whichever corner of its indented and mountainous shore you look, the panorama, mood, and tonal palette are entrancing, not least because of constant changes brought by the time of day and seasons. On top of this, each of the 11 lakeside villages has its own very specific identity, the 70,000 Mayan inhabitants speaking one of three languages (Tzutujil, Quiché, or Cakchiquel) and proudly clinging to their traditions. You can't help but be seduced by all this, nor by the grandeur of the setting, but remember that as this is also Guatemala's most popular tourist resort you won't be alone.

Central hub

Most people visiting Atitlán stay in **Panajachel**, a heavily commercialized and "gringo-ized" village still inhabited by ageing 1960s hippies and now entirely devoted to selling a stridently colourful range of local handicrafts. Child vendors are persistent, and morning ferries see entire families laden with wares heading in from their lakeside villages to "Pana." This remains the main hub for all Westernized restaurants, services, organized tours, watersports, and para-gliding. The latter kicks off from high on the slopes above Santa Catarina Palopó and, for those with no experience, can be done in tandem with an instructor. Unfortunately, the morning I had arranged to be swept through the airstreams, my para-sailing partner was nowhere to be found.

In their turn, foreigners in search of authenticity head either around or across the lake. This is where you will see tiny Mayan villagers (rarely standing taller than 1.5m, or 5 feet) trudging up hillsides with backloads of firewood or farm produce, sometimes carrying a baby in a sling, and kitted out in exquisite traditional handwoven and hand-embroidered costumes, usually in blazing colour. This, too, is where you can climb a volcano, ride on horseback through cloud forest, or even learn to weave. Ever since I watched Mexico's smoking Popocatépetl from a safe distance, I have searched out friendlier craters. The nocturnal sight of flowing rivers of incandescent lava and the sporadic booming of Arenal in Costa Rica was another seismic landmark, and now, in its turn, Lago de Atitlán's volcanic line-up was magnetizing me. Here I hoped actually to ascend the slopes of a volcano at last.

The ascent of Volcán San Pedro is very strenuous; the other activities on offer are less demanding.

★ Santiago, Panajachel, and other lakeside villages offer perfectly adequate accommodation where you can recover from your daytime activities.

No specialist equipment is required for this tour, aside from good walking shoes for the climb up Volcán San Pedro and a torch for power cuts.

SEISMIC SHUDDERS

Volcanoes are an integral part of Central America's highlands. Their cloud-wreathed cones create a moody backdrop, although only 32 of Guatemala's 324 "eruptive foci" are actually recognized as volcanoes. And although they may add instant drama to the landscapes of the Sierra Madre, they can also spell human tragedy. From the origins of the Lago de Atitlán, once a gigantic crater whose subsequent explosions created new craters and fissures, skip to 1976, when a serious tremor left many local homes and churches in ruins. Today, of the three silent volcanoes edging the lake's southern shore, only one (Volcán de Atitlán) is active, although this is limited to emissions of sulphurous gases.

UNDER THE VOLCANO

My chosen destination for pursuing my volcano was Santiago Atitlán, a Tzutujil Maya village sprawling over the lower flanks of the twin-peaked Volcán Tolimán (3,130m, or 10,300 feet) and looking across a narrow lake inlet to **Volcán San Pedro** (3,020m, or 9,900 feet). Behind Tolimán looms the mother of the lakeside volcanoes, Atitlán itself (3,540m, or 11,600 feet), whose crater contains steam vents that can safely be treated as a sauna. Both Atitlán and Tolimán are for serious hikers only, their ascents requiring two days and equipment for camping overnight on the saddle that links the two. The pay-off is, of course, spectacular views over the 125-sq-km (48-square-mile) lake and south to the Pacific Ocean. However, I hardly considered myself a seasoned climber and nor did the idea of a potentially damp, chilly night enthuse me. San Pedro was the one for me, touted as the "beginner's" volcano and apparently climbable in three or four hours with a little less for the descent. As the ferry chugged across the lake from Panajachel, and San Pedro's lofty, cloud-shrouded cone came closer, this alleged accessibility did seem somewhat exaggerated.

There are no organized volcano tours from Santiago Atitlán itself, but potential local guides abound. In the meantime, I had joined forces with Joe, a strapping, dauntingly fit young Englishman whose avowed intention was to conquer ten peaks during his Central American travels. Gazing serenely at San Pedro he announced that, in his view, if we left at 6am we should be back soon after midday. As an absolute novice in these matters, I happily concurred. After rapid negotiations on a darkening street corner, a squat little man called Francisco finally agreed to an acceptable rate for the half-day's climb, told us that he would supply breakfast, pick us up from our respective hotels, then lead us upwards (triumphantly?) to the summit. Hands were shaken, a small advance paid, and appointments made for the following morning.

GUIDED SAFETY

If you don't go to them, they come to you: Santiago's guides are legion and, if necessary, your hotel will arrange one for you. It is preferable to employ a guide with an official nameplate, though few speak anything other than their local dialect and Spanish, and nor are they loquacious. Be clear about what your guide is providing and what you have to bring (don't forget purified water, a wide-brimmed hat or cap, and sunblock). The guide's main role is a protective one as there have been several armed attacks on hikers around Lake Atitlán in the last few years. Always ask in advance about the safety of a trek and take only a minimal amount of money; leave all documents and valuables in your hotel safe.

RIGHT Para-sailing above Santa Catarina Palopó—not for the faint-hearted!
LEFT Reputedly the largest in Central America, Chichicastenango market is a kaleidoscope of vibrant colour

Morning climb

As I sat at the hotel jetty awaiting Francisco's canoe, the sun rose behind me, adding a warm glow to an otherwise monochromatic but breathtaking scene. Opposite loomed San Pedro and, in between, a soft layer of morning mist hovered above the lake, enveloping the silhouettes of fishing canoes. Visually at least this could have been a scene from far back in the Mayan past, although my ears picked up the sounds of a lorry labouring along the muddy road above and the rhythmic thud of a generator in Santiago, both joining the dawn chatter of the birds. Fishermen were either seated in their canoes using nets to catch the elusive black bass (mistakenly introduced to the lake a few years ago; its aggressive nature has subsequently spelt the death-knell of most other species) or punting through the mist. One canoe heading towards me turned out to be propelled by Francisco and Joe, so the three of us were soon crossing the inlet. From my "seat" (improvised from a crate), I took a short turn with the paddle and, about 20 minutes later, we were mooring in the reeds at the base of San Pedro beside other sturdy little handmade canoes.

As I was the least proficient climber, Francisco and Joe suggested that I should set the pace, so off I strode. Far from crossing a stark volcanic landscape as I had romantically imagined, the path edged a patchwork of cultivated fields that were to vary little for about a third of the way up. The crops were corn, sometimes entwined with bean vines as a variation, avocado trees, and coffee bushes. Later, and much higher up, we passed workers attacking the fields with their hoes, who just managed to raise their heads to say *buenos dias*. Later still, the track had twisted upwards sufficiently to offer some fabulous views over the lake and well beyond the headland of Santiago. Like a Chinese watercolour, a succession of peaks at the other end of the lake receded into the haze, while in the foreground a hawk sailed through the silent air. There was a rare harmony of sound, light, and sight that did wonders for the soul.

Francisco had been yawning frequently and now muttered something about breakfast, to which Joe, steadfastly serious, responded that we should wait for the next plateau with a view. So onwards and upwards I struggled, until Francisco finally showed us a small patch of wild, damp grass that he lopped at with his machete. Hey presto! There was the view! Out of his little shoulder bag came a napkin of warm tortillas and a tin canister of scrambled egg and tomato. That was the sum total of our breakfast (a major item in our financial negotiations the night before), but it enabled me to recoup some of my rapidly diminishing energy while indulging in another magnificent vista.

Volcanic exhaustion

From then on things deteriorated, for me at least. The path became steadily steeper, and even the panoramas disappeared behind a wall of uninspiring bushes, saplings, and undergrowth. By now the sun was higher and, without the breezy open spaces of the fields, we were

channelled through an increasingly airless corridor. Meanwhile, my underexercised heart was beating madly, my enforced stops becoming ever more frequent, and my water consumption rising. Joe, ever phlegmatic, suggested I look down at what I had achieved rather than balking at what remained. Even Francisco tried to encourage me with his English "Let's go!", but somehow my heart, or rather my lungs, was not in it. After 2½ hours of steady climbing, Francisco announced that we were not quite at the halfway mark and that the trail continued at the same gradient, if not worse (I estimated it was 80 degrees, a figure a local resident later agreed with). This inspired a lifetime's decision:

FUSION OF BELIEFS

As with all Mayan communities, an important aspect of Tzutujil culture is religion. Although Catholicism was brought by the Spanish when they unified the various local communities to found Santiago Atitlán in 1504, and the lofty 1540s church of San Francisco sees streams of worshippers, ancient Mayan beliefs have by no means been eradicated. In some cases, local forms of worship have even fused with Christianity: the idol Maximón (pronounced "Mashimon") is Santiago's homegrown example.

masochism was not on my agenda and I was going to turn back, renouncing the conquest of my volcano.

Francisco stated that he could not let Joe continue on his own, nor could he let me sit and wait for them both—it was simply too dangerous. Luckily, Joe was unphased, having accompanied inexperienced climbers like me in the past, and in fact seemed far more concerned about an overnight attack on Atitlán, the big one, that he was planning for the next day. For him, San Pedro was just a warm-up. So down we went, or rather down I skidded, so relieved that I turned my tendency to slip on the damp ground into a new sport. Later, my feelings of inadequacy were alleviated when I learned (even Francisco admitted it) that the majority of people stop even below the point where I turned round, so before you follow in my footsteps remember that the San Pedro volcano is no easy stroll. However, if you climb just part of it in the early morning before clouds descend, you are assured of some uniquely moving views.

Tzutujil culture

Santiago Atitlán itself, the lake's largest town, with 47,000 Tzutujil inhabitants, has much to offer, despite its rough and ready aspect. Skilful weaving and embroidery are, as in most highland villages, practised by the women, all of whom still wear the traditional embroidered, handwoven *huipil* (tunic) and belt over a woven wrap-around skirt. Specific to Santiago is the *cinta*, a woman's headdress made from a coiled red belt. Some men still stride around in embroidered and striped baggy shorts, with a wide, handwoven cummerbund and a stiff cowboy hat, although most have been seduced by Western styles. Santiago is also known for the imported techniques of tempera and oil painting, exploited particularly by the Chavez family, who own several art galleries locally. Woodcarving is another prolifically practised local craft. You don't have to go far to find these skills, as the main street leading uphill from the jetty is lined with commercial outlets.

Maximón

My first sight of Maximón's shrine was, dramatically enough, during a thunderstorm. I had been accosted by a tiny, wizened, barefoot old lady whose toothless whispers of this name beguiled me. As the rain intensified, I followed her along backstreets before turning into a ramshackle side-alley where laundry dripped on one side. Beckoning, she led me into a magical room where paper garlands, artificial fruit, flowers, and light-bulbs entirely draped the ceiling, while a suspended string basket stuffed with waste paper and old cigarette packets pointed to an unexpected sense of propriety. Seated or slumped around a table, six men were knocking back beer and corn alcohol (*cusha*), chatting away as if happily ensconced in a bar. The difference was that the entire scene was illuminated by flickering candles, while in front stood the curious effigy of Maximón.

The statue is dressed in a Western-style jacket and hat, accessorized with countless scarves of the fake Hermés variety, and completed by a giant cigar in his mouth. Beside him are donated bottles of Quetzalteca, the local tipple, cigarettes, and an ashtray; this is all for

The area surrounding Lago de Atitlán

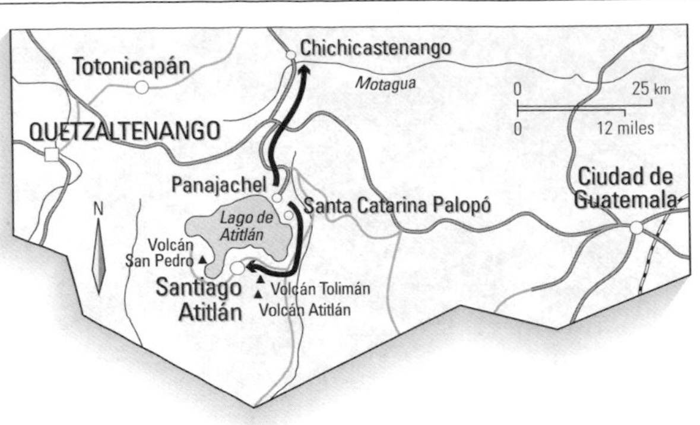

the smokin', drinkin' Maximón, the Mayan pastiche of a "legless" Catholic priest who, legend has it, was defrocked for debauchery. Another account of his origins maintains that he commemorates Judas Iscariot. After being asked by the affable *cofrade* (a member of the respected brotherhood, or *cofradía*, which acts as guardian of Mayan customs) to contribute to the fund, I then sat back to watch the proceedings. As the rain hammered down on the tin roof, dripping worshippers came and went, some kneeling to chant and swing copal incense in perforated tins, its smoke and pungent aromas intensifying the atmosphere. One danced, bottle in hand, accompanied by a drinker strumming a guitar. Somehow, I felt invisible but also privileged to witness this electrifying and completely natural performance.

Chichicastenango

Eager to see more of these Mayan practices, I set off one Sunday for **Chichicastenango** (known as "Chichi"), about an hour's drive north of Panajachel. I went the easy way, by tourist minivan that leaves Panajachel at 9am and returns about five hours later. Said to be Central America's largest market (it is also held on Thursdays), Chichi is now heavily geared to tourists although it remains a unique window on indigenous costumes and crafts. Above all, it shows how idolatry and Catholicism blend in an extraordinary cocktail of processions, ritual, and worship. In the 1540 **church of Santo Tomás**, famous for having harboured the Popol Vuh, the sacred book of the Quiché, I watched groups of petitioners squatting beside candles and rose-petal offerings as they proffered their handwritten requests to the priest. After he patiently read and blessed each one, the priest conducted mass. Meanwhile, another worshipper threw glasses of rum at a saint's statue, apparently in the hope of being cured of a drink problem, while on the church steps outside a stream of murmuring Mayas swung cans of smouldering incense.

Across the square at El Calvario, out of bounds to non-Mayas, more incense-swingers gathered outside. Here, I was accosted by a small boy who led me to the outskirts of town to see the rituals of a shaman (doctor-priest) at the crowded shrine of the pre-Hispanic goddess Pascual Abaj. On our way back we passed a group of magnificently clad *cofradías*. After I was told that other ceremonies take place at the cemetery and at numerous ancestral shrines in the surrounding hills, I began to understand the depths of ancient Mayan belief.

A Ride Through the Clouds

From my hotel in Santiago Atitlán I could just see the end of the lake inlet, where a

CHURCH ETIQUETTE

When visiting Santo Tomás in Chichi, it is essential to observe the "no photography" signs and to enter the church only from the side-entrance in the cloisters. El Calvario is out of bounds to foreigners. Great care should be taken in general when photographing these Mayas, who are increasingly weary of their photogenic status.

Horseback riding is the best way to see the cloud forest, home of the rare quetzal bird, near Santiago Atitlán

high mountain ridge rises to a lookout point, or *mirador*. This lush area of cloud forest nurtures numerous birds, including the quetzal (*Pharomachrus mocinno*), Guatemala's national bird, though few people are lucky enough to catch sight of one. To reach the *mirador*, it was a toss-up between a five-hour hike or a horse ride. I opted for the latter, and set off along the lakeside road in search of a small ranch run by an enterprising American couple who organize breakfast, lunch, and dinner rides with gourmet food thrown in. Pick-up trucks are the local form of *colectivo*, and when I finally flagged one down that was going the full 7km (4 miles) to my destination, it was, for once, not the proverbial can of Mayan sardines.

The ranch owner, Jim Matison, soon had me astride a horse that turned out to be sweet-tempered enough to put up with me, an exceedingly rusty rider, for the next couple of hours. Off trotted Jim, closely followed by two pit bull terriers that acted as vociferous guard dogs. From the road, our trail turned off through corn and coffee fields before crossing the local airstrip, then cut alongside the rockface and cloud forest before finally ascending to the ridge. In the distance the hacking of an axe rang out, a reminder that although the cloud forest is supposedly protected, there is little to stop ongoing destruction. Above all, such deforestation means that the brilliantly plumed quetzals are increasingly scarce.

Although most of the forest we rode through was secondary or tertiary growth, the scale of the misty landscapes and stark rocks was mesmerizing. As expected, when we finally trotted up to the *mirador*, it was thoroughly enveloped in clouds; Pacific views are reserved for breakfast and dry season rides, so mine did not qualify. Later, as our horses descended skilfully and at an increasingly confident speed, down came the deluge that had been threatening since we set off—and magically, out came an enormous rubberized poncho from my saddle. Now completely shielded from the elements, my feet firmly anchored in the leather stirrups, and my hands gripping the high pommel of the traditional Guatemalan saddle, I felt some affinity with the conquistadors who rode this way 500 years ago.

The local "chicken" buses are cheaper but slower and less comfortable than the tourist minivans

GOING IT ALONE

Internal Travel

It takes 3–4 hours to reach Panajachel from Guatemala City and about 2–3 hours from Antigua. All depends on whether you brave the local "chicken" bus (so called because of their poor state) or opt for a more comfortable tourist shuttle bus (usually a minivan seating up to ten passengers). If you start from the capital, remember that all shuttles go via Antigua, as this is where the majority of tourists are concentrated. A distinct advantage, apart from the comfort factor, is that shuttles will pick you up and drop you at your hotel. Local "chicken" buses also operate directly between Guatemala City and Santiago Atitlán.

A pricier alternative, but fun and not excessive if you are travelling in a group, is to charter a small plane. From Panajachel, there are four public ferries a day to Santiago Atitlán as well as negotiable water-taxis.

When to Go

During the rainy season (May–October), the lake is usually placidly mirrorlike at daybreak but by midday clouds have formed around the peaks and rain soon follows. Mid-July to mid-August produces the exceptional *canicula* of hot, sunny weather. The dry season (late November–April) sees higher temperatures and clear blue skies, but cold nights in December–January. Throughout the year, the *xocomil* (a Cakchiquel word meaning the wind that carries away sin) whips waves across the lake most afternoons, putting an end to all watersports.

Planning

The Lago de Atitlán can easily be slotted into an itinerary combining Antigua, Guatemala's beautiful old capital, and other towns of the *altiplano* such as Quetzaltenango, Huehuetenango, or Chichitenango. Apart from choosing your season according to what you intend to do and perhaps booking your hotel in advance, there is little to be planned. Tourist services are plentiful, though not always reliable, so be prepared for the occasional disappointment. Some tours may not take place out of season for lack of clients.

Remember that Easter is Guatemala's high point of the year—good hotels will therefore need booking in advance. Atitlán and, above all, Panajachel are very popular with domestic tourists at this time. This, too, is when Santiago Atitlán's statue of Maximón is brought out for parade and changes its "home" for another year, a procession that is well worth seeing. On Easter Sunday, indigenous people from all round the lake gather at Panajachel in their most outstanding costumes, while Chichicastenango also has stirring celebrations, surpassed only by the Festival of Santo Tomás on December 14–21.

Travellers' Tip

❏ An alternative market to the overpoplar one at Chichi is held every Tuesday and Friday morning at Solola, 8km (5 miles) from Panajachel. The town sits 550m (1,800 feet) above the lake, so offers great views. You can walk back to Pana along the road or across the hill. The Friday Solala market is the liveliest, and is particularly strong on food and crafts.

What to Take

❏ Walking boots.

❏ Torch.

Health

As in most places in Central America, be careful about any fresh food you eat. It is best to choose cooked vegetables and avoid salads. In Atitlán be careful of fresh fish. Always drink bottled or purifed water. Make sure your typhoid, tetanus, and polio inoculations are up to date before you leave home.

OTHER ACTIVITIES IN THE AREA

There are many energetic activities available around and about Atitlán, including para-gliding (not in the rainy season), windsurfing, kayaking, and scuba-diving. For those in search of something less strenuous, there are also nature trails, boat tours of the lake, and weaving courses. For further details, see the Activities A–Z section of this guide.

Mayan Heritage

by Fiona Dunlop

The Guatemalan lowlands of the Petén region harbour over 300 archaeological sites, most of them blanketed in dense tropical forest. King of them all is Tikal, while the nearby lake island of Flores makes the perfect base for exploring other lost Mayan worlds.

At Tikal, in a green, silent world abandoned by man, you have to project yourself back over a thousand years to visualize the days when priests climbed the steep steps of temples to burn copal (incense), imbibe hallucinogens, and make offerings to the gods. Below, hundreds of enthralled Mayan worshippers would watch and pray. Today, you can find these people's descendants to the south in towns dotted around **Lago Petén Itzá**. This is where you will discover those same slanting eyes and sloping foreheads depicted in countless Mayan stelae and bas-reliefs, and where you will come to realize that although Classic Maya civilization went into drastic decline in the ninth century the people themselves are still very much alive.

Boating on Lago Petén Itzá

Flores, the largest of several lake islands, is connected by a causeway to the much duller, more mundane Santa Elena on the southern shore. Together, these twin towns form the state capital of the Petén. Rising above the island's elevated plaza and visible from afar are the twin towers of a 1960s church that replaced the original colonial structure. This dated from the Spanish conquest of the Itzá, in 1697, the last indigenous group to succumb to conquistador swords. The cobbled streets radiating downhill from the church are lined with houses painted in a seductive palette of bright greens, pinks, yellows, and blues. Although it may feel as if you are somewhere in the Mediterranean, this is a remote watery oasis in the middle of a vast swathe of subtropical humid forest. Together with Mexico's Selva Lacandón and border areas of Belize, the Petén forms the Maya Biosphere Reserve, established in 1990 and covering an incredible 1.8 million ha (4.5 million acres).

So, what better place to hire a kayak in order to imitate the Mayan *cayuco* (canoe) transport of a millennium ago? And also perhaps to honour the audacious American pilot Charles Lindbergh, who landed his seaplane on this very surface in the 1930s. Like most other activities in Guatemala, my kayak rental was a straightforward affair and I was soon skimming across the water. Three hours floated by easily as I passed canoes filled with firewood and was rocked gently by the wake of motorboats ferrying passengers across the lake. Rural life was easily visible: pigs rooted for food and horses grazed in front of tiny thatched huts along the shore; while at times I closed in on long stretches of pristine

All you need for this trip is stamina, and a resistance to heat and humidity. Trekking gets more difficult in the rainy season, when insect numbers also increase.

★ All the activities described can be undertaken from the comfort of a hotel base. Longer treks that include camping can be organized through tour operators.

Good walking boots are essential, as is a rain poncho during the wet season. Take binoculars for observing the wildlife and a compass to avoid losing your way on the jungle paths.

forest with highly audible and visible birdlife. In contrast, groaning across the causeway linking Flores to the mainland were bright yellow secondhand American schoolbuses belching exhaust fumes.

As the sun started to sink, I paddled over mercurial water in which the ripples were tinged a metallic yellow and blue. A fisherman shouted a greeting, neotropical cormorants sailed regally by, beaks in the air, and a dazzling white egret watched me from a tree-stump. Drifting from the shore was a combined sensorial assault of woodsmoke, Guatemalan marimba music, and the screams and shouts of children. Gradually, the night orchestra of cicadas warmed up as the birds settled down and mist accumulated magically over the rain forest. In a few hours I had seen countless facets of this community, and it was only very reluctantly that I paddled back to the darkening shore to return, wet through, to my hotel.

LOOTING

Guatemala possesses an estimated 2,200 Mayan sites spread over 40 per cent of its territory. Guarding them all is, for the moment, an impossible task for this developing country, and even the 100 or so guarded sites are not exempt from the threat of looting. Yaxhá's famed stelae have been targeted on several occasions: one was airlifted from its jungle site by helicopter; while in October 1997 looters levered another into a pick-up truck using a small tree, and left behind the bullet-riddled corpse of an accomplice. In 1996 an armed gang held up workers at Yaxhá and stole eight polychrome pots; in this case although the looters may have earned $200–500 per pot, a collector would be willing to pay up to $100,000.

ITZÁ CONSCIOUSNESS

That evening, I discussed the Petén's ethnic composition with a local guide. There are an estimated 1,800 Itzáes, but only about 50 families actually speak their native language. Most of them live across the lake, in San José, where efforts are being made to revitalize and teach Itzá Maya after years of active discouragement. These once bellicose people of Chichén Itzá fame emigrated from the northern Yucatán to the Petén rain forest between A.D. 1200 and 1450. Lago Petén Itzá (*petén* means island) became their base, and the largest lake island their capital, Tayazal. After the Spanish army from Mérida finally conquered them, in 1697, Tayazal was renamed Flores. More recent arrivals into the region are the Kekchi Maya, who came from the southern Yucatán peninsula after the Spanish conquest. Since the 1960s,

MAYAN ASTRONOMY

The numerous structures of Tikal's El Mundo Perdido form part of an astronomical observatory, a field in which the Maya excelled. Although they were not alone among Mesoamerica's early peoples to observe planetary movements, the Maya were the most advanced in their calculations as they were brilliant mathematicians. Spring and autumn equinoxes, and summer and winter solstices became excuses for major celebrations, while all rituals, declarations of war, or auspicious planting periods were calculated according to complex cycles of *katuns* and *baktuns*. A *tun* was equivalent to a basic Mayan year of 360 days, a *katun* was 20 *tuns* (20 years), and a *baktun* was 20 *katuns* (400 years). Dates were based on the Long Count, a cyclical and linear system of time calculation that started in the equivalent of 3113 B.C. Tikal's renowned stelae include Stele 29, which bears the earliest Long Count date known in the Mayan lowlands—the equivalent of A.D. 292.

when agrarian reform laws offered free land to all-comers, the Petén population has multiplied five-fold, with many emigrants from the Guatemalan highlands.

The next day, I took to the lake again to visit **San José**, supposedly the most traditional of the lakeside communities. This time I chose the lazy option of a ferry, but the journey from Flores entailed two consecutive boats: the first to San Benito, then, from a different jetty across the promontory, the main, hourly ferry. Forty-five minutes later, I climbed onto some stone steps and looked up at San José. The old church dates from colonial times, but growing prosperity is visible in the newly built lakeside promenade, and the increasing ethnic consciousness in the Itzá translations on Spanish road signs. Modest thatched houses side with modern concrete, while between here and neighbouring San Andrés, women and girls wash laundry in time-honoured tradition in the lake. Even in Flores, locals without bathrooms wash and bathe in the lake, a mere 100 yards from an Internet café. The contrasts persist, but in supposedly less traditional San Andrés, when I enquired how to reach a lakeside eco-lodge a few miles away, I was immediately offered a lift. In a truck? No, only a canoe would do.

The lost world of Tikal

Along a surfaced road 65km (40 miles) north of Flores lies **Tikal**, Guatemala's most important archaeological site. In 1956, when there were no roads and the jungle had been choking the ruins for over a thousand years, this 120-sq-km (46-square-mile) site was impressively excavated and restored by the University of Pennsylvania over a four-year period. The airstrip where prop planes used to disgorge enthusiastic archaeologists is now a car park, and the simple jungle lodges where they stayed have become tourist eco-lodges. But there is still no electricity and the community cellular phone (installed in 1997), kept at the back of a souvenir stand, charges up on solar power. Generators ensure hotel guests do not lack the usual facilities (within restricted hours), but otherwise Tikal remains refreshingly primitive and undeveloped. Another of its bonuses is that the immense **Parque Nacional Tikal** (**Tikal National Park**), covering 575sq km (222 square miles) is a rich source of tropical flora and fauna, due in part to man's long absence.

Contrary to the habits of most tourists, who indulge in the masochistic practice of rising at 4am in Flores in order to scramble up a Tikal pyramid for sunrise by 5:30am, I chose to spend two nights at Tikal itself. It is a wonderful feeling to unlock your hotel's front door before daybreak and then follow a path through the jungle by torchlight. A few birds were stirring when I reached the ticket-booth, where I was met by the forest ranger who would accompany me, an essential arrangement for independent travellers if entering before the official opening time of 5:30. Roberto was a cheerful, sure-footed type who set a pretty snappy pace in the pre-dawn shadows. We decided to head for the pyramid in El Mundo Perdido rather than Temple IV, Tikal's highest structure, which hardly has room on its steps to accommodate the sunrise voyeurs. Suddenly, out of the darkness and mist between the tall tropical hardwoods, loomed a towering wall. This unexpected visual shock turned out to be the rear of Temple I; it was at this point that I fully realized the scale of what I was about to explore.

After a strenuous half-hour we reached our target, the main pyramid (Structure 5C-54) in an area of 38 structures that are thought to pre-date the central plaza by about 500 years. Still groping in the fast-disappearing night, we climbed the steep, narrow steps to the 35-m (116-foot) summit of what is thought to be Tikal's oldest excavated edifice, probably built before A.D. 300.

The view from the top of Tikal's El Mundo Perdido (Structure 5C-54) is well worth the steep 35-m (116-foot) climb

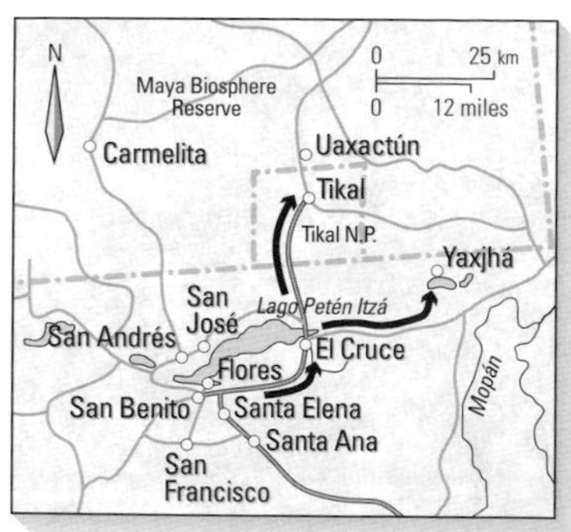

The area surrounding Lago Petén Itzá and Tikal in the Guatamalan lowlands

The eastern sky was already growing lighter, turning first pink, then yellow, and giving outlines to the dark and misty sea of treetops and a luminous clarity to the horizon. And then up she came, the golden orb that was worshipped by the Maya alongside the moon, their circular forms being perceived as so sacred that it is thought the Maya did not make or use the wheel for fear of abusing them.

The handful of Australian, German, and Swiss tourists who were with us on the summit were equally moved by this visual feast. Gradually, as the air warmed up, we could focus on the roofcomb (raised roof feature) of Temple I and on its opposite, Temple II, on the unassailable Temple III (also called the Temple of the Jaguar Priest), and on Temple IV (Temple of the Double-Headed Serpent), all of which were now emerging above the mist-shrouded canopy. Suddenly, a brilliantly coloured toucan swept by, later followed by warblers and flycatchers—this was their moment as the morning chorus grew. Roberto now took his leave, after making sure I knew my exact location in this vast site, and gratefully pocketing his tip. From El Mundo Perdido, I hiked onwards, climbing over the foundation walls of a triple ballcourt, exploring the labyrinthine, bat-ridden back rooms of the Palace of the Windows, and clambering up more steep steps in order to conquer other Mayan summits.

Zoological interest

Temple IV, Tikal's tallest structure at 65m (228 feet), can be climbed only by a series of steep, rickety wooden stairways—not to be attempted by anyone who is even remotely prone to vertigo. While I was meditating on the view from its summit, a silver fox (*Vulpes cinerero-argentatus*) suddenly rounded the corner, completely unphased by the crowd of lens-snapping foreigners. Below, troops of fearless spider monkeys (*Ateles geoffroyi*) were crashing around in the branches of lofty ceiba, mahogany (*Swietenia mahagoni*), and sapodilla (*Manilkara zapota*) trees. Later in the afternoon I was to hear the eerie wails and cries of the much larger howler monkey (*Alouatta palliata*), said to imitate the jaguar's call in order to keep predators at bay. Cat species that live here include jaguars (*Panthera onca*), margays (*Felis wiedii*), jaguarundis (*F. yaguarondi*), and ocelots

OPTIMUM VISITING TIME

What is special about Tikal is its vast scale and aura of mystery. You can explore, sit in the shade of trees or pyramids, watch birds, insects, and animals, and dream about ancient times—and you may be completely alone. The central paths and structures are well-trodden, but beyond that are numerous less frequented trails and ruins; invest in a decent site map from the museum shop and, if you intend to explore thoroughly, take a compass as the jungle paths can all look identical. Above all, choose your visiting times carefully: start at dawn, take a break from about 10am to 3pm in order to recharge, then benefit from the unexpected emptiness of late afternoon, by which time most bus groups have headed back to Flores. You can stay on after closing time if you are accompanied by a ranger (remember to tip well).

(*F. pardalis*), but they are rarely seen. Armies of sharp-snouted coatimundis are visible throughout Tikal, especially towards dusk, but most noticeable of all are leaf-cutter ants, industriously transporting vast tracts of jungle across paths and through undergrowth (they are known to strip tropical forest of about 15 per cent of its total leaf production in order to create a sticky mulch used for food). Armadillos, javelinas (peccaries), porcupines, weasels, and deer are also said to be common sightings in Tikal National Park.

Yaxhá: into the unknown

After Tikal, I was fired with enthusiasm to visit some of the lesser-known and less frequented Mayan sites. So far, 314 have been registered in the Petén, but few are accessible by road and even fewer by paved road. After discussing the possibilities with local guides, and not having the time to embark on a long trek, I decided to squeeze the sites of Yaxhá and Uaxactún into a one-day trip by four-wheel drive, chauffeured by the enthusiastic Otto. However, the night before our 6am departure it rained heavily and ceaselessly, as it often does in the Petén. As the wet and soggy morning announced itself, Otto drew up at my hotel. Seated demurely in the boot of his jeep were his two young daughters (six and eight years old), who, he declared, would accompany us without any problem around Yaxhá. Uaxactún was now struck off our agenda as the road would be too muddy and hence time-consuming. Also accompanying us were two young Japanese archaeology students, Yuki and Mitsu, both of whom belonged to the strong, silent, though eternally smiling category.

Yaxhá lies 60km (37 miles) northeast of Flores, half the journey served by a surfaced main road that continues to Tikal, and the rest by a rough, unpaved stretch that passes farmland before entering unadulterated jungle. We bounced along, our wheels occasionally churning madly in the mud that had built up overnight, but eventually arrived unscathed. This extensive site borders the large, crocodile-ridden lake of Topoxte, whose island contains ruins of a ceremonial centre. According to the Maya, the rain forests are the children of a torrid union between sun, water, and earth, a union that also produced Yaxhá (meaning green water, and referring to the colour of precious jade). The city was, in fact, founded in A.D. 751 as a result of a schism in Tikal's ruling family but, like all other Mayan cities, by around A.D. 900 its 500 or so structures were abandoned. It was first discovered by Europeans in 1904, but excavation work started properly only in 1993, aided by German backing. The site is believed to be Guatemala's third-largest from the Classic era, and its highlight is one of the Mayan world's most extensive constructions and examples of urban planning: a double acropolis surrounded by patios, plazas, and other monumental edifices.

Jungle magic

For us, the only visitors that day, it was an eye-opening experience to be led by park rangers through what still remains an untamed and largely untouched site. Huge grassy mounds sprouting trees

JUNGLE INCOME

Jade palms are, curiously, the most important source of employment in the Maya Biosphere Reserve, as their fronds are used as fillers by florists the world over. Other tropical-forest income sources include the lofty evergreen allspice tree (*Pimienta dioica*), used to produce a culinary powder that combines the aromas of nutmeg, cloves, and cinnamon, and whose fruits are picked by *pimenteros* in climbers' spiked boots; and the sapodilla tree (*Manikara zapota*), a type of spruce tree whose resin (called chicle) is tapped to make chewing-gum.

Descending the main pyramid at Yaxhá accompanied by the calls of howler monkeys hidden in the dense jungle below

from their summits were in fact Mayan pyramids, while the howler monkeys we heard grunting away around midday obviously felt safely distant from mankind. Numerous beautifully carved stelae have been uncovered here, some of which are displayed under shelters at the base of the pyramids. Otto's knowledge of the jungle, too, was illuminating, as were the asides he made to his daughters, switching from Spanish to Kekchi Maya to German, the latter inherited from his grandfather, one of many migrant Germans who came to Guatemala in the 1920s as coffee-growers.

From the *nabakaj* (priests' enclosure) at the summit of the main pyramid—still under excavation—we surveyed a sweeping vista of jungle and lake, visualizing the wild cats roaming in the former and the snapping jaws of crocodiles in the latter. Back on lower ground, we watched our feet carefully, as the prolific local wildlife includes the deadly fer de lance and coral snakes (*Bothrops asper* and *Micrurus fulvius*). Otto reassuringly showed us the jungle leaf that should be chewed to produce a pulp that is applied to a snakebite, as well as others used specifically for mosquito bites, for losing weight, for countering asthma, or for curing diarrhoea. Picking our way through the mud, we passed lofty hardwoods, pimienta (*Pimenta dioica*, or allspice), chicozapote (sapodilla tree), strangler figs (*Ficus aurea*; parasites that slowly throttle the life out of their host tree), and endless examples of the decorative xate (jade palms, of the genus *Chamaedorea*). At this time of the day, however, we saw few of the 300 or so bird species that make Yaxhá one of Guatemala's best birding destinations, although spider monkeys were volubly present.

Exhausted by our trek and early morning start, we all slept on the way back to Flores, but Otto's energy was far from diminished. Taking a fast left turn from Santa Elena, we bumped a few miles along another dirt road to the **Aktun Kan caves**. This extensive network of interlocking caverns, which includes a 4-km (2½-mile) underground tunnel leading to San Benito, is packed with weird and wonderful rock formations. Typically, local imagination has lent names to the various stalactites and stalagmites, although resemblances are not always obvious. As we skidded over the damp stone, our way crudely lit by blinding light-bulbs, it was hard to imagine the Maya using this lugubrious setting for ceremonial purposes. A pyramid with a spiritual view, yes. But a dripping cave? It seemed far better to leave it to the bats.

GOING IT ALONE

INTERNAL TRAVEL

The small international airport of Santa Elena receives several flights daily from Guatemala City, from Belize, from Cancún and Chetumal in Mexico, and, three times a week, from Palenque. Otherwise, there are comfortable express-bus connections with the capital and with Río Dulce, both journeys vastly improved since the road was surfaced. The 488km (303 miles) from Guatemala City can now be covered in a long day's drive, as compared with the six days necessary in the 1920s.

Numerous tourist minivans run between Flores/Santa Elena and Tikal, as does a very slow public bus, which also connects with Uaxactún. Jeep or car hire is available in Santa Elena.

WHEN TO GO

The high season is December–February, the first part of the dry season, which continues until June. However, from March to May, humidity hits 90 per cent and temperatures can rise to 45°C (113°F), so this period should be avoided. The heaviest rain falls from late September to early December, corresponding with the hurricane season. The *canicula* (heatwaves) of the Petén take place five days after the spring and autumn equinoxes, and last about three weeks. Annual average temperatures in the Petén are 22–30°C (72–86°F) and annual rainfall is 1,265mm (50 inches).

Ferries at Flores awaiting passengers to cross Lago Petén Itzá; you can also negotiate private boat hire

PLANNING

If you are heading for the Petén in the high season, it is essential to book accommodation, particularly if you want to stay on the site of Tikal. The same goes for plane tickets if you intend to fly there. If you want to explore some of the less visited Mayan sites, contact local tour operators to see when they have any expeditions planned. The Petén has endless potential for camping treks that combine jungle and wildlife with Mayan ruins, but these need to be organized in advance. By forming your own group of four people you can create a tailor-made itinerary at reasonable cost. The minimum for this is two people, but it is necessarily more costly. In the high season, there are frequent low-cost day trips from Flores to Mayan sites such as Ceibal, Uaxactún, or Yaxhá, but out of season there is a problem with filling the minivans.

TRAVELLERS' TIPS

- The Petén and the site of Tikal are classic stop-overs on the Ruta Maya (Mayan Route), which traverses the Yucatán peninsula and Belize, and then continues to Honduras beyond Guatemala. It can easily be combined with Palenque in Mexico (see page 62) and a beach resort such as Lívingston (see page 92) or one in nearby Belize.
- For visitors wanting to remain within Guatemala, the Petén can be combined with both Río Dulce (see page 92) and the Lago de Atitlán (see page 76) on a two-week holiday.
- In the Petén, be prepared for rain at most times of the year.

WHAT TO TAKE

- Insect repellent.
- Torch.
- Penknife.
- Sturdy walking boots.
- Sunblock.
- Rain poncho.
- Long-sleeved shirts and trousers in lightweight cotton.
- Compass.

HEALTH

Your combined tetanus and polio immunization should be up to date, and typhoid is also advisable. As this is a malarial region during the rainy season, it is advisable to take the appropriate medication (check with your doctor for the latest recommendations), starting two weeks before arrival and continuing six weeks after departure. If you go on a camping trip or long trek, make sure your guide is carrying the appropriate snake-bite antivenom.

Cruising Around Río Dulce

by Fiona Dunlop

Few people visualize Guatemala as having an outlet on the Caribbean Sea, and even fewer know of the black Garifuna community that lives there. This is the place to relax before exploring the waterway of Río Dulce, where yachtspeople and jungle-trekkers cross paths.

Pirates once captained the most commonly sighted vessels on the Río Dulce, in the days when the "Golfo Dulce" was the only outlet through which Guatemala's produce was shipped back to the colonial mother country of Spain. Schooners and catamarans are today's sleek equivalents, their skippers hailing from all over the globe; they are seen above all in late summer, when this inner sea becomes a favourite hide-out from the Caribbean's notorious hurricane season. Then, as the river finally drains into the sea, another community comes into sight: that of the Garifunas. These proud Afro-Caribbeans, who are descended from shipwrecked slaves and Carib Indians, and who also have settlements in coastal Belize and Honduras, maintain a strong identity and culture, as well as purposefully keeping their Guatemalan hometown of Lívingston accessible only by sea. This was to be my starting point for exploring the natural splendours of the Río Dulce area.

For this tour you must enjoy clambering in and out of boats and canoes and getting wet, as the Río Dulce area is prone to rain. Jungle-trekking requires a basic level of fitness.

★ There is a good range of hotels along the Río Dulce and in Lívingston, so basic comforts are assured.

Take binoculars for bird-watching, a snorkel and mask for expeditions to Punta de Manabique, and footwear suitable both for boating and wet weather, and for jungle-trekking.

If you come to Río Dulce from Guatemala City with your own transport, make sure you stop to visit **Quiriguá**, the most important of the 25 Mayan sites discovered in the Lago de Izabal region. The site lies about 4km (2½ miles) off the main Ruta al Atlántico, hidden among extensive Del Monte banana plantations. If you don't have a car, you can reach it by taking a Guatemala City bus from Fronteras (on the Río Dulce), followed by a *colectivo* pick-up for the last stretch, but allow plenty of time for the journey.

Quiriguá reached its zenith in A.D. 600–900, and hence was contemporaneous with Honduras's majestic Copán and an important trading post between it and Tikal. The highlight is a group of towering stelae, the tallest (Monument 5) almost 8m (26 feet) high. These upright stones, beautifully carved with images of animals and glyphs, stand on a grassy expanse in front of less impressive pyramid ruins. The tropical forest setting of towering ceiba and teak trees nurtures plentiful wildlife, not least mosquitoes, so take insect repellent as well as a hat and water.

To Lívingston

As I sat on the jetty in the decrepit banana port of Puerto Barrios beside a string of rusting cargo ships, I wondered how long it would take to reach Lívingston, somewhere over the watery horizon. A *colectivo* motorboat had just left when I arrived, but despite the depressing lack of fellow passengers, boat hands assured me that I would be off within 40 minutes. Sure enough, locals and tourists started rolling up with bundles and backpacks, and soon 12 of us were speeding across the waves. To our left (the south), the mainland was cloaked in dense jungle, its regular deep green treeline occasionally broken by palm trees or a house, and backed by the Montañas del Mico, the last bumps of the Sierra de las Minas range. On the water, the occasional fisherman threw a net from a canoe, while egrets and pelicans swooped between us. The scene was looking increasingly idyllic, and made a welcome change from the potholed streets and cargo containers that characterize Barrios, better known for its seedy bars, brawls, and brothels. Within 45 painless minutes we had thudded across the Bahía de Amatique and were docking at **Lívingston**.

This small, far-flung town, less than 20km (12 miles) south of the Belizean border, soon grows on you, particularly if you are coming from Guatemala's cool highlands or need to recover from the physical challenges of the Petén. Here, humidity and hot temperatures nurture a lushly tropical vegetation, where tall coconut palms and breadfruit trees overshadow bushes studded with red hibiscus or clumps of white lilies. Water surrounds you as Lívingston occupies a promontory, its handful of streets running uphill from the harbour on the Río Dulce side, then downhill to the narrow grey-sand shore of the Bahía de Amatique, part of the Caribbean Sea. Walk south and the village soon peters out, the jungle taking over. The sleepy backwater image is accentuated by the lack of cars; most people use bicycles (with toddlers often curled up in the basket) or their feet—up to a point. Stay on the two main streets, and you will be seduced by the easy communication and relaxed attitude of the 3,000 or so Garifuna inhabitants, as well as by numerous open-air restaurants. Stressed visitors soon become soothed by the background strains of reggae or by the rhythms of Lívingston's home-grown drummers.

Siete Altares

Its encirclement by jungle and sea makes Lívingston short on hiking destinations. An exception is the **Siete Altares waterfall**, a stunning beauty spot. This can be reached by motorboat or by a circuitous hike totalling about six hours, and which still necessitates a brief encounter with water. Those with yet more energy can continue the hike to **Playa Blanca**, a beautiful white-sand beach—something that is severely lacking closer to Lívingston. In the recent past, several muggings have taken place along this isolated path, so all visitors should be accompanied by a guide. I was advised to look for someone called Rojillo, who I eventually found in his front yard, sitting on an upturned crate and preparing a bucketful of fish.

The next day, after a few false starts, three of us were led out of town by Lester, Rojillo's sidekick, a cheerful Garifuna in

GARIFUNA ORIGINS

Long before Columbus reached these shores, Carib Indians from Venezuela started to emigrate north to islands of the Caribbean. After conquering the local Arawak Indians, they settled down to farm and fish, calling themselves Garifuna (meaning brave people). In the mid-17th century, when a ship carrying blacks from West Africa to the Spanish Caribbean colonies ran aground on the island of St. Vincent, its survivors paired off with local Indian women. This produced a new people—the black Caribs. In 1795, as a result of rivalries between Spain, England, and France, these Garifuna were rounded up, some were massacred, and the survivors finally dumped in 1797 by the British on Roatán, an island off Honduras. From there, their tiny community multiplied and spread to Belize, Honduras, and Guatemala. They are now estimated to number about 70,000.

LEFT and BELOW Lívingston sits on a promontory, with the Río Dulce on one side and the Bahía de Amatique on the other. Its Garifuna inhabitants are descended from Carib Indians and West African slaves

his early 20s. Under one mutilated arm was tucked a lengthy machete in an embossed leather sheath—he seemed reassuringly prepared for the unpredictable. Rosa, from Guatemala City, and her Italian friend, Giovanni, were my two young companions. Our route eventually left behind the clapboard houses and Lívingston's colourful, rambling cemetery to follow a muddy path through a tropical no man's land. Occasional fields of corn or beans (the frijoles variety) appeared between coconut palms and wild papayas as we slowly climbed to the *mirador* (lookout point). From here we could see the mountains of Belize on a not-so-distant marine horizon.

Aside from three diminutive Kekchi Mayas bent double beneath huge loads of firewood, we encountered no one. As

GARIFUNA SPECIALITIES

Garifuna restaurants dish up generous portions of grilled fish, lobster, and *tapado*, a divine coconut broth containing clams, prawns, crabs, and fish. Other dishes concentrate on prawns (try a succulent *ceviche de camarón*), conch (*caracol*), or the catch of the day, while *pan de coco* (coconut bread) and *bocadillo* (burnt-sugar coconut) are homemade candies sold on the street by rotund matrons. In the evening, head for the Garifuna bar on the Calle de la Iglesia, where boy-drummers start warming up at around 10pm. Their rhythmical prowess is often matched by that of a girl waitress, who dances as if she has had a lifetime's experience behind her. Local crafts include articles made from coconut shells.

we hiked onwards, pink land-crabs scuttled into their holes and the scenic wildness of the jungle intensified. Lester pointed out a San Juan tree (*Vochysia guatemalensis*), whose wood is used for canoes and for drums. Lianas increased in number, looping and draping over the sturdy hardwoods, sand gradually replaced soil underfoot, and the rather fragile-looking Giovanni stripped off his T-shirt as the level of our water bottles descended. Finally, we arrived at Río Quehueche. Here, we were met by a precarious-looking canoe that luckily was paddled smoothly by its Kekchi owner. No doubt helped by the stabilizing effect of its five passengers, the canoe drifted calmly through thick mangrove stands where a rich birdlife added to the evocative *Crocodile Dundee* atmosphere. Crocodiles do exist here, but Lester claimed that he had never seen one. Fortunately, the canoe remained upright, so we didn't have to put his faith to the test.

Some time later, as I dived into the cool jade-green water of the "Seventh Altar", I decided that we had indeed been blessed. The waterfall consists of a succession of organically shaped, terraced pools where crystalline water runs over smooth, greenish rocks beneath a soaring canopy of tropical forest. Hardwoods shoot up 30m (100 feet), straight as a die, while creepers, lianas, ferns, and undergrowth compete for space on the steep banks. Some rays of sunlight filter through, but the air remains fresh in contrast to the hot, humid beachfront stretch of the walk. Lesser mortals stop at the first few "altars," all of which offer easy bathing, but it is the magical number seven, with its showering cascade and deep pool, that makes for perfection—although reaching it requires some slippery rock climbing. Invigorated, but with increasingly weary limbs, we trudged back to Lívingston via the more direct route, involving a straightforward 6-km (4-mile) walk along Playa Salvador Gaviota and another canoe crossing back over Río Quehueche.

Exploring the Río Dulce

Lívingston marks one end of a vast area of waterways that centres on the **Lago de Izabal**, Guatemala's largest lake, measuring 20 by 48km (12 by 30 miles). More superlatives enter the picture when you realize that this lake is fed by the country's longest river (the Río Cahabón, which offers spectacular whitewater rafting along its upper reaches) and receives Guatemala's heaviest rainfall—something I saw plenty of, much to my chagrin. Every morning, motorboats set off up the **Río Dulce** from Lívingston on a 2½-hour tour to Fronteras, making fleeting stops at some of the many sights along the 36-km (23-mile) route. The pay-off comes quickly, as just a couple of hundred yards southwest of Lívingston sheer cliffs rise to over 100m (330 feet), creating a dramatic, narrow canyon much favoured by cormorants, pelicans, gulls, frigatebirds, ospreys, egrets, and kingfishers.

The dazzling white limestone walls at the base of the cliffs appear man-made, so even and straight are their forms, but they are all part of the 400-million-year-old geological history of the Izabal region, which saw the creation of a complex mixture of karstic caverns and hills, depressions, rivers, lakes, and swamps. The Río Dulce's healthy ecosystem is visible in the prolific catches of the local fishermen, who manoeuvre their tiny *cayucos* (dugouts) behind curtains of creepers and lianas to keep safely away from the central currents. The centuries may go by, but Mayan traditions remain unchanged. Beyond lies impenetrable rain forest; the occasional thatched hut on the waterfront is a modest Kekchi home, accessible only from the river, which at this point is nearly 24m (80 feet) deep. In marked contrast, the Río Dulce is being increasingly targeted by Guatemala City's wealthier citizens for their weekend homes; undeterred by its inaccessibility, some even arrive by private plane at the local airstrip, to be spirited away by boat to their personal jetty. Their more extravagant constructions are visible further upriver.

Río Dulce's attractions include sulphurous hot springs, whose natural jacuzzi effect regularly warms the hiking-weary limbs of boatloads of visitors. I indulged in this late one afternoon, when jungle wildlife was stirring after a long, hot day. Birds shrieked and flitted above, then a howler monkey (*Alouatta palliata*) started its unworldly cry. In contrast, a short distance east of here is the **Ak' Tenamit Project**, a set-up that aims to alleviate the poverty of the local Kekchi Maya; buy souvenirs here in the form of handmade paper produced by the women's cooperative, or make a donation of money, books, or batteries.

Also near by is the tranquil, entrancing tributary of Río Tatin, a shallow, north-flowing river best explored by dinghy or canoe. Paddle upstream through dense tropical jungle and follow the right fork to a crystalline waterfall where Kekchi women often wash. Further upstream still is the **Gruta del Tigre** (**Tiger's Cave**). If you organize your trip well, you can return to Lívingston via a trail from the waterfalls—a hike of four or five hours. In a similar vein is **Río Lampara**, virtually opposite across the Río Dulce, which, for several miles, offers the same type of vegetation before ending in open ranchland. In the distance rises the profile of the **Cerro San Gil**, a 1,300-m (4,265-foot) hill protected as a nature reserve and perfect for mountain biking, horse riding, or simply hiking and bird-watching. Access to the hill is from the Bahía de Santo Tomás, just south of Puerto Barrios.

KEKCHI MAYA

The other side of Livingston's ethnic coin is the community of Kekchi Maya, the original inhabitants of this area. Although they live side by side, the Garifunas and the Mayas maintain very distinct communities and lifestyles. Both live off the sea, but only the Kekchi farm. Altogether, over 6,000 Kekchi live in about 50 isolated villages in the mountains of Río Dulce, often in conditions of extreme poverty.

OF MANATEES AND OTHER CREATURES

Eventually, the Río Dulce opens into El Golfete, a wide lagoon whose banks are now theoretically protected as the **Parque Nacional Río Dulce** (**Río Dulce National Park**). About 16km (10 miles) upriver from Lívingston you come to the **Biotopo Chocon Machacas**, an ecological reserve designed to protect the endangered Caribbean manatee (see box on page 99). Whatever you may be told in advance, it is unlikely that you will spot this creature as the water is cloudy and in any case the manatee has an exceptionally timid

nature. However, manatees aside, the 6,245ha (15,425 acres) of the reserve are a veritable treasure trove of biodiversity. It is the northernmost "Amazonic" ecosystem, where humid tropical forest nurtures a resident population of howler monkeys, boa constrictors (*Boa constrictor*), iguanas, tapirs, jaguars (*Panthera onca*), and 300 bird species, including the multi-coloured toucan. An easy 1-km (1,100-yard) trail gives a preliminary taste of this spectacular natural setting of tropical hardwoods, cohune palms, ferns, orchids, and bromeliads, but, better still, hire a guide to lead you into the heart of the rain forest on foot or by boat, or even stay at the campsite here. As ever, remember to take insect repellent and water.

FRONTERAS

The face of Río Dulce changed considerably when a bridge was built over the narrow channel between the Lago de Izabal and El Golfete, so linking the little towns of El Relleno (east bank) and Fronteras (west bank). Things are now developing further, with a vastly improved road northwest into the Petén

ABOVE The endangered Caribbean manatee inhabits the waters of the Río Dulce, although it is unlikely you will spot one OPPOSITE The hike to Siete Altares from Lívingston involves crossing the Río Quehueche by dugout

THE MANATEE

The formidable Caribbean manatee (*Trichechus manatus*) is a herbivorous mammal shaped like a torpedo; legend has it that early Spanish explorers believed these creatures to be mermaids. Although manatees are found in an area ranging from the Gulf of Mexico to northern Brazil, they are an endangered species and several sanctuaries exist to protect them. The slow-moving creatures measure about 3m (10 feet) in length, weigh 400–500kg (880–1,100 pounds), and need to eat the equivalent of 20 per cent of their body weight daily. In its natural habitat, a manatee can live for 50–60 years, but despite the species' protected status in Guatemala, they are still hunted illegally for their prized meat.

and another southwest to El Estor. In the rambling village of **Fronteras** (also called Río Dulce), a food market and stores offer essentials to yachtspeople from the nearby marinas, as well as to local *campesinos* (peasant farmers). The yachties' own specialist infrastructure just below the bridge (boat- and sail-repairers, fax and email offices, and the inevitable watering-holes) is the best place to enquire about yacht charters or alternative means of moving on to other parts of the Caribbean.

By the time I reached Fronteras, I had already seen the **Castillo San Felipe**, Lago de Izabal's famed historical landmark, from a distance and wanted to get a closer look at it. With a choice of boat or *colectivo* pick-up truck, I opted for the latter, which I flagged down after already hiking a fair distance along the newly paved road to El Estor (this name, incidentally, is a mutation of the English word "store"). Up I climbed into the open truck, to squeeze into a crowd of men and women, mostly clutching bags of fresh market produce. Along we bumped, past farmland and small wooden houses, until about 20 minutes later I was dropped outide the entrance to the castle.

This impressive stone construction, immaculately restored in 1955, has a series of narrow stairways leading along ramparts to towers and lookout points. An earlier tower, dating from 1595, originally stood on the site. This was destroyed by pirates and subsequently rebuilt by Captain Bustamante in 1604. By 1640, pirate attacks on the fort had intensified, the protagonists being such notorious characters as Diego the Mulatto (Pegleg's lieutenant), the English aristocrat Anthony Shirley, William Jackson, and William Parker, known as the plunderer of Santo Domingo and Puerto Bello. In 1651 the fort was rebuilt as the Castillo San Felipe de Lara but, despite renewed improvements to the fortifications and the installation of a portcullis, pirates seized it again and attacked the *bodegas* (warehouses). After the Dutch pirate Jan Zaques actually set fire to San Felipe, in 1684, a completely new design was agreed upon, and 100 new guard positions ensured a peaceful existence from then on.

Today, the landscaped grounds around Castillo San Felipe have been declared a national park, with safe swimming points signposted and picnic tables arranged under shady trees. In front of me lay the vast Lago de Izabal, but that's another story....

BOATING AROUND

If your group is big enough, it is far more rewarding to rent your own boat, plus canoes or a dinghy, in order to do proper justice to this beautiful region. Such an excursion can be arranged at the Lívingston dock or at Fronteras, though serious negotiation is needed. An alternative area to head for is the Punta de Manabique, a finger-like peninsula north of Puerto Barrios and opposite Lívingston. Much of the fun lies in the one-hour boat ride: you may spot sea turtles bobbing on the surface or dolphins leaping out of the waves, and you are certain to see pelicans, magnificent frigatebirds (*Fregata magnificens*), and seagulls. On the peninsula there are estuaries, sandy beaches, coral reefs, and cays that offer plentiful wildlife and good snorkelling. You can stay in the small settlement here (see box opposite), and local fishermen will cook up their catch for you. If you rise early with the cacophany of tropical birds in the jungle behind, head for the jetty to watch the glowing sunrise and the fishing boats heading out over the waves. The Canal Ingles (English Canal), which cuts through the base of the peninsula to the Gulf of Honduras, offers the perfect experience of dense Amazonian-style jungle.

GOING IT ALONE

Internal Travel

Comfortable long-distance buses connect Guatemala City to both Fronteras and Puerto Barrios in 5–6 hours. Alternatively, the domestic airline Inter (part of Grupo Taca) operates daily flights to Puerto Barrios. A rather ancient ferry runs from Puerto Barrios to Lívingston twice daily (at 5am and 2pm), but the *colectivo* motor launches are much faster and more convenient, running from dawn to sunset. You can also avoid Puerto Barrios completely by taking a *colectivo* launch from Fronteras, at the little *muelle* (jetty) in front of the Río Bravo café. These boats tend to link up with the arrival of buses from Guatemala City and from Flores around midday. At other times of the day you may have to wait quite a while. There is a ferry service from Puerto Barrios to Punta Gorda (Belize) on Tuesdays and Fridays.

When to Go

The Lago de Izabal and Río Dulce area receive Guatemala's heaviest rainfall, averaging over 3,000mm (120 inches) annually (more than twice that of other regions), so expect downpours at most times of the year. That said, there is less rain from December to April. Lívingston's humid tropical climate is alleviated by northern breezes (in Garifuna these are called *lugudi varana*, meaning breeze from the sea) and by winds from the west.

Planning

Yacht charters are about the only activity that needs advance organization here, as local treks and canoe and boat trips can only be booked on the spot—bicycles tend to work better than phones in Lívingston. Tour agencies on Lívingston's main street all offer identical treks to Siete Altares and Playa Blanca, as well as boat trips along the Río Dulce to Fronteras or up the Río Tatin, mostly with sandwich lunches thrown in. If you are part of a group, you can arrange a tailor-made tour. Canoes (*cayucos*) can be hired by the hour at Lívingston's main jetty for exploring the canyon or for fishing. Longer trips are available to the Islas de la Bahía (Bay Islands) in Honduras and to the Belizean cays, and *colectivo* launches also run to Punta Gorda in Belize, which could make a logical extension to your trip. For the latter, sign up on a boatman's list at the jetty.

Travellers' Tips

- ❏ Water transport is essential in this area as little is accessible on foot. Ideally, negotiate a price for several days with one boatman.
- ❏ You may easily be lulled into hedonism in Río Dulce, but it is worth remembering that behind the natural beauty lies severe poverty. Most of the Kekchi Maya were displaced to this region by political violence, and they now suffer from a lack of medical care, education, and family support. At the Ak' Tenamit Project, located about 9km (6 miles) upriver from Lívingston, just west of the Río Tatin estuary, international volunteers give essential grassroots help to the Kekchi villages. A women's cooperative here sells handmade paper products, and the medical clinic is open to the public. You can contribute financially or donate medicines, books, or batteries.

What to Take

- ❏ Light cotton clothes suitable for the hot, humid climate.
- ❏ Good walking shoes.
- ❏ Rubber or plastic sandals for canoeing.
- ❏ Snorkelling gear.

Health

Make sure your typhoid, tetanus, and polio inoculations are up to date. Vaccination against Hepatitis A is advisable although not essential. Seek medical advice on what anti-malarial precautions are recommended.

ALTERNATIVE BASE

An even more adventurous alternative to staying in Lívingston is to head for Punta de Manabique. The isolated community on this peninsula numbers about 500, and villagers have set up basic overnight facilities in thatched huts right on the beach. Remember to take your snorkelling gear for exploring the coral reef. See Contacts for details.

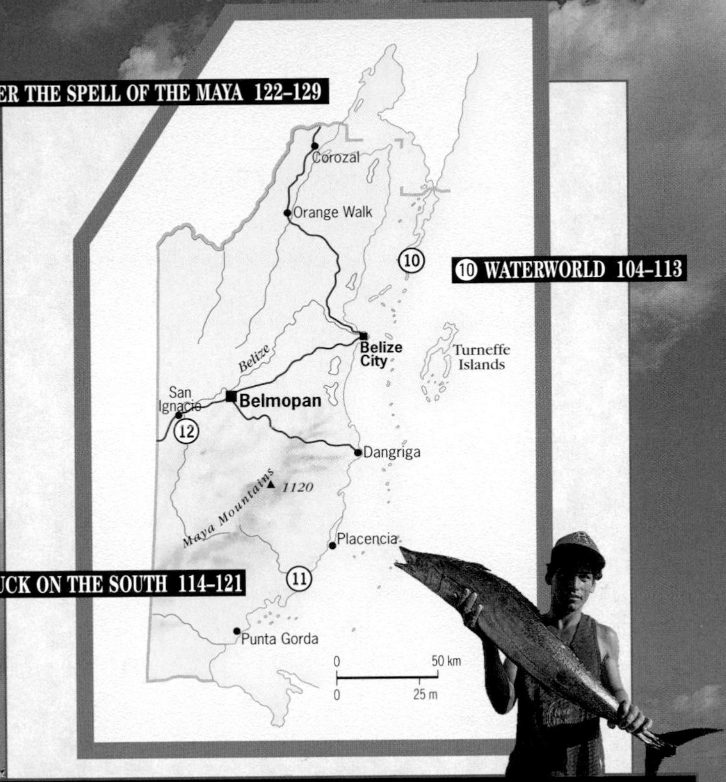

BELIZE

Belize is a giant advertising billboard proving that great things come in small packages: no other country in Central America offers so much for so little effort in such a tiny land mass. Hop off your plane and onto another, and within 15 minutes you can be touching down on a gem of an island, one of 200 cays that run the length of the country's 250-km (155-mile) coastline to rival Australia's Great Barrier Reef. If you drive inland for an hour to the Maya Mountains, you will find adventure travel experiences ranging from canoeing to caving, fishing, climbing, and jungle-trekking, as well as a fantastic array of wildlife that includes howler monkeys, iguanas, jaguars, tapirs, and hundreds of other, more exotic rare species. Or make a bit more of an effort and head south to another world, of peaceful Mayan Indian villages, primary rain forest, and jungle-covered ruins. Add to this an environmentally caring infrastructure, a helpful tourist board, and some of the friendliest and most laid-back people in the world, and you will soon realize that Belize really does have it all.

The beach at San Pedro on Ambergis Caye, the largest of Belize's offshore islands; ABOVE A San Pedro fisherman with a barracuda

Waterworld

by Carl Pendle

Running the entire length of the Belize coastline is an underworld wonder that rivals Australia's Great Barrier Reef. Over 200 cays are sprinkled along 250km (155 miles) of Caribbean waters, some no bigger than a mound of sand supporting a palm tree. I experienced two very different cays, Caye Caulker and Ambergris Caye, but for me the real adventure lurked beneath the waves.

Dark shadows circle purposefully beneath the boat. It's feeding time, and the rays and sharks aren't too fussy about what's on the menu. The sparkling turquoise water looks inviting, but our party of 12 is a little apprehensive about jumping in. Our captain, Paul, pulls a plastic bag full of sardines from beneath the stow and casts a handful into the Caribbean water. It's hot, but no one is bothered about getting burnt in the low morning sun. The boat tilts as we all lean on the starboard deck to watch the sardines being ripped apart. The stingrays are first at the table, followed closely by the sharks. Tails thrash and fins poke above the water as the creatures fight for the food in a spectacle that is simultaneously exciting and horrifying.

We are moored in Shark-Ray Alley, some 6km (4 miles) southeast of San Pedro town, the capital of Ambergris Caye, the largest and most developed of Belize's 200 offshore cays. What was supposed to be a gentle diving-snorkelling trip is turning into a Jacques Cousteau-style adventure, and the guests are—not surprisingly—rather worried about jumping into water that is teeming with sharks. The question on everyone's minds is, is it safe?

Reef encounter

My introduction to the Belize Barrier Reef had come courtesy of a Belize City tour on my first day in the country. As we sat parked next to the Baron Bliss tomb and lighthouse on the north side of town overlooking the offshore cays, my guide, Captain Nicholás Sánchez, turned around and said, "Please note this down carefully, because people are always getting it wrong. The Belize Barrier Reef is not the second longest in the world, but the fifth longest at 250km, not 298 or 290, as is

1 Almost all diving off Ambergris Caye is from boats run by local dive shops, which provide a divemaster who supervises and acts as a guide. In strong winds and high swells (greater than 1.5–1.8m, or 5–6 feet), the boat may have to move to another site or the dive may be cancelled for safety reasons. Hol Chan Marine Reserve is the most popular local spot with both divers and snorkellers, and as a result it can get crowded. There are plenty of snorkelling opportunities for those who do not dive.

★ The accommodation on Ambergris Caye is more comfortable than that on Caye Caulker. The trade-off is that Ambergris is a little predictable, and is certainly not as casual as its neighbour.

Although the water temperature is about 27°C (80°F) most of the year, it is cooler below the 3-m (10-foot) mark. A lycra bodysuit is usually adequate year round, but those who want more thermal protection may wish to pack a 3-mm (1/16-in) wetsuit. Divers may also wish to take their own buoyancy control device, regulator, fins, and mask, although all equipment (including weights) is included in the cost of an organized dive. Again, although tackle is usually included on fishing trips, serious anglers may also wish to take their own gear.

often misquoted. It stretches from Boca Bacalar Chico, on the Mexican border in the north, and stops at Hunting Caye at the bottom. The largest living coral reef in the western hemisphere would be a more accurate description."

A week later, after visiting the country's interior, I was back in Belize City and was ready to be whisked to Caye Caulker. I sat on a wooden park bench in the Marine Terminal waiting patiently for a boat to take me to Belize's second-most popular caye after Ambergris. Backpackers filed off an incoming boat and stood in the terminal looking lost, while a tall, gangling man tried to hurry them into taxis. Sleek, twin-engined powerboats leave from the terminal to Caye Caulker six times a day and to Ambergris three times a day. It's a fun way to spend 45 minutes, although most visitors opt for the convenience of a short 15-minute flight instead, with an eye-popping view of the cays scattered 1km (3,000 feet) below them like the trail of dice along a craps table.

The boat slipped out of the harbour, past others that sat three or four deep along the entrance. Once we reached the open ocean the captain released the throttle and away we lurched. The heads of all 19 passengers nodded violently as the hull thumped down over each wave. We scooted past cays, made unscheduled stops to let off a construction worker and a couple of Americans who were visiting an empty island, and finally docked at Caye Caulker.

It's impossible to get lost on **Caye Caulker** as it measures just 8km (5 miles) long and 800m (½ mile wide). Mestizo refugees from the Mexican Caste

BELIZE'S ATOLL REEFS

To the east of the barrier reef are three distinct atoll reefs, which are formed on two tiers of submarine ridges separated by deep trenches. Turneffe and Glover's lie on one ridge, while Lighthouse lies on a separate ridge further to the east. Right in the centre of Lighthouse Reef is the Great Blue Hole (see box on page 108). Turneffe and Lighthouse Reef provide some of the most pristine wall dives in the Caribbean, starting as shallow as 8–10m (25–35 feet) and dropping away to 1,000m (3,000 feet), as well as a number of interesting wrecks. Making the trip out is a must for any diver who has the time available. While it is possible to visit the Great Blue Hole on a long one-day trip from Ambergris Caye, divers who want to really explore the atolls should consider a two- or three-day trip, either on a "live-aboard" boat, or camping on the atolls. The dive operators listed in the Contacts section can provide varied itineraries.

THE UNDERSTATED MANGROVE

There are four species of mangrove in Belize: red, black, white, and buttonwood. Without the intertwined root systems of these mangroves, much of Belize's coastline would vanish into the sea. Their loss would also mean the end of a sensitive food chain as thousands of animals seek protection and sustenance among the mangroves' roots. Indeed, much of the fish and shellfish exported from Belize to tables all over the world has swum amongst mangrove roots at some stage in its life. Yet the precious mangrove is being threatened by development, which is causing a shift in the ecosystem. Some of the coastline is being destroyed by builders, who rip up huge tracts of mangroves to make way for beachfront hotels and cabanas. Unfortunately, Belize has no laws to prevent the clearance of the mangroves, and unless something is done soon the country may face environmental disaster.

wars in the mid-19th century were the first permanent settlers here, preceded by Mayan visitors and British buccaneers. The word caulk means to make watertight, and it is believed that the name of the island originated from boat-repairing activities. The island has also been a coconut plantation, a base for commercial lobster fishermen, and, since the 1960s, a popular tourist destination.

The slower the better

The island is still stuck in the 1960s, and it seems that the "Go Slow" signs along the sandy streets are more an attitude to life than a legitimate warning for the handful of cars. With my bag dragging in the sandy street, I made my way from the wooden ferry pier to the Rainbow Hotel, straight ahead and then left before the sea on the opposite shore. There are only

three streets—Front, Middle, and Back—which lie parallel to one another, with a few token lanes stretching east to west in between. Scruffy clapboard houses lined my route, and electric golf carts hummed past me.

The next day I went with guide Ellen McRae on a tour of the new national park and marine reserve that surrounds the island. It covers 40ha (100 acres) of land

to the north, and just over 11km (7 miles) of water from north to south 1.5km (1 mile) off the cay's east coast. Ellen is a marine biologist and has been studying the environment around this cay since 1975, and was also instrumental in setting up the new park. I sat at her untidy kitchen table and listened as she explained a few of the environmental

ABOVE Diving at Hol Chan Marine Reserve, just off Ambergris Caye
LEFT Hurricane Mitch, which hit the region in October 1998, caused extensive damage on Caye Caulker. Hurricanes are, however, generally rare
BELOW A fisherman sorts through his conch catch

BLUE HOLES

Blue holes are common in several countries, but the largest of them all, the Great Blue Hole, is found right in the centre of Lighthouse Reef to the east of the barrier reef. It measures 400m (¼ mile) in diameter and 145m (475 feet) deep. The Great Blue Hole was once a cave at the centre of an underground limestone tunnel complex, whose ceiling collapsed as a result of a major earthquake to form a sinkhole. The upheaval also had the effect of tilting the land to an angle of around 12 degrees. At the end of the last ice age, sea-levels throughout the world rose and the sinkhole was flooded. All along the walls of this former cavern are overhangs and ledges, housing stalactites, stalagmites, and limestone columns. Some of the stalactites hang at an angle as a result of the tilting, while those that continued to form after the earthquake start off at an angle and end perpendicular. Aside from their geological interest, there is very little else to see in blue holes—marine life and coral are scarce due to the lack of direct sunlight hitting the sides or penetrating as far as the bottom.

concerns the area faces. One of Ellen's main worries is the increasing problem of ill-planned, short-term profit-generating developments that have been springing up on Caye Caulker and Ambergris Caye. The fragile ecosystem of the reef cannot stand the onslaught of increasing pollutants generated by these developments, and unless legislation is put in place to control them, the very thing that draws visitors—the reef itself—will be destroyed.

In the afternoon Ellen took me to the north of Caye Caulker. With her husband at the helm of our boat, we cast off and headed out in the rain and wind. We passed the Split, a channel created by Hurricane Hattie in 1961 that cuts the island in two; it is now a popular spot with swimmers and sunbathers. The north of the island is virtually uninhabited. Just past the Split huge forests of mangroves pack the shore, and although they may not present the picture-postcard image of a coral island, they do play a vital role in protecting the coastline from erosion, and harbour fish, crustaceans, and other flora (see box on page 105). We headed to the far north of the island in the boat, but here the effect of Hurricane Mitch in 1998 had been so destructive that it was difficult to penetrate the mass of branches and debris to get a look at some of the interior's plant species.

THE CONTRAST OF AMBERGRIS

The following day I headed to **San Pedro**, the only town on Ambergris Caye. After 30 minutes the speedboat landed at a small pier, from where a taxi drove me past the airport and out of town to Royal Palm Villas, five minutes away. I was struck instantly by the roads, which were made of hard-packed earth covered in a layer of soft sand, and by the fact that there were so few vehicles—people were walking, cycling, or humming along in electric golf carts. The apartments I was staying at were a whole world away from the party atmosphere of the town centre, with its busy bars, restaurants, hotels, and dive shops.

Ambergris Caye is 32km (20 miles) long and 1.5km (1 mile) wide. Mirroring its entire length is the reef, where waves crash over into the shallow waters of the lagoon to create a frothy white horizon line. There are more than 50 named diving sites within half a mile of the cay's shores, each with a mooring buoy so that anchors do not destroy the coral. With few exceptions, underwater visibilty is close to its maximum for anywhere in the world at 50m (165 feet) as the reef lies 13–26km (8–16 miles) from the mainland and so is little affected by river outflow and rain runoff.

It was on Ambergris that I joined a day trip to two well-known offshore diving-snorkelling sites, at Hol Chan Marine Reserve and Shark-Ray Alley. Fifteen minutes out from Larry Parker's Reef Divers school, the boat moored at a blue-green oasis called **Hol Chan Marine Reserve**, a protected site since 1987, and the first of its kind in Central America. *Hol chan* is Mayan for little channel, and refers to the deep valley that cuts through the barrier reef here. The 13-sq-km (5-square-mile) underwater Disneyland of the reserve teems with fish and tourists. Six other boats were moored up with us, and I began to wonder how the coral reef manages to survive the onslaught of these hordes. Still, the fish don't seem that bothered.

The divers got ready. They pulled on their wetsuits, spat into their masks, and hefted their BCDs and tanks onto their backs before carrying out their equipment checks. This time I was one of the snorkellers, and soon enough the empty blue sky was replaced by a traffic jam of fish. As the bubbles cleared from my mask, fish mingled around me. A grey snapper lurked behind a fan of coral, a jazzy stoplight parrotfish (*Scarus viride*) flitted past, and a skulking barracuda patrolled the fringes of the action. Below me were the divers, their bubbles floating to the surface like marbles, and the only sound was my irregular breathing pattern in the snorkel tube. Back on the boat, I found I could not relate my experience to the pictures on the fish chart, and my appetite was whetted to don scuba equipment and learn more about the species found on these reefs. Diving here is a personal, sensuous experience, and is the reason why so many people want to try it for themselves. In all honesty, the cays are little more than platforms to the reef.

Touching a stingray

At **Shark-Ray Alley**, just inside the reef south of the cay, no one wanted to go swimming. Paul threw more sardines into the water and told us to jump in before

DIVING ORGANIZATIONS

Scuba-diving is an exciting and fulfilling sport, but requires a basic certification to ensure skills and safety; such certification is also a necessity when arranging dives with an operator on holiday. Beyond the basic course, more advanced levels of amateur certification can be achieved, together with speciality training in areas such a wreck diving or rescue techniques. There are a number of clubs and associations worldwide that provide the necessary training and certification; the majority of dive operators offer at least the basic course, which lasts 4–5 full days, includes both theoretical and practical aspects, and culminates in a written examination. For further general information on diving, along with details of dive operators in the region, see the Activities A–Z.

- **British Sub Aqua Club (BSAC)** This is the world's largest diving club. It is a non-profit organization based in the U.K., and it has been recognized for over 40 years as a promoter of training, exploration, and safety to the highest standards (website: www.bsac.com).
- **National Association of Underwater Instructors (NAUI)** Formed in the U.S.A. in 1960, this association provides training and certification to high standards (website: www.naui.org).
- **Professional Association of Diving Instructors (PADI)** Founded in the U.S.A. in 1966, although PADI International (larger than the parent association) is based in Bristol in the U.K. PADI certifies 55 per cent of all divers worldwide, and is recognized for its promotion of safety and training supervision (website: www.padi.com).

ABOVE Part of the charm of Caye Caulker lies in its lack of development: the majority of houses are wooden clapboard, usually brightly painted and raised up on stilts LEFT A scuba diver encounters a ray. Rays are not at all shy and divers often have to push them aside

all the sharks disappeared along with the food. Was it safe? Yes, because in fact the sharks here are nurse sharks (*Ginglymostoma cirratum*), which, as their name suggests, are totally harmless. I sat on the side of the boat, and held my hand across my mask to keep it in place as I slipped backwards into the water. Shark-Ray Alley has neither coral nor shoals of fish, just a swarm of southern stingrays (*Dasyatis americana*), nurse sharks, and the odd barracuda swimming in 2.4m (8 feet) of water. The stingrays are not shy in the least, and hover so close that pushing them away is the only option to stop their advances. The sharks are more elusive. They hug the seabed, keeping out of everyone's way, pacing up and down to catch the odd scrap that filters through the canopy of stingrays congregating above.

Tunnel vision

Inspired by my snorkelling trips, I was keen to discover more about the reef and its species, and so called in at Gaz Cooper's Dive Belize at the Sunbreeze Beach Hotel to arrange a dive for the following day. As a PADI-qualified diver I faced no problems, and simply had to decide whether to dive in the morning or afternoon. In the end I opted for a morning dive that combined Victoria Tunnels and Cyprus Canyons, leaving me free to spend the afternoon lazing on the beach. These two sites lie on the reef just to the south of San Pedro, 20 minutes away by boat, and are within a short distance of each other. As each site has just one mooring buoy, the only divers present at any one time are those from your own boat, so there is no chance of overcrowding (on my trip there were just four other divers plus the divemaster).

We reached **Victoria Tunnels** a little after 9am on a fine and sunny day, and after kitting up and carrying out our checks we started our dive 25 minutes later. The dive plan was for a multilevel dive, starting at 27m (90 feet) and rising to shallower depths where we could spend more time. The whole dive was expected to last about 35 minutes, but the divemaster had overall control and would be checking the calculations constantly on his dive computer. The water was a comfortable 26°C (79°F), and the visibility an amazing 40m (130 feet)—among the best you will find anywhere in the world.

We dropped down along the anchor line in a cloud of silver bubbles, and the colours of the reef quickly came alive. Several large red groupers glided away as we descended a canyon in the coral formation of the Victoria Tunnels. Technically speaking, these canyons are spur and groove topology, the spurs ridges of hard corals partially colonized by soft corals and algae, rising 12m (40 feet) above the intervening grooves, which are filled with white carbonate sand and scattered fragments of coral. Many of these limestone formations have caves or tunnels in them, hence the name of the site.

We passed blue and stoplight parrot-fish (*Scarus coeruleus* and *Sparisoma viride*) grazing noisily on the reef as the divemaster led us towards a tunnel entrance. He signalled that those who wanted to go through the tunnel should follow him, but otherwise we could pass over the top to the next canyon. All but one buddy pair chose to venture into the tunnel, whose narrow entrance required careful buoyancy control to negotiate. Beyond this the passage opened out into a cavern, where light spilling in from the exit ahead caused shadows to dance off the sides. Suddenly, we spotted the large silver shape of a tarpon (*Tarpon atlanticus*) at the cavern's mouth, its silvery scales glistening magically, but the 70-kg (150-pound) leviathan slipped majestically away as we emerged into the sun-dappled water. And then from nowhere came a remora (*Remora remora*), which followed us and tried persistently to attach itself to my tank, obviously mistaking me for a nurse shark or boat!

As we climbed slowly out of the canyon, we glided over coral gardens and marvelled at the variety of fish swarming around us, including yellow jacks, a black grouper, red snappers, and parrot-fish, along with myriad other reef species ranging from blue chromis and damselfish to queen and grey angel-fish. As we neared the end of the dive, we saw a large green turtle (*Chelonia mydas*), which tolerated us watching it for a while before gracefully gliding away towards the dark blue depths.

We returned to the boat after a safety stop, and relaxed for 1½ hours as we motored to the next site at **Cyprus Canyons**. This was to be another multilevel dive, starting at 24m (80 feet), and the site offered even greater visibility at about 45m (150 feet). Again, the topology is a series of canyons of coral, the sides of which contain layers of many hard and soft corals in a multitude of varieties and colours. On this dive we spotted a moray eel peering out of its hole, and again a legion of reef fish that included jacks, groupers, snappers, parrot-fish, angel-fish, and even an inquisitive barracuda. After 25 minutes we returned to the boat to remove our equipment, and congratulated ourselves on two very satisfying dives.

The attractions of the cays really do lie offshore, among the fantastic coral formations and the amazing marine life they harbour. For me, the whole dive and snorkel experience was thrilling, and has fired my enthusiasm to see more of one the world's greatest reef systems.

GOING IT ALONE

Internal travel

There are regular flights to both Ambergris Caye and Caye Caulker from Phillip Goldson International Airport in Belize City; the flight time to both is less than 30 minutes. If you don't want to fly then the boat is a fun alternative. Boats leave the Marine Terminal in downtown Belize City, and offer a regular service to both islands: six times a day to Caye Caulker and three times a day to Ambergris Caye. There are also unscheduled boat services to the islands, which can be arranged privately by asking around on the islands or at the terminal, but expect to pay more. There is no need to hire your own transport while on Caye Caulker as the island is so small, but you might want to hire a golf cart on Ambergris depending on your hotel's location.

When to go

Belize has a subtropical climate, so be aware that afternoon downpours are common. The rainy season is from June to August. Coastal temperatures are around 28–30°C (82–86°F), cooler than those on the mainland. This part of Belize is also lucky with rain, which averages under 1,800mm (70 inches) a year, and while hurricanes do occur they are rare and form only between July and November.

Planning

People rarely stay overnight in Belize City, and instead tend to hop on a plane and head straight for the cays. This is a shame as despite its bad press Belize City has some good hotels and restaurants, and a Belize City tour with Captain Sánchez (see Contacts) makes for a very entertaining introduction to the country. Belize Zoo is another must for visitors (see box on page 123).

There are hundreds of dive shops and tour companies that offer trips to this reef and that beach, and certainly more than can be listed here. Your hotel should be able to arrange tours for you; if not, ask other tourists for their recommendations or turn up at the docks, where someone will offer you advice. Note that the only decompression chamber in Belize is in San Pedro, Ambergris Caye.

Travellers' tips

- Crime is a problem in Belize City; do not carry valuables or large sums of money, and do not wander around at night.
- When in the water do not touch or disturb coral as it takes several decades to regenerate. Remember also that sand raised by fins can suffocate the coral. Keep at least 60cm (2 feet) away to protect both you and the reef.
- Toothpaste applied to insect bites will soothe the itchiness temporarily.

What to take

- Many divers pack their own buoyancy control device, regulator, wetsuit, fins, and mask, although all equipment is included in dive packages. Don't take a speargun as it will be confiscated at the airport. Do remember to pack all diving certification.
- Although most fishing trips include bait and tackle in the price, more serious anglers will want to take their own gear.
- Insect repellent.
- Suntan lotion.
- Waterproof bags to keep valuables dry during boat excursions.

Health

Sand flies can be a problem when the wind drops, so use insect repellent. Use a high-factor suntan lotion to prevent burning, and wear a T-shirt when snorkelling to protect your back.

UNDERWATER PHOTOGRAPHY

Aside from the obvious problems of keeping your camera and film dry and salt-free when filming underwater, you must also consider pressure changes, optical distortion, and the lack of light. Use a fast film—400 ISO and above is ideal—and as light levels vary bracket your exposures if you are able to. Use a wide-angle lens to overcome illusions caused by light refraction, and add a red filter to your lens to counteract the increased proportion of blue light at depths greater than 3m (10 feet). Finally, remember that your safety, and that of your dive buddy, always comes before trying to get a good picture.

Stuck on the South

by Carl Pendle

Monkey River village is a small community of only 250 people some 120km (75 miles) south of Belize City. The villagers lost everything when their only income source, the banana, was wiped out by disease in the 1940s. Today, life is still a struggle, but the locals have one advantage: they live in one of the most beautiful and untouched parts of Belize.

The jeep was dead in the mud. I jammed the gear lever into first and revved the engine, then tried the same in reverse. Nothing. The wheels span and whined, spitting out mud onto the flooded, potholed road. The towering jungle on either side of the road patiently watched and waited. As the choking heat seeped into the open window, it brought with it black flies which began to feast on my legs.

"You're over the worst," a lone cyclist had said when I passed him ten minutes earlier, "Monkey River is only a mile away." But around each corner the cratered minefield had stretched on and on. The locals know never to travel on this road after a heavy downpour; it is only tourists who get stuck, and a man in the village does a booming trade fishing them out. It doesn't usually rain this hard in Belize in January, when I made my trip. The dry season was only a month away and the heaviest rains have normally stopped by October. However, down here, in the deep southern district of Toledo, it is traditionally much wetter—over 4,000mm (160 inches) of rain fall a year compared with under 1,800mm (70 inches) in the north of the country.

The road I was following stops at Monkey River. It doesn't have a name and there are no signposts. The nearest respectable road, if you can call it that, is the Southern Highway, which winds its way even further south to Punta Gorda, the last stop in Belize before Guatemala. The people here refer to this area as the "forgotten land" as it is the poorest part of Belize, with bad roads, isolated villages, and very few tourists. The few visitors who do come here simply stop at Monkey River village to cruise up and down the river, and then return to their hotels in better-known resorts such as Placencia further up the coast.

I decided to leave the jeep with its tyres sunk in the mud. I had lodged stones under the wheels, rocked the suspension, and waited to be rescued, but all to no avail. There was no choice but to leave my suitcase in the car, pack my valuables into a small backpack with my remaining water, and go to find help. The muddy trail was completely deserted. The only signs of life were the tracks

In the wet season the dirt road leading to Monkey River village is impassable to all but the most experienced drivers; at this time of year it is much easier to reach the area by boat from Placencia.

★★ You will not find any luxurious hotels at Monkey River, but there are some very comfortable cabanas with outstanding views. If you want both comfort and convenience, the best alternative is to find a hotel on the Placencia peninsula.

If you're a birder or wildlife enthusiast you will already have packed your binoculars. Most of the tours last all day, so take good walking boots and a small backpack if you plan to go jungle-trekking. Mosquitoes and sand flies can be a problem, so a good repellent is essential.

embedded in the mud from a truck, the pencil line of the bicycle that had passed earlier, and the pawprints of a jaguar.

The 1½-km (1-mile) walk to the village turned into 3km (2 miles), then 5km (3 miles), until an hour later the track ended at a river, opening up to face the Caribbean Sea. On the far bank of the river a group of women and children chatted to one another below the stilts of a wooden house. Along the shoreline four men perched in their longboats. One of them spotted me and motored across to the mouth of the river to see what was wrong.

"Ya car stuck man," he said. "No problem." With the help of my rescuer, Winsley, and a friend of his who owns the only truck in the village, we dragged the hire car out and parked it at a neighbour's farm, and then Winsley ferried me to my final destination, Bob's Paradise, a ten-minute boat ride north of the village.

JAGUARS

The jaguar population is rising in Belize, but it is still very rare to spot this elusive nocturnal hunter. The jaguar (*Panthera onca*) is the largest cat in the Americas and the largest spotted cat in the world, and the greatest concentration of these hunters north of the Amazon Basin is found in Belize. Their name derives from the Mayan Indian word *yaguar*, meaning he who kills with one leap. The Maya held the animal in such high regard that they believed it was related directly to the Mayan sun god.

Boat trips up Monkey River, which can be arranged locally or through the larger resorts, offer great opportunities for spotting numerous bird and animal species

BELIZE DRIVING

The roads in Belize are generally poor. The Southern Highway leads all the way down to the southern border, although most of it is unpaved. During the wet season the highway's surface turns to porridge, and when it is dry clouds of dust can block your vision, especially after a truck has driven past. Note that buses drive dangerously fast, and watch out for the frequent narrow wooden bridges as these are wide enough for only one vehicle. A four-wheel-drive jeep or truck is essential for these roads. Also check the insurance cover; I had a puncture, which I thought would be considered normal wear and tear for the roads, but subsequently found I was not covered by my insurance (even if I had taken out the hire company's insurance, I would still have been liable for the first $900-worth of damage). It is therefore best to arrange your own insurance before you travel.

RETREATING TO BOB'S

Most visitors to Belize don't make the effort to travel so far south. Many of those who land at Belize City simply hop on another plane bound for the cays, and so face no such problems reaching their destination. Down here things are a little different, but with persistence rewards are found in the thriving wildlife, the easy pace of life, the lack of tourists, the waters that team with fish, and in the hospitality of the people.

The skiff bounced over the water to Bob's retreat. Along the shoreline mangrove trees lined the beaches, their roots intertwined like praying hands. Pelicans flapped their wings inches above the water, patrolling the shallows for signs of fish. At a gap in the mangroves, nestled amongst coconut trees, Bob's Paradise came into view. A wooden jetty projected into the sea from the beach and Winsley pulled up beside it. Some people were gathered underneath a thatch-roofed bar. The bar lady pulled another beer from the fridge, two Labradors sniffed suspiciously around my ankles, and two or three locals sitting on the tall mahogany bar stools stared at the comings and goings. Then someone pointed out Bob, barefoot and wearing scruffy shorts and thick, black-rimmed glasses smudged with grease. He shuffled over, and we shook hands and had a laugh about my recent troubles with the car. He is an animated talker, gesturing constantly with his hands.

Bob had retired early as a teacher in Florida and, after moving from one Caribbean island to the next, finally settled here, buying this 30- by 25-m (100- by 80-foot) beach lot. For many years he lived alone on the beach in just a tent, then he cleared an area and built a house for himself and three cabins for tourists. He equipped the cabins with all essential amenities, powered by a diesel generator at the back of the property. No roads lead here, and there are neither phones nor shops. This perfect retreat is accessible only by boat. There's just you, the beach, the view, the bar, the hammocks, and the sunsets. But what more could anyone want?

TALK THE TALK

That evening at the bar I chatted to Anthony, a wiry old Creole who does the odd favour for Bob in return for some rum. Creoles are descended from African slaves and British settlers, and make up 30 per cent of the Belizean population. The Creole language is short and thumpy, with very few words of more than one syllable, and with every sentence rounded off by "man." I found it almost impossible to understand Anthony, for while the odd word did sound familiar it was totally lost in context. Creole is spoken in most of the villages in Belize, each of which has its own dialect. Still more confusing is the fact that everyone has a nickname, and some people have more than one. Anthony is known as Bing or Painless, while Winsley, my rescuer and subsequent guide, is called Babe, presumably because of his round, child-like face.

Ready for Monkey River

Babe arrived at 7am the next morning to guide me on a trip up the **Monkey River**. An early start was essential so that we could see animals while they were still feeding. The skiff whisked past the headland and into the murky waters of the river. The banks were alive with movement, and even with my untrained eye spotted a bat falcon (*Falco rufigularis*) nestling between the branches of a mangrove. Snowy and great egrets (*Egretta thula* and *Casimerodius albus*) lurked amongst the bushy undergrowth, while in the treetops scaly green iguanas (*Iguana iguana*) sparkled in the morning sun. The locals eat iguanas, and hence call them bamboo chickens. But the real bush delicacy is a scruffy looking, rabbit-sized rodent called the gibnut, or paca (*Agouti paca*). This was even served to Queen Elizabeth II on one of her visits, leading the press to christen it the "Royal Rat."

The boat continued to cruise slowly on up the river. There were so many birds it was hard to keep track of them all. A kingfisher darted past, a pair of parrots crossed high over our heads, and two king vultures (*Sarcoramphus maximiliani*) drifted by and came to rest on a branch, their reddish heads, grey scarves, white bodies, and black-tipped wings easily distinguishable against the bright green canopy. Fish jumped, turtles popped their heads up, a Jesus Christ lizard (*Basiliscus vittatus*) lived up to its name by dashing across the water, and sac-winged bats dozed below the overhanging branches. Along the banks grew battalions of wild cane, together with a range of palms, black bay cedar (*Guazuma ulmifolia*), and many other species beyond Babe's identification skills. There are only 12 licensed guides for this tour, nearly all of them based in Monkey River village. They undergo a thorough training programme, but some are better than others. Babe is the first to admit that he doesn't know all the scientific names of the plants or wildlife, but in any case the local names are certainly more entertaining.

Wildlife on the River

Babe moored the boat and started the jungle tour. Mosquitoes soon honed in on us, persistently trying to find suitable entry points on our bodies. This land was once used to farm mango, sugarcane, and casava, a plant harvested for its root. An old house stood in the jungle, almost unrecognizable as the roots of trees flowed like a river into its brickwork.

By the side of the trail a wooden stump protruded from the ground. Babe spotted a large tarantula in all its black and orange livery inside the stump. Tarantulas are the largest spiders in Belize and are usually harmless. Aside from a buzzing insect life, Belize is blessed with over 4,000 species of flowering plants, 700 species of trees, and 540 species of birds. The boa constrictor (*Boa constrictor*) is easily the largest snake in Belize, sometimes reaching up to 4m (12 feet) long, and is one of just 54 species of snakes, nine of which are venomous.

We spotted a small black snake diving into the undergrowth, but a loud grunting noise echoing in the moist air diverted our attention. "Howler monkeys," whispered

ETHNIC MIX

Belize is a mix of races. Aside from the Creoles, who make up 30 per cent of the country's 200,000 inhabitants, there are the Mestizos, descended from Indians and Spanish, and forming the majority at 44 per cent. Mayan Indians, once the original people, now form only 8 per cent of the population, while the rest is divided between the Garifuna, Mennonites, Chinese, Lebanese, and a few minorities. It is a widely integrated culture that somehow works.

BIRDER'S PARADISE

Belize was made for bird-watchers. There are 540 species of birds, close to 200 of which migrate annually. The country also has six distinct geographic areas, providing a wide variety of habitats: north and south hardwood forest, mountain pines, coastal savannahs, mangroves, and the island environments of the cays. More than 40 per cent of Belize is protected by national parks, forest reserves, wildlife sanctuaries, and private reserves. Birding is a year-round activity, but is particularly popular during the mating season, which starts at the beginning of March and runs through to the start of the rainy season.

Babe, and then strolled off in their direction. By a stand of large trees a troop of four or five chubby cheeked howlers (*Alouatta palliata*) stared inquisitively down at us. Everything was calm until Babe hacked his machete into the base of the nearest tree to provoke the monkeys into barking. For the next few minutes the forest vibrated as the monkeys worked up a chorus of deep, throaty whoops.

On the way back to the boat we saw a line of leaf-cutter ants marching across the trail. Babe told me that the jaws of a soldier leaf-cutter ant are ideal for stitching a cut. The ant should be placed over the wound until it bites the skin shut, then its body is twisted off so that the pincers are left behind, stapling the wound shut.

A huge variety of birds live along the river banks

VILLAGE LOST IN TIME

We docked back at **Monkey River village** and embarked on a quick tour. Only 250 people live here, in simple wooden houses racked up on stilts. Many of the people abandoned the small coastal settlement when banana blight struck their crops in the 1940s, and most never returned. The banana industry is flourishing in Belize once again, and tankers cruise in and out of nearby Independence village, the country's modern-day banana capital. Monkey River village, however, now depends entirely on tourists for its survival.

There are three hotels in the village, all of them quite modest. The biggest is

The resort of Bob's Paradise lies down the coast from Monkey River village. It can be reached only by boat, and so offers its guests the perfect retreat

Sunset Inn, owned by Clive Garbutt, one of the area's leading guides. There are also a few restaurants and bars, but the biggest attraction is the simplicity and reclusion of a community that is surviving on the fringes of the jungle. Sandy streets have names like Lover's Lane, Lemon Street, and Cashew Street. The beach has gradually been eroded and a few run-down houses battle with waves that beat a path to their front doors. As we walked along the beach reggae music boomed out at us from a pair of scratchy speakers. We passed the school, its doors and windows open wide to let in the cool ocean breeze. Opposite the classrooms sits a derelict wooden house that was once the health centre. The local nurse now treats the sick by herself and delivers all the babies. There used to be a playground, but all that's left is a dusty, potholed soccer field.

The amenities are much better at **Placencia**, further north up the coast. The town sits on the end of a scrawny peninsula that sticks out of Belize's navel, about 160km (100 miles) south of Belize City. A dirt road runs 42km (26 miles) along this spine, a hellish drive that explains why so many people choose to fly. Placencia was a fishing town in the mid-1800s; before then, so the story goes, buccaneers used the peninsula as a harbour. Today, it relies on tourists for most of its trade. People come here for the lazy, laid-back feel of the town. The streets are concrete paths that wander through the soft sand, and stilted wooden houses lie scattered around the town at random. The peninsula is so narrow in places that you can stand in the middle and see the Caribbean Sea on one side and a mangrove lagoon on the other.

Despite its remoteness, the Placencia peninsula has been discovered by developers, some of whom are building here while others try to sell land for $50,000 a plot. Halfway down the peninsula, on Maya Beach, is a group of well-run resorts. One of these is Singing Sands, where a cluster of cabanas has been tastefully built only a few yards from the sea. Further down is the Nautical Inn; when I arrived here the owners, Ben and Janice Ruoti, were having a traditional evening's entertainment. Ben had hired some local dancers from the nearby village of Seine Bight, and they were ready to begin.

The Garifunas

Seine Bight is a shanty town 11km (7 miles) north of Placencia with a population of about 750 people, most of them under 18 years old. It is unique because it is only one of four villages in Belize that are home to the Garifuna people, descended from escaped African slaves and Caribbean island Indians. The cultures fused accidentally when two Spanish ships carrying Nigerian slaves were shipwrecked in 1635 off the St. Vincent coast. Some survivors managed to swim ashore, and so began the relationship with the local Indians. In 1797 the British deported 2,000 Garifunas to an island off the northern coast of Honduras, and from there they dispersed to form small communities in various Central American countries, including Belize. Every year on November 19 Belizean Garifunas celebrate their arrival in the country with nine days and nine nights of solid dancing and drinking. Garifuna Settlement Day is now a national holiday in Belize.

Under the cover of an open, thatched cabana, a lady starts to thump a rhythmic beat on her drum. Other members of the gathering join in, some rattling maracas or banging on bits of wood, while a few wiggle in time with the beat. Six teenagers take centre stage and pair up, boy and girl. A lady comes over to the small audience and announces that the adolescents will be performing the Punta dance of pleasure. The boys begin by thrusting their pelvises towards the girls, who in turn twist and squirm towards them. As the beat quickens so does the thrusting, until it all gets rather steamy. Then one of the girls collapses in a fit of giggles. The tension breaks.

On the bumpy journey back to Singing Sands, we stopped to watch a boa constrictor dragging its heavy body across the road, our car headlights illuminating its progress. Some months earlier a jaguar had been spotted a bit further up this same road. We swerved around the snake, and then passed a group of construction workers watching a Mike Tyson fight on a television rigged up in the open air. The bright screen cast a green light over their faces. Hopefully the inaccessibility of this area will preserve its charm, so that travellers who make the effort to come will be able to dodge snakes and experience the joys of being stuck in the mud!

BELIZE'S NATIONAL SYMBOLS

- The black orchid (*Encyclia cochleata*), the national flower, is green, yellow, and purple, and blooms nearly all year round on trees in damp areas of Belize.
- The mahogany tree (*Swietenia mahagoni*) can grow to a height of over 30m (100 feet). The tree is part of the Belize flag and inspired the country's motto: *Sub umbra floreo* (I flourish in the shade).
- The keel-billed toucan (*Ramphastos sulfuratus*), Belize's national bird, has a beautiful, brightly coloured bill measuring 50cm (20 inches) in length.
- Baird's tapir (*Tapirus bairdii*) is the unglamorous-looking choice of national animal. It is related to the horse and rhino, and is one of the rarest animals in the world.

GOING IT ALONE

INTERNAL TRAVEL

Regular flights to Placencia from Belize City are offered by Maya Island Air and Tropic Air. The flight takes just under an hour, and a return ticket costs around $120.

There are a number of car-hire companies at Belize City's Phillip Goldson International Airport. Drive on the right-hand side of the road, and make sure you hire a four-wheel drive if you plan on heading south. Petrol is expensive, and the drive to Placencia from Belize City will take about 3 hours in good conditions. It is a 4-hour drive to Monkey River village from the city. Do not embark on the drive if it has been raining as the road will be a muddy quagmire; instead, go to Placencia and hire a boat to transport you for the final section.

WHEN TO GO

Belize has a pleasant subtropical climate. Most people visit during the dry season (November–May), although it is still very pleasant until August. The south does receive much more rain than the north of the country—3,300–4,000mm (130–160 inches) is not uncommon.

PLANNING

Not many people stay at Monkey River village, although there are three clean, modest hotels in the town. Bob's Paradise and the Monkey River House lie a bit further down the coast; both offer more luxury although they are accessible only by boat. Day trips and excursions along Monkey River can be booked through many of the larger resorts in the region. I arranged my tour locally at a cost of $25, and for this price was picked up directly from Bob's. Day trips from Placencia, 20 minutes away by boat, will cost about $50. During the dry season the level of the river gets very low, so to explore its banks at this time hire a kayak.

TRAVELLERS' TIP

- ❑ There are no real shops at Monkey River village, so stock up on essentials before you arrive.

WHAT TO TAKE

- ❑ Binoculars.
- ❑ Good walking boots.
- ❑ Insect repellent.

HEALTH

The local area is not a harsh environment, but do take the normal precautions when sunbathing or jungle-trekking. Anyone who intends to spend time in the jungle should take anti-malarial tablets—check with your doctor for the latest advice.

BIRD PHOTOGRAPHY

- ❑ Birds have a very keen sense of sight and hearing, and this alone makes them difficult subjects to photograph. As a bird will often assess you as a threat it will tend to fly as soon as it spots you. To take good picture you will therefore need to keep out of sight using either natural cover or a man-made hide.
- ❑ The best time to take pictures of birds is when they are taking off or landing (following a bird in flight is very difficult, even with today's most sophisticated auto-focus cameras): simply prefocus and press the shutter when the bird flies past your area of focus. Birds tend to stick to the same routes to their nesting or feeding areas, which makes it quite easy to follow the direction of their flight and to get a good panning shot.
- ❑ Try to use a fast film such as 400 ISO or above. Your shutter speeds can then be set fast enough to capture the bird without the image being blurred. Alternatively, it might be possible to use a flash: the brief duration of the flash will freeze any movement. However, this does mean that you might have to set your camera on a tripod and hide until a bird passes in front.
- ❑ Finally, remember that you should never approach a nest too closely as the parents may subsequently abandon it or damage the eggs.

Under the Spell of the Maya

by Carl Pendle

Many millions of years ago, when Belize was covered in water, the Maya Mountains reigned over the seascape. Today, these same mountains dominate the skyline of what is now called the Cayo District, in the western interior bordering Guatemala. I chose to stay at the foot of these mountains to experience nature at close hand and to discover what the ancient Maya had left behind.

By the flickering spotlight of our headtorches, we start to dance. The three of us wail and holler, wave our hands in the air, and stamp our feet in the cold river. Our chanting disturbs a cluster of bats that are dozing in a hole over our heads, and they join in the spectacle. The guide, José García, bends down and picks up some clay from the riverbed, then gestures that Rob and I should do the same. We knead the clay between our fingers while continuing to sing, and then plaster our faces with the thick, gritty paste.

The medicinal trail tour consists of a very gentle walk. Near by, at Cha Creek, there is a range of activities to suit all fitness levels. Those searching for something even more adventurous can try the caving tours on offer at Caves Branch.

★★ Cha Creek is a very luxurious jungle resort. Caves Branch, on the other hand, is not for those who like to be pampered.

The only really necessary piece of equipment is a good pair of hiking boots.

We are 2.5km (1½ miles) deep inside a 5-million-year-old cave under the Maya Mountains in central Belize, and are preparing to meet the Monkey God, the Mayan god of happiness. The Maya called the Underworld Xibalba (pronounced "She-bal-ba"), and often visited the ancient caves of this system to talk to their gods. Over 2,000 years ago, in the spot where I am standing, women and children were sacrificed as an offering to these gods. Broken pieces of pots are scattered here, black ash from their fires scar the cave floor, and children's bones have been discovered in the debris. With José and me is Rob Pywell, an

ABOVE Ix Chel Farm and Chaa Creek lie 13km (8 miles) south of San Ignacio along this unpaved "road"
BELOW RIGHT Dr. Rosita Arvigo, founder of the Ix Chel Tropical Research Foundation, leads tours of the farm herself
LEFT José García, my guide, using "inner tube" transport

Englishman from London. We are all alone in the cave, and no one knows we are here apart from Ian Anderson, the owner of Caves Branch, a jungle resort that specializes in this type of underground adventure. Ian is under strict instructions to come looking for us if we don't return by 5pm.

Right now, however, we are in the capable hands of José, a 20-year-old guide who is one of five who work at Caves Branch. He leads us, shivering and caked in mud, over to a shelf and we scramble up it. At the top we switch off our head-torches and stand very still. In the eerie silence I swear I can hear mumbling voices. A man with a deep, husky voice is talking and some children are giggling. It doesn't feel right and I panic, fumbling in the dark for the switch on top of my torch battery. The beam cuts through the darkness to illuminate a face carved into the limestone wall. My mouth drops, my heart quickens, and then I look around to notice that José has disappeared.

START OF THE JOURNEY

My introduction to Belize was much more sedate. After an overnight stay in Belize City, which allowed just enough time to pick up a rental car and grab a local tour with Captain Sánchez, a guru on local history, I headed towards Guatemala along the Western Highway. The road took me past **Belize Zoo**, and then through small towns with names such as Cotton Tree, Orange Walk, Mount Hope, and Unitedville. I saw children in neat uniforms leaving school for their lunch break,

BELIZE ZOO

The zoo in Belize City is pretty unusual as far as zoos go. For one, winding pathways lead you through lush vegetation to create a jungle atmosphere, so that although the animals are caged you feel they are still within their natural habitat. Hand-lettered signs introduce each animal, all of which are native to Belize. The use of humour also helps to break down the usual stiffness of zoos: the sign for the puma reads, "You say Puma and I say Cougar. You say Mountain Lion and I say Red Tiger. Puma, Cougar, Mountain Lion, Red Tiger. Let's call the whole thing *Felis concolor.*" Money is tight here, but with such imagination and a genuine conservation ethic, Belize Zoo deserves all the attention it gets.

BOB'S TIPS

Bob Jones, owner of Eva's Restaurant in San Ignacio, has been living in Belize since 1984. Here are his top tips for travellers:

- Don't organize any tours with people who approach you on the street.
- Don't buy anything that looks suspicious from people in the town.
- Make sure you pack a torch.
- If you are coming from the U.K., take U.S. dollars rather than sterling.
- Take the best hiking boots you can afford, and make sure you wear them in before you arrive.

women with black umbrellas raised over their heads to protect them against the sun, and quaint wooden houses on stilts lining the quiet road. Occasionally, the peace was disturbed by an impatient local trying to overtake, or by a British Army truck ferrying troops to their nearby bases. On the radio Love F.M. played classic tunes, interspersed with announcements from the D.J. naming locals who had died recently and where people should pay their respects.

An hour into my journey, the Maya Mountains rose ahead of me into the grey clouds like a stack of chimney pots. I was headed for Ix Chel Farm, just 8km (5 miles) past the town of San Ignacio in Cayo District. This small, dusty town is a stepping-off point for travellers who are seeking an alternative to Belize's well-publicized coastal resorts. Cayo is the largest district in the country, blanketing more than 5,000sq km (2,000 square miles) of diverse landscape where paths meander through thick jungle, waterfalls gush down mountains, and creatures pop out of the undergrowth. There can be few more magical areas left in the world.

At the turn-off from the highway, a dusty gravel road twisted 6km (4 miles) into the jungle. My jeep rocked past a grapefruit orchard and a few wooden houses where pigs stretched out in the mud. The road finally ended at the farm. Three people were planting seedlings in a freshly dug border around a courtyard of buildings, and I asked one of them where I could find Dr. Rosita Arvigo.

Ix Chel Farm is a unique establishment dedicated to helping people understand the medicinal powers of tropical plants. It was founded by Rosita Arvigo, a Chicago-trained herbalist and naprapathic physician (a practitioner who normalizes nerve, artery, vein, muscle, and ligament function through stretching and therapy of deep connective tissue). In 1981 Rosita moved to Belize with her family, bought a 14-ha (35-acre) piece of uncleared jungle along the Macal River, and set up a small practice as a natural healer in nearby San Ignacio. Fate then brought her into contact with an old Mayan bush doctor called Don Elijio. After a ten-year apprenticeship with this ancient healer, Dr. Arvigo dedicated herself to the study of ethnobotany and traditional medicine. As a result, she set up the Ix Chel Tropical Research Foundation in conjunction with the National Cancer Institute, with the aim of searching for plants that have anti-cancer and anti-A.I.D.S. properties. With the help of Don Elijio she has been able to send over 2,000 plants to America for exhaustive tests. At the time of writing, ten of these are showing promise and three are undergoing clinical trails.

In the foreword to Dr. Arvigo's book, *Sastun*, Michael Balick, a director at the New York Botanical Garden, states that, "Fewer than one-half of 1 percent of the planet's 250,000 species of higher plants have been tested for medicinal benefit. But from that one-half of 1 percent that have, some 25 percent of all our prescription pharmaceuticals have been discovered." From this statement alone, it was clear to me that something special was going on down at the farm.

BOB'S PLACE

Dr. Arvigo was busy, so I decided to head into **San Ignacio**. It didn't take long to find Eva's Restaurant on Burns Avenue, a scruffy meeting place that acts as an information supermarket for travellers of all types. The restaurant and unofficial tourist office is run by Bob Jones, an Englishman who moved to Belize in 1984 after leaving the British Army. I walked into Eva's just after 2pm, sat down on a white plastic chair, and glanced at the blackboard menu. A few lonely backpackers propped up the bar, caressing their bottles of Belikin beer, four Americans sat at a table in the far corner, and next to me a young man stared at a computer screen in an effort to compose an email. Bob proved very generous with his advice, and gave me a long list of hotels and guides he trusts. In the few hours I sat in the restaurant, Bob introduced me to a school teacher, a landscape artist, a Vietnam veteran, and someone called "Pops," who visits Eva's every day for a ritual three bottles of beer. All day long, characters like these come and go.

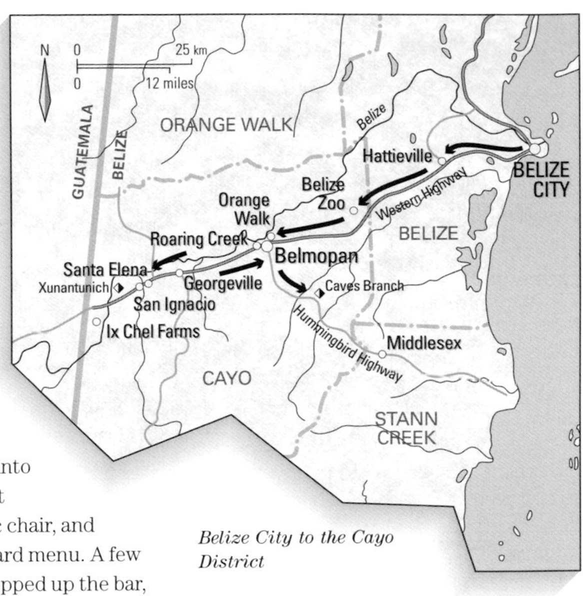

Belize City to the Cayo District

There isn't much else to do in San Ignacio apart from taking a look at the Hawkesworth suspension bridge. This miniature of New York's Brooklyn Bridge connects San Ignacio to the neighbouring village of Santa Elena. The police station near the bridge is a fine example of a typical colonial building, recalling the days of the British Empire when San Ignacio was a major logging camp.

The Medicinal Trail

Early the next morning a group of 19 people, mostly Americans, had gathered at Ix Chel for a tour of the medicinal trail. Under the pointed peak of an open cabana we listened as Dr. Arvigo talked. First, she recounted the story of Ix Chel, the Mayan goddess of medicine.

Apparently, Ix Chel was the overseer of four domains: as a young maiden she was in charge of childbirth and weaving, and as an old lady she looked after medicine and the moon. Dr. Arvigo showed us an illustration of the goddess that depicted her kneeling down, a snake in her hair, jade beads dangling from her neck, and a tree branch in her outstretched hand.

NATURAL REMEDY

The wild yam (*Dioscorea* spp.) is one species that clearly demonstrates why pharmaceutical companies should continue researching tropical plants for medicinal gain. During the 1930s a biochemist called Russell Marker noted that the Nahuatl women in Mexico were eating yams to avoid getting pregnant. Professor Marker successfully isolated a substance in the yam called sapogenin, which eventually led to the production of the birth control pill. Traditional herbalists also recommend that drinking the chopped and boiled flesh of the tuber can relieve the pain of rheumatism and arthritis.

After the talk we were led along a white gravel path that circled through the jungle. Along the way were varnished wooden signs pointing to 35 medicinal plants, some of which we stopped at and others we ignored. And the whole time Dr. Arvigo held us captivated with her stories. She told of the jackass bitter (*Neurolena lobata*), a tall, bright yellow herb found all over the Yucatán Peninsula which is used to treat malaria, intestinal parasites, ringworm, and sores. The leaves of the plant are boiled to make a tea that contains a potent agent called sesquiterpene dialdehyde. Rosita spent a long time talking about the red gumbolimbo tree (*Bursera simaruba*), whose shaggy bark is valuable for dealing with skin ailments. It is found all over Belize growing next to poison wood trees (*Metopium browneii*), venomous plants whose black sap causes a very serious burn. A few days earlier, I had been speaking to one of the gardeners at Belize Zoo, who showed me a scar that had resulted from an encounter he had had with a poison wood tree. His skin looked as if it had been melted, and the scar stretched from his elbow to just below his wrist. Unfortunately, at the time of the accident he didn't know the antidote was a strip of gumbolimbo bark.

BUTTERFLY FARM

At the butterfly breeding centre at Cha Creek you can witness the full life cycle of the *Morpho peleides*, commonly known as the blue morpho. The butterfly begins life as a pale green egg disguised as a droplet of water. After eight days this egg hatches and the emerging caterpillar starts to eat. The caterpillar is bright red and yellow, which warns predators that it is highly poisonous. At the pupa stage the morpho turns bright green and hangs upside down from a leaf or small branch, then two weeks later the butterfly breaks out of the pupal case to stretch its crumpled wings. The adult spends its time feasting on rotting fruit and searching for a mate. When the morpho's wings are closed, the complex brown markings on their underside act as a camouflage, but when it flies you can admire its beautiful metallic blue uppers. Before the butterfly dies—just a few days after emerging from the pupal case—it lays its eggs, and the whole cycle starts again.

ABOVE The beautiful blue morpho butterfly
RIGHT Limestone curtain formations in Foot Print Cave
BELOW A welcome shower at Caves Branch

The tour took just under two hours and ended in the so-called "Granny's garden." In a clearing near a hut was a cactus that is a cure for headaches, and orange marigold flowers that are used to relieve fevers or mixed with orange peel to rid the body of evil spirits.

SILENCE OF THE MAYA

Another afternoon I visited the nearby Mayan site of **Xunantunich**, meaning stone maiden. I headed west along the Western Highway for 20 minutes and stopped my jeep by a rickety wooden ferry on the outskirts of San José Succotz. It was a hot and dusty day, and the Mopan River looked inviting. A round

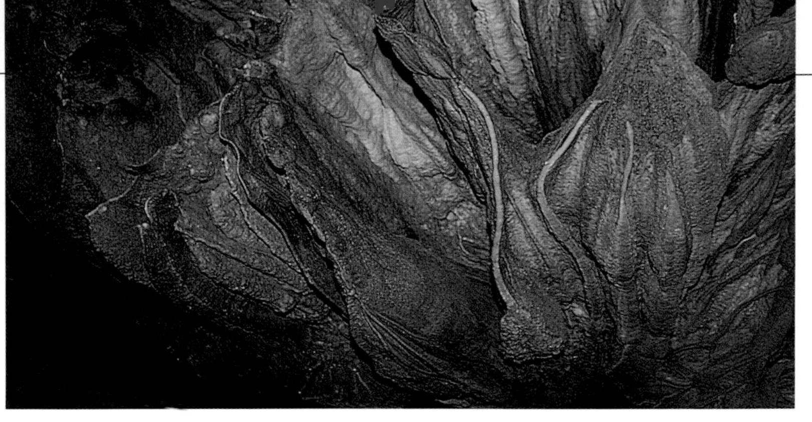

man in his 40s waved me onto the ferry, and the bridge creaked and swayed as I mounted the ramp. It took only a few minutes to get to the other side, and I felt guilty as I watched the ferryman puffing and straining as he winched us across. After a further five-minute drive along a gravelled road, I reached my destination.

The city of Xunantunich flourished in the Classical period over a thousand years ago, when between 7,000 and 10,000 people lived here. Up until the early part of the 20th century the ruins were covered in jungle, but when the city was rediscovered it was excavated and reconstructed. The frieze on the east side of the lower temple was restored in the early 1970s, when an exact copy was plastered over the top of the original. It is hard not to be struck by the mystery surrounding the Maya when you enter this stunning place. I walked to the south and cranked my neck to peer up at the top of the El Castillo pyramid, 40m (130 feet) above the grassy plaza. This was the tallest known manmade structure in Belize until the discovery of Canaa at Caracol. I climbed to the top of the temple and stood there for some time, enjoying the 360-degree panorama of the forest below.

The next day I headed along the Western Highway again, this time in the direction of Belmopan, the capital of Belize. I was headed for **Caves Branch**, where I intended to join a guided cave tour. Just past Roaring Creek town I turned right onto the Hummingbird Highway, which follows a beautiful route, twisting through jungle, gliding past orange groves, and cutting through the Maya Mountains. Thirty minutes later, after dodging construction vehicles that were involved in resurfacing the road, I saw a sign for Caves Branch. A gravelled road led me to a cluster of cabanas in a clearing by a river. As I waited for the guide to prepare the equipment, I spotted an otter swimming gracefully beside a rotting log on the far side of the river. The sighting caught me by surprise, and the hairs on the back of my neck tingled at the sheer delight of it.

The guide, José García, introduced me to the other tour member, Rob Pywell. He then looked down at his watch and said we would leave in half an hour. He told me to change into a pair of shorts and a T-shirt, and declared that the hiking boots I had on were perfect for clambering about inside the slippery caves. The three of us hopped into an old truck. As we went on our way I watched the road passing below us through a hole in the floor, and tried to keep off the rain that poured in through the broken sunroof. We bounced down the entrance road back to the highway, turning off after ten minutes and eventually parking in an orange grove.

Inner tubing

We grabbed an inner tube each from the back of the truck and hiked down to the river. José started to talk about the caves we were heading for, stopping every so often to point out the wildlife along the way. He crouched beside some tracks in the mud, which belonged to an ocelot and a tapir, and without looking up was able to identify a brown jay singing in an orange tree. José told us that the ancient Maya believed that evil spirits lived in the caves. Apparently, even today three-quarters of Belizeans refuse to enter these once-sacred places and José himself expressed his belief that the spirits still exist. Most of the caves in Belize have been carved from limestone by the erosive action of water over millions of years, creating fantastic formations.

We placed the inner tubes in the river and battled against the flow until we reached the entrance to **Foot Print Cave**, named after prints of shamans (priest-doctors) were found on the floor. A huge submerged tree served as a walkway to the cave entrance, where we sat back in our tubes once again and splashed inside. The cave system stretches for 11km (7 miles), and along its entire length flows a meandering river. It is still so undiscovered that some areas have yet to be mapped; we wouldn't be going any further than 3km (2 miles) in. José asked us not to touch anything, so as to preserve the fragile microclimate. Even the grease from our fingertips could destroy a structure that has taken thousands of years to form—a stalactite, for example, takes 1,000 years to grow just 65cu cm (4 cubic inches). Statistics such as these really put things into perspective.

Spending a day in these caves is not for anyone who is claustrophobic or is scared of the dark. The headtorches are the only source of illumination, and should they break you would be plunged into darkness like you've never experienced before. However, Rob and I were in safe hands. José had been well trained and was a member of the Belize Cave Rescue Squad. He has never been called into action and Caves Branch is proud of its immaculate safety record. It was also comforting to know that if our torches broke we would get out safely, as navigating his way out of the cave in complete darkness was part of José's training.

As we started our journey the light from the entrance faded into a faint white tear in the fabric of the darkness. Then it vanished altogether, and we were plunged into a thick, lonely emptiness. I felt uneasy for a moment, and then relaxed at the sheer beauty of where we were. Bats flew from holes in the roof and described giant loops above our heads. Our lamps momentarily illuminated huge caverns where massive fingers of rock pointed accusingly down at us, and José's high-pitched voice echoed around the 30-m (100-foot) high chamber as he talked about the rock formations.

We stopped at a sandy beach flecked with smooth pebbles that had been brought in by the river. Here, José pointed out a scorpion spider perched on top of a rock, its long stringy legs and cockroach-like antennae wriggling under our lights. Beside the spider were cave crickets, and dangling from the roof were sticky threads used by cave worms to catch flies. I found it amazing how such creatures can adapt to a life without light.

Heart of darkness

The deeper we went into the cave the thicker the air became: when the torch shone across the caverns its beam illuminated motes of dust formed from bat excreta.

By 3pm we were caked in mud and ready to pay our respects to the Monkey God. José had asked us to switch off our lights, but after five minutes I could stand the loneliness no longer. José had disappeared, leaving Rob and me in a momentary state of panic until our torch beams picked him out giggling to himself a short distance away.

On the journey back, José asked us to switch off our lights again and float downriver in the darkness. The silence was so complete that it felt unnerving, yet I also found the experience relaxing and tranquil. At times I felt the presence of something close, never really knowing if my imagination was playing a cruel trick or if there really was something there. Perhaps in the mystical world of the Maya some things are better left unexplained.

GOING IT ALONE

INTERNAL TRAVEL

It is very easy to reach Cayo District from anywhere in Belize under your own steam: the Western Highway is a very good road, and hiring a car from Phillip Goldson Airport in Belize City is a straightforward affair. Some resorts in Cayo will even pick you up from the airport if you arrange it in advance.

WHEN TO GO

Belize has a subtropical climate with a fairly constant temperature, rarely falling below 16°C (61°F). Temperatures around San Ignacio are slightly cooler than at the coast. Most people visit Belize during the dry season (November–May) and avoid the hurricane season (July–November). The Maya Mountains area does get more rainfall than the coast, although not as much as the south: Cayo District receives an average of 1,750–3,300mm (70–130 inches) a year. River levels rise during the rainy season, so the flow of rivers in the caves will therefore also be higher, although tours are not usually cancelled.

PLANNING

Ix Chel Farm doesn't have a restaurant or accommodation, so it's either best to book a room at the nearby Cha Creek or just plan to visit the farm for the day. San Ignacio is only a half-hour drive away and has a number of cheap places to stay. Most lodges have email and accept bookings online. If you are happy to wait until you get to San Ignacio, then Bob Jones at Eva's Restaurant will find somewhere for you to spend the night, usually at quite a saving. Check with Bob via email as to the availability of hotels during the peak season (see Contacts).

TRAVELLERS' TIPS

❑ Along the medicinal trail be careful not to touch any of the trees unless you know it is safe to do so: the poison wood tree, for example, looks very harmless but its bark inflicts a serious burn. Wear long trousers and long-sleeved shirts if you do go into the jungle to protect your skin against poisonous plants and insects.

❑ If you go on a cave tour be prepared to get wet. Good footwear is essential, although it can be hired if you don't want to walk around for days in soaking boots. My guide advised me to wear shorts and a T-shirt, but I found I got cold in the cave as we jumped in and out of the water. Take a light water-resistant jacket to cover yourself up when you are not in the water, and a waterproof bag to keep items such as cameras dry.

WHAT TO TAKE

❑ Hiking boots and a change of footwear.

❑ Torch.

❑ Insect repellent and a mosquito net.

❑ Water-resistant jacket and waterproof bag for the cave tour.

❑ Long trousers and long-sleeved shirts.

HEALTH

It is advisable to take precations against malaria; consult your doctor for the latest recommendations. Asthmatics and those with breathing difficulties may face problems with the dust inside the caves.

BELIZE'S MAIN MAYAN SITES

❑ **Altun Ha** Belize's most famous Mayan site, a small but rich trading community and ceremonial centre from 600 B.C. to A.D. 900.

❑ **Caracol** A vast city covering 88sq km (34 square miles), dated 300 B.C.–A.D. 1150. Features the 42-m (138-foot) high Caana "sky-palace."

❑ **Cerros** A trading port in the Pre-Classic period.

❑ **Cuello** Has a Late Pre-Classic stepped pyramid. On private land.

❑ **Lamanai** Occupied 1500 B.C.–Spanish conquest. Has a 34-m (112-foot) high temple.

❑ **Lubaantun** A trading centre dated A.D. 700–800. Unexcavated.

❑ **Nim Li Punit** May have been a satellite of Lubaantun (see above). Only partially cleared.

❑ **Xunantunich** A ceremonial centre during the Classic period—see main text.

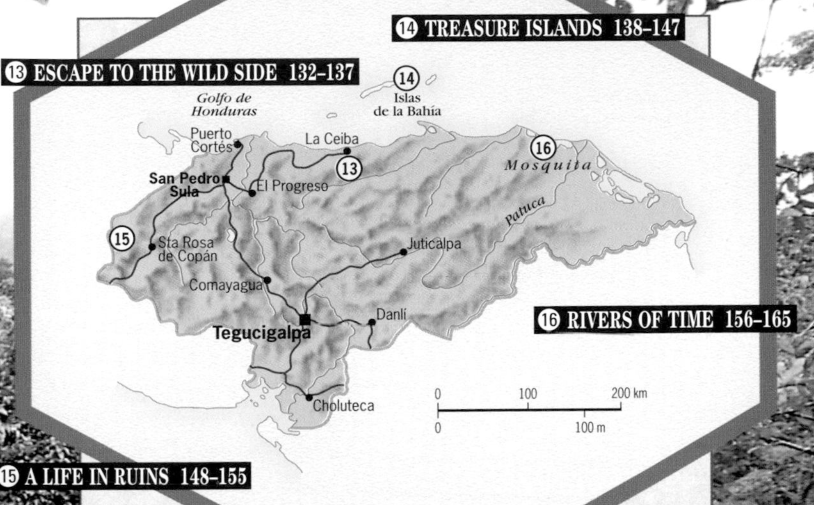

⑭ TREASURE ISLANDS 138–147
⑬ ESCAPE TO THE WILD SIDE 132–137
⑯ RIVERS OF TIME 156–165
⑮ A LIFE IN RUINS 148–155

HONDURAS

Honduras is the second-largest country in Central America after Nicaragua, and yet has only 6 million inhabitants, fewer than tiny El Salvador. It can be divided roughly into three distinct geographical regions. The northern Caribbean coast is a thin strip of low-lying land fringed on the ocean side with beautiful, palm-tree-lined beaches and sprinkled with Garifuna villages. To the northeast lies the vast, almost uninhabited, Mosquitia region, where access is possible only via rivers and lagoons. Inland, the major part of the country sits on a plateau dominated by range after range of mountains that are dissected by dirt roads and inhabited by small farming communities. There are plenty of places in Honduras that will appeal to the adventure traveller, including 40 protected areas, 20 national parks, and two UNESCO World Heritage Listed Sites—at Copán and Río Plátano. From jungle-hiking and scuba-diving to ancient Mayan culture and untouched indigenous villages, Honduras has everything boasted by the better-known Costa Rica and more, yet remains one of the lesser-visited countries in the region.

Following a jungle trail through the Parque Nacional Pico Bonito, Honduras

Escape to the Wild Side

by Steve Watkins

The northern coast of Honduras has become the adventure travel centre of the country. There are several protected nature areas within easy reach of the town of La Ceiba, so it doesn't take long to escape to the wilderness. I explored two of the more diverse parks, Refugio de Vida Silvestre Cuero y Salado and Parque Nacional Pico Bonito, in just one day.

The northern Caribbean coast of Honduras, around the port town of La Ceiba, is squeezed between the sea and a daunting range of high mountains. From these mountains a number of rivers tumble via waterfalls and narrow gorges to emerge on the flat coastal plain, where they slow considerably, twisting their way through mangrove swamps and dense rain forest to the Caribbean Sea. This is one of the country's most diverse natural regions, a fact reflected in the number of local reserves and national parks. I visited two of them, the Refugio de Vida Silvestre Cuero y Salado (Cuero y Salado Wildlife Refuge) and Parque Nacional Pico Bonito (Pico Bonito National Park) to gain a taste of the extremes on offer.

Visiting the Cuero y Salado Wildlife Refuge is not physically taxing, but you will need to have a reasonable level of fitness for the half-day jungle hikes in the Pico Bonito National Park.

The one-hour burra trolley ride from La Ceiba out to Cuero y Salado is great fun but lacks comfort. The small train (if it is working) is slightly better, though not as entertaining. Hiking in Pico Bonito is hot and sweaty work, but you can cool off in the superb natural swimming pools near the waterfalls. La Ceiba has a full range of hotels to suit every budget.

No specialist equipment is needed for this trip, aside from a good pair of hiking boots and binoculars for viewing wildlife.

There is something magical about train travel in an exotic location, the sense of movement, the clickety-clack of the wheels on the track, the sound of the engine, and the smell of tropical lushness; it is one of my favourite forms of transport. When I heard that access to Cuero y Salado was possible only via an old railway run by the Standard Fruit Company, I began dreaming of steaming iron-rooster engines…how dreams can deceive. On my arrival at La Unión, a tiny village about 30km (20 miles) west of La Ceiba from where the trains depart, I was surprised to see a rusty, narrow-gauge line struggling to keep its rails above the grass. The "station" was a run-down wooden shop selling bottled soft drinks and a wide variety of cheap snacks. From the murky depths at the back of his store, the owner informed Joáquin, my guide, that the Standard Fruit train, known simply as the *motocarro*, had broken down the day before and that we would have to take a *burra* instead. Now, my Spanish is quite reasonable, and hearing the word *burra* brought visions of my relaxing train ride turning into a jolting journey on the back of a stubborn old donkey. Thankfully, however, *burra* is the affectionate term given to the second-class form of travel to the wildlife refuge…a tiny flat-bed rail cart that is poled along by two men. It wasn't quite the Orient Express, but it looked like fun none the less.

The wildlife refuge is around 9km (6 miles) from La Unión, and the *burra* ride takes an hour. With my legs crossed under me, I settled into the middle of the narrow trolley and watched with admiration as the two polers heaved the ponderous beast into action. Remarkably, they got the trolley moving along at such a pace that I began to wonder how we were going to stay on the crooked track. At times, we bounced over the rail joints, which brought huge smiles to the polers' faces and looks of alarm to mine. Although the mode of transport did not match my dream, the tropical scenery certainly lived up to expectations. The rail line was built around 1972 to give easier access to Standard Fruit's coconut plantation processing plant, and the line now runs through parts of the plantation and past small lakes and streams. In the distance we could see the pyramidal outline of Pico Bonito's summit. The poling work looked extremely taxing, so I was amazed to learn that the polers make three or four return trips every day, amounting to up to eight hours' non-stop work. No wonder they looked so fit.

Decimated coconuts

As we arrived at the very rustic processing plant at the village of **Salado Barra**, a handful of children came running out to greet us. Mounds of shredded coconut husks lined both sides of the track and seemed to spill from every gap in the plant's old corrugated-iron panelling. Inside, a couple of women loaded husks into rudimentary shredding machines while a teenage boy sat in a corner pre-chopping the husks with a machete. One of the more experienced workers came over and gave us an impromptu demonstration of how to split and remove coconut husks on an upturned spike. He did it so quickly that I missed it and had to ask him to do it again.

The village is home to around 85 families, who live in wooden houses raised high on stilts to protect against flooding. Their subsistence way of life is based on harvesting coconuts and fishing, which is carried out from simple dugout canoes called *cayucos*. Recently, a new accommodation block was built here for travellers who wish to stay for a night or two so that they can further explore the 13,250-hectare (32,740-acre) **Cuero y Salado Wildlife Refuge**.

After signing in at the visitor centre, where some of the park's less likeable inhabitants—scorpions and deadly coral snakes—were displayed in jars of alcohol, we boarded a small boat for the ride out onto the Río Salado. The refuge comprises of a system of natural canals and inlets formed by three rivers, the Río Cuero, Río Salado, and Río San Juan, which run out to the white sandy beaches bordering the Caribbean Sea. In 1987, Cuero y Salado became a national wildlife refuge, principally because it is home to a number of Caribbean manatees (*Trichecus manatus*), one of the world's most endangered species. Our guide explained that since Hurricane Mitch, when the river system flooded, the manatees seem to have temporarily moved away as the aquatic plants

COMPLETELY NUTS

If you have ever knocked a coconut off a shy at a fairground, then you will have won one of the world's most useful fruits. The oval-shaped coconut, which grows on coconut palms (*Cocos nucifera*) in clusters of ten or more, has many uses. The outer, hard husk can be shredded (as you see at Cuero y Salado) and woven into ropes. The inner, white kernel is dried to produce copra, which yields oil used in soaps and candles. The kernel is also a favourite food in the tropics, whilst the coconut milk found inside is a delicious additive to drinks and food dishes (try coconut rice in restaurants along the northern coast of Honduras). The palm trees also have their uses: the leaves are handy for thatching roofs and for making mats and baskets, while the tree's roots are a mild narcotic.

ABOVE Sitting on a pile of coconut husks at the processing plant in the village of Salado Barra
BELOW Waiting for the burra *on the way to Cuero y Salado*
OPPOSITE The 15-m (50-foot) waterfall along Río Bonito—a welcome sight at the end of a jungle trail through the Pico Bonito National Park

they feed on were washed out to sea. The creatures are still spotted, but not as often, although the guide was sure that they would return once the underwater plants regrow.

Out on the black waters of the Río Salado, we saw some of the estimated 196 species of birds that live in the protected area. Easiest to identify were the oropendolas (*Gymnostinops montezuma*), whose raucous cries and bright yellow tail flashes make it impossible for them to keep a low profile. High in the treetops, we spotted the bird that most people associate with tropical destinations, the toucan. The most common species in the park is the outrageously coloured keel-billed toucan (*Ramphastos sulfuratus*). Its bright yellow chest and face contrast sharply against its jet-black body, while the front of its huge yellow and green beak is tipped with a scarlet red splash. It certainly made an impressive spectacle as it swooped down from a branch and flew across the river.

Howls of protest

The fearsome reputation of the crocodile (*Crocodylus acutus*) is due mainly to its primordial looks and sharp teeth. It is very rare for these reptiles to attack humans, but of course the consequences when they do so always make headline news. Although I knew I was safe, I still felt overawed when I saw one lying patiently on the riverbank. As our guide cut the engine and we drifted closer, my heart rate increased accordingly. When we were just a couple of boat lengths away, the crocodile suddenly launched into the water with a violent slap of its tail, and from the shallows continued to keep a wary eye on us. I made sure I kept my hands as far away from the edge of the boat as possible! Further upriver, we heard the unmistakable, throaty roar of a howler monkey (*Alouatta palliata*). The primates were in the trees right above the river, and it seemed that we had disturbed them during their early afternoon siesta. They looked as if they would rather just go back to sleep, and protested at our invasion of their feeding territory rather halfheartedly from reclined positions. It was only when we roared back at them that they managed to liven up! After an enthralling couple of hours on the water, we returned to the village and set off on our return *burra* trip to La Unión.

Climbing Pico Bonito

One of the most challenging adventures in Central America is to climb the 2,436-m (7,992-foot) Pico Bonito. It is remote, steep, and trail-free in the upper sections, and just getting to the base of the peak can take experienced hikers four to five days. After so much effort, it takes a certain mental fortitude and a good deal of experience of rock climbing with ropes to ascend to the summit. The whole trip takes seven to ten days, and has been completed by only a small élite group of people. Beware of taking the challenge lightly—my guide told me that one Japanese group never came back.

Jungle trail

On the way back to La Ceiba we stopped off at the **Pico Bonito National Park**, the country's largest national park, dominated by the 2,436-m (7,992-foot) Pico Bonito. The peak itself has seldom been scaled—see box below. The park covers over 107,000 hectares (264,395 acres), of which 80 percent is untouched wilderness, and is home to a large variety of forest habitats and an array of rare wildlife, including jaguars (*Panthera onca*), armadillos, and quetzal birds (*Pharomachrus mocinno*). There are hardly any trails into the park's interior, but there are several short ones that follow river valleys into the lower hills. I joined José and Russell, two hiking guides from La Ceiba, on a three-hour round trip that followed the Río Bonito up to a beautiful waterfall.

The narrow trail was muddy following the previous day's rain, so we moved slowly to start with until we became used to the conditions. As we headed through secondary growth forest, we crossed a small stream and climbed a steep bank, at the top of which we began to see the larger-leafed plants that indicate primary rain forest. Lizards scuttled off into the floor litter as we approached, and occasionally José stopped to point out interesting plants, including one that has remained virtually unchanged for millions of years.

The highlight of the hike for me was the 15-m (50-foot) waterfall at the end of the trail. Here, a thin veil of water serenely cascades down into a half-moon-shaped rocky gorge. All too soon, however, it was time to return. Although civilization is just an hour away from both Cuero y Salado and Pico Bonito, for a few precious hours that day I had been for a walk on the wild side.

GOING IT ALONE

WHEN TO GO

The prime time for visiting the north coast region is during the dry season (November–April). Outside of these months afternoon downpours are the norm.

PLANNING

It is reasonably straightforward to organize an independent visit to Cuero y Salado. Reservations must be made at least one day ahead with the Fundación Cuero y Salado (FUCSA) in La Ceiba, which will help arrange *burra* or train transport from the village of La Unión and the boat tour in the refuge. Prices are very reasonable ($15 for the 2-hour boat trip and $5 for two people on a *burra*), and there are discounts for groups. There is a $10 fee for entering the refuge. Buses to La Unión leave La Ceiba's San José bus terminal from 8:30am (the last one returns around 4pm), or you can take a taxi for about $10 each way (make sure you arrange a return pick-up time as there are not normally taxis in La Unión). Pico Bonito is slightly more awkward to get to and is probably better visited through an organized tour, especially if you don't have to your own transport. Several tour operators in La Ceiba, including La Moskitia Ecoaventuras and the San Pedro Sula-based operator MC Tours (see Contacts), organize trips to both Cuero y Salado and Pico Bonito.

TRAVELLERS' TIPS

- Although there is the option of taking the Standard Fruit Company's *motocarro* train to Cuero y Salado, the experience of riding a *burra* should not be missed.
- The workers at the Salado Barra coconut factory are very friendly and don't mind if you wander around taking photographs. Ask for a demonstration of coconut splitting.
- Hiking in Pico Bonito National Park is hot work, so take plenty of drinking water with you even on the short trails.

WHAT TO TAKE

- Sun hat.
- Sunglasses.
- Waterproof jacket or plastic poncho.
- Mosquito repellent.
- Sunblock.
- Hiking footwear.
- Binoculars.

HEALTH

Medical precautions against malaria should be taken before you leave home (consult your doctor for the latest information), and insect repellent should be used liberally, especially in the Pico Bonito National Park. Sun protection and a hat are also very important as you are exposed tofierce sun for long periods in Cuero y Salado.

NATIONAL PARKS IN HONDURAS

- **Celaque NP** Accessible by four-wheel drive from Gracias, then a challenging hike up the mountain. This is one of the best-preserved cloud forests in the country, with a high degree of biodiversity. There are also four high peaks within the park.
- **El Cusuco NP** Situated to the west of San Pedro Sula, and accessible from there on a one-day trip. A substantial cloud forest with several well-maintained walking trails. There is a fair chance of seeing a quetzal bird amongst the huge ferns and towering trees.
- **La Tigra NP** Only an hour's drive from Tegucigalpa. Mainly a secondary growth cloud forest with some interesting birdlife and a wide vairiety of orchids. At one entrance is the old mining town of Santa Lucia, home to the first American consulate in Honduras.
- **Punta Sal NP** Located west of Tela on the north coast. This park is based on beautiful lagoons and mangroves that teem with birdlife—over 350 species have been spotted between December and May. There are also idyllic Garifuna villages along the beaches.
- **Sierra de Agalta NP** Situated in the north-central region near Juticalpa. Probably the least-visited but most impressive of the country's national parks, with over 400sq km (150 square miles) of virgin forest, many endemic wildlife species, and spectacular waterfalls.

Treasure Islands

by Steve Watkins

The fabulous Bay Islands off Honduras's north coast swarmed with British pirates in the 17th century. Today, they are a major destination for adventurers seeking more modern "treasure"—adrenalin and relaxation. I visited Roatán and Guanaja for an exotic cocktail of diving, kayaking, biking, and hiking, mixed with a dash of Caribbean culture.

Considering that the Bay Islands can be reached by air within 20 minutes from the Honduran north-coast town of La Ceiba, it is remarkable that they are so significantly different from the mainland. Set in the enticing blue waters of the Caribbean Sea, the three islands of Roatán, Guanaja, and Utila have a unique culture that stems from a rather turbulent history of conquest and piracy, and from the modern influences of tourism. In order to gain an insight into the individual natures of Guanaja and Roatán, I spent a week exploring the adventure-sport options both above and below the water.

Flights and ferries to the islands leave from La Ceiba, the north coast's largest port town. **Guanaja** is the second-largest island after Roatán, measuring 18km (11 miles) long by 6km (4 miles) wide, and is the furthest of the three from La Ceiba, a 35-minute flight away. Due to a lack of fresh water on the main island, Guanaja's 10,000 inhabitants are mainly

2 Diving is not too physically demanding, but it does require an average level of fitness. Operators demand that divers have their basic certification. Sea-kayaking and mountain biking also require a reasonable fitness level, while the short hike on Guanaja is relatively easy-going.

★ The Bay Islands have accommodation to suit every budget level, with a surprising number of reasonably priced hotels that are exceptionally good value. This is an ideal destination for travellers looking for a combined adventure and traditional beach holiday.

All specialist equipment is supplied for diving, although you may wish to take your own. No equipment beyond what is provided is needed for kayaking, hiking, or mountain biking.

squeezed onto two tiny cays just off the southeast coast, where they live in wooden houses raised above the water on stilts. The total lack of cars and narrow waterways between the houses has resulted in the cays being dubbed the "Venice of Honduras." Guanaja was the hardest hit area of the country when Hurricane Mitch arrived in October 1998. Over a period of just three days, the

ABOVE The club at Bayman Bay on Guanaja.
INSET The logo of the Bayman diving resort
BELOW At West End on Roatán, locals escape from sandflies (a common irritant in the Bay Islands) by sitting on the jetty instead

storm wall stalled over the island and completely transformed it from a dense tropical forest into a bare mountain landscape. I arrived just three months after Mitch, and already the vegetation was starting to grow back, although the new-look island with its freshly revealed mountains was appealing in any case.

From Guanaja's airstrip, I took a water-taxi along the manmade canal that cuts through mangrove swamps at the island's waist to reach the northwestern shore. A brief ride across the ocean took me to the new pier at the Bayman Bay Club Dive Resort. The resort is set high up on the mountainside, and has gained a reputation for being one of the most idyllic in the Caribbean. As I took in the 14 luxury, rustic bungalows (there were originally 18, but four were destroyed by Mitch), each with breathtaking views out over the ocean and a crescent-shaped white-sand beach, the feeling of relaxation that washed over me was hard to ignore. I sat on my balcony, sipped my welcome cocktail, and soaked up the sun's rays.

HENRY MORGAN, PIRATE AND POLITICIAN

Born in Wales in the U.K. in 1635, Henry Morgan was kidnapped as a boy and sent to the Caribbean island of Barbados as a servant. Eventually, he worked his passage to Jamaica, and there began to mix with the pirates who were making vast fortunes from raiding Spanish cargo ships. Inspired, he secured his own vessel around 1666, and, with the express approval of the Jamaican government, began a reign of terror that surpassed most other pirates' efforts in the region. His attacks covered countries as far afield as Cuba, Panama, and Venezuela. In 1672, he was brought to justice in England for sacking Panama City, but King Charles II was so moved by his loyalty to the Crown that he appointed him governor of Jamaica! Morgan continued his buccaneering ways despite his new title, until he was suspended from political duty for piracy in 1683, five years before he died.

LIZARDS AND FORKED TAILS

I was here to explore, however, and Alice, Bayman Bay's enthusiastic joint operations manager, had recently cleared some of the walking trails in the hills above the resort. I donned my hiking boots and we headed towards Pando Ridge on a narrow trail that zigzagged up the slope. At the crest of the ridge, it was possible to see almost the whole island, from Sandy Rock Hill in the northeast to West Peak and Grant's Peak in the southwest. Small lizards scampered through the undergrowth, while magnificent frigatebirds (*Fregata magnificens*), with their mighty wingspans and forked tails, glided overhead on the updrafts. We returned via an impressive lookout point above the resort. Over dinner, served up in the sumptuous wooden bar and restaurant, I chatted with the other guests about their day's diving experiences. Steve, an American businessman and very experienced diver, had visited many dive locations around the world, but he and his wife returned annually to Guanaja because they believe the diving is some of the best to be had.

Unfortunately for me, an out-of-season rain front moved in overnight, so that by morning large whitecaps were clearly visible on the distant reef and waves were pounding ashore, making it impossible to launch the dive boats. With only one day free for diving during my three-day stay (there are restrictions on diving and flying within a 24-hour period), I resigned myself to diving only on Roatán.

Thankfully, the waves calmed down enough for me to get out in a sea kayak later in the day. Paddling a sit-on-top kayak out through the waves was immense fun, so much so that I decided to stay in the bay area and just play in the surf. When a decent set of waves arrived, I paddled forward hard and waited for the inevitable curl of white water to catch me from behind. Sometimes, I caught the waves just right and rode them into the beach, while on other occasions I was ignominiously dumped into the water. As the sun began to set, I caught one last wave and enjoyed a thrilling surf before being tossed into the white water as it finally broke.

The next morning, before leaving Bayman Bay for my afternoon flight, I borrowed some snorkelling gear and kayaked up the coast to a small spur known as Michael's Rock. The storm had long gone, and it took less than half an hour to paddle over the crystal-clear waters to the beach next to the spur. There was not a soul in sight, so I had a brief taste of the Robinson Crusoe-style isolation so many holiday brochures promise but few deliver. Amongst the brain corals and swaying fans, I spotted an array of exotic fish, including angel-fish (*Pomacanthus paru*), parrot-fish (*Scarus lepidus*), and various groupers. With my appetite for underwater adventures whetted, I packed my bags and headed for Roatán, confident that the weather would improve enough to go diving.

DIVE THE WORLD

Learning to dive is relatively easy, and there are several dive outfits on the Bay Islands that offer Professional Association of Diving Instructors (PADI) courses resulting in qualifications that are recognized around the world. Open Water beginners' courses, leading to a qualification that allows you to dive to 40m (130 feet), last from three to five days and are reasonably priced. Utila, the third of the three Bay Islands, claims to be the cheapest place in the world to gain your qualification, and as a result is very popular with backpackers. As a prerequisite to the course you must pass a simple health test and be able to swim. The syllabus includes classroom instruction, a straightforward multiple-choice exam, and several dives. One-day taster courses and more advanced courses, which teach you skills such as wreck diving and rescue diving, are also available.

A PIRATE'S REFUGE

Although it is only 3km (2 miles) wide, **Roatán** is the largest of the Bay Islands as it stretches like a sinewy slice of bacon for over 50km (31 miles). Pech Indians originally inhabited the island, but after Columbus arrived in 1502 the indigenous population was completely wiped out—either killed or shipped off to Cuba as slaves. In the 17th century, Roatán became a major base for British pirates, and was so popular that over 5,000 of them were living here by the middle of the century. The most famous of all was Captain Henry Morgan, the buccaneering governor of Jamaica, who used the town of Port Royal as a base for his raids on Spanish ships—or, for that matter, any other ships that entered his waters. It wasn't until the end of the century that British forces regained control of the region. In 1797 Garifunas were forcibly moved to the island by British troops after an uprising on nearby St. Vincent. Since then, these people have meshed their own African and Caribbean cultures with the English influences to develop the exuberant island culture that you see today.

Remarkably, despite the fact that it lies just a few miles west of hard-hit Guanaja, Roatán escaped virtually unscathed from the grips of Hurricane Mitch and is still covered in lush, tropical forest. The island is completely surrounded by a spectacular coral reef that forms the lower sections of the world's second-largest reef system, after the Great Barrier Reef in Australia, and that is renowned for its large variety of coral and excellent underwater visibility. The most popular part of the island with divers is **West End**, just a 15-minute taxi

ABOVE Water visibility in the Bay Islands is among the best in the world at around 30m (100 feet), allowing you clear sightings of the myriad fish species LEFT Making equipment checks and donning gear on the way to the dive site

ride from the airstrip. After checking in at the lovely Posada Arco Iris on Half Moon Bay, I spent the rest of the afternoon snorkelling in perfectly calm waters right in front of the hotel.

Early the following morning, I wandered down the sandy main street to the Sueño del Mar Dive Centre and booked up for a day's diving. The schedule was for a wreck and cave dive, with a shallower second dive on a coral wall. There are over 60 named dive sites just offshore around the island, so there is no need for long boat trips. After being issued with equipment and having loaded the boat, the four other divers and I barely had time to get our gear on before we arrived at the marker buoy above the wreck. Mike, the guide, and divemaster Claudio checked everybody's gear, and then explained the profile of the dive and gave some background on the wreck. *El*

Aguila (*The Eagle*) originally sank in shallow waters off the neighbouring island of Utila, but it was salvaged, made safe for diving, and then re-sunk off Roatán to create the biggest wreck dive in the Bay Islands. At 80m (260 feet) long, the old cargo ship suffered further damage when Hurricane Mitch's storm waters broke its body into three sections. "It's a real wreck now," quipped Mike. The *El Aguila* lies at a depth of 33m (110 feet), and we were going to spend 12 minutes at that level exploring the ship. Mike emphasized that if someone didn't feel comfortable with entering the narrow rooms, then it was easy enough to stay on the outside and simply meet the other divers at the far end. One by one, we manoeuvred our heavily laden bodies to the boat's rear platform and took a giant step off into the big blue Caribbean waters.

Rusty radiators

True to Mike's word, the visibility was superb, and as we descended along the buoy line shoals of fish came over to check us out. The rusting, contorted hulk of *El Aguila* could clearly be seen below, contrasting sharply with the bed of white sand. Starting from the stern, three of us followed Mike in through a narrow doorway, now tipped awkwardly to one side, and entered the main deck. Old radiators and piping still hung from the walls, and where the ship's captain used to stand fish now swam. It was a bizarre feeling. Through the narrower gaps it was difficult to judge how low to go as the scuba tanks almost doubled the width of our bodies, and occasionally they did snag on the metal panels. From the main deck we moved left into another, more enclosed room, where light streamed through a far doorway. Slowly, we made our way through it, passed under a jutting mast, and emerged from the bow into the brilliant blue light of the open water. Even though we hadn't spotted the green moray eel (*Gymnothorax funebis*) that has apparently taken up residence in the wreck, it was one of the most thrilling dives I have undertaken, and the fun still wasn't over.

For the remaining 30 minutes of the dive we moved to a shallower reef area at a depth of around 12–18m (40–60 feet), where Mike had promised to take us into a cave if we had a minimum of 80 bars (1,200psi) of air left. A quick check of our gauges confirmed that everyone who wanted to go for it still had enough reserves, so Mike took us in one at a time. The entrance, situated in an impressive wall of weird and colourful coral formations, was large enough to swim through, but then the cave narrowed and it became impossible to avoid brushing against the walls. The tunnel bent around in a U-shape, and twice opened up into bigger chambers where beams of sunlight funnelled through small holes in the cave roof. In the second chamber it was possible to see out through another hole to where the other divers were waiting for us, but the gap was just too small to get through, so we turned around and made our way back out. Claudio and I still had

CORAL REEF FORMATION

Coral reefs are fragile colonies of organisms that can live for hundreds of years. They are made up of tiny animals, red algae, and molluscs, and are found only in tropical waters where the temperature remains above 20°C (68°F). Tougher corals, such as brain coral, can survive in turbulent waters, but fans and disc-like corals need calm waters to thrive. They all rely on sunlight to grow, so are found only in the upper reaches of the oceans. Threats to the existence of coral reefs are on the increase. Ocean pollution, greater levels of ultraviolet light penetrating the Earth's ozone layer, and commercial activities such as uncontrolled diving and fishing all damage the coral, often permanently.

plenty of air left, so while the others made their way back to the boat we ventured into some of the deep channels that cut through the coral walls. In amongst the deepwater sea fans (*Iciligorgia schrammi*) and various brain corals—including boulder brain coral (*Colpophyllia natans*)—we saw small blue and yellow blueheads (*Thalassoma bifasciatum*), bright yellow cleaner wrasse (*Labriodes dimidiatuis*), more rainbow-coloured parrot-fish, and the head of a shy moray eel poking out from beneath a rock. The experience was sublime, and I felt disappointed when my gauge reached 50 bars (700 psi) and we began the swim back to the boat. A three-minute safety stop at 4.5m (15 feet) allowed excess nitrogen to escape from our bodies. Back on board, the other members of the group were just as enthused as I was, especially with the dive through *El Aguila*.

Underwater Rock and Roll

For our one-hour surface interval before the next dive, we returned to the Sueño del Mar, where I sipped a drink and munched on a chocolate bar to restore my energy levels. As it turned out, however, this wasn't such a great idea, for during the interval the wind picked up and the sea became quite choppy. By the time we reached the second site, things were getting quite rough, and the rocking boat did no favours for my chocolate- and fizzy-drink-filled stomach. For this dive, Claudio acted as guide as well as dive-master, so I buddied up with another diver. It was a relief to get off the boat and into the water. The turbulence had reduced visibility a little, and the wave surge made accurate movement rather tricky. Still, the wall began quite deep, at around 24m (80 feet), where things were somewhat calmer. The range of coral was quite incredible, and it was all in very good condition, with the luminous purple sponges (*Aplysina archeri*), resembling big, hollow candles, just edging ahead in the "Best in Show" awards.

Not to be outdone, the fish turned out in force, too, and we were treated to a swim through a beautiful shoal of blue ocean surgeonfish (*Acanthurus coeruleus*). Meanwhile, lone barracudas (*Sphyraena barracuda*), looking like silvery missiles with an attitude problem, stalked the reef in search of their next victim. These are the pirates of the underwater world, and can strike at great speed. The way the barracudas eyed us, it seemed that even we were not too big for a main course, but it is, in fact, very rare for them to attack divers. The highlight of the dive was seeing an enormous crab, which would have had more than a fair chance of winning a wrestling match with a gorilla, tucked away in its cave. After an hour of drifting through the magical coral dreamscape, we surfaced to find that conditions had worsened. It was quite a challenge climbing into the bucking boat, but once aboard we were all too busy talking about the dive to feel queasy. For one ecstatic diver, it had been the last dive in her quest to gain her PADI Open Water qualification, and she was now free to dive anywhere in the world. In the evening, we all met up for a beer in the stunningly situated Sueño del Mar open-air bar, and danced the night away to the vibrant beat of the weekly disco.

Island Tour

Roatán is such a big island that it seemed only fair to get a taste of the hilly inland areas before I left, so on my final morning I hired a bike from Captain Van's Rentals and rode for 45 minutes down to West Bay at the far end. The roads were not too steep, and I met only a handful of cars. After enjoying a detour onto a short section of single-track trail that led through a forest to a small isolated cove on the south side of the island, I rejoined the main track and swooped down the hill into **West Bay**. This is the place to head if you really want to get away from it all. Here, a sprinkling of lovely small hotels, bungalows, and private holiday homes butt onto what is probably the most attractive beach on the whole island. The sand beyond the palm trees was dazzlingly white in the strong morning sun, and the sea was as clear as bottled spring water. It seemed incredible that only a handful of people were there to enjoy it with me. West Bay also has some of the best snorkelling on the island, although there was barely a soul in the water. I spent a couple of hours swimming around in my own private tropical fish tank to get my final fix of underwater adventure. The Bay Islands may have been a treasure hunters' dream in the years gone by, but I think that the riches modern adventurers can experience here would turn old Henry Morgan green with envy.

Hiring a mountain bike will give you the chance to escape the beach for a day to explore Roatán's hilly, forested interior

GOING IT ALONE

INTERNAL TRAVEL

Getting to the Bay Islands is easy and relatively cheap both by plane and by ferry. Airlines that serve the islands from La Ceiba include Grupo TACA/Isleña, SOSA Airlines, and Rollins; prices are the same, so it's a case of finding the most convenient times. The first flights leave around 6am and the last around 5pm. There are regular air links from La Ceiba to San Pedro Sula and Tegucigalpa. Once a week, on Fridays, Caribbean Air has a direct flight from Miami to Roatán. There are no direct flights from Roatán to Guanaja, although there is a new twice-weekly boat service (Sundays and Wednesdays at 5:30pm, returning on Mondays and Thursdays at 5am) run by Seaways. Safeway Marine Company runs the *MV Tropical* ferry service from La Ceiba to Utila and Roatán. Seaways also runs the *Nautica* ferry on the same routes. Schedules change frequently, so it is always wise to check in advance.

WHEN TO GO

The best time to visit the islands is during the dry season (April–August), when diving visibility is superb and a cool sea breeze helps to ease the effects of the high temperatures. It is perfectly reasonable to visit during the rainy months, too, as the precipitation tends to fall as short, sharp afternoon downpours. Visibility for diving is not quite as good during the rainy season, but accommodation and flights can be cheaper and the sun still shines most days. September is the usual tropical storm season, but it is extremely rare for the islands to experience hurricanes on the scale of 1998's Mitch as they normally track further to the north.

PLANNING

There are plenty of good-value hotels in the medium-price bracket, but fewer options at the lower end on both Roatán and Guanaja. Booking ahead is only essential during the peak holiday seasons and on dry-season weekends, when mainlanders head over for a break. Dives can usually be organized the day before, or even on the same day during quiet periods. There are plenty of operators, so someone should be able to fit you in, and as many return to base between dives you can just go for an afternoon or morning rather than a whole day.

TRAVELLERS' TIPS

- ❑ Make sure you reconfirm your return flight from the islands as soon as you arrive. The booking system is rather haphazard, and the computers are often down. If you do find yourself at the airport without a confirmed return ticket, just hang around and make out that you have a range of connecting flights that will be ruined if you don't get on board. It is not unknown for an "extra" space to be found, sometimes on top of the cargo at the back of the plane! As the airlines run all their routes with few planes, delays are common, so don't schedule things too tightly.
- ❑ Not all dive operators are the same. Ask other divers for recommendations and check the operator's equipment for yourself before booking any dives. Remember: it is your life at stake! If you are diving for a few days, then "multi-dive" packages work out much cheaper.
- ❑ Many resorts include free kayak use and snorkelling gear in their package prices. If not, they are easily and cheaply rented from various stores and dive shops around the islands.

WHAT TO TAKE

- ❑ Sun hat, sunblock, and sunglasses.
- ❑ Mosquito repellent, coils, and net.
- ❑ Hiking footwear.

HEALTH

Mosquitoes are a problem on the islands, so suitable malaria precautions should be taken before you leave home (consult your doctor for the latest information). Some areas, particularly on Guanaja, also have plenty of irritating sandflies; although they don't carry disease, their bites can be very itchy. The sun is intense in these latitudes, so sunblock, a sun hat, and sunglasses are essential, especially when you are out on the water kayaking or on a dive boat. Decompression chambers are available on Roatán for treating diving-related problems. There is a voluntary insurance scheme in operation locally, which, for $2 per diving day, covers all emergency helicopter transfer and treatment costs (these are very expensive, so if your travel insurance doesn't cover you then it is definitely worth paying). Details are available at all dive centres.

A Life in Ruins

by Steve Watkins

The Maya dominated the heart of Central America for over 700 years, leaving in their wake magnificent stone cities. For artistic expression, the city of Copán in northwestern Honduras ranks among their greatest achievements. I explored the ruins to learn about the absorbing history of the Maya, and visited Rosalila's Temple, a stunning recent discovery.

While Europe stagnated in the Middle Ages following the demise of the Roman Empire, the Mayan civilization was entering its golden age, with an empire stretching from southern Mexico to El Salvador. The Maya created impressive cities with monumental structures, the most accurate calendar known at the time, and a trade network that included the great cities of central Mexico such as Teotihuácan. Of all their creations, however, none can match the city of Copán for artistic richness. In 1980, UNESCO justly listed Copán as a World Heritage Site, and since then it has been the scene of major archaeological investigations that have advanced the understanding of Mayan lifestyle and the roles of their rulers. I took a two-day tour to the ruins with San Pedro Sula-based operator MC Tours to see at first hand why Copán is so highly rated.

1 This adventure is not physically demanding, although you can certainly build up a sweat climbing the oversized temple stairways!

★ Exploring Copán and its surrounds is an ideal family adventure. The site itself and the two museums (one at the ruins, the other in town) will keep all age ranges enthralled for a couple of days. Accommodation to suit all budgets is available in the nearby colonial town of Copán Ruinas.

No specialist equipment is needed for this trip.

The ruins sit in a lush river valley beside a tight bend on the Río Copán, and are surrounded by high mountains that continue to the northwest to become the western highlands of Guatemala. During its heyday, around A.D. 600, Copán's influence covered an area of over 130sq km (80 square miles), probably the largest domain of any Mayan city, and its centre was home to over 27,000 people. Over

DISCOVERY AND ADVENTURE

After its first sighting by the Spanish in 1576, European interest in the ruins of Copán was not seriously renewed until 1839, when John L. Stephens and Frederick Catherwood visited during their expedition to several Maya sites. The riches of Copán kept Stephens, the writer, and Catherwood, the artist, occupied far longer than the other sites they went to, and they detailed their findings in the famous book, *Incidents of Travel in Central America, Chiapas and the Yucatan,* which is still available. As you read through the pages and admire Catherwood's superb drawings, you cannot help but feel a tingle of excitement. In 1855, the Peabody Museum in Cambridge, U.S.A., authorized Alfred Maudslay to conduct excavations at the site, and he made moulds of many of the stelae and altars so that they could be reproduced in the British Museum.

4,500 structures have been identified in the valley, ranging from massive temples to simple mud huts. However, as with modern cities, it is in the centre of Copán that the most astounding buildings—dubbed the Principal Group—are found.

The first decision to make when you arrive at the site is whether to visit the museum or the ruins first. To take advantage of the wonderful early morning light, and figuring that the exhibits would mean so much more once I had seen where they came from, I headed towards the ruins through a lovely avenue of trees. Even at such an early hour, a large team of workers was out tending the grounds, a sign of just how much importance is credited to Copán by the Honduran people.

A DISGUISED RABBIT

The entrance avenue opens out onto the spacious **Great Plaza**, oriented in a roughly north–south alignment. It is probably the most impressive plaza in the Mayan world, and is dominated by eight enormous, carved standing stones, called stelae, which mainly represent the self-promotion campaign of just one king, Waxaklahun-Ubah-K'awil (nicknamed, I was thankful to learn, 18-Rabbit). Copán was ruled by a dynastic succession of kings over a period of about 400 years from around A.D. 400. It was 18-Rabbit, the 13th ruler, whose reign lasted from A.D. 695 to 738, who commissioned the city's most accomplished stone masons, scribes, and artists to create six of the intricate stelae. The inspiring, powerful images depict the king in the various guises of the ancestor spirits that were central to Mayan mythology. By linking himself with the gods in this way, 18-Rabbit reinforced his own control and the legitimacy of the dynasty.

However, 18-Rabbit's success in creating a dynamic city at Copán and his subsequent expansionist war tactics, which saw neighbouring cities vanquished, eventually resulted in his own demise. In A.D. 725, 18-Rabbit led an attack against the nearby kingdom of Quiriguá (see page 92) and installed one of his own nobles, Cauac-Sky, as ruler. Quiriguá grew in strength and became more independent until, in A.D. 738, Cauac-Sky attacked Copán, captured 18-Rabbit, and sacrificed him. As I wandered around the stelae, marvelling at the three-dimensional sculpturing that brings 18-Rabbit's reign to life, I could not help but reflect on what other wonders he may have created had he lived longer.

I headed south, back down the plaza and past the isolated low temple of Structure 4, to reach Copán's "sports stadium," known as the **Ballcourt**. Such I-shaped courts exist at numerous sites throughout the whole of Mesoamerica (the name given to the pre-Columbian region of Indian civilizations that stretches from north-central Mexico to El Salvador), but details of the actual

DECIPHERING THE GLYPHS

For the uninitiated, like myself, it seems incredible that archaeologists and iconographers have uncovered such detailed stories about Mayan history from a seemingly limitless jumble of stone pictures and markings. It took a long time for the initial breakthroughs to happen, but since Heinrich Berlin published evidence in 1958 that Mayan sites have unique "emblem glyphs," a sort of coat of arms, progress has accelerated. As more information was recorded and knowledge pooled from the various regions, patterns started to appear. Tatiana Prouskouriakoff first recognized that groups of stelae usually related to just one ruler, while by 1973 the late Linda Schele and Peter Matthews had deciphered the entire dynastic history of the rulers at Palenque in Mexico. There is now a proper Mayan syntax that allows scholars to build up words from various glyphs, and, who knows, maybe soon there will be Maya–English dictionaries!

ball-game played remain something of a mystery. It is thought that two teams of two or three players had to keep a rubber ball off the ground without using their hands or feet. However, the purpose of the game is a rather contentious issue. Many scholars believe that far from just being a recreation sport, ruling nobles, possibly from rival cities, played the ball-game as part of a ritual ceremony, and there is some evidence to suggest that the losers were sacrificed. Copán's Ballcourt was rebuilt several times throughout the Mayan heyday, but large macaw heads, which can still be seen, were always part of the design. Macaws and quetzals were particularly significant symbols at Copán, probably inspired by the founder of the dynasty, Yax K'uk' Mo', whose name translates as Blue-Quetzal-Macaw. The gently sloping platforms on either side of the Ballcourt were once covered in smooth white stucco to allow an even bounce of the ball, and there were markers, or "goalposts," at either end. It must have been quite a spectacle to witness the plaza's pyramids packed with spectators cheering on their favourite team.

Royal propaganda

One of Copán's most famous features is the **Hieroglyphic Stairway** on the temple known as Structure 26, at the southern end of the Ballcourt. Although the stairway had an unsightly tarpaulin roof stretched over it to protect it from the elements when I visited, it was deeply impressive none the less in both its scale and high level of craftsmanship. Consisting of over 1,250 hieroglyphic stone blocks, it is the longest continuous pre-Columbian script ever found in the New World, and was an audacious piece of propaganda aimed at redeeming a faltering dynasty.

Following 18-Rabbit's untimely demise and the disruption it caused to the dynastic power base at Copán, his successor, Smoke Monkey, struggled to reassert control—a state of affairs reflected by the lack of public building that took place during his short reign of ten years. When his son, Smoke Shell, the 15th ruler, came to power in A.D. 749, he began an enthusiastic campaign to re-establish the glory of the royal lineage. Smoke Shell's first public works were the reconstruction of Structure 26 and the creation of the incredible Hieroglyphic Stairway, at the very core of the city.

The hieroglyphs chart the entire history of the Yax K'uk' Mo' Dynasty, placing particular emphasis on their conquests (and conveniently glossing over 18-Rabbit's defeat). Rising up the stairway from the open mouth of an inverted snake, the mythological Mayan Vision Serpent that helped bring forth the ancestors during ritual ceremonies, are lifesize sculptures of the last five rulers of the dynasty in full battle regalia. As you look up the impressive, high stairway, it seems hard to believe that the nobles and peasants who had doubted the ability of the royal family to continue the glorious expansion of Copán could possibly continue doubting Smoke Shell after seeing such a powerful piece of work. Yet Copán was entering its twilight years.

From the stairway, I strolled along the base of the immense, steeply stepped north façade of **Temple 11** to Stela N, the final piece of public work found at the site. Both of these structures were built by Smoke Shell's successor, Yax Pac, the 16th and last great ruler of Copán, who reigned from A.D. 763 to 820. Far from being a passive overlord of the dynasty's breakdown, Yax Pac continued the inspired efforts of his father to reclaim power, and was responsible for a comprehensive public building programme, of which Temple 11 was the finest achievement. To get a better look at it, I followed a narrow trail from the lower plaza level up through the forest, where roots of towering ceiba trees are intertwined with the tumbled blocks of unexcavated mounds.

Sunrise over Structure 22, adjacent to the Acropolis on the northern side of the East Plaza and part of Copán's Principal Group

Some convenient steps led to the temple's upper platforms, from where there were remarkable views over the entire Great Plaza and Ballcourt, and off to the mountainous backdrop, a fact that wouldn't have been lost on Yax Pac. From here, during ceremonies that he performed at the open mouth of a terrifying Witz Monster façade (*witz* is the Maya word for mountain, which is what the temples represented), he would have been an imposing figure to the masses below.

UNDERWORLD KILLINGS

On the ground at the northeastern corner of Temple 11, I came across a giant head grinning at me manically. His rotund face, wrinkled skin, and huge teeth brought back memories of some of the figureheads I had seen from Olmec sites, which flourished on the east coast of Mexico prior to those of the Maya. The Olmec are widely regarded as the first major civilization in Mesoamerica, and many scholars believe that traders from there created the first Mayan settlements. This giant head at Copán belonged one of four statues that were placed at the corners of Temple 11. The figures represented the mythological beings that held up the four corners of the sky, symbolized by the temple's roof.

On the lower, south-facing levels of the temple, Yax Pac created a vision of Xibalba, the submerged, ancestral Mayan Underworld, with imagery that, over 1,200 years later, still manages to strike an uneasy chord. Deteriorated crocodile masks and several conch shells across the top of the small platform stairway indicate that everything below that level on the West Court is the underwater world of Xibalba. At the upper corner of the staircase, the fearsome face of the axe-wielding executioner god, Chac Xib Chac, stares out as he emerges from the water. Sacrificial victims, normally from enemy cities, were rolled down these steps to the "false ballcourt" below, where the Lords of Death awaited them with messages from the ancestors. Only relatively recently have Mayan scholars begun to understand the violent and warring nature of the Maya people, after decades of thinking that they were a peaceful civilization of star-gazers.

Despite the undoubted positive effect Temple 11 had on Yax Pac's rule, problems at Copán continued to mount. Members of the burgeoning nobility class became increasingly convinced that they could get by without a king at all. There are signs, such as the construction of smaller temples outside of the Acropolis, that increasing numbers of challenges were being made to Yax Pac's authority. More significantly, the city's success had led to overpopulation of the valley, and the natural resources were being strained to breaking point. In order to appease the people's growing anxiety, Yax Pac commissioned the impressive **Altar Q**, and set it at the base of the other great pyramid he constructed in the West Court, Temple 16. This is the area where much of the current archaeological

A 52-YEAR TIMER

Mayan scholars recorded time on a unique double calendar system. One calendar ran for 260 days, meshing 20 named days—including Ahau, Cauac, and Akbal—with 13 numbers. Known as the *tzolkin*, this calendar began with the day 1 Imix and ended with 13 Ahau, before starting again. Each day was associated with omens, and priests used the calendar to guide every aspect of Mayan life. The *tzolkin* was then meshed with a 365-day calendar, the most accurate of its kind until the Gregorian calendar was introduced in 1582. This "Vague Year," which didn't take account of the quarter-day gained each year which results in our leap year, consisted of 18 months of 20 days, with a five-day period added at the end (this was a notoriously ill-omened time of year). Working together, both calendars covered a period of 52 years.

nvestigation is being carried out. While workers wheeled barrows of excavated earth to a special sieve beneath a ceiba tree, I admired the replica square altar (the original is in the site's museum). It shows in wonderful relief the 16 kings of Copán, four on each side, starting with the dynasty founder, Yax K'uk' Mo', and ending with him handing over power directly to Yax Pac. However, things didn't improve for Yax Pac, and the altar was his last effort to link himself with the ancestors. His power gradually seeped away towards the nobility as he tried to cajole their support by allowing them to enact some of his ceremonial rights.

A TEMPLE SANCTUARY

Altar Q portrayed the royal dynasty as having come full circle to meet its founder, but little did archaeologists realize how true that was. In 1989, Honduran archaeologist Ricardo Agurcia Fasquelle was working in a tunnel that led into the interior of **Temple 16**. At all Mayan sites, great importance was attached to building new structures over the top of the old ones, the earlier building being ritually destroyed in the process. Archaeologists had known that Temple 16 had been constructed in this way, but had no idea of its inner secret. Agurcia came across a fantastic four-level temple, now dubbed **Rosalila**, which was almost completely intact. It is thought that the tenth ruler, Moon Jaguar, constructed the temple during his reign (A.D. 553–73). This was sensational news in the archaeology world, as nothing had ever been found like it before in the Mayan region.

Subsequent investigations below Rosalila in 1991 by Robert Sharer and David Sedat of the University of Pennsylvania revealed the base of another temple, called **Margarita**. Inside, they found tombs containing the remains of founder Yax K'uk' Mo' and his wife, and many artefacts still painted as brightly with reds, greens, and yellows as the day they were interred. These major discoveries helped put many pieces of the Copán puzzle into place, and gave archaeologists the inspiration to initiate the building of a full-scale replica of Rosalila in the museum. As the official public opening of a section of the Rosalila Temple was still a month away when I visited (in March 1999), I received special permission from Professor Cruz, Copán's director since 1967, to enter this temple and another, nicknamed **Ante** and due to be opened at the same time.

Findings in Ante link parts of its construction with the seventh ruler, Waterlily Jaguar, and the charismatic 11th ruler, Butz' Chan or Smoke Serpent, who had the second-longest reign (A.D. 578–628) after Yax Pac. The narrow, dusty tunnels twisted and turned, and I was glad Roberto, my guide, was there to show me the way. In a narrow passage that separated the inner and outer temples, huge macaw masks were still partially covered in red stucco, a fine plaster used to coat the walls and clearly visible after over 1,400 years. It was enthralling, and I paused to imagine how magnificent the city must have looked in its heyday.

FACING A SERPENT

We emerged at the back of the Acropolis, and made our way to the north side of Temple 16 on the Jaguar Court, so called because of the dancing jaguar figures that adorn the plaza steps around a face mask of Venus, the Sun God. Roberto unlocked a simple wooden door sunk into the temple's side, and we entered a cramped tunnel where the hot, stale air clung to my skin. I began to appreciate just how tough archaeological work must be in such oppressive, confined conditions. Turning a corner, we entered a slightly longer reinforced passage built especially to allow easier access for tourists. A side tunnel led to a corner of Rosalila's second level. Here, a sculpture of an ancestor spirit emerging from the gaping mouth of a Vision Serpent looked out through the protective Perspex window. Further along the wall, elaborate sculptured swirls symbolizing the serpent's body led

ABOVE Within Temple 16 is a fantastic four-level temple filled with Mayan treasures BELOW Stela B, in the Great Plaza, dates from A.D. *731 and is one of several depicting the great king 18-Rabbit*

to another mask. It wasn't until later, when I saw the spectacular, colourful replica in the museum, that I realized just how large the temple is, and how incredible it was that Yax Pac had managed to construct Temple 16 over the top of it without damaging it. The fact that Rosalila was left intact shows how central Yax K'uk' Mo' was to the glory days of Copán, and how much he was revered by 15 subsequent kings over a period of more than 400 years. It was thrilling to catch a glimpse of such emotive history.

Later, I visited the wonderful open-plan **museum**, where some of Copán's most important façades and artefacts are displayed and described. As I walked around the impressively colourful replica of Rosalila Temple, my mind turned to wondering about how such a great civilization could have disappeared so rapidly. Of course, the Mayan people didn't vanish altogether, and still make up a significant proportion of the population in highland Guatemala and the Mexican state of Chiapas, but the region's powerful cities were abandoned over a reasonably short period of time. Although overpopulation certainly led to a degradation of the agricultural land around Copán, and, as we have seen, political pressures from the nobility upset the dynastic power base, it seems strange that these factors would cause people to leave. Modern-day examples of overcrowded cities, such as Mexico City, seem only to attract more and more people, with increased trade bringing in the necessary supplies to feed everyone. The Mayan cities all traded with one another and with settlements further afield, so food shortage should not have been an insoluble problem. In politics, the winners normally want to take over and put their own stamp on great cities, not abandon them. It appears that there was a purposeful change of attitude among the people towards the whole notion of city living and central control. Nobody really knows for sure what happened, but with each new discovery at sites such as Copán the answer is perhaps brought ever closer. After such a mind-provoking insight into the magnificent Mayan world, I just hope I will still be around when they find it.

GOING IT ALONE

INTERNAL TRAVEL

Independent travellers can reach Copán Ruinas from San Pedro Sula by bus. Cheny Buses have four buses a day (two, at 2pm and 3pm, are direct and much faster—3 hours—for only a little extra cost). There are no direct buses from Tegucigalpa, so you need to travel from the capital to San Pedro Sula first. Buses also run from Guatemala City to Chiquimula, from where local buses run to the Honduran border; there is usually a connecting bus waiting on the Honduran side for the 1-hour journey to Copán (if there isn't, then it is reasonably easy to hitch a lift on a pick-up truck).

WHEN TO GO

Copán can be visited at any time of year, but is probably best during the dry season, especially from December to April. National holidays and school holidays are the busiest times, and are therefore best avoided if at all possible.

PLANNING

There are numerous ways of visiting Copán to suit all types of budgets. Several Honduran tour operators, including San Pedro Sula-based operator MC Tours (see Contacts), offer complete packages to the ruins, including accommodation at the wonderful colonial Hotel Marina Copán. Tours are also operated from Guatemala City and Antigua in neighbouring Guatemala, but these include very long road journeys; because of this the day tours on offer are hardly worth joining as the time spent at Copán itself amounts to little more than a couple of hours. There is accommodation to suit every budget level in Copán Ruinas, including Los Gemelos, Popul Nah, and Hotel Marina Copán. It is just a 20-minute walk out of town to the ruins, or taxis can take you there in 5 minutes. The ruins open at 8am, and there is no entry fee after 4pm (throw-out time is 5pm). There are separate entry fees for the park, museum, and the Rosalila Temple.

TRAVELLERS' TIPS

❑ It is most definitely worth getting up early to be at the site for opening time as there is a good chance that you will virtually have the whole place to yourself. It is also worth staying there until closing time as herds of wild deer wander around the Great Plaza and Acropolis after most visitors have left.

❑ It is worth hiring one of the multi-lingual guides on site as they can bring the history to life.

❑ Take drinking water with you as the restaurant is a fair walk from the ruins and it can get very hot during the middle of the day.

❑ Don't rush your visit. Take some time to sit down on the temples and imagine the life of the Maya.

❑ A useful, affordable book, *History Carved in Stone* by Fash and Agurcia, is available at the site and in town. It gives good background information and is very readable.

WHAT TO TAKE

❑ Sun hat.

❑ Sunglasses.

❑ Mosquito repellent.

❑ Comfortable footwear.

❑ Torch.

❑ Drinking water.

HEALTH

Mosquitoes can be a problem at the site in the early morning and late evening, so take precautions against malaria before you leave home (consult your doctor for the latest advice). The site is quite open and the sun can be very strong in the middle of the day, so wear a sun hat and drink plenty of water.

BELOW Pauahtun head, Temple 11

Rivers of Time

by Steve Watkins

Vast and virtually roadless, the rarely explored, river-laced Mosquitia region of eastern Honduras is sparsely inhabited by indigenous peoples who live in tiny, rustic settlements. For five days I ventured on a variety of small boats into the World Heritage Listed Reserva de la Biósfera Río Plátano to visit Pech, Miskito, and Garifuna communities.

On the map of Central America, La Mosquitia stands out for one reason only—an almost total lack of roads. This remoteness inspired Paul Theroux to used it in his famous book *The Mosquito Coast*, about an American family setting out on a doomed attempt to live a totally self-sufficient life, later turned into a film starring Harrison Ford. Even with the increasing interest in adventure travel worldwide, the numbers of travellers who have made it into this region remains remarkably small. Mosquitia is inhabited by indigenous Pech, Miskito, and Garifuna people, who live traditional subsistence lifestyles, and so offers a real opportunity to take a step back in time. Access is possible only by private boat and there are no scheduled services, so I took a five-day tour with local guide Roberto Marin, who helped to smooth the journey to Las Marías, deep in the **Reserva Biósfera Río Plátano** (**Río Plátano Biosphere Reserve**).

Travelling around Mosquitia by boat is not physically stressful, but the long river trips do require patience. The jungle hikes on offer vary from relatively easy-going hour-long walks to very challenging, multi-day treks.

For luxury and pampering, look elsewhere. This is a very remote region where all facilities are basic and travel is by dugout boats. You will get wet, although this is a small price to pay for a rare chance to spend time with the indigenous communities and to sample life as they see it. Accommodation is in simple, yet comfortable huts, and the food consists of staples such as rice, a potato-like vegetable called yuca, and eggs.

Hiking footwear is required for the jungle treks; other essentials include a mosquito net and a comprehensive medical kit.

The flight from La Ceiba to Palacios, the small coastal town that serves as an entry point to northern Mosquitia, lasted only 50 minutes, but it was an adventure in itself. With fellow travellers Martin and Michael, students from Germany, Roberto and I flew in an old 14-seater, propeller-powered plane over dense jungle dotted with the occasional thatched hut and dissected by contorted brown rivers. We came in very low over Laguna Balcalar, and the plane landed on the rough grass strip of Palacios "airport," bouncing across the soccer pitch in the process! Roberto told us that during matches the players just run off the pitch if a plane is coming in, and then continue as normal.

Hypnotic boats

Palacios lies on the northwestern corner of the Reserva Biósfera Río Plátano, which covers over 850,000sq km (328,000 square miles). The reserve was created by the Honduran government in 1980, and accorded UNESCO World Heritage status in the same year. It protects an area of mangrove swamp and tropical rain and cloud forest with the lowest population density in Central America—just three inhabitants per sq km (eight per square mile). From Palacios, Roberto organized a

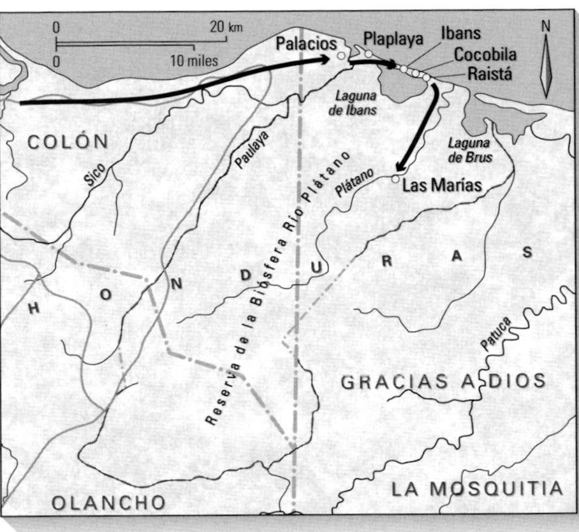

The Reserva de la Bíosfera Río Plato, Eastern Honduras

boat to take us to our first night's stop at the village of Raistá, on Laguna Ibans. The small wooden boats with onboard engine and rudimentary steering wheel used locally are known as *tuk-tuks*, so called because of the rather loud and hypnotic "tuk-tuk" noise made by their feeble one-cylinder engines. With our gear loaded in waterproof bags, we waded through the shallows to board our *tuk-tuk* and set off to negotiate the watery highways of Mosquitia.

To shorten journeys between the rivers and lakes of the region, a series of linking canals has been built by hand. From the wide waters of Laguna Bacalar, we made a tricky manoeuvre against a strong current to reach the narrow, overgrown entry to Canal Siblablá. The canal was so narrow and twisting that Roberto had to paddle up front in order to turn the boat's bow more quickly around the corners. The two sides of the canal contrasted sharply. To our left, the flooded, tree-stump-dotted landscape demonstrated how even biosphere reserve status has failed to stop encroachment by cattle farmers, who have to clear acres of land in order to sustain mere handfuls of cattle. To our right, a tangle of forest brought back memories for Roberto, who was born in nearby Plaplaya, of how the canal used to teem with monkeys. The monkeys may have moved away, but numerous exotic birds still ply the route for food.

THE WORLD'S GREATEST PLACES

In 1972, the United Nations Educational, Scientific, and Cultural Organization (UNESCO) adopted an international treaty, simply called the Convention, that aims to protect world cultural and natural heritage through a network of World Heritage Listed Sites. Natural site candidates are judged against four criteria: the property should either represent major stages of the Earth's history; contain on-going processes in the evolution of ecosystems; include areas of superlative natural phenomena or beauty; or contain significant natural habitats, including those of threatened species. Chosen sites are deemed to be of "outstanding universal value," and thus "belong" to the people of the world with a duty of care transcending national boundaries. The 146 member countries of the United Nations and the sale of World Heritage products provide annual funding of around $3 million; these very limited funds are primarily used to protect sites on the World Heritage in Danger List. In 1996, UNESCO added the Reserva de la Biósfera Río Plátano to this list owing to continuing encroachment by farmers, loggers, and poachers in the south and west of the reserve, combined with a lack of a suitable management plan.

The canal emerged onto Río La Criba, which runs parallel to the coast. The river gets its name from a local corruption, originally "Black Riba," of the English name for it, Black River. Beyond Plaplaya, we entered Laguna de Ibans, a large lagoon with two islands, Cayo Sicotingni and Cayo Halover. We slipped between the latter and a narrow spit of sand that separates the lagoon from the ocean. At Ibans, a mainly Miskito village, we pulled into shore to offload one of our passengers, a teenage boy. In the shallows, a young girl scrubbed away furiously at clothes placed on a wooden table while her even younger sister looked on. A group of older women gathered at the first thatched hut to welcome home the boy, and to take a good look at the strangers—us. As so few travellers make it into this remote part of Honduras, the novelty factor remains relatively high.

The butterfly family

Ibans has been steadily growing over the past few years, and now forms an almost continuous community with neighbouring Cocobila, also a Miskito village. It was

41 years ago that William Bodden decided to move from Cocobila to set up the village of **Raistá**, our overnight stop, a few miles further east. Thanks to his outright purchase of a large block of land and subsequent refusal to sell any of it, the settlement remains a unique, one-family village of around eight wood and thatch houses. Now in his 80s, William Bodden remains the central character and patriarch, and he greeted us, in surprisingly fluent English, on our arrival. All around him, numerous grandchildren played among lines of drying, multi-coloured clothing. William used to work for the United States-based United Fruit, which farmed the area's rich coconut supplies. The company no longer operates here, however, and today the vast majority of the community's money is gained through tourism and from a commercial butterfly project.

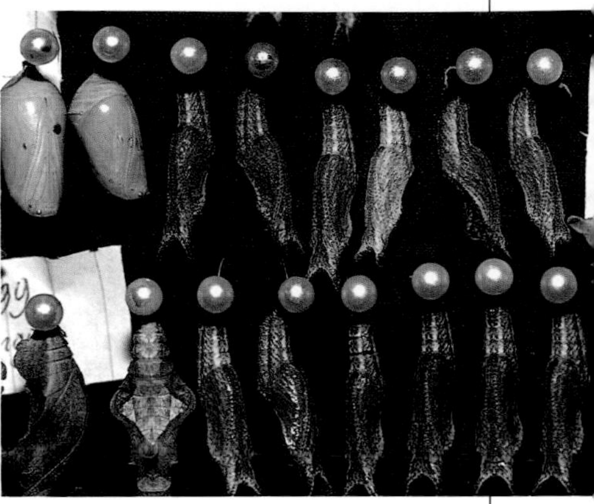

ABOVE Butterfly pupae pinned in racks and ready for sale at Raistá Butterfly Farm
LEFT Village hut, Las Marías
BELOW One of the grandchildren of William Bodden, founder of Raistá

Since March 1992, William's son, Eddy, in association with MOPAWI (a non-governmental environmental development agency), Roberto Gallardo (a Peace Corps volunteer), and the San Diego Zoo, has developed the internationally successful **Finca de Mariposas Raistá** (**Raistá Butterfly Farm**). A limited number of exotic butterfly species are captured locally for breeding. When the offspring reach pupa, or chrysalis, stage, which generally takes 7–14 days, they are sold to the San Diego Zoo for between $1.50 and $4 each. With Eddy acting as our guide, we took a tour around the farm. In the first cabin we

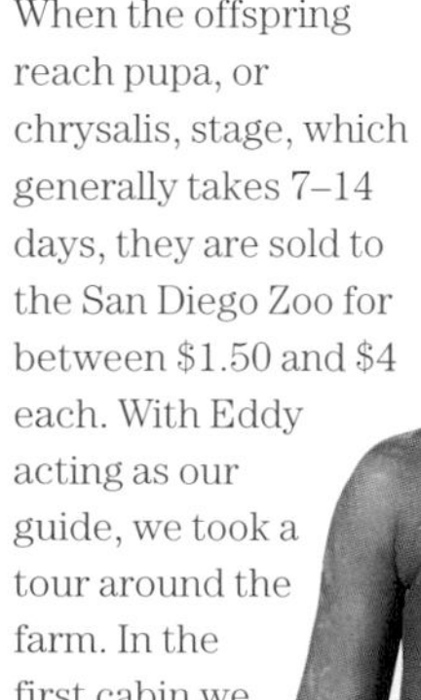

saw the rabbit-style hutches where the pupae are initially formed on plant offcuts placed upright in soft-drinks cans, and racks of colourful pupae hanging from silver-headed pins like exotic earrings in a jewellery display case ready for transfer to San Diego Zoo. Eddy showed us chubby, bright green pupae that resembled small chilli peppers. Remarkably, these are eventually transformed into the magnificent, iridescent blue morpho butterflies (*Morpho peleides*) that we later saw in the large adult enclosure. These beautiful creatures are so popular that they carry the top, $4 price tag. The farm's success has also created an economic incentive for the local inhabitants to protect the forests where the butterflies thrive, and this in turn has additional benefits for eco-tourism.

While several of the Bodden grandchildren entertained themselves by swinging wildly on a hammock strung between two trees, we relaxed on the porch outside our wooden bungalow. This was one of the family's houses, and we had been given a spare room at the back. Hung on the living-room walls and standing on tables were fading brown photographs in silver frames, while the sofas were finished off with delicate lace covers. It seemed strangely grand for the remote jungle setting, but it felt very homely none the less. After a delicious meal of rice, beans, fried *yuca*, and roast meat, we wandered down the dark track to Cocobila for a drink. There are no bars in the village, but people like to gather at the local store to sup on one of the two national beers, Salva Vida and Port Royal, both reasonably good. Cocobila's store sells everything from sacks of rice to fancy women's shoes, all at inflated prices due to high transportation costs—a cargo ship makes a twice-monthly trip here from La Ceiba.

LOST CIVILIZATIONS

The Mosquitia region has remained relatively untouched by archaeologists, despite compelling evidence that an advanced civilization once lived here. Over 80 archaeological sites are known to exist, and one of them, the mystical Ciudad Blanca (White City), was probably a large city that rivalled the size of the more famous Mayan sites of Central America. Only aerial reconnaissance has been carried out so far, and the local indigenous people are loathe to allow any exploration of the ruins. A veil of silence descended every time I asked about their exact location.

Cheap teeth

The next morning, we rose early to start the long trip to Las Marías, a tiny Pech village on the Río Plátano. Our boat was waiting in Nueva Jerusalem, a one-hour walk east of Raistá through the village of Belén. After cutting through a brief section of forest, the trail opened up near the Belén airstrip and we watched as a six-seater SAMI plane landed on the waterlogged runway. Along the way through Belén, wooden houses, raised high on stilts for protection against floods, steamed as fire smoke seeped through their palm roofs. At a small store near the end of the village we stopped to buy canned fruit juices, and on its wall I spotted a handwritten sign notifying residents that a dentist was going to be working for a few days in the village hall. Each tooth treated would cost only seven lempiras (around 50¢), and I couldn't help thinking how my dentist back home could justify his extortionate rates!

For the five-hour river journey to Las Marías we were going to be travelling first class. The fastest, most comfortable boats in Mosquitia are the long, wooden launches powered by outboard motors. For the trip upriver against the powerful current of the Río Plátano these boats are almost essential, but the price of the ride is relatively expensive due to high fuel costs in the region. Many local people

PLIGHT OF THE BOY DIVERS

With increasing pressures being placed on Mosquitia land by commercial logging and cattle-ranching interests, the indigenous Miskito families are finding it harder to eke out a subsistence living. To earn money, many young men and teenage boys have taken to hiring themselves out to commercial boats as lobster divers. The work is well paid—up to $500 for a two-week trip—but the dangers to their health are immense. Little or no training is given, and their equipment is very poor quality. As the lobsters are caught in water that is 30–45m (100–150 feet) deep, the divers are exposing their bodies to serious pressures, and almost every veteran diver suffers from decompression-related illnesses. Around 20 divers die suddenly each year from embolisms, and most use drugs or alcohol to numb the pain. Robert Armington, an ex-U.S. Special Forces operative, has set up diving schools around Cocobila to teach basic safety routines, a move that has already significantly reduced the problem in the immediate area.

cannot afford to hire the launches, and instead spend an incredible 15 hours paddling upstream in their own dugout canoes to cover the same distance. Loaded up, we set off into a tiny, overgrown canal where the long boat struggled to negotiate the tight bends through the mangroves. Following recent heavy rains, a tree had fallen across the waterway. Locals had chopped a gap in it big enough to accommodate a dugout canoe, but our launch got well and truly jammed. Roberto and the driver jumped into the tannin-stained water to try to rock the boat free, while we huddled at the rear end in an attempt to lift the bow. Eventually, we inched the boat through the gap and entered the wide, fast-flowing waters of the Río Plátano, just inland from its mouth, where Caribbean waves crashed ashore.

Although much of the lower section of the river was bordered by only secondary forest (areas of regrowth after virgin, or primary, forest has been cleared), there was plenty of wildlife around. Two large greyish-white jabiru storks (*Jabiru mycteria*), with their black necks and brilliant red throat flaps, stood tall and motionless, like sentries at a royal palace, on the riverbank. These birds can grow up to 1.5m tall (4 feet) and have a wingspan of around 3m (10 feet). All along the river's edges we spotted various species of river turtles basking on fallen trees, although if our boat got too close they slid off and splashed into the water. Meanwhile, up in the overhanging trees, alert belted kingfishers (*Megaceryle alcyon*), with their distinctive white collars, eyed the water for the slightest movement that revealed the whereabouts of their next fish snack. With little to do except relax, we sat back and soaked up the jungle atmosphere, as bright green parrots and scarlet macaws (*Ara macao*) screeched and squawked overhead. Some passing boats carried so many people, goods, and even dogs that their sides were barely above the water-level, but nobody appeared to be perturbed by what seemed like an imminent sinking. As the sun dipped below the silhouetted palm trees on the west bank, a large group of waving children greeted us at Las Marías.

FAR FROM THE MADDING CROWD

Supposedly founded around 1945, when a Miskito Indian woman, Francela Carington, came alone from Barra Patuca to settle in **Las Marías**, the community subsequently became predominantly Pech as Indians moved downriver from Buena Vista from 1949. Today, the village is mixed, and the majority of the 460 inhabitants live on the west bank, while seven or eight families have settled on the

opposite side. In addition to their second language of Spanish, each of the indigenous Mosquitia groups has a distinct language, with Pech being related to a macro-chibcha language that has its origins in northern South America. We were staying in a recently constructed wooden lodge with palm-frond roof, owned by the Tinglas family. It was wonderful sitting out on the front deck listening to the gentle flow of the river, the dusk

ABOVE A full pipante *(canoe) sets off along the Río Plátano from Las Marías*
LEFT Guide Roberto points out the petroglyphs upriver from Las Marías

birdcalls, and the croaking toads. There is no electricity in the village, so the only illumination came from the cool white light of the moon and the warm orange glow of our candles. Although it had been a long boat journey to reach La Marías, it was only that evening that we really began to understand just how remote the community really is.

There has been steady progress in the development of ecotourism in Mosquitia, and recently around 300 travellers have visited Las Marías annually. One of the main attractions is a trip further upriver to see some ancient petroglyphs carved in riverside boulders. After a filling breakfast of delicious fried plantain (a cooking banana), rice, and eggs, we shouldered our daypacks and walked the short distance through the forest to the main village centre to catch our third type of boat in three days. Above Las Marías the river becomes very shallow, and there are several small rapids that make it impossible for motor-powered boats to pass. The journey is therefore made in tiny, roughly hewn dugout canoes called *pipantes*, which are powered by two men with wooden poles, just like the gondolas in Venice. The boats are able to carry just two passengers in the middle, two polers up front, and a paddler/navigator at the back, sit very low in the water, and feel incredibly unstable. When Roberto had settled into his seat, I gingerly made my way into the wobbly wooden front chair, which seemed to have been designed for infants. As the two polers flexed their sinewy muscles and pushed us away from the shore, I felt certain that the *pipante* would turn over at some stage during the four-hour journey, and felt thankful that my gear was packed away in a waterproof bag.

A rapid recovery

In the distance, the impressive rock spire of Pico Dama dominated a horizon clad in virgin rain forest. The peak is a sacred mountain in Pech mythology, and can be climbed if you have 14 days to spare, advanced climbing skills, and a penchant for serious jungle-trekking. However, our challenges were with the rapids, and it was amazing to see the stop-go techniques employed by the boatmen in order to inch the canoe through them. The line of entry was crucial, and occasionally the paddler at the back had to use the river flow to steer the boat across stream in order to change our approach. At one particularly powerful rapid, the polers momentarily lost control and the canoe began to slide backwards through the white water. The level rose up over the sides, and it looked as if the "abandon ship" command was about to be given. The polers quickly recovered their footing, however, and jammed their poles into the stony riverbed to halt our reversal of fortunes. Once the canoe was stationary, they began to coax it onward again.

On reaching a small rocky island in the middle of the river, Roberto announced our arrival, and we disembarked, waded through the water, and cast our eyes over the first petroglyph. A simple, happy smiling face was carved in a small boulder set in the shallows, and beamed out at us as if in welcome. A short distance upriver was a more elaborate petroglyph, shaped like a fancy piece of wrought ironwork, which seemed to have more significance. However, virtually nothing is known about the carvings or the people who made them. With ominous storm clouds gathering, we settled back into our seats and began the rather more rapid return to Las Marías.

The next morning we rose at dawn to get an early start for the long trip back downriver to our final night's rest point at Plaplaya, Roberto's home village, near Laguna Ibans. **Plaplaya** is a Garifuna village, where life follows a different beat, the sound of Punta. The Garifuna were sent to Honduras from St. Vincent by the British in 1797, and are descended from African, Carib, and Arawak Indian stock. After watching the sunset on the deserted, white-sand beach on one side of the village, we enjoyed a night of traditional Punta dancing in the village hall. To the pulsating rhythm of large drums, a circle of old and young women developed, and in the middle a teenage girl began to gyrate and shake as if possessed by the music itself. Joined by a young boy, they danced intertwined but never actually touching, the sweat pouring down their faces as the beat intensified. Around them, the crowd began singing tribal chanting songs. It was quite a show. Even though it was organized especially for us, the dancers relished the chance to lose themselves in the infectious beat and seemed almost oblivious to our presence.

At 5am the following day, as the glorious golden sunlight lit up the river, we boarded our final *tuk-tuk* for the ride back to Palacios. Originally I came to see exotic wildlife and the ancient stone carvings, but I found that the indigenous people and their incredible lifestyle made this journey to Mosquitia an exceptionally rewarding trip. I probably wouldn't choose to follow in Harrison Ford's footsteps and try to live there, but it was refreshing to see that a happy life is possible without all the modern conveniences.

GOING IT ALONE

INTERNAL TRAVEL

There are daily flights to Palacios from La Ceiba and Trujillo with Isleña Airlines, Sosa, and Rollins. SAMI is the only company that flies to Belén.

WHEN TO GO

The best time to visit Mosquitia is during the dry season (November–April). February–March is the best season for spotting birds as many migrant species stop off in the region.

PLANNING

Several tour operators run various trips into the Mosquitia region. It is possible and cheaper to travel independently, especially if there is a group of you, but you really should employ a local guide to smooth the way, particularly if you do not have a good command of Spanish. Boat travel is expensive, especially along the section from Raistá to Las Marías. There are no scheduled services, so it's a case of organizing things as you go. There are set prices for the *pipante* trip from Las Marías to the petroglyphs, and don't forget that you have to pay two polers, a paddler, and the head organizer. There are very reasonable set prices for meals and accommodation in the different villages. Bargaining is not really possible.

TRAVELLERS' TIPS

- ❑ Don't panic in the *pipantes*. Keep your weight low in the boat and don't make any sudden movements. The canoes may feel completely unstable, but the boatmen are very experienced and accidents are rare. In any case, the water is very shallow in most places.
- ❑ Make sure you reserve your return flight as soon as you arrive at Palacios. The booking system is rather haphazard, and if you don't confirm you may not get out.
- ❑ Tempting as it may be to go without a guide, a good one can save you lots of hassle and money, and can provide a fascinating insight into the local communities and wildlife. Hiring a guide also brings much-needed revenue to the area, and in turn helps to persuade inhabitants to preserve the wild environment.

WHAT TO TAKE

- ❑ Sun hat, sunblock, and sunglasses.
- ❑ Waterproof jacket or plastic poncho.
- ❑ Mosquito net, plus string and cup hooks to hang it.
- ❑ Mosquito coils and insect repellent.
- ❑ Hiking footwear.
- ❑ Sandals—the rafting style is preferable.
- ❑ Torch.
- ❑ A good book—there's little to do at night.

HEALTH

Both malaria and dengue fever are present in the Mosquitia, although they are not common. That said, medical precautions against malaria should be taken before you leave home (consult your doctor for the latest information). Insect repellent and mosquito coils should be used at dawn and dusk in particular, and mosquito nets are essential for night-time. The sun can be very strong indeed, and you are exposed for long periods on the boat trips; wear full-length clothing, a hat, and sunglasses, and apply plenty of sunblock. Also drink lots of water—either take bottled water with you from La Ceiba or pass the local water through a high-quality, iodine-based filter (these are supplied on organized trips). The food in established ecotourism centres, such as Raistá and Las Marías, is all cooked hygienically and should therefore be safe to eat. If in doubt, check with your guide. Ensure that you have a comprehensive medical kit and know how to use it—professional help may be a long time coming in this remote region.

FURTHER READING

- ❑ Parent, Derek, *La Mosquitia—A Guide to the Land of Savannas, Rain Forests and Turtle Hunters* (self-published, 1994; available on the Internet: www.amazon.com, or by fax (U.S.): 1-800/677-1821). Fills the rather gaping hole in information contained in the more established guidebooks. An in-depth look at Mosquitia's indigenous people and their languages, wildlife and flora, climate, health issues, travellers' routes, local guides, and accommodation.

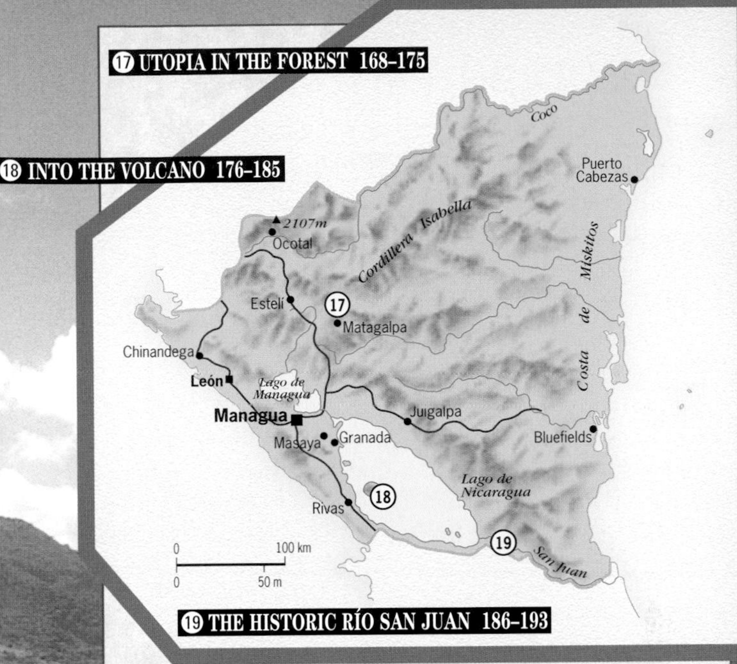

NICARAGUA

Politically, economically, and environmentally, Nicaragua has had more than its fair share of problems. In December 1972 an earthquake flattened Managua, killing 6,000 people, the country was torn apart by the Sandanistas revolution in the late 1970s and by the Contra war in the early 1980s, and then rampant inflation wrecked the economy in the late 1980s. These and other atrocities have taken their toll, but despite it all the resistance of the people continues to shine through.

Nicaragua is the largest country in Central America, covering 129,500sq km (50,000 square miles), yet only 4 million people live here, most of them in and around the capital, Managua. In between the land and oceanic borders lie three distinctive regions—the Pacific lowlands, north-central Nicaragua, and the Caribbean coast—which cover an immense geographical diversity ranging from idyllic islands and smoking volcanoes to lush jungles and glorious beaches. Despite this ecodiversity it is, however, the people who are the country's most endearing feature. Their friendliness and forgiveness in the face of adversity is why Nicaragua will eventually bounce back. Tourism is unlikely to embrace the country in the way it has Costa Rica anytime soon, but for the determined traveller who is hunting for a genuine experience, this is the place to find it.

View over Matagalpa, the third-largest city in Nicaragua

Utopia in the Forest

By Carl Pendle

High up in the cool mountainous air of Nicaragua's north-central highlands is an oasis called Selva Negra (Black Forest). It is a hotel, restaurant, coffee plantation, and nature reserve all rolled into one, and is set amongst 500ha (1,200 acres) of fertile land. I came here to spend a few days relaxing in this protected virgin forest, where the huge assortment of wildlife and fauna kept me spellbound.

The tranquillity of Selva Negra was a long way from my initial introduction to Nicaragua. A lightning storm greeted my plane on its approach into Managua from Miami, huge, jagged forks lighting up the city as we banked towards the runway. The few tourists on the Nica flight looked rather apprehensive, and rightly so, but for the locals it was just another typical tropical storm.

My guide, Juan Carlos Mendoza of Careli Tours, met me at the airport. I paid $5 for my tourist visa, breezed through immigration, picked up my bags, and was outside within 15 minutes of landing.

1 At Selva Negra the pace is dictated by you. You can spend the entire break sitting in the restaurant drinking coffee, reading, and admiring the breathtaking views, or get up at dawn to spot the rare birds and then take off on a hike along one of the 14 trails. The trails themselves cater to all levels of fitness, from a four-hour mountain ascent to a 15-minute lakeside stroll.

★★ Compared with much accommodation in Nicaragua, Selva Negra is very comfortable indeed. The cabins are well-equipped, the food is excellent, and the people are very friendly.

Take binoculars for viewing the wildlife in the jungle and around the cabins. Good walking boots and a waterproof jacket are essential if you plan on going trekking. Don't forget your camera and pack plenty of fast film to cope with the low light levels in the forest.

In the cold chill of the waiting air-conditioned minibus, Juan welcomed me to Nicaragua, "the land of lakes, mountains, rivers, volcanoes, sea, and sun." It was not all good news, however, as Nicaragua is also a land of earthquakes. There had already been 100 tremors on the day of my arrival, and the paper Juan carried warned of the possibility of another on the scale of the December 1972 disaster, when Managua was flattened and 10,000 people died. Juan joked that the hotel I was staying in, the plush Hotel Intercontinental, had survived the last one and would no doubt survive another. Although it is harrowing to realize that, on average, there is one earthquake in Nicaragua every month, I guess it's all part of the adventure.

As you would expect, I didn't sleep well that night, and was glad to leave the smog and confusion of Managua behind as we headed for Selva Negra the next morning. Half an hour into the journey, and in the distance lay creased, rain-forested peaks, lush valleys, and the shimmer of sunlight bursting through cool grey clouds. We were headed for the beautiful-sounding Sierra Isabela mountains, 1,200m (4,000 feet) high and home to the most beautiful rain forests in Central America. Selva Negra lies a good two-hour drive northeast of Managua, most of it following the busy Pan-American Highway. At the town of Sébaco you branch off towards Matagalpa, where a steep, winding road wiggles its way to Jinotega. An old rusted tank perched on a grassy bank along this road indicates Selva Negra's entrance.

THE FURNITURE-MAKER

Along the way we stopped by a wooden house set atop a small hill overlooking the Pan-American Highway. A sign outside read "*Artesanía El Caminante*" (artist of the passers-by). Juan introduced me to the owner, Asención Zeledon, a furniture-maker. He was a small man with gold-capped teeth and a greying moustache who wore an upturned baseball cap, which he removed every so often to scratch his head. Asención is famous in Nicaragua for the garden furniture he crafts by hand from a hardwood called *chaperno*, which he gathers from the forests surrounding his house. This land is, unofficially, his. After the war the government gave him 36ha (90 acres) as a reward for his bravery as a guerrilla fighter; subsequent governments have taken all but 8ha (20 acres) back. It started to rain hard as Asención explained all this, the water gushing through holes in the grass shelter and spilling onto the furniture. We left him and his family to put away a couple of chairs and a table that would have cost me only $80—a cheap price to pay for four days' hard work.

We passed through **Sébaco**, set in a valley of the same name. Thousands of years ago this was once a huge lake, and today the fertile region produces most of Nicaragua's vegetables. In the town there were big wooden carts loaded with all kinds of fruit and vegetables. Carrots, beets, garlic, rice, and onions were piled precariously high in carts and on stalls, and were strewn on mats at the side of the road for sale to passers-by.

Just 10km (6 miles) beyond Matagalpa stood the tank marking the entrance to **Selva Negra**. It was blown up by a bazooka during the revolution against Anastasio Somoza in the late 1970s, and although it is an odd landmark for a hotel, history is all part of the landscape here. The minibus turned right and wove along the mile-long private road to the resort. Sword-like trees called *esbadilla* lined the road, while just behind them lay a huge swathe of coffee plants—thousands upon thousands of them—set amongst taller trees whose fronds shaded the delicate beans from the harsh sunlight.

EDDY AND MAUSI

We were met by owner Eddy Kühl, who along with his wife Mausi founded this resort in 1975. He led me along the road, and then into the jungle where slippery paths branched out to wooden cabins scattered under the canopy. There are 24 of these half-timbered cabins, each with *en suite* bathroom and shower, a comfortable bed, and clean towels. Some also have a television, refrigerator, open fireplace, and spacious lounge area. These are rustic, walk-in-the-woods sort of places, with pretty curtains, framed pictures on the walls, and outstanding views to the lush, green forest; at certain times of the year the roofs of the cabins are even covered with a mass of pink and red flowers.

That afternoon Juan and I met up

WILDLIFE GALORE

Selva Negra is a zoo. Even the most nonchalant animal lover will be stunned by what can be seen even in the short space of time it takes to eat breakfast. Hummingbirds of unbelievable colours sip nectar just inches from your table, parrots flutter over the lake, and the mountain behind the restaurant is alive with the sound of bird music. At Selva Negra there are 175 species of birds, 85 different varieties of orchids, a plethora of butterflies, and thousands of insects. The luckier bird-watchers might spot a toucan, and it is rumoured that the elusive quetzal bird also hangs out here. Larger creatures include sloths, mountain lions, ocelots, howler monkeys, armadillos, and tapirs.

with Eddy and the energetic Mausi at the restaurant, which overlooks a wonderful man-made lagoon. The view was breathtaking: the sun peeked through wispy clouds, a faint steam rose off the water, an overwhelming backdrop of forest filled the sky, the water rippled from a feeding bass, a necklace of red flowers tumbled around the bank, and there was a serene stillness that was truly magical.

German settlers

Eddy talked for hours about the history of the immediate area. In the 1880s, he told me, a band of 30 German settlers, all in their 20s, arrived in these mountains on an invitation from the Nicaraguan government to try to grow coffee. In return for their expertise, the Germans received some land. They made this their home, naming the coffee plantations after places in their motherland, such as Bavaria, Alsacia, and Hammonia (Hamburg). Both Eddy and Mausi are descendants of these early German settlers, a link they keep alive with Germanic touches all around the resort. There's sauerkraut on the menu, the cabins look Bavarian, and Mausi even organizes an annual Oktoberfest party.

My plan of attack for the next morning was to combine jungle-trekking with a bit of bird-watching. I was desperate to spot the elusive quetzal bird (*Pharomachrus mocinno*), reputed to be one of the rarest birds in the world. It is a striking creature, swathed in long green, red, and white feathers, and is usually only ever seen at altitudes over 1,400m (4,600 feet). Juan knew a little about these birds, but for accurate identification he packed his Costa Rican bird book (there is no comparable publication available on native Nicaraguan birds).

Monkey troubles

That night a loud thumping on my cabin roof woke me at 3am. I lay still, straining

ABOVE There are 14 trails at Selva Negra; the Indiana Jones Trail leads up to the top of the reserve
LEFT Horse treks into the surrounding area can be arranged from the resort

to hear the noise again above the rush-hour traffic of insects chirruping and clicking away. There was another rustle. It sounded too heavy for a squirrel or a bird, and although there have been sightings of mountain lions, ocelots, and sloths in the resort this could only have been a lone howler monkey (*Alouatta palliata*). During the day their familiar haunting bark can be heard echoing from deep within jungle, but thankfully it is rare for them to howl at night.

In the morning Mausi got a message over her radio that one of the workers had spotted a sloth asleep in a tree on the plantation. Sloths are slow-moving animals, so I had time to finish my typical Nicaraguan breakfast of *gallo pinto* (rice and beans), scrambled eggs, and two freshly baked tortillas before Mausi drove me to the edge of the plantation for a closer look. The supervisor waited for us beside the road. In his right hand dangled a long machete, which he used to point to a tree amongst the young coffee plants. We followed him up a steep, muddy embankment. A two-toed sloth (*Choloepus meganychidae*) had curled itself tightly into a ball and was wedged between two branches. On hearing our approach, it woke up and then slowly and deliberately moved its front legs, exposing two long claws. It hung upside down to get a better look, its large eyes peering at us for a few minutes, and then coiled itself back up into the tree.

Bird-watching

Juan and I hiked across the plantation to connect with a trail that would lead us to the top of the mountain. There are 14 trails at Selva Negra, catering to all fitness levels. On the way up birds sang in the thick landscape, at times swooping down to heckle us, and then disappearing. Trying to identify them proved difficult without a pair of binoculars, although Juan managed to recognize the chirrup of a hummingbird and the familiar call of a rufous-naped wren. I spotted the red plumage of a woodpecker and heard the cry of a great kiskadee (*Pitangus sulphuratus*) which, legend has it, is a sign of good news.

Eventually we stumbled upon the Indiana Jones Trail, which links up with the so-called Fountain of Youth and comes out at the top of the reserve. The paths were easy to follow, although some were narrow and occasionally a fallen tree blocked our route. We strode over rocks, slipped on moss-covered logs, and fought off stray branches. Juan pointed out wild avocado trees and banana plants, as well as cedar and mahogany.

The route steepened near the top, so that at times we were on our knees, grabbing roots and branches to pull ourselves up in the wet, slippery conditions. In the distance came the echoing beat of a howler monkey. It was cool at the top, but the fresh air felt good against my hot skin. This was the roof of the reserve at 1,400m (4,600 feet), although it is well short of the country's highest point, Pico Mogotón (2,107m, or 6,913 feet), near Ocotal next to the Honduran border.

JUNGLE SAFETY

The Peter and Helen Trail at Selva Negra was named after a British couple who became lost in the forest during their stay. The jungle paths all look very similar, so it is essential that you take some precautions before you set off on a hike. Let the staff at the resort know where you are going and what time you expect to return, and take a compass with you to avoid walking in circles. If you do get lost and darkness falls, stay where you are and wait until daybreak before setting off again. Wear ankle-high walking boots for support, and take plenty of water, a lightweight waterproof jacket, and insect repellent.

We traversed the ridge until we came across the Peter and Helen Trail, which would lead us back to the hotel. On the way down we passed leaves the size of elephant's ears, poisonous spikes protruding from bushes, deep blue butterflies, and fast-flowing streams. We stopped once so that Juan could drink from the river using a cup he made from a leaf. The trek took four exhausting hours, but it was worth every minute.

Eddy joined us for lunch at the restaurant after our walk and talked a bit about the guests who come to the resort. Selva Negra attracts a good mix of nationalities. Half of all visitors here are Nicaraguans, followed by Americans and Canadians, Germans, Dutch, and British. The cabins are usually all booked at weekends, but during the week finding accommodation is generally not a problem.

COFFEE TOUR

In the afternoon Mausi gave me a tour of the plantation. As we bounced down the uneven roads along its edge, Mausi talked about their ecologically sound farming techniques. She showed me the water-powered generator, and how they collect methane for use in the workers' kitchen. Worms are kept to feed off the kitchen waste, so that the compost they produce can be used on the vegetable patch. Pesticides are rarely applied, and when deemed essential are targeted at the problem area rather than blanketing the whole plantation needlessly.

Mausi stopped at a clump of coffee plants to show me some ripe beans. She knelt down by a bush and snapped off a red bean, then popped it into her mouth, crushing the outer shell between her teeth and sucking out the "honey water." I tried extracting the sweet juice, but crushed the entire bean on my first effort. I got it right the next time, however, and the sweet gelatine oozed over my tongue.

The plantation workers aren't paid very much, but they are treated well. The permanent workers are given their own houses (there are 64 basic brick homes

GROUNDS FOR SUCCESS

There are 200ha (500 acres) of coffee at Selva Negra, with 4,000 bushes to every 0.8ha (2 acres). Between November and early February over 600 workers are employed to harvest the coffee by hand. Each bush is picked four or five times during the season, with, on average, one bush yielding 450g (1 pound) of coffee. It takes three years for a bush to reach maturity, but it will then carry on producing fruit for another 30 years. Selva Negra produces 150 tonnes (300,000 pounds) of coffee a year, two-thirds of which is exported to America and one-third to Europe. Coffee is Nicaragua's number one export, although Mausi was quick to point out that the producer receives only 2 per cent of the price paid by the customer for a cup of coffee.

on the south side of the resort), fresh water, access to medical care, and an abundance of food, and Mausi has even set up a school for the workers' children. The temporary workers live in long, dormitory-style brick shelters that house over 300 people. We stopped off at the kitchens, inside a long, dark building with a tiled roof that looked like an old stable. Inside, the cook was busy making tortillas (she makes 500 every day), while two large pots were bubbling away over a pile of smoldering logs. Both pots were full to the brim, one with rice and the other with a dark brown mixture of beans. The cook was a large lady with deep-set black eyes, most probably a result of having to rise at 12:30am to prepare breakfast for 4am.

That evening Eddy entertained us with more stories. In the 1920s these mountains saw the birth of guerrilla fighting, and it was also here that Eddy himself fought with the guerrillas against Somoza. He was shot at on numerous occasions, and in September 1978 decided to go into exile in Costa Rica. He left his mother and a schoolfriend in charge of the resort, which at the time was often used by both the Contras and Sandinistas.

Horseback outing

Rain greeted us the next morning for our horseriding trek to a nearby village. The horses were brought up to the restaurant from the stables, and Juan and I waited in the rain as a stablehand tightened the saddles and adjusted the stirrup lengths. My mount was a small white and tan horse that hung one leg limply in the air as if it was lame. The man bent down and attached a spur to my right foot. Juan and I mounted our horses and headed towards the main road, passing the tank and following a gravel path on the opposite side that offered beautiful, uninterrupted views to a lush valley.

After an hour we stopped at the small village of **Parsila**, where we tied the horses to a barbed-wire fence next to the shop. Inside, several children were huddled around a black and white television set playing Super Mario on a Nintendo machine. They looked around, but didn't seem bothered by us. The owner greeted us and then fetched two Pepsis from the refrigerator. She placed them on the wooden counter next to a three-tiered shelf that housed some toilet paper, matches, cigarettes, a box of Alka Seltzer, lollipops, and some homemade cakes sealed in plastic bags. We chatted to her and another local, and asked them about a community of blonde-haired, blue-eyed people Eddy had talked about. The shop owner told us that these people lived in the mountains and kept to themselves. She said they were descended from the gringos who came to Nicaragua to work on the roads in the early 1900s.

We left the village and headed deeper into the hills. It was here that we passed two old ladies with fair skin and blue eyes. We said hello but left it at that, feeling awkward about asking any more questions. We turned back soon afterwards as our horses were tired of struggling on the steep, muddy roads.

Coffee seedlings waiting to be planted out. Selva Negra's coffee plantation contains around a million bushes in total

We later told Eddy about our chance meeting with the two old ladies, and in turn he recounted some interesting facts he'd read in a book called *The Naturalist* by Thomas Belt, published in 1874. Eddy said that Charles Darwin considered this to be one of the finest naturalist books ever written. In it were a couple of paragraphs referring to a blonde-haired, blue-eyed community living in these mountains. In contradiction to Parsila's shop owner, Belt states that these people were related to the buccaneers who arrived in the region via the Río Grande.

HOMEWARD BOUND

On our last afternoon Mausi took us to the edge of the plantation to show us the wide, sweeping views down to the city of **Matagalpa**, Nicaragua's third-largest city. We stopped here on the way back to Managua to look around the cathedral and to people-watch in the nearby plaza. We saw women cooking food over barbecues, children shining shoes, and old men chatting amongst themselves under the shade of some trees. This town saw some of the fiercest fighting during the war, and as a result there are many wounded veterans and single-parent families in the community. Matagalpa is also where Carlos Fonseca, the founder of the guerrilla movement, was born; his house is now a museum.

We left the safety and peace of the hills behind us and headed for Managua. On the way back two people tried to force our van to a stop by holding a length of rope across the road as a barrier. Apparently, this is a common means of extracting "donations" to repair the potholes in the road. Further on, people were selling bass, parrots, monkeys, and armadillos by the side of the road. We pulled up beside the two men who were selling the armadillo. One of them held the animal up towards the window of the minibus; it was still alive but its legs had been tied together. Armadillos are quite rare, and the man was asking $9 for it.

If you are looking for an escape from the sometimes harsh realities of everyday life in Nicaragua, or need to draw breath after active adventures elsewhere, then I suggest you head for the tranquillity of Selva Negra, where the animals are protected, hunting is banned, and your energy levels will be restored by the plentiful local food, fresh mountain coffee, and traditional homemade German cakes.

GOING IT ALONE

INTERNAL TRAVEL

The journey to Selva Negra in a tour company's private bus takes about 2 hours. Public buses do make the trip from Managua, but they are slower. Take the bus bound for Jinotega and ask to be dropped off at Selva Negra by the rusted tank; the ticket costs about $2.

WHEN TO GO

As is the case for the rest of Nicaragua, it is best to visit during the dry season (December–April). I went in October during the rainy season (May–November), but although it often rained in the afternoons the temperature was a very pleasant 20–25°C (70–80°F).

PLANNING

It is very easy to organize a trip to Selva Negra yourself by contacting the resort direct. Both Eddy and Mausi speak very good English if you want to call, or you could book via email. Tour operators will gladly arrange your trip, but they will add on their own charges for transport, guide, and administration.

Three or four days at Selva Negra is ample time to relax, eat, and enjoy walks in the jungle. Horse riding is very inexpensive and can be arranged from reception (in the restaurant). It is advisable to break up your stay with day trips out to Matagalpa and Jinotega. It is quite possible to arrange these yourself or through a tour operator.

TRAVELLERS' TIPS

- If you go by public bus be vigilant in the bus station at Managua as pickpockets abound. Keep your backpack in sight at all times—insist on having it with you in the bus, and do not leave it in the hold or on the roofrack.
- If you go by minivan or drive yourself, do not stop for anyone except the police along the road to Selva Negra. Always be alert when driving.
- The guided tours of the Selva Negra coffee plantation are highly recommended.

WHAT TO TAKE

- Mosquito net (these are not provided in the cabins).
- Binoculars for viewing the jungle wildlife.
- Waterproofs.
- Walking boots.
- Warm clothes for the evenings—remember that it is much cooler in these mountains than in the rest of Nicaragua.

HEALTH

Selva Negra is largely free from mosquitoes owing to its altitude. Beware of fire ants, which can deliver a very painful bite; the ants' nests are visible on the ground as small mounds of earth.

Ingenuity and local materials can produce wonders!

Into the Volcano

By Carl Pendle

Climbing a 1,395-m (3,833-foot) volcano swathed in thick jungle has to be one of the most thrilling and challenging episodes in my life. It took four hours to reach the summit and three hours to get back down, all undertaken in the most terrible of rainstorms, and I have no idea how I managed it.

Twenty-four-year-old Ramiro Carrillo-Valle doesn't look like much of a guide. He is wearing worn-out rubber boots, jeans, and a thin T-shirt. He's carrying a small, red backpack, a neatly coiled rope dangling from its opening and a bayonet taken from an AK47 sticking out of a side pocket (a machete, he says, would be too cumbersome). He doesn't speak much English, and he can't even remember how many times he's scaled the volcano we are about to climb; he thinks its more than 15, but less than 20.

Nic, a fit-looking American from San Francisco, is also along for the climb, and we have both come very well prepared—you would be foolish not to. We each have sturdy walking boots, quick-drying trousers, a waterproof jacket, and a backpack full of energy-replacement foods and plenty of water.

Climbing the Madera and Concepción volcanoes demands a seriously high level of fitness: the trekking is extremely hard, sometimes up very steep slopes. It is possible to trek some of the way and turn back when you are tired. It is wise to have your fitness assessed professionally before you attempt this expedition.

The hotels on Isla de Ometepe are very basic, often lacking hot running water, and therefore suit only backpackers and hardened travellers. If you want comfort then plan a day trip to the island, taking the last ferry back to the mainland at 4pm.

If you plan to trek up one of the volcanoes then sturdy walking boots and some waterproofs are essential. A small backpack is useful for carrying emergency provisions such as a basic first-aid kit, plus insect repellent, high-energy bars, and lots of water.

Our driver drops us off at a path running along the edge of a field at the base of the volcano. I strain my neck to look towards the top, but the summit is still hidden under a thick layer of cloud. I bend down to tighten my boots and then fidget with my backpack to make sure it is comfortable. Of course, I am just delaying the inevitable. The driver looks at Ramiro, then at Juan Carlos Mendoza from Careli Tours, at Nic, and finally at me, the shortest in the group. He asks me if I lift weights. Not really, I reply. He then bets me $10 that I won't make it to the top. I take him up on his offer, safe in the knowledge that a 62-year-old Japanese lady had scaled the volcano a few weeks ago. Surely it could pose no problems for a fit 33-year-old?

Expedition plans

Juan had been preparing me all week for the trip up Volcán Madera, the easternmost of two volcanoes on Isla de Ometepe. Like me, he was a little apprehensive about scaling its 1,395-m (3,833-foot) forested flanks to reach the crater lake at the summit. Ometepe is one of 365 islands in Lago de Nicaragua, of which 300, known as Las Isletas, lie within a mile of the colonial city of Granada. Ometepe is shaped like a bone; on the west side is Volcán Concepción, a perfectly pointed volcano 1,610m (4,430 feet) high which last erupted in 1957. Lava from past eruptions has formed a connecting bridge between the two volcanoes, called the Tistian isthmus. One day Ometepe will no doubt have modern hotels and proper tourist facilities, but right now it is perfect for anyone who is willing to shun creature comforts in order to experience an eco-tourism diamond and a never-to-be-forgotten adventure.

Both volcanoes can be climbed. Concepción is a classically shaped volcano, very similar in appearance to Mount Fuji in Japan, but it doesn't have the lush forest of Madera and the volcanic ash makes climbing quite hard work (Juan described it like trying to scrabble up a sand-dune). Madera is also a difficult climb, but there is more to see as its slopes are covered in a lush forest that is home to an abundance of wildlife. At the top is a beautiful lagoon with a waterfall and natural springs. We decided Madera would be the better option.

Start of the adventure

We left Managua at 8am and headed south in the air-conditioned Careli Tours bus towards the city of Rivas, 110km (70 miles) away along the Pan-American Highway. During the two-hour trip we passed through many small towns, the most interesting of which were Dirioma and Diria. Apparently, these are famed centres for witchcraft, and people come from all around in search of alternative medicines to cure a range of strange ailments. Juan told us that the witches prescribe racoon's penis to men looking for the woman of their dreams. This particular treatment is quite expensive, so Juan told us, as a racoon's private parts are rather difficult to come by!

Rivas itself is a small town bound on the east by Lake Nicaragua, and lies just 30km (19 miles) from the shores of the Pacific Ocean to the west. It is here that the site for a canal connecting the Pacific and Atlantic was once targeted. The American millionaire Cornelius Vanderbilt, owner of the Accessory Transit Company, first transported passengers and freight through here to San Juan del Sur. There had always been plans to build a canal in Nicaragua, but lobbyists for the Panama scheme highlighted the dangers of building such a waterway through a country with so many active volcanoes, and Nicaragua's bid was rejected.

Not far from Rivas, on the Pacific coast, is the town of **San Juan del Sur**. The area is renowned for its fine beaches and for the fact that sea turtles come ashore to lay their eggs at Chococente and La Flor. During the months of September and October, these peaceful animals lay their eggs on many beaches along this Pacific coastline. Although their nesting sites are protected, turtles' eggs can still be seen on sale in the markets of Managua (astonishingly, this is legal as long as the trader has permission from the Ministry of Natural Resources).

Lake port

A short drive beyond Rivas is the Lake Nicaragua port of **San Jorge**, from where the ferry runs to Ometepe. We were early so we waited in the ticket shop, shuffling through the postcards in an attempt to get some idea of what to expect on the island. Two boys stared at the television, and on the walls hung swordfish and shark trophies, reminders of the unique freshwater game that can be caught in

BE PREPARED

When attempting a peak such as Volcán Madera, it is common sense to be well prepared. Your body can only store enough carbohydrate for about three or four hours' hard exercise, so on a long walk you need to keep your energy levels topped up. Glucose tablets are worth taking, as are electrolyte-powder sachets, which contain a mixture of sugar and salt. Mix the powder with water to replace any liquids and valuable minerals you may have lost during the climb.

the lake. Outside, two men were cleaning a car by the water's edge, while to my right a row of restaurants stood bleak and lonely in the pouring rain.

We walked the short distance to the jetty and boarded the ferry. The boat could only have been 12m (40 feet) long, just about capable of carrying a few cars or a largish truck. There were two decks for the foot passengers, both equipped with padded vinyl seats that faced a television set fitted into a wooden panel. The boat was three-quarters full, mainly with locals, although in front of us sat a small group of American backpackers. Two girls walked around both decks trying to sell packs of chewing-gum that swung from metal loops secured around their necks. There was also an onboard shop that sold sandwiches and a selection of drinks ranging from coffee to shots of Johnny Walker. I looked through my porthole towards the island, hoping for a view of the volcanoes, but all I could make out was a thick band of vegetation along the coastline.

ISLAND LIFE

Some 35,000 people make their home on the 276-sq-km (107-square-mile) **Isla de Ometepe**. There are only two major towns—Moyogalpa and Altagracia—while the rest of the coastline is dotted with small villages. Their inhabitants live off fishing and farming. The land is very fertile and many types of crops can be grown in the tropical climate. Plantain, similar in appearance to the banana, is grown in large quantities and forms part of the staple diet of Nicaragua. Rice, tobacco, coffee, watermelons, maize, and an assortment of citrus fruits are also grown on Ometepe.

We were met at Moyogalpa by a minibus that took us out of the busy port, over an old landing strip, and towards San José del Sur. Just past the village, we turned off the gravel road down a potholed track, and after five bone-jerking minutes arrived at a beach where some men were building a boat from long planks of cedar. On a clear day it is possible to see Costa Rica, which lies only 15km (9 miles) away. We walked down the beach to Charco Verde, known locally as the Devil's Lagoon. Legend has it that a kind of farm from hell exists under the lake as punishment for those who sell their souls to the devil in exchange for wealth during this life. Walking back from here we passed an *elequemen* tree, whose bark is supposed to be a cure for arthritis. A butterfly wafted by, and Juan pointed to a groundcover plant whose leaves close up when you touch it. We also spotted a termites' tunnel winding its way up a tree, and a blue heron (*Ardea cinerea*) shuffling about on a bowed branch.

Ometepe is a haven for wildlife: even from our noisy minibus we managed to spot howler monkeys (*Alouatta palliata*) and many species of birds. Within just one hour Juan had pointed out parrots, sandpipers, egrets, cranes, fish-hawks, frigatebirds, and ducks. The island's inhabitants are keenly aware of the importance of its wildlife, and there are many signs by the side of the road educating people to "Protect Your Wildlife."

BEACH RESORT

We were heading for Juan's favourite place in Nicaragua, **Santo Domingo**, a very small, peaceful beach resort on the isthmus joining the two volcanoes. We stopped here for lunch at a hotel and restaurant called Villa Paraiso, owned by a doctor and his Austrian wife. A friendly waiter escorted us to our table, which was near coconut palms and papaya trees that swayed in the welcoming sea breeze. We all ordered fresh-caught tilapia, a spiky-finned fish that was introduced to the lake 25 years ago from Africa. While we ate, a buzzard circled overhead. We also managed to attract the gaze of the hotel's two pet monkeys, which had wrapped themselves around a couple of guests seated near by.

The constantly smoking crater of Volcán Masaya, the most spectacular of Nicaragua's 58 volcanoes

That afternoon we drove to Altagracia for a tour of the **Ometepe Museum**, where a schoolgirl took our money and pointed towards the first exhibit. This is not a very glamorous place, but there are archaeological remains on display that date back to pre-Columbian times. Most of the exhibits aren't dated so as to deter thieves, but we saw pottery, ceramics, decorative figures, and some jewellery. Outside were large stone statues engraved with petroglyphs made by the Chorotegas, an Indian tribe that migrated south from Mexico. It is believed that the Chorotegas, along with Nahuatl tribes, came here because a prophecy told them to find an island with two mountains rising from a freshwater sea.

We made our way back to Moyogalpa along the same gravel road. There is, essentially, only one road on the island that skirts the coastline. It splits on the east side, one branch leading to Balgue in the north and the other winding to Mérida on the south coast. The road terminates at these two towns so that the rest of the island is accessible only by horse or boat, or on foot.

At **Moyogalpa** Nic, Juan, and I checked into the Hotel Pirata. This is one of only three hotels in the town, all of which are quite basic but adequate for a few days. That evening, while we were strolling around the town, a man invited us into his house. Inside, he showed us a cabinet full of ancient Indian artefacts. There were old pots, jewellery, and stones depicting wide-eyed faces, while outside he had a treasure trove of larger items. His proudest find was some burial pots shaped like gourds. Everything, he told us, was for sale. I asked if this was legal, but he didn't answer the question directly and said instead that there was so much "treasure" lying about that the authorities don't seem to take much notice. We left the house empty-handed, and went back to our hotel for an early night.

EXPLOSIVE REGION

The whole of Central America is an active seismic region, where the Pacific tectonic plate is colliding with the Caribbean plate and being subducted under it. As the Pacific plate is driven down into the mantle, it melts to create lava, which is then forced up to the surface through fissures in the crust. It is this eruption of lava that leads to the formation of volcanoes. Earthquakes are also common in Nicaragua, and are the result of pressure releases along the tectonic boundary. Volcán Concepción on Ometepe Island is an active volcano, and has erupted 24 times since 1883—the last one took place as recently as 1986.

EARLY START

The driver picked us up at 5am outside the hotel, the motor of his Mitsubishi jeep thundering away. We made the figure-of-eight drive to Balgue on the other side of the island, passing Santo Domingo beach where we had been the day before. It rained for most of the journey, although the sun did shine once or twice through a tiny slit in the blanket of clouds that still covered both peaks. Just before Balgue we stopped outside a lone house to pick up our guide. No one was in, so we moved on to another house where the sleepy owner greeted us dressed in shorts and shabby flip-flops. He looked at us and then said, "I'm not taking you up that volcano, it would be like going to hell." Instead, he gave us the name of a young man in the centre of town who might agree to help us.

Ramiro said he would guide us. While he packed his belongings, Nic and I wandered over to the local store to buy a Coke. Freshly baked bread was laid out in wicker baskets on the counter, and we couldn't resist a couple of small loaves. We told the girl serving us that we were going to climb up **Madera**. She gasped with horror and told us we were mad. She was 22, had lived in the village all her life,

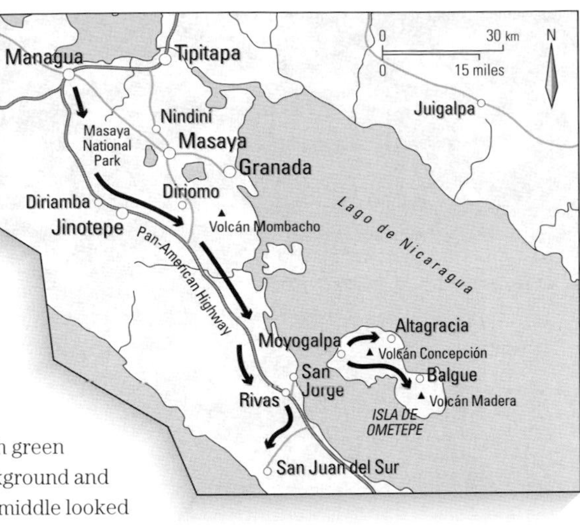

The volcanic area by Lago de Nicaragua

and had reluctantly climbed the volcano for the first time the previous year with some friends. She showed us pictures of her adventure: five of them smiled triumphantly out of one photo, taken at the lagoon. I thought the lush green cape of forest in the background and piercing blue lake in the middle looked worth any hardship.

The trek started sedately enough through open fields of rice, changing to denser plantations of plantain that led us to a wooden building called Magdalena Farm. A young girl greeted us and asked if we wanted breakfast. This is the last building on the route, and it is also acts as a check-in point for anyone attempting the ascent. There was a simple restaurant and bar with basic lodging suitable for hardened backpackers. We said no to breakfast and instead headed straight off into the thick forest.

Ramiro and Juan set a fast pace. I struggled to keep up, and was glad when they stopped to pick the fruit from a plantation of cacao (cocoa) trees. These were held sacred among the native Indians, who used the seeds as a form of currency. Ramiro cut a pod down and opened the outer flesh with his bayonet; inside were broad-bean-sized seeds packed together tightly and surrounded by a white casing. At least the bitter chocolate taste provided some diversion from the thought of another six hours' climbing.

After a further hour Ramiro and Juan paused by some large, dark stones beside the muddy path. They had been engraved with playful images of faces and swirling patterns. Eventually we stopped for a late breakfast at the second shelter of three on the mountain. Here, Ramiro peeled the lid off a plastic bowl to reveal a brown, stodgy mass of beans, rice, and plantain. I poured a sachet of electrolyte powder into my water bottle, sipped on the salty, sweet mixture, and gazed at the uninterrupted view to the curved bay down below at Santo Domingo. Behind us howler monkeys barked while parrots darted near by. We were only at the 540-m (1,770-foot) mark, with 855m (2,805 feet) still to go.

At the three-hour point my calf and thigh muscles started to feel numb. The rain came down so hard that I no longer cared about trying to keep dry, and even my fingers had become wrinkled from the constant wetness. I had to stop every fifteen minutes to catch my breath.

Reaching the Top

Eventually we made it, and climbed down the lip of the volcano to the crater lake. Ramiro tied his rope to a tree stump, and we took it in turns to lower ourselves gently down the near-vertical slope so that we could walk the rest of the way to the lake. The mist was so thick that we could see only as far as the grassy bank. We took a few pictures in the rain, not really stopping to think of our achievement as we knew that we had three more hours to go before we would be back

ABOVE Ferries to Isla de Ometepe dock at Moyogalpa, in the west of the island
LEFT Creating a rope picture: one of the many crafts on view and on sale in the city of Masaya

down again. We scaled back up the lip of the lagoon and started our descent.

The rain fell harder, if that was possible, forming a river in the muddy path. Ferns and leaves lining the way licked our arms and faces, while exposed roots crisscrossed the route like trip-wires. At first, the walk down was easy, but after two hours my legs started to lock up. I stopped to rest, wondering if I'd ever make it. I fell over a lot, mostly from exhaustion, and was so tired that I almost missed a howler monkey sitting on a branch just a few feet above my head. It didn't look very concerned by my presence, as I slowly ducked under its tail and looked back at its dark face. And then up ahead I heard the chattering of women and children. The others had stopped to clean their boots in a pool where two women were washing their

clothes, bashing and scrubbing them on top of a worn stone.

At last Magdalena Farm appeared in a clearing. We all stopped here for a drink. I pulled off my boots, peeled away my sodden socks, and then slumped in one of the hammocks with a beer. I smiled for the first time that day and wondered how I ever did it.

Ramiro invited us for a coffee back at his house, fortunately only a short walk away. Inside the living room a boy was watching *Conan the Barbarian* on the television. I pulled up a wooden rocking chair and looked around the room. There were coffins scattered all over the house—there was even one in the main bedroom. It turned out that Ramiro's father is the village carpenter, and he was stocking up in the expectation of a busy summer. I asked him if he minded the coffins being stored in his house, but he simply smiled at me and said he wasn't afraid of death.

More volcanoes

Ometepe is not the only place in Nicaragua where you can see a volcano. The country has 58 volcanoes in all, the most spectacular of which is Masaya (meaning where the grass burns), just 27km (17 miles) south of Managua. It is still active, and the smoke billowing out of its huge cone is a fearsome sight. The volcano last erupted on March 16, 1772, when it spewed out the 15-km (9-mile) lava flow that now forms part of the **Parque Nacional Masaya (Masaya**

MASAYA STATISTICS

- The temperature below the crust in the volcano's crater reaches 850°C (1,562°F).
- The crater measures 500m (1,650 feet) in diameter and 200m (650 feet) deep.
- The volcano discharges 1,000 tonnes (985 tons) of sulphur a day and has been smoking for over 200 years, since its last eruption in 1772. The emissions have created an environmental disaster as nothing grows for 30km (20 miles) along the path of this deadly smoke, which fortunately is usually blown from east to west, away from Managua.

National Park), the first such park in Nicaragua.

The park opened in 1979, and contains a unique tropical savannah and dry forest ecosystem covering an area of 54sq km (21 square miles). A tarmacked road leads all the way up Masaya and the adjacent Nindirí. There are three craters at the top, of which Santiago is the only one still active—it emits sulphurous gases. At the entrance to the park is an excellent museum, so we paid our 40-cordoba fee and drew up outside. We then drove the 5km (3 miles) to the top of the crater and parked in the large car park, where a woman was selling coconuts for 5 cordobas. We walked to the edge and peered into the eye of the crater. Smoke bellowed out, sounding like a rushing wind and blending into the clouds. Occasionally a load cracking noise echoed from below as the crust split.

The Indians believed that Masaya was the entrance to hell, and would throw children and virgins into it as a sacrifice to appease the gods. A cross at the summit was placed there in 1529 by Father Francisco Bobadilla to exorcise demons from the volcano. There are some marvellous views over the park towards the capital. Lava flows dating back some 300 years scar the landscape, most of them still black although lichens, mosses, and other simple plants are colonizing on the bare rock. There is plenty of wildlife here, including coyotes (*Canis latrans*), skunks (*Mephitis mephitis*), racoons, opossums, and bats, although they only appear at night. In the toxic wasteland around the volcano live parakeets and numerous odd-looking insects that have adapted to the conditions.

To the east of the volcano is Masaya lagoon and, adjacent, the lovely city of **Masaya**. The latter is a renowned centre for arts and crafts, where you can find cloth, leather goods, pottery, and cheap hammocks at the local market. Look out also for the cayman crocodiles (*Caiman crocodilius*) that swim in the market's fountains.

It is possible to combine a trip to Masaya with a visit to **Granada**, which lies only 15km (9 miles) away. This charming city, like so many in Nicaragua, also sits in the shadow of a volcano. Volcán Mombacho (Flat Volcano), one of the biggest in the area at 1,400m (4,593 feet) sets off Granada beautifully. Eruptions from this volcano formed the 365 islands on Lake Nicaragua. It sides are swathed in rich vegetation, coffee is grown on the slopes, and it is home to many rare orchids and two endemic species of butterfly. Below, Granada's colourful Spanish buildings and classical Italian architecture have made this city the number one destination in Nicaragua. A tour in one of the many horse-drawn carriages that leave from the old square is the best way to appreciate Central America's oldest colonial city.

Of all the volcanoes in Nicaragua I will remember Madera the most. That unforgettable feeling of conquering one of nature's giants will stay with me for ever. And how can I forget the look on the taxi-driver's face when he saw us all return, refusing to believe that I had made it? He looked at me, staring deep into my tired eyes, and laughed. I didn't care if he believed me or not, and I'd forgotten about the bet. I had made it. I knew it, the volcano knew it, and every muscle in my body knew it.

GOING IT ALONE

INTERNAL TRAVEL

There are 58 volcanoes in Nicaragua, a good number of which can be climbed. It is always best to take a guide as it is very easy to get lost on the bigger volcanoes such as Mombacho, Madera, Concepción, and Masaya. Managua is a good base for all these volcanoes.

The ferry from San Jorge to Moyogalpa costs $1.50 per person and $10 per vehicle. There is a regular bus service on the island, with buses leaving every hour from Moyogalpa. It takes about 2 hours to get to Balgue on the other side of the island, only 29km (18 miles) away; hiring a jeep will halve that journey time. Whatever form of transport you opt for on the island, plan on having an uncomfortable journey.

WHEN TO GO

Volcano treks can be undertaken at any time of year, but the dry season (December–April) is obviously the best time. Even then, rain is not unusual in the forests surrounding some of these volcanoes.

PLANNING

The best way to organize a trip up a volcano is through a tour operator in Managua. That said, it is very easy to find a guide on Ometepe Island by asking at any of the hotels or *albergues* in Moyogalpa. Often even that isn't necessary: I was stopped twice whilst walking down the main street and asked if I needed a guide to go up either Madera or Concepción. Such guides will usually be young, however, so be wary if you are approached by anyone who doesn't look fit.

TRAVELLERS' TIPS

- Meals are not usually provided by guides, so take a packed lunch and plenty of water. High-energy bars and glucose tablets are also recommended for a quick boost.
- Guides will often point out a range of edible plants on the trek, but if you choose to taste the temptations of this jungle supermarket do so only in moderation as a stomach cramp halfway into a 7-hour trek will be very uncomfortable. The guide will also drink water from fresh mountain springs, and will often suggest that you do the same. This water should be pure, but if you are in any doubt use a water-purification bottle.

WHAT TO TAKE

- There are no specialist shops on Ometepe, so stock up before you arrive.
- Walking boots.
- Waterproofs.
- Binoculars for viewing wildlife, although if they are heavy it may not be worth it.
- Torch (power cuts are quite common on Ometepe).

HEALTH

At Masaya there is a strong smell of sulphur from the smoking volcano, which can affect people with asthma or breathing difficulties. Be careful when drinking from streams or trying edible plants recommended by your guide as you may consequently suffer stomach upsets.

LAKE ACTIVITIES AND SIGHTS

Lake Nicaragua is the largest lake in Central America, measuring 8,157sq km (3,150 square miles). It is thought that it was once part of the Pacific Ocean along with Lake Managua, until volcanic eruptions cut it off and the salt water gradually turned fresh. Saltwater species evolved over time, so that today the lake is home to the world's only freshwater shark, *Carcharhinus nicaraguensis*, as well as to freshwater swordfish and tarpon. Other marine species migrate to the lake along the Río San Juan. Such unusual and abundant fish species make the lake a popular fishing destination, and many locals will be able to recommend a guide.

If you have time then a journey to the Archipiélago de Solentiname, opposite San Carlos at the southern end of the lake, is well worth the effort. The main island is Mancarrón, whose local artists are famous for their naïve paintings and colorful balsa woodcarvings. The archipelago is remote and secluded, and consequently is a haven for wildlife.

The Historic Río San Juan

By Carl Pendle

In the far south of Nicaragua, the graceful Río San Juan hides many of the best-kept secrets of this fascinating country. The only way to discover them is to take a boat out of San Carlos, on Lago de Nicaragua, and explore the historic waterway.

The view out of my plane window should have been an eco-traveller's dream: untouched islands, wild tropical forests, and miles of virgin shoreline outlining Lago de Nicaragua, the largest lake in Central America. I should have seen pockets of neatly tilled fields, cows grazing idly, and the white trails of boats zigzagging between the lake's 365 islands. But this simply was not the case as the tiny single-engined plane was cruising through thick clouds on its 45-minute flight to San Carlos, a small town at the head of the historic Río San Juan in Nicaragua's deep south. We were 15 minutes into the journey, had already passed the Isla de Ometepe to the west, and were heading for the islands of the Archipiélago de Solentiname, which sit like limpets just off San Carlos.

The skies finally cleared just before the plane landed in San Carlos. Down below, beyond the wing, I could make out a few of the 36 islands that form the Solentiname Archipelago. The peaceful-looking islands are home to an abundance of wildlife and a thriving community of artists and poets. We left them behind as the plane banked sharply left for our final approach into San Carlos. We passed inches over coconut palms and banana plants before landing firmly on the bumpy

This trip doesn't require much in the way of fitness; it is a "sit back and enjoy the ride" sort of adventure.

★★ Don't expect any luxury hotels along the San Juan. There are comfortable lodges overlooking this magnificent river, but that is all. Many of the hotels do not have hot running water.

Take binoculars so that you get a good view of the wildlife from the boat. A blow-up neck pillow or a beach ball would be useful for the hard seats on the boat, and don't forget your mosquito net.

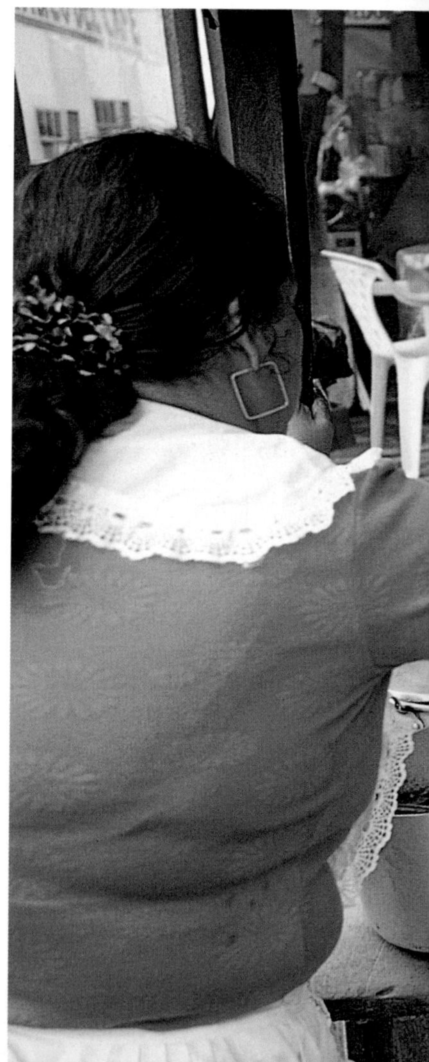

grass and gravel runway. Two soldiers watched us land, while a line of beaten-up blue jeeps, posing as taxis, waited patiently next to a primitive shelter and two wooden outhouses. This was the start of my journey down part of the Río San Juan, a 191km (119-mile) giant that empties into the Caribbean Sea on the other side of the country. This is the watery heel of Nicaragua at the border between neighbouring Costa Rica, where the San Juan's course describes an epic journey past spectacular wildlife, over rapids, and

RIGHT and BELOW San Carlos, on the southern shores of Lake Nicaragua at the head of Río San Juan, is a poor town whose inhabitants work hard at making a living

into forgotten communities.

Many visitors to Nicaragua don't make the effort to head towards the Río San Juan. It's tucked out of the way, unchartered, undiscovered, and very much a mystery. The short daily flight is by far the easiest way of accessing this area; otherwise, it necessitates a six-hour drive along a bumpy road from Managua or a tedious, diagonal 12-hour crossing over Lake Nicaragua from Granada. The area's hub is **San Carlos**, an apocalyptic town with dusty streets, untidy houses, and a desperation carved from utter poverty. As soon as I landed in San Carlos it was impossible not to be fazed by the destitution. From the moment the blue taxi took me from the airport along the unpaved and potholed roads to the centre of town, I knew that the five hours I had to spend here waiting for the boat to take me downriver would pass very slowly indeed.

A poor town

San Carlos hasn't always been a poor, forgotten outpost, but once played an important military role in protecting the area from looting pirates. The wealthy cities of Granada and León in the northwest were particularly vulnerable to attack from pirates, as were the gold-rich Spanish boats that lumbered past here bound for eager kings and queens in Europe. Today, all that remains from those days are the ruins of a fort that overlooks the corrugated-metal roofs of a small community living off the trade and tourists the river brings them. There is a pleasant restaurant called El Mirador next to the fort's old walls, which are embedded with three rusting cannon pointing over the river towards Costa Rica and the start of the **Guatusos Wildlife Refuge**. It is a good viewpoint and local children gather here to fly their homemade kites.

I decided to walk around the town. There were stalls selling shoes, tourist trinkets, car parts, and the usual colourful display of fruit and vegetables. One old woman sat on a wall selling a strawberry-coloured drink, which she carefully ladled from a huge basin into plastic bags pierced with a straw. I saw a small girl walking up and down the main street in her dirty pink dress and worn-out flip-flops shouting "Enchiladas! Enchiladas!", while many of the boys carried shoe-shine boxes, lugging them hopefully into the bars, their hands pitch-black from the polish and their faces smudged from the dirt of their job. It seemed that everyone was trying to get by as best they could.

The real adventure begins

Past the streets of San Carlos, out towards the rippling muscle that is the river, lies a different adventure altogether. It tempts you past the richness of nature and beyond huge conservation areas into jungles, and lets you into its rawness. The history of the river is also as much part of its attractiveness as its natural beauty. It took the Spanish a while to

IMPORTANT WATERWAY

Square-riggers, galleons, schooners, and even paddle-steamers have all journeyed along the Río San Juan, and the river also acted as a major artery for American boats heading for the 1849 gold-rush in California. It is odd to think that east-coast Americans would venture this far south to get to places like San Francisco; but they came in their thousands thanks to Cornelius Vanderbilt, a New York millionaire who formed the Accessory Transit Company. Passengers would board his boats at Greytown (now San Juan del Norte) to ride up the Río San Juan and across Lake Nicaragua to San Jorge port, where they picked up a stagecoach to the Pacific port of San Juan del Sur, only 18km (11 miles) away. Like today, it must have been a pleasant journey, and was certainly quicker and safer than taking the land route across North America.

DEPTH CHANGES

Over the years the geology of the San Juan's bed has changed, sometimes through nature, but more often through the effects of man. One local story tells of a Spanish galleon that travelled up the river on its way to Granada, but never made it back because an earthquake struck the area and changed the depth of the riverbed, thereby making it impassable for the vessel. Later on, the Spanish filled the river with rocks to make the route treacherous for pirates.

find a river that linked Nicaragua to the Atlantic, but they did so in the early part of the 16th century. They must have been dazed by the 45 rivers leading in and out of Lake Nicaragua, and by the size of the lake itself—it is the tenth-largest freshwater lake in the world at 8,157sq km (3,150 square miles). Lake Nicaragua is even home to the world's only freshwater shark, *Carcharhinus nicaraguensis*, which is thought to have adapted to the conditions after the lake was cut off from the Pacific during volcanic eruptions. Once the gateway to Europe had been discovered, the San Juan became a busy artery, carrying ships loaded with gold, silver, and spices. By the 17th century English, French, and Dutch pirates had moved in to take what they could from the Spanish.

Careli Tours, the Managua-based tour company that had arranged this trip, had warned me that the public boat ride from San Carlos up the San Juan to El Castillo was an uncomfortable five-hour journey in cramped conditions. The only consolation was the price: for just $3 I could get a ride, albeit a very slow one, up this magnificent river with the locals. The other option was to hire a private boat, but this privilege would have cost me over $200. After waiting five hours in San Carlos and facing the prospect of another five on a rickety boat, I decided that there must be a quicker way of getting to El Castillo. Boats were everywhere, moored to restaurants and bars, and tied to the wooden stilts of houses—even the children put putted around in crafts resembling boats. Surely one of them was going to El Castillo?

CATCHING A RIDE

After lunch I wandered over to the main gate of the port and indicated to the harbour-master that I wanted to go to El Castillo. He waved me through the gates and introduced me to the captain of a long, thin boat moored at the grassy bank. After scribbling frantically in my notebook to communicate where I wanted to go, I was told that it would cost just $4 for a place on the 22-seater boat.

Nothing is ever guaranteed in Nicaragua, so I took no chances in securing my place on the boat and arrived half an hour before departure—as indeed had many of the other passengers. The seats were arranged two by two all the way down. Being so thin, the boat wobbled whenever anyone shuffled about. I settled near the very front, thinking that I had reserved one of the best seats. Down by my feet were strewn bags full of groceries. A boxed Barbie doll, some matches, and vegetables peered out of one; another contained what looked like coloured water, but as I bent down to take a closer look a rancid aroma filled my nostrils. The bag apparently bulged with the sloppy entrails of some animal, and was later delivered to another boat that passed by us on the river.

Our boat rose out of the water as we picked up speed, the hull see-sawing and creating a frothy wake that splashed into my lap. The two people in front of me took the brunt of the spray, and sat huddled behind a clear polythene sheet tucked up to their necks. The 2½-hour journey went by quickly. The river was mesmerizing. My eyes darted from side to side, scanning the banks for movement, and watching the surface of the water for the rise of a tarpon or a snook. The Río

San Juan varies in width as it journeys towards the Atlantic, and along the way the banks are densely populated with a forest of trees and bushes that define the river like a badly trimmed hedge. The water itself is calm and smooth, its surface only occasionally broken by a turtle's head or the darting stutter of a swallow diving for insects. A few houses line the river, all very basic and mostly made from wood with corrugated-metal roofs. Cattle and horses roam the banks, mingling between the crops that thrive in this tropical climate.

There was a short stop at a town called Sabalos, where three passengers got off. As they did so, children played in the water, demonstrating their diving skills over the canopy of our boat. On the other side of the bank some pigs wallowed in the mud and a few locals stared at us from a bar. Bags of rice sat on the harbour wall awaiting collection.

LEGENDS OF BRAVERY

El Castillo's fort was built in 1675, along with 12 other such fortifications along the length of the river. Its main aim was to block the route for European pirates attempting attacks on Granada and León. In 1762, a 19-year-old woman named Rafaela Herrera helped defend the fort from a British invasion, and today is remembered for sinking some of the attacking fleet as an act of revenge after her father was killed during the fighting. English buccaneer Henry Morgan also fought here, as did a young Horatio Nelson in 1780, when 50 British ships and 2,000 troops attacked the Spanish and briefly held the fort until disease forced them to depart.

THE RIVER TOWN

From Sabalos, it was only a half-hour ride to El Castillo. During that time the shape and atmosphere of the river changed. It became busier as people punted their way down the river in dugout canoes while others whined past in their speedboats. Here we also had our first sight of the rapids; the water was so shallow in places that only an experienced pilot would know where to go.

The boat finally eased into **El Castillo**. Some young boys filled the landing area, eager to help people out of the boat or offering to carry their luggage for a small tip. Everyone hopped out and scattered through the small town, leaving me to head up some wide steps towards the fortress that gave El Castillo its name. Except for a pig tied up to a post, I was alone in the grassy plaza in front of the heavy, triangular building. I walked up the ramp and peered around the corner, checking which way to go. Fortunately, a diagram near the entrance pointed out the various vaults of the fortress. I climbed some more steps, stopping near the top at a classroom and small library. Below here was the museum, where a lady waiting by the door charged me 5 córdobas to look around the few illustrated pictures and artefacts that documented the fort's turbulent history. Unfortunately for me, everything was in Spanish, but it was still worth a look none the less. I rested at the bridge of the fort, turning around to look at its strategic location on the river. The murky waters arched around the town, flowing quickly after the recent heavy rains.

El Castillo viewed from its fort, built by the Spanish to block the route for pirates attempting attacks on Granada and León

RESCUED BY AMERICANS

That afternoon I was supposed to have been met and taken to my pre-paid hotel 20km (12 miles) further downriver at Refugio Bartola. But nobody came to pick me up, and as the phones had been down all day I had no choice but to stay in town at the nearby Albergue El Castillo. Thankfully, I had brought a little extra cash with me.

Later on I met a couple of Americans called Paul and Kevin, who were staying in the same hotel. Paul was working for USAid and Kevin for World Relief Corporation, a religious charity that advises and educates farmers on how to make better use of their land. Luckily, they were heading to San Carlos the next morning in their private boat, and offered me a ride. On the journey back Paul and Kevin wanted to visit the **Indio Maíz Reserve**, opposite the hotel where I was originally booked to spend the night.

By 7am the next morning we were seated in our boat ready to leave El Castillo for the 20-minute ride south to the reserve, which sits amid a 360,000-ha (900,000-acre) protected conservation area. The land here is such virgin territory that many species of plants and insects haven't even been classified yet. The wardens who look after the reserve are rightly proud of this land, and realize that, as eco-tourism is still in its infancy here, the trees are worth far more up than down.

We docked at the reserve and took a guided tour along a 2-km (1¼-mile) trail that encircles an area of secondary forest growth. The original primary forest that was here was destroyed by fire during the war, although you would never have known such devastation had occurred as there are now towering trees and thick undergrowth. The muddy path wound past gum and wild almond trees (*Prunus fascicula*), around lakes, and under palms that the locals use for roofing, and all along the route we heard the sounds of the jungle, from the songs of rare species of birds to the buzzing of insects. Our guide introduced us to the stench of a hogweed plant and pointed out the so-called big-man tree, used to treat malaria and dengue fever, and to help people with low blood pressure. Although we never saw them, he told us to be watchful of snakes, especially the fer de lance (*Bothrops asper*), literally translated as point of the spear. This is an aggressive snake and is among the most dangerous in the world as its venom is highly poisonous and it will bite without provocation; farmers in particular are in constant danger of being bitten whilst tending their crops.

Back on the river we saw a feast of animals, although not any cayman crocodiles (*Caiman crocodilius*), which are reported to live here. Our six-seater boat paused long enough to pick out howler monkeys (*Alouatta palliata*) feeding quietly on some leaves, and we spotted flocks of egrets, lonely herons frozen in their pose, and swallows dive-bombing the surface of the water.

Disaster strikes

Although we reached San Carlos safely, I never managed to leave it that day. My flight was cancelled due to heavy rain in Managua. I had no money, and knew nobody. Again, Kevin came to the rescue and offered me a ride back to the capital in one of World Relief's jeeps. The 289-km (180-mile) journey was slow and painful, as although the roads were straight, they were extremely bumpy. Then, two hours into the journey, a car coming the other way flagged us down to tell us that the road was impassable as a bridge had collapsed up ahead. We turned back to San Carlos, hoping to catch the boat for Granada, but that had departed early for fear of getting caught in the bad weather. That night I stayed with a friend of Kevin's in town.

The next day things improved, and my plane eventually departed into the same grey clouds that had shrouded my arrival two days earlier. For want of a view to admire, I reflected instead on the Río San Juan and its progress into the next century. Perhaps it is a good thing that a canal linking the Atlantic and Pacific never was built here, for if it had been, this area would certainly have lost much of what it has to offer today. There remain few such untouched places in the world, and if you don't mind the hardships and are prepared for the unexpected, then this part of Nicaragua will reward your patience many times over.

GOING IT ALONE

Internal Travel

The port of San Carlos can be accessed in three ways: you can rent a sturdy jeep and battle the bumpy, 6-hour road trip from Managua; catch a boat from Granada; or, by far the easiest option, catch a plane from the capital's Augusto Sandino Airport.

La Costeña operates daily flights to San Carlos in a single-engined 15-seater plane. It is only a 45-minute flight, and a return ticket costs $100.

The boat journey to San Carlos from Granada departs on Mondays and Thursdays at 2pm, arriving in San Carlos 12 hours later. The same boat leaves San Carlos for Granada on Tuesdays and Fridays at 3pm. A single ticket costs 40 cordobas ($4). A public boat leaves San Carlos for El Castillo, a journey of 5 hours, but as it is cheap it tends to be quite crowded. The other option is to charter a private boat, which will be much faster and more comfortable but obviously substantially more expensive. The army continues to monitor all boats that leave San Carlos, but the strict rules on who can charter boats seems to be relaxing. You can also simply turn up at the port, where you will be able to hop on a boat that will take you downriver quickly and cheaply.

When to Go

Most of the Pacific lowland is warm year round. The rainy season runs from May to November, although the rain is rarely constant and usually falls as heavy downpours in the afternoon. December through January is a good time to visit as the weather is drier yet the countryside is still green. During March and April, the hottest time of year, it can be very dusty, especially when the wind blows.

Planning

To save yourself a lot of hassle it is definitely much easier to book things through one of the good tour operators in Managua. That said, it is possible to organize the trip yourself: many of the hotels in San Carlos and El Castillo will have rooms available in the low season, and booking the flight is straightforward.

You can easily travel to Costa Rica from San Carlos via Los Chiles, 20 minutes away along the Río Frío. From Los Chiles there is an excellent highway to San José (5–6 hours). You can therefore plan any combination of tours starting in Costa Rica and continuing to Nicaragua, or vice versa. San Carlos is an international entry point for Nicaragua, so if you enter or exit the country through this town normal immigration and customs procedures and costs will apply.

Travellers' Tips

- ❑ It is essential to ensure that your name is on the flight list for the journey back to Managua. Go to the La Costeña office in the centre of San Carlos and actually watch the staff write your name down for the return flight. The plane is notorious for being overbooked, so if yours is not in the top 15 names on the list you could well have to wait for the following day's flight. Also remember that the flight may be delayed or cancelled during the rainy season due to bad weather.
- ❑ It is not necessary to have a guide for this trip, but one can be arranged through a tour operator in Managua or by asking around in San Carlos. If you don't speak Spanish, remember that very little English is spoken in this part of Nicaragua and tourism is still very much in its infancy here.
- ❑ It is possible to travel the entire length of the Río San Juan. To do so it is best to negotiate with a guide in San Carlos.
- ❑ The river and lake are fantastic for fishing, and many of the locals will be able to recommend a good guide who can help you land that dream fish.

What to Take

- ❑ Spanish phrasebook.
- ❑ Basic first-aid kit.
- ❑ Blow-up neck pillow to act as a cushion for the long boat ride.
- ❑ Lightweight waterproof jacket or small umbrella to keep the spray off during the boat ride.
- ❑ Mosquito net and insect repellent.

Health

Don't swim in the water; the locals say it is unpolluted and the children play happily around its banks, but don't take the risk as you are a long way from a well-equipped hospital. Be wary of snakes but don't be paranoid about them. Most of the time they won't bother you, especially if you stick to footpaths.

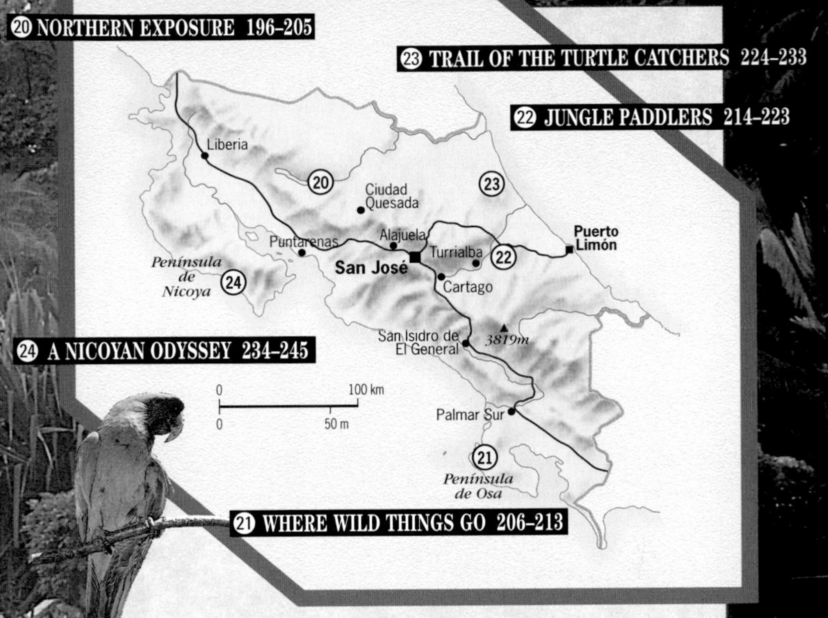

COSTA RICA

For such a small country, Costa Rica boasts an incredible diversity of landscapes, from lowland tropical rain forest and high mountain paramo to pristine beaches and spectacular coral reefs, all of which are are home to a bewildering range of wildlife. Add to this diversity a well-developed tourism infrastructure and it is easy to understand why the country is experiencing a surge in popularity amongst travellers who come in search of a real adventure without all the hardships usually associated with travel in the region. Although it does lack the indigenous cultures of other Latin American countries, Costa Rica is in the premier division for adventure and wildlife. It offers most outdoor activities imaginable, and a host of opportunities for encountering exotic flora and fauna. If you so wish, you are almost guaranteed to see monkeys, toucans, turtles, and crocodiles, and you can see them whilst biking, hiking, kayaking or four-wheel driving. With facilities to suit every budget level, Costa Rica is a good choice for first-time travellers to Central America and for those who want a hassle-free action holiday.

*Tabacón Hot Springs, Costa Rica, with Volcán Arenal looming in the background; ABOVE A Great Green Macaw (*Ara ambigua*)*

Northern Exposure

By Steve Watkins

Northern Costa Rica is a cocktail of vast farmsteads, quirky churches, labyrinthine caves, and brooding volcanoes. I took to the roads in a four-wheel drive, braving the country's haphazard motorists, and followed a scenic tour along the highland route from San José to La Fortuna.

The most hair-raising adventure in Costa Rica has to be driving. Almost every taxi-driver I met in San José told me so, and it did look a bit scary from the passenger seat. I wondered how my nerves would survive when I took to the driver's seat for a long journey north through the country's coffee-rich highlands to a place where nature's awesome power can be seen on a daily basis. The region surrounding Volcán Arenal (Arenal Volcano) is one of the most popular destinations in the country, and I wanted to find out why, on my own.

From watching traffic on previous trips, I had gained the impression that driving in Costa Rica is based on three principles: rights of way do not exist; both sides of the road are fair game for all traffic at all times; and no matter how slow you drive or how hard you concentrate, the potholes will always get you in the end. It certainly isn't something to be undertaken by the faint-hearted, so if you find driving in the rush hour a stressful experience at home it is probably best to take a bus or hire a car and driver. However, the freedom of exploration offered by having your own transport is invaluable, even in a country with such an efficient bus system. If you do go it alone be sure to hire a four-wheel drive.

This tour is open to most levels of fitness, with nothing more challenging than a few gentle hikes. Visiting La Caverna del Venado (Venado Cave) is more adventurous though, and whilst it doesn't require high fitness levels, it does need a positive attitude, a love of water, and no phobias about either bats or enclosed spaces.

★★ Generally, this tour is fine if you are looking for a fairly soft adventure. The only exception is the caving, where you will get wet and dirty. Accommodation can be arranged to suit all budget levels.

All specialist equipment is provided for the caving. Lightweight hiking boots are useful for the waterfall and jungle hikes. No other special equipment is needed.

The quickest way out of the capital is to follow the toll-road via Alajuela, before taking the well-signed right turn towards Grecia, 18km (11 miles) to the northwest. On leaving the Pan-American Highway, the road immediately starts to twist and climb into lush, green country where the hills are dominated by sugarcane and coffee. Along the roadside, the low, wooden homes all have richly decorated gardens overflowing with bright flowers, for the Costa Ricans revel in the natural beauty that flourishes all around them. Don't admire them for too long, however, or a big truck may be upon you before you realize it.

Grecia is a small, unassuming agricultural centre dealing in pineapples and sugar, but the main reason to stop here is to visit the remarkable metal **church of Las Mercedes**. After the initial church burnt down in a fire, it was rebuilt in 1958 using sheet metal imported from Belgium. Painted rust-red with bright white piping around the windows and doors, the twin-spired church looks rather like a toy, but with its solid, riveted walls, it will certainly survive longer than the first one.

An ox-cart family

The back roads in this area are in better condition than the main highways, have far less traffic on them, and generally pass through prettier landscapes, so although they may be slower, I found them much more relaxing. Just 15 minutes or so from Grecia I drove into **Sarchí**, home of Costa Rica's famous painted ox-carts (*carretas*). With several factory shops to choose from along the main road, I decided to stop at Fábrica de Carretas Chaverri, the oldest factory in town. By chance, Joaquín Chaverri Jr., the 65-year-old son of the factory's founder, was there. Sitting on a slightly faded but still colourful old cart that was painted by his father 50 years ago, Joaquín took great pleasure in explaining the legend of the ox-cart. Pulled by two oxen, these sturdy, cedarwood vehicles were once used, unadorned, to move sugarcane, coffee beans, and firewood along the poor-quality dirt tracks in the rugged highland mountains.

As there were no other forms of transport available, the carts were also often used to take family members into town, especially to church on Sundays. With the families dressed in their best clothes, the carts looked scruffy in comparison, so, around 1910, it occurred to local men to paint them. The level of competition soon grew—just as today's young lads compete to have the best-looking car in town—and led to an explosion of elaborate designs, many inspired by Moorish images. By the 1930s, a family's status was judged by how pretty its ox-cart was, and the wealthier families invested in two carts, one simply painted for the fields and another more elaborately decorated for parading around town. Top ox-cart artists commanded great respect and good wages. Designs included flowers, birds, animals, and a variety of symmetrical patterns all linked by one common factor: bright colour. It must have been a cheery town centre indeed on Sundays or during weddings. As cars became more widespread in the 1960s, the art form of the ox-carts became more important than their usage, and artists dedicated themselves to creating new, more elaborate designs.

By the 1970s traditional usage had all but died away and demand for the carts fell sharply at a local level but grew internationally. The boom in tourism brought new buyers to town and Sarchí's factories altered their production to suit the new market. Lighter woods were used

SINGING OX-CARTS

Sarchí's ox-carts were more than just a method of transport; they were an indication of a family's status. Before it became popular to paint them, it was the resonant quality of the rhythmic clanking sound of the mahogany wheels on iron axles, affectionately known as the "song of the ox-cart," that distinguished well-made, expensive carts from cheaper, mediocre ones. It is claimed that each cart had such a distinct sound that wives could tell from over a mile away when their husbands were coming home from the fields.

FAKE SPEEDING FINES

There are increasing incidences of hire cars being stopped by police in order to levy "on-the-spot" fines. One couple I met paid $80 after negotiating the fine down from $200. In truth, there are no fines that need to be paid immediately. Ask the police officer for his name, number, station, and a written report about the nature of the offence, and then insist on going to the station to pay the fine. If you really weren't speeding then he will probably give in at this stage and let you off with a warning. There are many legitimate speed traps set up on roads across the country, especially at weekends and during public holidays.

to make smaller carts that were easier to export. These days, business is healthy again and the factory shops now resemble supermarkets, though the carts are still hand-painted in the attached workshops. Each cart takes around four days to complete. Joaquín has been painting carts since he was 13 years old, and his obvious love for the singing *carretas* and his scheme to train new painters ensures that this wonderful art form will endure.

FANTASY GARDEN

After a brief stop in Sarchí's main plaza to admire the beautiful pale pink church, I headed for Naranjo and onto the main road north to Zarcero. Apart from being too timid to overtake a very slow truck on a twisting section of road, I was actually starting to drive like a Costa Rican, paying scant regard to people walking in the road, cutting corners, and making turns without indicating.

Zarcero would be an ordinary highland town if it were not for Evangelisto Blanco. Since 1964, he has single-handedly and single-mindedly (he works seven days a week, year round) created a unique collection of giant whimsical cypress-bush sculptures. Fantastic elephants, dancing couples, raging bulls, and a tunnel of arches have turned the square into a bizarre playground for the imagination. Again, my luck was in, for Evangelisto was there, clipping away with his shears. The quiet, humble man showed me photographs of his past creations and spoke with passion of the ideas he has for new figures. I asked him where his inspiration comes from. Pointing to the heavens, he simply replied "*El Maestro*" (the Master). Within the confines of tiny Zarcero, Evangelisto has created something that may well be unique in the world…inspiration indeed.

Shortly beyond Zarcero, the scenery began to change. I had now crossed over the

LEFT A footbridge leads across the river to the restaurant at La Garza ranch hotel
RIGHT New crops growing near Zarcero. Much of the rich farmland in the foothills of the Cordillera Central is given over to coffee and sugarcane

main ridge of the Cordillera Central. Villages became few and far between, and pockets of cloud forest lined the roadside. Where the land was cleared it was strange to see herds of black and white Holstein dairy cattle, and with its green fields and rolling hills the scenery looked remarkably like England. I was soon snapped out of my delusion. The road dropped sharply through San Carlos to the timber town of Florencia, in the hot and humid lowlands, where palm trees and sugarcane dominated the landscape. Rather than head to popular La Fortuna, a small town nestling at the base of Arenal Volcano, I decided instead to try the more tranquil setting of La Garza ranch hotel on the main road to Muelle San Carlos. It was starting to get dark and the road had deteriorated into a mass of huge potholes that were hard to spot; I missed a few by swerving across the road but there were always more lying in wait. Thankfully, La Garza was not too far away.

Located in a 90-year-old hacienda, with over 1,000ha (2,500 acres), **La Garza** is a working dairy and plantation ranch owned by the Cantillo family.

CAVE FORMATION

Limestone caves like La Caverna del Venado are mainly formed by the solvent action of water and of acids contained within water. Over thousands of years the acidic water solution dissolves the limestone to create chambers, so the bigger the chamber the older it is. At Venado, the effects of downward seepage of surface water are combined with the highly erosive action of the underground Río de la Muerte. The river has created long, narrow tunnels with smooth sides, while the seepage has formed the half-dome-shaped rooms and the many fanciful rock formations.

Aberlado Cantillo, a pioneering cattleman, bought the property in 1947 and developed it into the largest ranch in the area. His son, Carlos, now runs the property and has harnessed the financial power of tourism without compromising the hacienda's work. Just 12 beautiful wooden bungalows line the bank of the Río Platanar, each with an uninterrupted view across the plains to **Arenal Volcano**. As part of the move towards attracting eco-tourists, Carlos has established a private biological reserve that protects a large area of forest on the edge of the plantation. Howler monkeys, poison-dart frogs, and toucans can all be seen here, and horseriding tours take in both the forest and the plantation area.

UNDERGROUND ADVENTURE

However, I wanted to venture further afield and decided to spend the following day exploring the volcano area. I was up at dawn, and drove towards La Fortuna to watch the sunlight creep down the broad flanks of Arenal. During the rainy season (May–November), the summit is regularly covered in cloud and, true to form, clouds soon welled up from the plains to cloak the crater. **La Fortuna** is a one-street town with only 5,000 residents, but because it is located near the base of Arenal Volcano it has become the main centre for adventure activities in the north. Small tour agencies fill every spare building and the competition keeps prices at very reasonable levels. Perhaps the best-value adventure is a trip underground into the extensive **Venado Cave** system. As I had my own transport I could cut out the agent, so I drove northwest out of La Fortuna on the road to San Rafael de Guatuso. After about 25km (15 miles) a small left turn led to a rollercoaster road to Venado village, where the bitumen ended for the final short, rough section to Las Cavernas farm (not very well signed, but ask in the village for "Las Cavernas"). The farm has showers (very cold!), changing rooms, and a small restaurant for cavers.

Northern Costa Rica

By chance, I met Gustavo Quesada, an adventure-mad Costa Rican from San José who had assisted in mapping the 2.5-km (1½-mile) long cave system. He was taking his cousin, Tim, a lively middle-aged American, and Priscilla, a young expat Costa Rican now living in California, on a private tour and invited me to join them. Wearing helmets and headlights supplied at the farm, we strolled down into the valley and clambered through some trees to the cave entrance. Any thoughts of avoiding getting wet ended as we stepped through the doorway into a knee-deep pool. The cave has been carved from the limestone hills by the ominously named Río de La Muerte (River of Death), and was undoubtedly used and explored by the indigenous Guatuso people, who named the cave Gabinarraca. In modern times, Frenchman Robert Vergnes conducted the first serious exploration of the cave in 1962, but it has been the subsequent work of the Anthros Speliological Group that has made most contribution to the knowledge of the whole system.

Blind as a Bat

Our headlamps pierced the darkness, lighting up the creamy brown sidewalls along a long, narrow stretch with a high roof. Occasionally, a bat would cross the light beam, causing me to duck instinctively even if it was flying away. The further in we walked, the warmer and more humid it became, making T-shirts and shorts the ideal clothing. The roof got lower and the turns tighter as we passed through a beautiful waterfall, and we soon found ourselves scrambling around rocks, squeezing through holes, and wading through rivers. Beautiful stalactites, thick-based stalagmites, and wonderful hanging tables made the cave look like a wierd fantasy landscape from a science-fiction movie. At one point we saw a large, round stalactite that looked like a pumpkin and, to my surprise, we came across a spider species that has adapted to life in the cave by becoming more sensitive to heat and movement to compensate for its loss of sight in the pitch-black environment.

In Room 5, where a stunning rippled wall looked like the pipes of a church organ, Gustavo asked us if we wanted to continue. To reach the Room of the Virgin, not normally included on general tours, we would have to crawl through a very low, narrow, water-filled tunnel. An instant and unanimous "Yes" reflected the amount of fun we were having. Gustavo wasn't joking about the tunnel. The roof was so low that there was only enough room for our heads, but not the helmets, above the level of the water. Holding our helmets and headlights to see where we were going, we shuffled on our hands and knees through the 10-m (25-foot) long passage to emerge in a tiny chamber. For Tim, this was the end of the road. The final section to the Virgin Room involved a seemingly impossible tight squeeze between two rocks. Tim was certainly not overweight, but to get through you needed to be as slim as a hungry whippet. It took some stern mental control to avoid panicking when I was halfway through and squirming to manoeuvre my rib cage around a slight bulge in the boulder. It was certainly worth the effort. The room was immense and had a white-limestone, multi-level waterfall at the end. There wasn't much time to spare as Gustavo was keen to get back before the afternoon rains arrived, which, if heavy enough, had the potential to swell the water levels in the cave and trap us.

After lunch, we made a brief excursion to the Río Fortuna waterfall, just 6km (4 miles) out of town along a very rough dirt track, suitable only for four-wheel-drive vehicles. From the car

LEFT The stunning limestone formations in the extensive Venado Cave system include this organ-pipe wall in Room 5
BELOW Volcán Arenal's near-perfect cone looks peaceful in the dawn light, but appearances can be deceptive: it is, in fact, one of the most active volcanoes in the world

park, it was a short walk to a lookout over the spectacular fall, which plummets 30m (100 feet) from a V-shaped cleft in the black cliff into a round, emerald-green pool that is surrounded by rain forest. To get closer, we followed a long, twisting, muddy trail (with steps and rope handrails in very tricky parts) down a steep slope through the forest. The thunderous roar grew louder until, at the base of the fall, it was almost impossible to hear each other speak. The water was freezing but Tim and Priscilla braved a swim, only to find that the currents continually pushed them back to shore. Having had all the pleasure, we then had to endure the exhausting climb back up to the car park.

RIVERS OF STONE

Perhaps the most popular activity with visitors to La Fortuna is volcano-watching, in the hope that they will witness one of Arenal's reasonably regular eruptions. There are numerous volcano tours on offer in town, including hikes to old lava flows and night-time walks to watch the new lava tumbling from the crater. However, there is a cheaper option for people willing to go it alone. **Jungla y Senderos** is a resort complex situated right below the volcano on the road to Tilarán. Entry is only $5 for the day and there are plenty of trails, lakes, and lava flows to explore. With a four-wheel-drive vehicle, or by walking for around 45 minutes up a steep track, it is possible to reach the first of two breathtaking lakes, where a lookout platform gives spectacular views across the clear, green water to the volcano. From the back of the lake, which has basic hut accommodation on its shores, I hiked up a volcanic-ash trail onto the lower slopes of Arenal. After 30 minutes the trail ran into the old lava flow, which dates back 6,000 years, and then continued above the tree line. Unfortunately, cloud had enveloped the summit. A slight rumbling from above didn't make me feel like hanging around for it to clear, so I hurriedly made my way back to the lake, only to realize that the rumble was an imminent thunderstorm and not an eruption after all.

After a very active day, I met up with my fellow cavers again and we treated our bodies to a night at the luxurious **Tabacón Hot Springs**. Heated by the lava of Arenal, the water that emerges in the wonderfully landscaped, tropical grounds of Tabacón is a perfect 38°C (100°F) all year round. A revitalizing massage in the health centre and a pummelling under a hot waterfall made the stresses of the day simply melt away. As darkness descended, we sat in the main pool, sipped ice-cold beers from the poolside bar, and waited for the moment that everyone comes to see. Loud gasps greeted the eventual eruption of thick, red, glowing lava that poured out of the crater and began running down the slopes, like luminous honey down the sides of a jar. The display can even feature mini explosions of red-hot rocks, accompanied by rumbles and crashes, although it does all depend on the weather—clouds often hide the summit during the rainy season.

Arenal was dormant from about A.D. 1500 until July 28, 1968, when a large earthquake shook the region and blew the top off the volcano with devastating consequences. Two villages were destroyed by lava flows and at least 65 people died. These days, the daunting, conical profile of Arenal dominates the surrounding flat plains, and it remains one of the most active volcanoes in the world. A foolhardy few insist on climbing to its summit, but it was far more enjoyable to observe it from the safety of the hot springs. Watching the lava creep down the black slopes above us, I asked Gustavo why we were issued with luminous-green identity tags on entering Tabacón. "Oh, one of the villages destroyed in 1968 was right here," he replied. It seems that even the so-called softer adventures, such as driving and relaxing in tropical hot springs, carry an extra edge in Costa Rica.

GOING IT ALONE

Planning

It really is a tough decision between driving yourself, where the freedom to explore is maximized, and going by bus, which limits you to the main areas. Perhaps the ideal, though more expensive, answer is to hire a car and a driver. This service is available via most of the major car-hire companies (located in San José). It would certainly make the journey more pleasurable, because although driving is quite fun once you get used to the roads, it does require total concentration, leaving little time to admire the scenery. It is wise to shop around as prices and standards of vehicles can vary quite alarmingly. Fuel is reasonably priced.

La Garza hotel offers tours to Arenal and Venado Cave, or you can find numerous agencies in La Fortuna, which run all the above trips and many more; recommended agencies include Sunset Tours and Aventuras Arenal. Organized tours to Venado Cave normally leave early in the morning, so if you are going independently and want to join a group get there by eight o'clock (you may have to pay more for a private tour).

When to Go

The dry (and therefore busy) season in northern Costa Rica is December–April, when accommodation should be booked in advance. During the rainy season (June–October) there are still sunny spells, prices drop considerably, and there are fewer visitors. At this time the waterfalls are more spectacular, although Venado Cave may be closed during periods of heavy rain.

Travellers' Tips

- ❑ Remember to take your driving licence (international licences are not necessary) to hire a car.
- ❑ Many hire cars have had a rough life by the time you get behind the wheel; be careful tocheck the previous-damage sheet meticulously and go around the car thoroughly before you leave the hire office. Don't be afraid to point out minor scratches, open the bonnet and boot, and check under the car. Such caution could save you your substantial deposit. There is always a non-waivable collision damage clause that means you have to pay the first part of any damage bill. This can be quite high.
- ❑ If you wish to purchase a large craft item from Sarchí and have it shipped home, then it is worth buying it at one of the more established stores. They have good track records for fulfilling orders and packing them in a such way that the risk of damage is minimized.
- ❑ Caving is a very soft sport, but you should avoid the temptation to wander off from the group during the tour. The route may seem obvious, but it can soon become complex and there are numerous tunnels that look remarkably similar without the advice of a knowledgeable guide. If you do get lost, then stop and stay in one place as trying to find your way back may take you further off course, thus making the job of trying to locate you even harder.
- ❑ Do not be alarmed by the close proximity of flapping bat wings in the cave. The bats have very advanced radar systems that allow them to manoeuvre precisely around your ears!
- ❑ Refuse any "guide" who offers to take you up Volcán Arenal. Such an ascent is incredibly dangerous—over the years several people have paid the ultimate price for ignoring the warnings.

What to Take

- ❑ Sunglasses.
- ❑ Cassette tapes for the journey (radio stations are hard to tune into).
- ❑ Old clothes for caving.
- ❑ Good waterproof headtorch.
- ❑ Swimming costume for the hot springs.
- ❑ A good map, such as Berndtson & Berndtson's 1:650,000 laminated *Costa Rica—Road Map*.
- ❑ Hiking boots.

Health

Malaria is not a high risk in the highlands, although medical precautions are still recommended (consult your doctor). In Venado Cave there are large amounts of bat droppings, and while there have been no reports of subsequent illness, it is advisable to wear old clothes and to dispose of these after your visit. Some people wear a facemask to reduce any possible risk of infection through inhalation.

Where Wild Things Go

by Steve Watkins

Costa Rica's wildlife-rich Parque Nacional Corcovado (Corcovado National Park) is probably the most pristine rainforest area remaining in Central America today. There are no roads in the area, so I took an exciting all-inclusive boat tour to Marenco Lodge in Bahía Drake, from where I hiked into Corcovado and joined a snorkelling trip to a nearby island.

In Central America, where progress is often measured by how many trees can be replaced by cities, a rain forest on the Osa Peninsula holds out against development with the defiance of Davy Crockett trying to keep the Mexicans at bay in the Alamo. Awkwardly jutting out like a geographical afterthought from Costa Rica's southern Pacific coastline, the peninsula contains an undiscovered gem in a crown full of wilderness jewels, namely Corcovado National Park. The reserve has been described as the most biologically intense place on Earth by *National Geographic*, and is home to the most outstanding tract of coastal rain forest remaining in the region. It is not all trees and wildlife, though. Just getting there, in these roadless lands, involves a fascinating boat journey along the remote Río Sierpe, while a host of deserted beaches, stunning waterfalls, and the beautiful Isla del Caño (Caño Island) promised to provide ample entertainment during my four-day stay.

By bus, it is a six-hour journey from San José to the town of Palmar Sur, gateway to the Osa Peninsula, but by plane it

2 This adventure is quite easy-going and is suitable for most fitness levels. Hiking in the hot and humid Corcovado National Park is the most testing part, but will be tailored to your ability.

★★ The tour requires an adventurous spirit as it is in a very remote area, and involves thrilling journeys in small boats on the open ocean and treks through wild rain forest. The comfort levels depend on the unpredictable weather conditions. The accommodation at Marenco is rustic but comfortable.

Good-quality snorkelling equipment is provided, but as it is heavily used you may want to bring your own mask, snorkel, and fins. Hiking boots are essential for the rain-forest treks.

is a mere hour and the flight offers spectacular views over the Cordillera de Talamanca and the Pacific coastline. Despite the extra cost, Keith, a friend from England, and I chose the latter option and boarded Travelair's 12-seater plane at San José's Tobias Bolaños Airport. When the mountains petered out we came in to land over the tops of vast banana plantations. A bus transfer took us to Sierpe Lodge, departure point for our boat trip down the Río Sierpe to Marenco Lodge in Bahía Drake (Drake's Bay).

Johnny, the guide, loaded our luggage onto the small, white, six-seater launch and fired up the outboard. Leaving behind the banana plantations, we passed Sierpe village and twisted and turned through tropical forest down the broadening river. Without warning, Johnny cut the engine and glided towards the right bank. A large spectacled cayman (*Caiman crocodilius*) was basking in the sun, its open jaws displaying an impressive array of sharp white teeth. Although caymans are territorial, Johnny

RIGHT Toucans are commonly seen in Corcovado; this is the keel-billed species, Ramphastos sulfuratus
BELOW Trails in Corcovado range from short hikes to tough multi-day treks

assured us that they would never attack a boat. Watching it menacingly slide into the brown water as we moved closer, I just hoped he was right. Further down the now broad river, we saw olivaceous cormorants (*Palacorax olivaceous*) perched on tree branches, their long black wings outstretched to dry off after diving for fish.

SURFER'S PARADISE

Nearer the river mouth, forest-draped hills emerged to the south, while on the riverbank rain forest gave way to mangrove swamps. As the tide was out the dense tangle of black mangrove roots was exposed. Johnny safely avoided two sandbars and soon we heard the roar of the open ocean. At its mouth, the river narrowed slightly as rocky outcrops jutted out from Playa Blanca. The surf was pounding and it became clear why we were all wearing life jackets. With great precision Johnny edged forward, watching the developing wave patterns in order to pick the right line of escape. As we slid through a narrow gap between two rocks, the surf ended and the Pacific Ocean began.

Bouncing over the waves, we cut across the arc of Bahía Drake towards Punta San José, passing a couple of eco-lodges on the way. **Bahía Drake** (pronounced "Dra-cay") gained its name after Sir Francis Drake landed here in 1579 during his circumnavigation of the world in the *Golden Hind*. As we pulled into a small, sandy cove guarded by sentinels of black rock, we found it hard to believe that a lodge existed there. A long sweeping beach stretched out to the north, hemmed in by coconut palms and thick forest, and there were few signs of any buildings. The site felt both imposing and remote. Taking off our boots, we jumped into the shallow waves and climbed the seemingly endless steps to **Marenco Lodge**.

The lodge is set high up on the headland and commands sumptuous views out over the Pacific Ocean and Caño Island. Established as a biological research station in 1982, the property was taken over by Costa Rican Señor Henrique in 1997 and is now a privately run tropical forest and wildlife reserve, with facilities to support further study. The 500-ha (1,200-acre) reserve is an important protective buffer zone at the northern end of the Corcovado National Park and has its own remarkable biodiversity. Within its lands are 140 species of mammals, 367 species of birds, 117 species of reptiles and amphibians, and over 6,000 types of insects. Thankfully, the thatch-roofed accommodation bungalows are well sealed! As for sealife, whales and dolphins are often seen in the coastal waters. Best of all, because we were there during the rainy season (May–November), only two other guests shared the experience, compared to the 40 or so that normally stay during the high season (December–January).

COSTA RICA'S NATIONAL PARKS

Over a quarter of Costa Rica's territory is protected as a national park, wildlife refuge, or biological reserve, a greater proportion of land than in any other country in the world. It was the determined effort of Swede Olaf Wessberg that started the process in 1955. He bought a house at Cabo Blanco, at the tip of the Península de Nicoya, and started a personal campaign to have the area surrounding it protected from the ravages of farming. In three years he had raised enough money to buy the area known today as the Reserva Absoluta Cabo Blanco (Cabo Blanco Strict Nature Reserve). In 1969 Santa Rosa became the country's first national park, and today there are 21 throughout the country, although it still takes much effort to protect them from development and farming pressure.

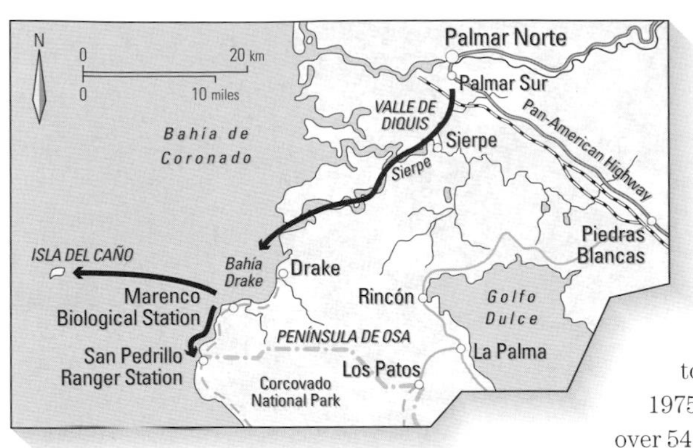

Parque Nacional Corvacado

SHRIEKING MACAWS

With the rest of the day to ourselves, we sat on our bungalow balcony and watched the incredible wildlife in our lush back garden. Delightful, tiny hummingbirds hovered from plant to plant feeding on nectar. Their wings flap so quickly (up to 80 beats per second) that they sound like mellow bees, and they are the only bird species that can fly backwards, courtesy of their fully rotating wings. In the taller trees, two chestnut mandibled toucans (*Ramphastos swainsonii*), with their ridiculously large yellow and chestnut bills and bright yellow chests, showed off their unique side profiles before swooping away like feathered torpedoes. The late-afternoon peace was shattered by the arrival of a flock of shrieking scarlet macaws (*Ara macao*). These large parrots, which mate for life, are impossible to ignore as their shocking red bodies, yellow, blue, and green wings, and raucous behaviour attract attention like a gang of spoilt clowns. Corcovado is home to the largest remaining population of scarlet macaws in Costa Rica, as numbers elsewhere have dwindled with the ongoing destruction of tropical forests.

RAINFOREST HIKE

The following morning, after enjoying a traditional beans and rice breakfast called *gallo pinto*, we packed our daypacks and headed down to the beach to catch the boat to **Corcovado National Park**. Light rainfall forced us to don the capes we had been supplied with for the 25-minute ride down the coast to San Pedrillo Station, the northernmost entrance to the park. Created in 1975, the park now covers over 54,000ha (134,000 acres) and protects at least 13 different habitats, including floating herbaceous swamp in the lagoon area, mangroves along the coast, coral reefs, and high forest on the plateau and in the mountains. The tree canopy, which includes mammoth ceiba trees (*Ceiba pentandra*), reaches up to a height of 60m (200 feet) in places, making it the tallest in the country, and the Lorena Plateau area has over 100 species of trees per hectare (2½ acres). It is also home to some of the world's most endangered species, such as the virtually extinct harpy eagle (*Harpia harpya*) and Baird's tapir (*Tapirus bairdii*), an enormous, long-snouted animal that is one of the world's most ancient large mammals. No wonder *National Geographic* spoke so highly of the park.

There are several long and arduous multi-day trails that run through the park; hikers need to carry substantial amounts of equipment and food, and must have a reasonable amount of rainforest hiking experience. However, most visitors will get a good feel for the area by taking a day hike. With Johnny as our guide, we set off to do a relatively short walk into the northern section, which included a visit to a waterfall. From the rear of the San Pedrillo Station, where rangers are always available to advise on routes and to help should any problems arise, we took a stepped trail up into the damp, dark forest. We didn't have to wait long to see some wildlife. The steps were covered with hermit crabs of various sizes. They crawled around until they sensed our

DEADLY AMPHIBIANS

Poison-dart frogs come in seven different varieties in Costa Rica, three of which exhibit bright colours that help predators to recognize them again if they survive their first taste of the potent toxin secreted from the frog's skin glands. This toxin was used by the Choco Indians of Colombia to poison their blowdart tips, hence the frog's name. In Corcovado, my guide picked up a green and black poison-dart frog knowing that the Costa Rican varieties do not have as powerful a toxin as the blue and red ones of South America, which are potentially lethal for humans. However, it is not wise for visitors to the country to pick up any of these frogs as they can all cause enough of a reaction to spoil your trip for a few days.

ABOVE Although the tiny green and black Costa Rican poison-dart frogs are not as toxic as their blue and red South American counterparts, visitors should never touch one RIGHT Cooling off in a waterfall along Río San Pedrillo, Corcovado

movement, then instantly recoiled into the mobile shell-homes on their backs. A little further on, Johnny pointed out a male red-headed tanager bird (*Cianerpes cyaneus*), with its bright red skullcap and yellow eyes, performing a little courtship dance for a female in a nearby tree.

A MILKY WAY

It took us an eternity to walk just a few hundred yards, as there were so many fascinating things to see and sometimes even feel. Golden orb spiders (*Nevila clavipes*) weave slightly yellow webs the size of dinner plates across the trail. We proved too big a catch and were left to peel the silky threads off our faces and arms while the spider faced up to a morning of reconstruction work. At a milk tree (*Brosimum utile*), Johnny pierced a small hole in the thick bark with his knife. True to its name, a milky sap trickled out; this is used as a cure for stomach upsets but is also supposed to be an aphrodisiac. Shortly after, the heavens opened, turning the trail into a stream, and we were forced to shelter in a large hollow tree. We left before the rain stopped as we were keen to escape the bats that whizzed over our heads inside the trunk.

There are some rather unpleasant serpents in Corcovado, including the venomous and aggressive terciopelos (*Bothrops asper*), known as the fer de lance, and coral snakes (*Micrurus fulvius*). One snake that it is not as dangerous as these is the boa constrictor (*Boa constrictor*). We didn't have such luck as to see one, but we did find a boa's nest surrounded by the feathery remnants of its last meal. Our most exciting find for the day was along a flat section of track right on the park boundary. Somehow, Johnny managed to spot a tiny green and black poison-dart frog (also known as a poison-arrow frog, and a member of the *Dendrobates* genus) leaping around in the leafy floor matter (see box).

As we approached the narrow headwaters of the Río San Pedrillo, the telltale sounds of rustling trees and dropping fruits could be heard just off the trail. High up in the branches, a troop of white-faced capuchin monkeys (*Cebus capucinus*) was scouring the tree,

poking pink noses into everything in search of food. One of them was hanging from a branch by its tail, picking at brown fruit husks below. These small monkeys, which have white fur on their faces and upper bodies, weigh up to 4kg (9 pounds) and can sometimes be seen foraging amongst leaf litter on the forest floor.

Swimmer's paradise

It was time for us to get our feet wet as we crisscrossed our way down the Río San Pedrillo, stepping over big buttress tree roots and ducking under thick liana vines along its banks. At a rocky outcrop, the river tumbled down an 8-m (25-foot) high waterfall, causing spray to rise up like morning mist from the lush valley below. Just a short distance further on, we arrived at our treat for the day, a lower but wider three-step waterfall with a beautiful, clear pool at the bottom, perfect for a tropical swim. Refreshed, we donned our soggy boots and climbed a steep, narrow trail that followed the river to the ranger station. Back at Marenco, we sat in the open-sided restaurant, reflected on an enthralling day, and watched a heavy thunderstorm roll in from the Pacific.

Island adventure

Some 17km (10 miles) due west of Marenco lies **Caño Island**, a biological and marine reserve which, when viewed from the mainland, looks like a giant cigar. Although it is only 3km (2 miles) long and just over 2km (1 mile) wide, the island also attracts interest from archaeologists, who come to study the strange stone spheres that are thought to have been sculpted by the pre-Columbian Bruncas Indians. No purpose has been found for the spheres, which can measure up to 2m (7 feet) in diameter, but they may have been used as part of burial ceremonies.

Just getting to the island proved an adventure, as we boarded the small launch with three others—Jeff, Patricia, and Heather—and set off across the open ocean. At times, the boat flew over the swell, landing with a slap that had us all hanging onto the handrails. About halfway across, we encountered a wonderful group of dolphins. For a few minutes they played around the boat, seeming almost to escort it towards the island. Their black fins and rubbery bodies intermittently pierced the surface, drawing cries of "There they are!" from whoever was fortunate to spot them first.

Later, as we approached the island, an olive ridley turtle (*Lepidochelys olivacea*) popped its head up to breathe just a few metres in front of us. Shocked to see us, it quickly dived again.

Parrots and porcupines

Snorkelling is one of the main attractions of Caño Island, and we soon donned our supplied masks, fins, and snorkels and waddled backwards into the breaking waves. Unfortunately, the island's coral reefs suffered from a sudden and unexplained dieback in 1984, possibly as a result of changing water temperatures linked to the El Niño current. However, even with below-average visibility (it improves during the dry season) the fish life was still impressive in the warm water. After a brief practice of clearing the snorkels by blowing hard into them on surfacing, we dove down deeper into rocky channels. It never ceases to amaze me just how much life hides in the ocean. Numerous species, including luminous-green parrot-fish (*Scarus lepidus*), porcupine fish (*Diodon hystrix*), and manta rays swam around us, virtually oblivious to our presence. However, we had forgotten to wear T-shirts and, after almost an hour facedown in the water, our backs were sunburnt.

Later, Keith and Jeff followed Johnny on a short trail up into the inland forest, Patricia and Heather soaked up the sun, and I explored the beach area. Hundreds of hermit crabs brought the sand to life, while brown pelicans (*Pelecanus occidentalis*) plunged into the ocean in search of fish. Between December and April humpback whales (*Megaptera novaeangliae*) migrate to this region from Alaska, and are frequently seen. Although I kept my eyes peeled in the hope of seeing one, we had obviously arrived a few weeks too early. Later, after lunch and more snorkelling, we began the journey back to the mainland over even choppier afternoon waves. Tiny flying fish leapt around the boat and the dolphins returned to play for a while. The view of Marenco perched alone on the densely forested coastline made us realize just how far from civilization we really were.

Wet and happy

Our final day was spent within the Marenco reserve. Several generally easy-going trails (not always clearly marked) run through the area. One such trail starts near the beach and leads south to the mouth of the Río Claro. A large, natural pool behind a high sandbank was perfect for a refreshing freshwater swim before we set off on an inland hike. However, just as we began climbing a narrow, red-dirt track a torrential rainstorm hit. Unperturbed, Keith and I continued up the steepening path while the trail, it seemed, was washed downhill in a growing stream. The clinging mud and clay below the water either snatched at our footwear or felt as slippery as ice. I couldn't help but remember Johnny telling me that snakes get washed from their burrows in rainstorms. Soaked through, we turned to each other and decided that this was a real rainforest experience! When the rain finally stopped, the trail dried up quickly. On the final downhill section we saw black mantled howler monkeys (*Alouatta palliata*) and rarer spider monkeys (*Ateles geoffroyi*) swinging through the branches, the latter's reddish-brown chests making them easier to spot. We were fortunate not to be pelted with fruit, a favourite scare tactic of spider monkeys when they encounter humans. Four hours after leaving the river, we finally emerged, muddied and triumphant, back at Marenco.

Heading back to San José the next morning was a wrench. This region is as wild and remote as it gets in Central America, almost overwhelming the senses with the natural diversity on offer. Having had a taste of its wildness, I yearn to return to take on one of the challenging multi-day treks deep into the Corcovado National Park. By so doing I will be able to immerse myself fully in one of the most outstanding wilderness areas on Earth.

GOING IT ALONE

Internal Travel

Travelair and Sansa have daily flights to Palmar Sur, which save a lot of time compared to the bus journey from the capital. The boats that serve the lodges around Drake's Bay will take passengers if they are not full, or boats can be chartered from Sierpe

Planning

Due to the remoteness of Corcovado and the lack of roads, it can take a lot of time and a substantial amount of money to organize a tour independently. Packages, such as those offered by Marenco Lodge, include the return airfare, boat transfers, and tours. They are available as two-, three-, or four-day options, and the longer you can afford the better; you won't get bored. However, it is possible to make the trip independently. You are allowed to camp in the region and in the national park so long as you have gained prior permission from the National Parks Service in San José, and sometimes it is possible to stay in the ranger stations. The trails through the park are long and hard so come prepared with food and water for at least eight days. Much of the water in the park is undrinkable, so ask the park rangers where fresh water can be found.

When to Go

The dry season (December–April) is a popular time to visit the Osa Peninsula, when snorkelling conditions are at their best. However, rainforest treks can be hot and package prices are at their highest. Whilst there are downpours most afternoons from June to October, trips can be arranged to avoid the worst of the rain. At this time prices are often discounted and there are fewer visitors.

Travellers' Tips

- ❑ If you travel by airplane, try to get a seat that offers a good view—away from the wings and engines—as the mountains and coastline are spectacular.
- ❑ If you feel a little queasy during the boat trips on the ocean, concentrate on the horizon and think of your favourite sport or television programme—in fact anything, apart from feeling ill.
- ❑ It is easier and more effective to wear a T-shirt for protection against the sun when you are snorkelling, but don't forget to put sunblock on the backs of your legs, neck, and arms.
- ❑ Take plenty of insect repellent and beware of the little black sandflies on the beaches, whose bites itch far worse than those of mosquitoes.

What to Take

- ❑ Swimming costume.
- ❑ Sunglasses.
- ❑ Sturdy hiking boots.
- ❑ Insect repellent.
- ❑ Binoculars.
- ❑ Waterproof/underwater camera.
- ❑ Rain jacket.
- ❑ A good book for evenings at the lodge.

Health

Malaria and dengue fever are a problem in the Osa Peninsula, so seek medical advice as to which anti-malarial precautions should be taken. Wear full-length clothing, apply repellents, and use a mosquito net. Also be aware of the danger of snakes, and carry antivenom (see box below).

DEALING WITH SNAKES

Snakes, whether venomous or not, strike fear into most people. In the Osa Peninsula there are plenty of them, but you are unlikely to see any as they sense movement and quickly absent themselves from the scene. The best way to be prepared for an encounter with a venomous snake during a rainforest trek is to talk to the park rangers, who normally have dead specimens or picture boards handy so that you can recognize the dangerous species. You will always have time to do something even if you are bitten, and the whole treatment procedure will be speeded up if you know what type of snake attacked you. For longer treks into remote areas, it is wise to carry and learn how to use antivenom; contact the National Parks Service in San José for information on where you can obtain it (see Contacts).

Jungle Paddlers

by Steve Watkins

In a country blessed with several top-class whitewater-rafting rivers, it is the Río Pacuare's wilderness route through primordial forest that makes it Costa Rica's most thrilling and rewarding. I tackled the raging currents on the more "leisurely" two-day tour option, and stayed overnight at a riverside jungle camp.

Blessed with a plethora of raging rivers, all of them emanating from the rugged Cordillera Central, Costa Rica is to whitewater enthusiasts what the Himalayan region is to trekkers and mountaineers: a Mecca that must be visited at least once in a lifetime. In addition to the multitudes of inexperienced paddlers who get their first taste of rafting here, many professional rafters and kayakers from around the world come to escape the winter months at home. The rapids are world class and the water is not so cold as to leave you speaking a few octaves higher. The most popular rafting rivers, the Pacuare and the Reventazón, run down the lush, virtually unpopulated Atlantic-facing slopes towards the Caribbean lowlands, where the Afro-Caribbean Garifuna culture reigns in the towns and villages, and banana plantations dominate the fields.

3 Rafting needs an average level of fitness, although people taking the one-day option need to be fitter. The ability to swim is not absolutely essential as the buoyancy aids keep you afloat, but confidence in turbulent water is, so almost all rafters can swim.

★ Camping is very comfortable at the exclusive river camp and the food is excellent. Whilst rafting, it is a fairly easy ride if you stay in the boat, but things can get a little rougher in the water.

All specialist rafting equipment is provided. Training shoes or well-fitting whitewater sandals that have Velcro fastenings or, preferably, plastic buckles (Velcro doesn't work so well in water), ankle straps, and rubber soles, must be worn (barefoot equals sore foot on the sharp rocks).

PACUARE BOUND

Although the Reventazón has the country's wildest water, with several Class V sections (see box on page 216), it is **Río Pacuare**, the river I was heading to, that is held aloft as the jewel in Costa Rica's bountiful collection of rafting options. Originating on the eastern slopes of the Cordillera de Talamanca mountains, which stretch all the way from San José to northern Panama, the Pacuare twists its way through pristine rain forest and deep canyons. In 1986, the government made it the first river in Central America to receive protected status as a "wild and scenic" river, and it is popularly rated

RIGHT El Nido del Tigre, the Coast to Coast Adventures overnight camp on the Pacuare BELOW The brightly coloured helmets and life jackets aid recovery if you fall overboard

APEX

COSTA RICA'S RAFTING RIVERS

Apart from the Pacuare, there are seven other rivers on both sides of Costa Rica's Cordillera Central that are run commercially. Unless noted otherwise, trips can all be booked via agencies in San José.

- **Corobicí** Class I–II; Pacific side. More of a "float" than a whitewater experience. Ideal for beginners, and a wildlife enthusiast's dream as it runs through the Parque Nacional Palo Verde.
- **General** Class III–IV; Pacific side. Long, remote, and full of big-wave rapids, the General is a real adventure, usually run over four days only during the rainy months.
- **Naranjo** Class III–IV; Pacific side. Trips are organized from the town of Quepos. This relatively new addition to the rafting list offers an exciting ride for experienced rafters, but only during the rainy months.
- **Parrita** Class II–III; Pacific side. A reasonably gentle river to the north of the Parque Nacional Manuel Antonio.
- **Reventazón** Class III –V; Atlantic side. With a name meaning bursting waves, this river offers something for everyone. The most popular section (indeed, the most popular raft trip in the country), the Class III run from Tucurrique to Angostura, will be lost to a dam project in 1999, but three other sections will still be feasible.
- **Sarapiquí** Class I–III; Atlantic side. A forest river that offers outstanding bird-watching and wildlife opportunities. Monkeys, toucans, and kingfishers may be seen. A good choice for new or inexperienced rafters.
- **Savegre** Class II–III; Pacific side. A truly beautiful river that runs through rain forest near the Parque Nacional Manuel Antonio. Trips are also organized from Quepos.

as one of the world's top five rafting experiences, filled with Class III and IV rapids. Despite its high ranking, it is accessible to anyone who is reasonably fit and who is looking for an adventure that, whilst being safe enough, still retains enough risk to get the adrenalin flowing.

As with most tours out of San José, I needed to set my alarm clock early to be ready for the 7:30am pick-up from my hotel. Our small group of seven comprised of John and Julie, newlyweds on honeymoon from the United States; Asako, a young Japanese girl; and Coast to Coast Adventures' head guide Matt and his assistant guides Goldie, Joel, and Edwin. I had planned on getting a little more sleep during the 2½-hour bus ride to the put-in point, but Goldie turned the journey into a fascinating guided tour of the history and wildlife of the places along the route. He pointed out things as diverse as the turkey vultures (*Cathartes aura*), known locally as the Costa Rican Air Force, circling above the coffee fields, and Volcán Irazú (Irazú Volcano), which last exploded the day John F. Kennedy came to visit. In the old colonial capital of **Cartago**, a brief stop allowed a visit to the grandiose **Basilica de Nuestra Señora de los Angelos** (**Basilica of Our Lady of Los Angeles**). It is home to a tiny black statue of the Virgin that is attributed with miraculous healing powers. On August 2 pilgrims come from all over Central America to bring lucky bracelet charms representing the part of the body they want healed. The charms are all hung in glass display cases as a rather eerie record of their visit.

Two is better than one

At Turrialba, a pretty town near the base of the daunting Volcán Turrialba, we breakfasted on scrambled eggs and the traditional *gallo pinto*, a mix of beans and rice, perfect fuel for energy-sapping rafting. From there, a short drive along a twisting road took us to Tres Equis, the put-in point for the rafts.

It is possible to complete the 29-km (18-mile) rafting section to Siquirres in a very long day (an option offered by several companies), but it is far more relaxing and rewarding to take two days over it. This allows rafters the chance to stay overnight in a comfortable riverside camp, and leaves time to explore some of the many waterfalls along the way. Another advantage is that it is possible to set off later than the hordes of day-rafters (as many as 30 boats a day use the river during high-season weekends), so that you can experience the wilderness scenery on a more personal level.

After changing into our shorts and T-shirts at the Tres Equis farmhouse, we strolled down the track and caught our first glimpse of the rushing white water slicing through the steep-sided, densely forested valley. On the boulder-strewn riverbank, we collected our blue helmets, yellow paddles, and red buoyancy aids, which fitted as tight as corsets. The bright colours help recovery from the water of both the equipment and the attached—one hopes—human.

As we gathered around the raft for a thorough briefing on safety techniques from head guide Matt, we learned that there are two very important things to remember. The first is never to let go of the T-bar handle of the paddle as, when swung around in the heat of the action, it can knock out the teeth or blacken the eye of a fellow paddler. Second, if you are flipped out of the raft in a rapid it is essential to remain calm and float on your back with your feet pointing downstream. Apparently, the urge to try to stand up can be very strong, but if one of your feet gets trapped under a boulder, the power of the current will push your upper body underwater so that it is then virtually impossible to surface again. "However, we have never lost anyone, yet, on the Pacuare," Goldie added with a reassuring smile.

High-flyers

To practise our paddling strokes and teamwork, the raft was kept on dry land. Rafting has a simple language all of its own. "Right back!" means those on the right paddle backwards while those on the left paddle forward. "Forward hard!" needs a huge effort from everyone, while "Get down!" signifies that we are in way above our heads and just need to hold on for dear life. The fun commands, however, are "High side left!" and "High side right!" These signify that the raft is in imminent danger of flipping over and everyone has to dive to the highest side to try to weigh it down. It became quite cosy with six bodies crammed onto one rubber tube and certainly helped us to get to know each other better.

Now it was time for the real action. With the first rapid just in front of the put-in there was no easing into it and we were soon paddling with all our might as the raft skewed sideways on entry. Water splashed over the front and oozed through my clothes, sending shivers down my spine. Once we had recovered our direction, we paddled the raft out of the rapid and all felt relieved that the first one was out of the way.

"OK, that was just a small one. Remember to paddle together," Goldie shouted from the rear. After successfully tackling the hole (a depression in the river bed that causes water to recycle through it continually) on El Segundo rapid, Goldie used the relatively calm section that followed to forewarn of the first major rapid. Dubbed Bienvenido (Welcome), this Class III section has plenty of holes and large waves. We were instructed to paddle hard around the initial hole as many rafts get caught there and tip over. Slight apprehension was visible on everyone's faces as the water dropped away in front of us and only turbulent spray rose beyond. "Forward hard!" boomed Goldie, but it was still difficult to hear him over the roar of the rapid. Reaching forward, eyes closed, I pulled strongly on the paddle, aware of nothing except the water crashing into my face. During a fleeting lull, I opened my eyes, saw that we were heading for a steep drop over a wave, and quickly shut them again. The bucking raft sent me sliding to the floor, and by the time I regained some composure the rapid was over. We all whooped and slapped paddles in a high five to celebrate both our survival and our reasonably synchronized teamwork.

Into the Tiger's Nest

In the afternoon, the traditional rainy season downpour arrived. The accompanying low mist only added to the feeling of exploration as we slid through rapids called Landslide, Piel Ojo (literally, by the skin of your eyes), and Bumper Rock, our confidence increasing with every stroke. Around the final few corners, a slate-blue ringed kingfisher (*Ceryle torquata*) flew just ahead of the raft to escort us to our overnight camp, hidden away in the trees at the river's edge. Built entirely from driftwood, the El Nido del Tigre (Nest of the Tiger) luxury camp was established by Coast to Coast Adventures in 1996. The name is taken from the giant ginger plants that cover the main camp area. When the plants reach a certain height they fall over to

create flattened areas in the shape of tiger paws. The hammocks, cold beers, and fresh fruit snacks proved popular as we deservedly put our feet up and listened to the screeches and twitters of the birds in the surrounding virgin rain forest.

Normal fare during my own camping trips is a sorry-looking jumble of mashed potato, tuna, and soup, so it was a pleasant surprise to be served a gourmet meal that evening of pasta and vegetable sauce followed by exquisite caramel biscuits with cream. Good food usually leads to a good sleep, and it was not long before we all wandered off, torches in hand, to the camp's spacious tents, raised above bug level on a series of wooden platforms. The orchestral accompaniment of the

LEFT Teamwork is an essential part of white-water rafting
BELOW By opting for the two-day tour you can take time out to enjoy the surroundings of El Nido del Tigre

river and the cicadas ensured a swift and soothing night's rest.

Swirling currents

Day two on the river is slightly shorter but features the biggest rapids. Over breakfast, the group seemed calmer than the day before and we enjoyed another helping of *gallo pinto* whilst watching an incredible, iridescent blue morpho butterfly (*Morpho peleides*) flutter around the camp. During colonial times, the French were so enamoured with the morpho's colour that they used the pigment in its wings to dye their money.

Back at the river, the previous day's rain had caused the water to rise even higher, and Matt assured us that our deliverance to Siquirres would be both rapid and eventful. Past the Ríos rapid we came to a curve in the river where the white water slammed against a black boulder the size of a detached house. Goldie issued the cry to arms and we all prepared to give every ounce of effort to the battle ahead. There was a real chance that the raft could strike against the rock and flip; the swim out would be long and bumpy. "Forward hard…harder!" bawled Goldie, and we all dug deep to drag our paddles through the swirling currents as powerfully as possible. Short paddle strokes allow the boat to turn more quickly, so our arms pumped up and down like the pistons of an engine in an effort to maintain control. The water was too strong though, and the boat hit the rock, sending us all of off balance and causing a telling pause in the paddling.

"High side left!" screamed Goldie as the raft was forced up the boulder face, and we all dived across to hang onto the safety line..For a brief moment the battle seemed lost, but somehow our combined weight managed to tip the odds in our favour and the raft came crashing back down. Within seconds, we had regained our places and were paddling furiously to extricate ourselves from the danger. Our celebratory high five when we popped out of the rapid was loud enough to send a couple of white great egrets (*Casmeroidus albus*) hurtling downriver.

Beyond the long and twisting rapid called Blind Man's Bluff, the water slowed and we had a chance to up paddles and admire the luxuriant scenery. The dense forest includes various species of palms, heliconias, and ferns, and giant ceiba trees (*Ceiba pentandra*), all of which cling like

WHITEWATER RIVER RATINGS

The Scale of River Difficulty, set by the American Whitewater Affiliation, is universally used to grade rivers:

- ❑ **Class I** Moving water with a few riffles and small waves. Few obstructions.
- ❑ **Class II** Easy rapids with waves up to 1m (3 feet) high and wide, clear channels that are obvious without scouting. Some manoeuvring is required.
- ❑ **Class III** Rapids with high, irregular waves often capable of swamping an open canoe. Narrow passages that often require complex manoeuvring. May require scouting from the shore.
- ❑ **Class IV** Long, difficult rapids with constricted passages that often require precise manoeuvring in very turbulent waters. Scouting from shore is often necessary and conditions make rescue difficult. Generally not possible for open canoes. Boaters in covered canoes and kayaks should be able to Eskimo roll.
- ❑ **Class V** Extremely difficult, long, and very violent rapids with highly congested routes that nearly always must be scouted from shore. Rescue conditions are difficult and there is significant hazard to life in the event of a mishap. Ability to Eskimo roll is essential for kayaks and canoes.
- ❑ **Class VI** Difficulties of Class V carried to the extreme of navigability. Nearly impossible and very dangerous. For teams of experts only.

tropical-print wallpaper to the almost vertical slopes of the valley. Snakes, including the very venomous terciopelos (*Bothrops asper*), jaguars (*Panthera onca*), southern river otters (*Lutra longicaudis*), and collared peccaries (*Tayassu tajacu*), a breed of wild pig, inhabit the forest, but it is highly unlikely that rafters will be lucky (or unlucky) enough to spot them. Throughout the entire route more than 20 spectacular waterfalls tumble into the Pacuare. At two of them, it is possible to manoeuvre the raft under the flow for an impromptu team shower. As we neared the impressive cascade at Río Frío, a couple of yellow-beaked collared aracari toucans (*Pteroglossus torquatas*) launched themselves from the treetops and swooped down behind us. At the falls, we reaped another benefit of taking the more relaxed two-day option on the river. Stopping the boat in an eddy, a current found at the edges of a river where the water actually flows backwards, we leapt out and hiked to the upper levels of the waterfall. Once there, we clambered above a deep, natural pool and jumped off into the clear green waters below.

A DAMMED FUTURE

Costa Rica justifiably has a good reputation for protecting its remaining wildlife and forest areas. However, this eco-friendly approach seems to have been abandoned when it comes to the country's wilderness rivers. By the time you read this, Río Reventazón will already be dammed near Turrialba to produce electricity, instantly wiping out the country's most frequently run rafting section. Possibly more disturbing though is a proposed project to dam the Río Pacuare at the Dos Montañas gorge, effectively wiping out all of the upper sections of the river and their world-class pristine rainforest habitats. Protests against the project are increasing, but the National Electric Company is pushing ahead to have the $1 billion dam completed by 2006.

THE BIG ONE

Our early morning success on the rapids and the relaxing break at the waterfall had lulled us into a false sense of security. Matt soon snapped us out of it. He explained that we were heading for the biggest, most technically challenging rapids on the river, called Upper and Lower Huacas. Everything that had gone before was really just training for this 150-m (150-yard) stretch of boulders and ledges that is normally Class IV but would be Class IV+ with the high river level. A swim on this section would be, to say the least, unpleasant. It was only now that the true value of having Matt paddling near by in the safety kayak became apparent. In the event of one or all of us ending up in the river, he would be able to reach us relatively quickly and could deploy the safety rope he carried in his bright orange throw bag.

As we neared the edge of the drop, we glimpsed the pounding froth below; my stomach had that heavy feeling that comes only when something serious is about to happen. I vaguely remember Goldie's voice urging us on, but all too soon the water was crashing over the bow as we were tossed about by the huge waves. At times, the raft rode so high up the wave faces that it was difficult to get the paddle into the water and the resulting air strokes made me lose balance. There was no time for panic, though. The boulders loomed quickly; the raft slid right, bounced against a large black rock, and rebounded left over a ledge. "Back paddle!" came the command, and we all fought to stop ourselves colliding with another boulder. To get through the big holes it is important to maintain momentum, and it took the biggest team effort of the day to get us through Lower Huacas and safely out to the tranquil waters beyond. The feeling of relief was quickly overwhelmed by the buzz of success, and we cheered as if we had won an Olympic gold medal.

Float to a new world

To savour our achievement, we stopped on a sandy beach for a delicious buffet lunch, served on the upturned raft. The action was not over, though. Back in the water, several Class III rapids—including Pinball, The Brain, and Magnetic Rock—followed in quick succession, before we slowed a little to admire another stunning waterfall. A real treat awaited us around the next corner: a deep, narrow gorge with vertical walls that looked like the gateway to another world. Called Dos Montañas (Two Mountains), this is perhaps the most spectacular section of the river. After we were given the okay by the guides, we all jumped into the calm water and floated downriver. This was the wilderness we had come in search of. Lesser swallow-tailed swifts (*Panyptila cayennensis*) flitted around the rock faces and black vultures (*Coragyps atratus*) circled above the canyon. For all we knew, the nearest civilization could have been hundreds of miles away. This moving experience was heightened even further by the knowledge that Dos Montañas is the proposed site of a dam (see box on page 221) that will destroy for ever the upper reaches of the Pacuare and end rafting trips on the river.

We clambered back into the raft as we exited the gorge, only to realize that we were indeed entering another world, for the mountains ended and the flatlands of the Caribbean coastal plain began. We were just two small rapids away from the town of Siquirres, the end of our exquisite and exciting journey through one of Costa Rica's most remote, untouched areas. We had learned not only how to paddle a raft, but also that even the most challenging of situations can be overcome with a little teamwork. Glancing back, I only hoped that I would return one day to find it still there.

Goldie, our experienced guide, sat at the back to steer the raft and to scout our route through the rapids

GOING IT ALONE

Planning

Numerous companies in San José, including Coast to Coast Adventures, Ríos Tropicales, Horizontes, and Aventuras Naturales, offer single- or multi-day trips to all the major rivers. All trip prices include return bus transport, specialist equipment, services of the guides, and food and drinks (no alcohol is allowed for obvious reasons) whilst on the river. Some companies include breakfast on the first day, usually at a restaurant *en route*. For multi-day trips, riverside accommodation (in tents or cabins, depending on the company selected) and food and drinks (including wine and beer for dinner) is also included. If you do not use one of the above companies, check with the tourist office in San José to ensure that the company you do choose has good-quality equipment and experienced guides.

When to Go

Most people visit Costa Rica during the dry season (December–April), when the rivers are low and temperatures are high. For rafting on the Pacuare, there are very good reasons for bucking the trend and heading there during the rainy season (June–November). The river is much more fun when the water is pounding down it, creating bigger waves and covering many of the boulders that slow progress and require greater effort to navigate around when the water is low. In the heat it can be a little uncomfortable exerting yourself all day, so during the rainy season you have the added advantage that you can enjoy the relief of the afternoon cloud cover. And even when it does rain, it is warm rain. Finally, there are far fewer tourists around at this time and the hotels are consequently cheaper.

Rafters' Tips

- Whilst rafting, don't apply sunblock to your forehead as it will run into your eyes, causing irritation, nor to the backs of your legs as you will slip off the rubber-tube sides of the raft.
- Double check any pockets for valuables before you set off and pack everything you are taking into one of the dry bags supplied for the purpose. Plastic bags just don't work in white water.

What to Take

- Sunblock.
- Peaked hat that can fit under a helmet.
- Whitewater sandals (make sure they fit properly or they will get ripped off in the white water) or training shoes.
- Strong insect repellent.
- A dry set of clothes, which can be stored in special waterproof bags on the raft.
- Waterproof camera; the single-use ones are good enough and are available in San José.
- Torch for the overnight camp.
- A retaining cord for your sunglasses.

Health

Precautions against malaria should be taken; consult your doctor for the latest medical advice. Do not wear contact lenses whilst rafting as they can be washed out; instead, wear glasses with a retaining cord. Use liberal amounts of sunblock.

El Nido del Tigre is a luxury campsite

Trail of the Turtle Catchers

by Steve Watkins

The Parque Nacional Tortuguero (Tortuguero National Park), on Costa Rica's Caribbean coast, is one of the last safe havens for many of the country's wildlife species. The area is crisscrossed by a network of jungle rivers and canals, and I found the best way to maximize wildlife-spotting opportunities was to take a peaceful kayak trip.

In 1970 there must have been a few wry smiles at the management meeting of Costa Rica's National Parks Service when they decided to call the brand-new Caribbean wildlife reserve "Turtle Catchers' National Park." After at least 400 years of virtually unrestricted access to the bountiful nests of giant turtles, the *tortugueros* (turtle catchers) suddenly found that they were banned from the only area of Costa Rica to be named after them.

Whilst there are no such entry restrictions placed on travellers, there is just one transport option when it comes to getting into this 19,000-ha (46,000-acre) park of dense jungle, sweeping coastline, and wilderness rivers. A complete lack of roads into the region means that the only way to get to Tortuguero is along one of the rivers, but at least there are plenty of them. The vast majority of visitors explore the area in motorized launches, but noise and wildlife don't always mix very well. The boatmen do cut the engines every time they spot something interesting, but by this time many other animals will have been alerted by the approaching racket and consequently disappear from view. One way to make things a little quieter is to venture into the park in a kayak. Keith, a friend from England, and I joined four travellers from the United States and guides Matt, Joel, Goldie, and Sue on a two-day Coast to Coast Adventures trip on the lower Río Pacuare. The river lies just south of the national park, so the trip allowed us to get some paddling practice in before spending a further two days exploring some of the lesser-known rivers that run into the park itself.

Kayaking demands a reasonably good level of fitness, although the rivers on the tour are calm and the pace is easy. Paddling against the current on a few short sections can be tiring.

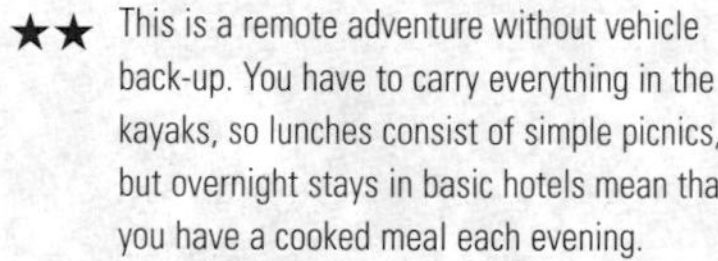

★★ This is a remote adventure without vehicle back-up. You have to carry everything in the kayaks, so lunches consist of simple picnics, but overnight stays in basic hotels mean that you have a cooked meal each evening.

All specialist kayaking equipment is provided.

STRAIGHT BANANAS

After unloading the kayaks near a banana-processing depot on the banks of the Pacuare, we took a brief look around the plantation. Sweating, muscle-bound men used leather waist straps to haul trains of banana bunches, wrapped in blue plastic raincoats, along an extensive overhead cable system that links the plantation to the depot. There, the plastic coats were stripped off and a team of women sorted the bananas for suitability; apparently the United States market prefers green, curvy bananas while European regulations insist on straighter, more yellow ones. Hundreds failed both tests and were ejected from a conveyor belt into a skip. The chosen ones were washed, broken down into smaller bunches, labelled and then packed into large cardboard boxes where they awaited their long journeys to the fruit baskets of the world.

Back at the riverbank, we packed our extra clothes, torches, wallets, and other personal gear into the dry bags supplied, picked up a buoyancy aid and paddle each, checked that our water bottles were full, and slid into the kayak cockpits. The lower sections of the Río Pacuare are wide and free from rapids, unlike the upper sections I had been whitewater rafting on earlier in the week (see page 214). Goldie, my partner in a double kayak, and I soon got into an easily paced paddling rhythm as we glided round the twists and turns of coffee-brown water. In order to spot wildlife it is better to stay close to one bank of the river, but not too close—snakes abound in the forest areas and it is not uncommon to see them curled around low branches that overhang the rivers. I am no expert on tropical wildlife, so it was great to have the knowledgeable Goldie pointing out things I would otherwise have missed, and regaling me with funny stories. One of his gems told how kids from the few local villages cut down banana trees and use them to ride down the river, balancing on the trunk by rolling it beneath their feet, just like the log runners of northern America.

SAFE KAYAKING

When you first get into a kayak it will feel as if it is impossible to stay upright as the boat twitches with every movement. However, by positively thinking all your weight into the seat and avoiding any sudden upper body movements (such as swinging around to spot monkeys), it will soon become clear that it is possible to avoid swimming with the crocodiles. Like all boats, kayaks become more stable the faster they go, so you will be fine once you are on the move. On the river, watch out for wakes from passing launches; try to paddle directly into them as they will destabilize a kayak if they are hit side-on. Most launches will slow down when they see kayaks, to reduce their wake.

LIFE IN SLOW MOTION

The riverbanks were alive with countless species of birds and butterflies. Graceful great egrets (*Casmeroidus albus*) perched their slender, white bodies on fallen trees, flycatcher birds darted above us in search of a meal, and magnificent, iridescent-blue morpho butterflies (*Morpho peleides*) fluttered across the water, looking like flashing Christmas lights. However, most of the day's excitement was generated by one of the least excitable animals on earth. High up in the Y-fork of a cecropia tree (*Cecropia lyratiloba*), Joel spotted the motionless frame of a brown-throated three-toed sloth (*Bradypus variegatus*). These incredible creatures, with snub noses, gangly legs, and clawed toes, are distantly related to anteaters. However, somewhere along the line of evolution sloths decided that even the relatively sedate life of the anteater was too hectic for them. Even when they do move—and you could wait all day to see this—it apparently looks like a slowed-down version of a slow-motion replay. They feed principally on cecropia leaves, which contain a chemical that acts like a sedative, rather similar to the effect eucalyptus leaves have on koalas in Australia. A slow digestive system also means that the sloths don't need to feed very often, leaving them free to do what they do best—absolutely nothing. Even with Joel pointing to the sloth, it was still very hard to see because its brown-grey body matched the tree perfectly. Needless to say, we didn't see it move.

Soon after we passed a small tributary called Río Madre de Dios (Mother of God River) on a sweeping S-bend, we began to hear the rumbling waves of the Caribbean Sea. The river widened considerably, and right at the mouth we pulled into a pretty beach lined with palm trees for a late picnic lunch. After digesting it rather more quickly than would a sloth, we played around on a partially fallen palm tree that made a solid, if rather narrow, platform for diving into the water. Only later, when we were safely back on the beach, did we remember that there are crocodiles in the river. Then it was just a short paddle to our overnight stop, a tiny, rustic hotel called the Cocotel Inn. Basic it may have been, but with a balcony overlooking the river, a resident, playful howler monkey (*Aloutta palliata*), and plenty of beer and rum, it satisfied all our relaxation and entertainment needs for the night.

Canal cruising

A subtle pink sunrise and rising mist greeted the early birds amongst us and boded well for a warm day out on the river. A plentiful helping of *gallo pinto*, the traditional Costa Rican breakfast of rice and beans, topped up our energy reserves, and we were soon loaded up and back in the kayaks. The Caribbean coast has always been a busy trade area for both local traders and those from Nicaragua in the north and Panama in the south. However, the sea voyage along the coast can often be affected by bad weather and is not navigable for ordinary villagers in their dugout canoes. The majority of inland rivers are navigable for

ABOVE A series of canals was built in Tortuguero to connect the rivers, thereby creating a protected inland waterway that allows safe passage for local traders in their dugout canoes
LEFT An impromptu diving board on the Caribbean shore
BELOW A kayak tour of Tortuguero offers ample opportunity for spotting wildlife, such as this spider monkey (Ateles geoffroyi)

THE BIG SLEEP

Every day Tortuguero's most inanimate inhabitant, the three-toed sloth (*Bradypus tridactylus*), manages to squeeze in 20 hours of sleep, a slumber broken only so that it can slowly consume the leaves and fruits that make up its diet. Its sight is poor (perhaps even seeing takes up far too much energy!) and it finds food high up in the cecropia trees using its sense of smell. Very rarely the sloth ventures down to the ground, where its performance does not speed up—even when it is travelling at maximum speed it manages only 0.16kmh (0.1mph), which means it would take almost 40 minutes to break the tape in a 100-m (110-yard) race!

canoes but they all run in a west–east direction. To overcome this, a network of inland canals was built to link the major rivers and to form a protected water highway that stretches all the way from Puerto Limón in the south to the Río San Juan on the Nicaraguan border. We were going to head a little way south down the canal that links the Pacuare with the Río Chirripó, before crossing a narrow land bridge to paddle back up the open ocean to return to the Pacuare's mouth.

Crocodile warning

Again, wildlife was the real highlight of the day. As we paddled next to floating fields of lilies, a northern jacana bird (*Jacana spinosa*) popped its head out from amongst the white flowers. These beautiful birds have a very self-conscious, awkward walking style caused by their extremely long, four-toed feet, designed to allow them to skip along on top of the lily pads. The birds are easy to spot as their yellow bill contrasts sharply against their brown body feathers. However, it was only when Matt paddled up close to it that we saw its real beauty, for as it took to the air the bright yellow undersides to its wings were revealed to us.

Where the riverbanks became muddier and sloping, spectacled caymans (*Caiman crocidilius*) lurked, waiting for a chance to slip into the water to snap up their next meal. Thankfully, in or out of our kayaks we were probably too big for them. However, the larger, more aggressive American crocodiles (*Crocodilus acutus*) in the river could cause severe damage should we have the misfortune of rolling over. As if to warn us to stay upright, we paddled past a wooden sign, almost covered by a tangle of branches, that recorded the demise of an Israeli researcher on April 9, 1997. Despite warnings from locals about the dangers of swimming in the river, he apparently persisted until a crocodile finally happened upon him and ate him.

As we turned into a narrow side channel that led towards the ocean, a ringed kingfisher (*Ceryle torquata*) dived into the water in front of Joel's kayak to take a fish. The commotion of the kingfisher and our arrival caused an explosion of yellow butterflies from a nearby patch of lily pads. It was a dreamlike experience paddling through the fluttering cloud of wings, and Goldie and I stopped to take a closer look. Costa Rica alone is home to a staggering 11 per cent of the world's butterfly species.

Pulling in to shore, we carried the rather heavy kayaks a few hundred yards to the open ocean. The surf was not too high and we were soon out beyond it into the calmer waters. Sea-kayaking can be rather exhausting, and with the sun beating down on us it seemed to take a very long time to reach the mouth of the Pacuare again. A thrilling ride into shore on the breaking waves took us to the Cocotel, where Matt arranged for the owner to take us back to the banana depot in his boat. With the kayaks trailing behind like a camel train, we relaxed and saw the Pacuare how most people see it;

the trip was certainly easier going, but the experience wasn't anywhere near as intimate.

INTO THE UNKNOWN

The Americans headed back to San José, while Matt, Goldie, Keith, and I drove to the remote village of **Quatro Esquinas**, situated on a tiny, never-before-kayaked tributary of the Río Suerte (Lucky River), which runs into Tortuguero village. Matt wanted to scout this new waterway with a view to running future trips on it. To get to a suitable put-in point we first had to get permission to carry the kayaks through a farm. After the wide open canals of the previous two days, it was a shock to see a river so narrow and shallow that two of us could have linked together and lain flat across the whole width without fear of drowning. However, like all ventures into the unknown, there was a tingle of excitement as we wondered where the river would lead.

At first, we could only just get the edge of our paddles into the shallow water, but we resisted the temptation to get out and walk. The river eventually deepened and began twisting around corners so sharp that we sometimes had to do three-point manoeuvres to get around them. As the high grassy banks gave way to thick overhanging rain forest, it felt as if we were the very first Amazon explorers. Caymans lined our route, looking so much more menacing from a distance of only 3m (10 feet). Usually, we could just see their watchful eyes breaking the surface of the water, but occasionally we would surprise one and watch in awe as it slid smoothly off the bank.

Ducking under vines and negotiating a path around sunken tree trunks, we gradually got closer to the Río Suerte. Near the junction, Goldie and I spotted a baby turtle basking on a half-submerged tree branch. We stopped paddling and glided closer, getting to within a few yards of it before it flopped back into the water. As we finally emerged onto the wider Suerte, I felt a sense of relief to get out of the enclosed confines of the tributary but at the same time a yearning to turn right around and go back into it.

Along the edges of the Suerte we spotted black mantled howler monkeys (*Alouatta palliata*) rummaging around in the canopy and spider monkeys (*Ateles geoffroyi*) swinging among the branches like gymnasts on the high bar. Eventually, the Suerte joined the canal that runs between Tortuguero village and **Cerro Tortuguero**, the only hill for miles around. The hill is 119m (398 feet) and can be climbed if you are very fit and like muddy, steep slopes. We headed towards the village instead, and paddled up to a riverside bar to enjoy a quick celebratory beer before dragging the kayaks out of the water.

Tortuguero village is tiny, hot, and very laid back. It is home to a wide variety of cultures, including Hispanic, Miskito, Nicaraguan Indian, and Afro-Caribbean. The locals live in brightly painted wooden houses, most of which are festooned with

EGG TIMING

From around the 1500s, turtle catchers (usually just local fishermen) plied their grim trade all along the Caribbean coast. The rich turtle meat was a local delicacy, and with the arrival of the Spanish it soon gained popularity in Europe, increasing enormously the demand for meat and for products made with turtle shells. Often, if the spears hadn't killed them outright, the turtles were kept alive during the long voyage to Europe, prolonging their suffering. The creation of the Tortuguero National Park and strict laws regulating the catching of turtles eased the creatures' plight, but illegal poaching of turtle eggs and continuing encroachment of humans into the park's boundary area still give cause for concern.

equally punchy bougainvillaea flowers. The main street is just a narrow dirt path that runs past a rustic children's playground, a pretty pale yellow church, a bakery, and several bars and restaurants. There are also several places to stay in the village if you travel here independently.

The main reason to visit the village is to go turtle-watching, so at eight o'clock that night we joined a tour that took us down to **Tortuguero beach**. This is Costa Rica's major nesting site for giant green turtles (*Chelonia mydas*), with over 20,000 of them coming ashore each nesting season, according to the resident Caribbean Conservation Corporation. The corporation maintains a visitor centre just north of Tortuguero village, with information on research and conservation of the turtles. We weren't there during the high nesting season (July to early October), but we hoped to see some turtles none the less.

Before heading for the beach we were given a lecture on how to behave with the turtles. No flash photography is allowed because it interrupts the egg-laying process, and under no circumstances were we allowed to leave the marked viewing area. It is important that such restrictions are adhered to as the turtles are easily disturbed. Our luck held, and soon we stood watching a solitary green turtle struggle up the sand before digging a nest with her rear flippers. It seemed to take an age, but eventually golf-ball-sized eggs began to drop into the hole. After carefully covering them with sand, she returned to the ocean to roam the waters of the Caribbean before her inevitable return during the next breeding season. We almost felt like applauding her, but were scared the noise would disturb the tranquillity of the scene.

Tortuguero is a world-class national park, and seeing it from just above water-level in noise-free kayaks is certainly an enjoyable alternative to other options. Judging from the number of visitors in motor launches who took pictures of us with the same wide-eyed enthusiasm that they snapped the monkeys, it certainly felt as if we were closer to the wildlife than them.

TORTUGUERO'S GIANT TURTLES

- **Green turtle (*Chelonia mydas*)** Found in warm coastal waters in the Atlantic, Pacific, and Indian oceans, the green turtle eats mainly turtle grass and other marine plants, and can weigh up to 180kg (400 pounds). Its attractive, heart-shaped main shell (carapace) has four plates and is dark brown and olive in colour. Males can grow to around 1.6m (5 feet) long and spend their whole lives in the ocean, while the slightly smaller females come ashore on the beach where they were born every two to four years to nest, when they can lay over 100 eggs.
- **Leatherback turtle (*Dermochelys oriacea*)** The severely endangered leatherback is now found mainly in the tropical, subtropical, and deeper temperate waters of the Atlantic, Pacific, and Indian oceans. This impressive turtle is the largest on Earth, the male growing up to 2.4m (8 feet) in length and weighing up to 860kg (1,900 pounds). Its unique carapace doesn't have the horny plates of other marine turtles, but instead consists of a dark, leathery skin that contrasts sharply with its white belly. Leatherbacks are strong swimmers and travel large distances in search of jellyfish, their principal food source.

*PREVIOUS PAGES Once you get the hang of paddling a kayak, you will be able to relax and enjoy the ride. This noise-free form of transport will also give you a much better chance of getting close up to wildlife such as (INSET) the spectacled cayman crocodile (*Caiman crocodilius*)*

GOING IT ALONE

When to Go

The dry season (December–April) is significantly busier than the wet season (June–October). The green turtles mainly nest from July to mid-October, so this is probably the best time to go. Although it obviously rains more during the wet season, there is usually some sunshine during the day, prices are cheaper, and hotels have more vacancies.

Planning

Owing to the lack of roads, travelling independently to Tortuguero is not easy and can prove quite expensive if you have to charter boats. Unless you have a lot of time, a good command of Spanish, and plenty of patience it is probably better to join an organized tour. There are a number of tours on offer in San José, many of which are reasonably priced. Coast to Coast Adventures is currently the only company that runs kayaking trips into the national park area, and they offer two-day trips as standard, although they can customize itineraries.

If you travel to the park independently and wish to kayak, there are a few places near the main jetty in Tortuguero village that rent out surf kayaks (the type where you sit on top). If you haven't paddled one of these before then practise near the village before you head off to more remote water as they can feel quite unstable. You really don't want to end up swimming with the crocodiles.

Tours to see the turtles are offered by numerous people in the village, but it is best just to go to the Quatro Esquinas ranger station at the northern end of the park, where rangers will show you where to go. Most organized tours include the turtle visit.

Travellers' Tips

- The Caribbean Conservation Corporation's research centre, just to the north of the village, has an excellent display explaining its work with the turtles. This is well worth a visit.
- Do not swim in the coastal waters around Tortuguero as there are strong currents and big surf that can cause problems even for experienced swimmers. If that isn't enough to put you off then the additional fact that sharks are very common in the area should do the trick. Swimming in the rivers is also unwise as there are crocodiles. In Tortuguero, the only safe respite from the hot temperatures is to find a shady tree or to take a shower at the hotel.
- If you take a motorized-launch tour around the canals it is best to sit at the front as many animals soon disappear with the noise. Arriving a fraction of a second earlier can make the difference between spotting a fleeing jaguar and only seeing more rain forest.

What to Take

- Brimmed sun hat.
- Sunblock.
- Waterproof camera.
- Binoculars with neck cord.
- Plenty of drinking water.
- Snack foods.

Health

Take medical precautions against malaria (consult your doctor for the latest advice), and wear full-length clothing, apply strong repellents, and use a mosquito net. Drink plenty of water whilst kayaking, and apply sunblock. Do not drink the tap-water in Tortuguero.

FURTHER READING

- Beletsky, Les, *Costa Rica: The Ecotravellers' Wildlife Guide* (Academic Press, 1998). A handy book that covers natural history, ecology, and wildlife habitats in a very accessible way.
- Janzen, Daniel H., *Costa Rican Natural History* (University of Chicago Press, 1983). A mighty tome to carry around, but it covers every aspect of natural history in the country, from history and archaeology to wildlife and weather.
- Stiles, F. Gary and Skutch, Alexander F., *A Guide to the Birds of Costa Rica* (Cornell University Press, 1990). Widely acknowledged as the bible on birds in the region, and beautifully illustrated with detailed colour plates of hundreds of species.

A Nicoyan Odyssey

By Steve Watkins

The southern part of Guanacaste's Península de Nicoya (Nicoya Peninsula) is remote and infrequently visited, and so offers a wild playground for adventure travellers. I opted for a tour using kayaks and mountain bikes to explore the beautiful Pacific beaches and inland hills of this unique region.

The southern sections of the Nicoya Peninsula, in Costa Rica's Guanacaste province, are among the most remote parts of the country. A lack of surfaced roads means that only the dedicated few get to see the richest natural treasures on offer. One way to gain better access is to use sea kayaks and mountain bikes, which can reach the parts that leave other modes of transport floundering. I chose to join an organized tour that carried the luggage between overnight stops, so that our small group was completely free to explore the wilderness beaches and hills.

Its physical separation from the interior of Costa Rica by two mountain chains, the Cordillera de Guanacaste and the Cordillera de Tilarán, has given

4 Sea-kayaking is easy to learn and needs only an average level of fitness, but is not recommended for those who suffer badly from seasickness. Mountain biking requires some cycling experience (preferably off road), a good level of fitness, and a positive attitude towards challenges, mud, water, and sweat.

★★ At times, the activities can be quite challenging, both physically and mentally, but there are good hotels, a comfortable campsite, and tasty food to make up for it at the end of each day.

All specialist equipment is provided for the kayaking, and bikes, helmets, and repair tools for the biking aspect. You may wish to bring special biking clothing such as shorts and gloves with padding and stiff cycling shoes (though training shoes will suffice), as well as your own cycling helmet.

RIGHT The lack of surfaced roads in the Nicoya Peninsula makes mountain biking one of the few suitable modes of transport
BELOW The 30-km (18-mile) route down the coast from Carrillo to Malpaís includes a mix of inland dirt tracks, beach sand trails, and a few river crossings

CHOROTEGA INDIANS

From around A.D. 800, the Chorotega Indians populated Guanacaste. Their name means 'people who escaped' in their own language, and stems from their breakaway from the crumbling Mayan societies further to the north in Guatemala and Mexico. They created elaborate pottery, used ceremonial skulls, and were very fond of jade, as were the Maya. Their homes were longhouse-style structures that surrounded a central religious worship area where they practised bloodletting and sacrificial rituals. It has been discovered that virgins were thrown into volcano craters as an offering to appease the gods, possibly when the Chorotega were suffering hardship after a volcanic eruption. In 1522, the arrival of the Spanish and their Western diseases was disastrous for the Chorotegas. The few who were not killed by influenza and smallpox were enslaved, leading to the rapid demise of their civilization.

Guanacaste a unique climate, with only 500mm (19 inches) of rain a year, ten times less than the Caribbean coast and significantly less than in the Cordillera Central. From December to April, the parched fields become brown and sallow, but come the rainy season (May–November) and the landscape is transformed into a lush pastureland of long, swaying grasses and dense-canopied trees that is intertwined by fast-flowing rivers.

Getting to the Nicoya Peninsula from San José takes five hours, so the Coast to Coast Adventures bus, topped off with sea kayaks and towing a trailer of mountain bikes, arrived at the pick-up point at dawn. Our group of five comprised John and Julie, a young honeymoon couple from the United States, and our guides Matt and Goldie, all of whom I had been rafting with on the Río Pacuare (see page 214), thus removing the need for introductions. From the capital, our route followed the Pan-American Highway as far as the crocodile-infested Río Tempisque; a ten-minute ferry ride then transported us over to the Nicoya Peninsula. The peninsula is rugged and hilly, and most of its roads are dirt tracks that during the winter months can become impassable to all but four-wheel-drive vehicles and mountain bikes. However, most of the road to **Playa Sámara** (**Sámara Beach**), our starting point, is paved, and twists through beautiful, rolling countryside where we encountered more cowboys on horseback than other vehicles.

SAFETY FIRST

From the Hotel Fenix, a small, friendly place with a clutch of comfortable self-catering villas right on the edge of Sámara Beach, we wandered off down the arcing, endless stretch of white sand and didn't see another soul. After lunch, the sea kayaks were prepared for a thorough training session on paddling and safety techniques out in **Bahía Sámara** (**Sámara Bay**). We donned our buoyancy aids and spray decks (a water-resistant, nylon skirt worn around the lower chest and attached to a rim on the kayak cockpit to keep water out), and listened to Matt as he explained the methods for getting out through the surf. This was a challenge that needed to be met head on. If you paddle hard and straight the kayak's sharp nose should punch through the wave. If you paddle too weakly you either end up back on the beach or ride up the wave and then possibly tip backwards end over end. Matt assured us that this only happens in surf that was much bigger than we were facing that afternoon. However, getting wet was guaranteed as part of the training involved learning how to right a flipped kayak in the open water. Any questions? "Are there any sharks out there?" I asked, fearing the answer. "Sure, but they stay further down the coast…

Península de Nicoya, Costa Rica

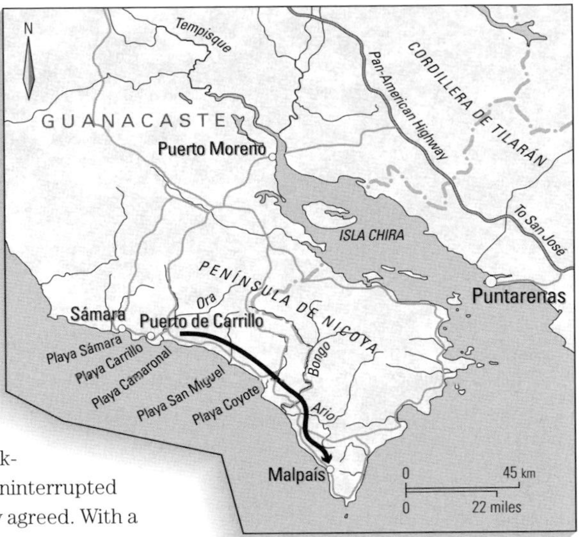

usually," replied Goldie with a mischievous smile.

The honeymooners were first up in a double kayak. Newlyweds are normally quite open to compromise so I didn't think anything of it when Julie requested the front cockpit, the prime seat for uninterrupted views, and John happily agreed. With a loud shout of encouragement from Matt they both started paddling with all their might. As the first wave hit them, it became clear why John had agreed so quickly to Julie's plea. The wave crashed over the bow and hit her full in the face. John sat behind his protective bridal shield and flashed a knowing grin as they made it safely to the calm water beyond the breakers. I would have laughed, too, but Goldie was already sitting comfortably in the rear cockpit of our double kayak.

GUANACASTE'S IDENTITY CRISIS

Does it belong to Nicaragua or does it belong to Costa Rica? Guanacaste has changed hands like an old dollar note. As part of the Spanish-run administrative collection of Central American countries known as the Captaincy General of Guatemala, the region was considered too small to exist independently and was granted to Nicaragua in 1787. By 1812, the Spanish felt that Costa Rica needed a greater population and more land, and so ceded the country control of Guanacaste. Just nine years later, the captaincy was dissolved as the various nations declared their independence from Spain; Guanacaste's position hung in the balance. Those who lived in the northern sections preferred to be under Nicaraguan control and those in the south chose closer affiliation to Costa Rica, while both countries' governments claimed ownership. At a crucial and close vote in 1824, the Guanacaste people voted to remain as part of Costa Rica.

ROLLING ESKIMOS

Unlike river kayaks, sea kayaks have a rudder that is operated by the rear paddler via foot controls, so moving in a straight line is quite easy. Problems for sea kayaks come when they are upside down in deep water. As they are so heavy—particularly the double ones—it is impossible to right a sea kayak using the Eskimo roll technique, which makes the boat flip back up without the paddler having to get out. With a gentle swell rolling underneath us, it was soon time for us to learn the technique for righting the sea kayak. Murky water and the thought of sharks made it difficult to roll over deliberately, but it was quick and painless. Taking a moment to calm myself, I pulled the spray deck off and

slipped out backwards; the buoyancy aid rushed me to the surface where the real work began. Goldie and I turned the kayak over and took it in turns to hand-pump as much water as possible from the cockpits. The tricky part is to get back in without tipping the boat again. While I grabbed one end to steady the boat, Goldie crawled carefully from the other end, like a soldier creeping under barbed wire, into his seat. I did the same and we were back in action. Matt was happy with our efforts, so we paddled around the bay before surfing some small waves back to the beach.

Blue sky and bigger surf greeted us the following morning. Loaded up with water, sunblock, and snack foods, we crashed out through the waves and set a course for Isla Chora, a squat, rocky island just off Punta Indio (Indian Point). From the island, breakers spread out across the mouth of the bay, seemingly blocking our route to the open ocean, but as we eased closer a gap appeared in the centre. The feeling of isolation grew as

ABOVE The Río Ora is one of several rivers that have to be forded along the bike route
RIGHT The sea-kayaking training session on Playa Sámara covers techniques and safety, and allows plenty of time to practise before you set off

quickly as the coconut palms along the coastline receded. For me, kayaking on the ocean had a similar effect to climbing mountains: both impart a refreshing sense of human insignificance in comparison to the wide-open spaces of nature. As we approached the breakers nearest the island, a flock of brown pelicans (*Pelecanus occidentalis*) skimmed the swell as they glided straight towards us with the awkward grace of old, heavy bomber planes. They waited until the very last moment to break formation and veer away from the collision course. The Nicoya Peninsula is a favourite breeding ground for these unwieldy birds, which feed by plunging spectacularly into the water to scoop fish up in their large, pouched bills.

Paddling south past the hill at Carrillo, where waves were battering into the coastline, we briefly spotted a giant turtle just ahead of our kayak. Possibly a leatherback (*Dermochelys coriacea*), it poked its head above the surface to breathe, and seemed as shocked to see us out there as we were delighted to see it. The sun was now blazing down and we reapplied sunblock to avoid getting frazzled. Without warning, the swell suddenly increased to the extent that Matt, in a single kayak, began to disappear from view behind the 4.5-m (15-foot) high waves. Some of them were threatening to break near us so we played it safe and paddled further out into the ocean.

A SHORT INTERVAL

By early afternoon, we were at the mouth of **Bahía Carrillo** (**Carrillo Bay**), our overnight stop. As we surveyed the rather intimidating surf that extended right across the beach, no single place seemed better than any other to get ashore. Matt went first; it was hard to keep track of him once he was in the white water. Just when it seemed he had been swamped by a wave, he popped up on the beach and signalled for us to follow. On the way towards the action zone, Goldie counted the time interval between each wave to give us an idea of how long we had to paddle ashore before we would be hit by a wave from behind. Fifteen seconds didn't seem long enough to me to reach the beach. We lined the boat up straight at the beach and paddled cautiously forward, waiting for a wave to pass under us just before it broke. "Paddle hard!" screamed Goldie, and we pumped away, feeling the kayak surge with each stroke. As I suspected, we were still short of the beach when 15 seconds elapsed and a breaking wave turned us sideways. Reaching out with our paddles, we braced ourselves against the white water and enjoyed a thrilling, if somewhat bumpy, ride into the shore. On a high, John and I teamed up to go back for more, but following two exhausting runs out through the big surf we finally gave in to the lure of lunch.

After a relaxing night at the Italian-owned Hotel Sueño Tropical, where we feasted on delicious pasta dishes, the kayaks were packed away and the mountain bikes readied for an early departure. South of Carrillo the coastline becomes even more remote, and our 30-km (18-mile) route to Malpaís would include a mix of traffic-free, inland dirt roads, hard-packed sand trails on the deserted beaches, and a few major river crossings. With the bike saddles adjusted, front suspension forks checked, and helmets secured, we set off to conquer—or maybe just survive—the reddish-brown dirt trails that lay ahead.

Initially, we followed a narrow, tree-shrouded track alongside the Río Ora. Pools of brown water proved irresistible to the child within us and we tried our hardest to splash each other. Given the hot and humid conditions, the muddy showers were actually a welcome relief. After wading, bikes on shoulders, across the wide, thigh-deep Ora, the first of the day's four climbs arrived all too soon. It wasn't that long, but what it lacked in length it certainly made up for in gradient. The heat was sweltering and the sea breeze was blocked by small hills between the track and Punta Camaronal on the coast. Even for the fitter ones amongst us, it was a struggle up the twisting incline in the still, hot air, and we soon sucked our water bottles dry. Thankfully, Matt had extra supplies for us to refill them at the top. As with any challenge, it felt great to have overcome it and, on the equally steep descent, we reaped the rewards of our efforts. Cool winds and spectacular views down the verdant coastline instantly erased any lingering aches we were suffering.

At **Pueblo Nuevo**, a tiny wood-shack village where horses wandered the main street and the only human activity was a groundsman mowing the local soccer pitch, we pulled into the aptly named Café Maravilloso (Marvellous Café) for several bottles of much-needed lemonade. Only one more climb lay between us and the overnight stop. Thankfully, it was one of the easier ones and we were soon on the flat road towards our camp on **Playa San Miguel**. The ocean looked so inviting after a hot day in the saddle that we all took the plunge. Later, relaxing in rocking chairs on the bar's veranda, we enjoyed a moody sunset below gathering storm clouds.

Beach nesting

The highlight of that night was seeing a green turtle (*Chelonia mydas*) come ashore to nest on the beach just a short distance from our camp. To add to the drama, bolts of fork lightning lit the whole scene. Oblivious to our small group watching from behind, the turtle struggled as far up the beach as possible before digging the nest. Using her rear flippers, she dug for over 20 minutes to scrape out a 60-cm (2-foot) deep round hole. Matthew, an English volunteer working alone on the local turtle project, asked whether I should like to count the eggs. As each golf-ball-sized, slimy egg (they are covered in a mucus that prevents fungal growth) popped out into my hand, I had to place it in a collecting bag. The eggs are taken to a protected hatchery at the project centre to ensure that animal predators, such as dogs and racoons, and human thieves do not take them. It was an awesome experience. I was scared of breaking the soft shells, although Matthew assured me that they were very durable, and I had no idea that the turtle would lay so many eggs—98 in all. The large quantity of eggs ensures that a reasonable number survive, although only about 3 per cent reach maturity). I felt more than a little guilty watching the turtle spend another 20 minutes or so carefully covering the now empty nest, but it was a memorable sight to watch her return down the beach to the ocean.

The storm passed right over us that night, but it wasn't until the following day, when the rain had long gone and the sun was shining again, that we really felt its effect. From San Miguel the 35-km (22-mile) trail crossed four major rivers

RETURN TO THE NEST

Sea turtles have perhaps the most fascinating reproduction cycle of any species. They take 50 years to become sexually mature and then return annually, after decades of wandering the oceans, to lay their eggs on the very beach where they were born. It is still unclear how they navigate with such accuracy. An unwelcome impact of the coastal resort developments north of San Miguel has been the disturbance of the turtles' nesting process. Females normally lay eggs under the cover of darkness, so the bright hotel lights in the new resort areas scare them off. Also, the hatchlings are guided to the ocean by the dawn sky and they are disorientated by other light sources. Protection projects, like that at San Miguel, have momentarily saved sea turtles from extinction, but the pressure is still on and six out of seven species remain endangered.

ABOVE There are plenty of opportunities to cool off along the way
RIGHT The deserted sands of Playa San Miguel
BELOW Though deep, the Jabilla Narrows still proved fordable

and the rain had caused water levels to rise. Matt was uncertain whether the rivers would be passable but we all wanted to try anyway.

After the hills of day one, it was pure pleasure to whiz along the hard-packed sand of lovely Playa San Miguel. Warm sunshine, a cooling breeze, and the mesmerizing sound of the ocean brought on a carefree feeling, and we snaked down the beach, creating wavy tyre-track patterns. The euphoria was short-lived, however, for 20 minutes into the ride we arrived at the swollen waters of the Estero Jabilla (Jabilla Narrows). Matt scouted it and felt that it was safe to cross. With our bikes hoisted overhead, we edged out into a current that was strong but not dangerous. By the halfway point, the water had crept up to our waists, causing a few raised eyebrows, but thankfully it didn't get any deeper than our midriffs before we emerged on the opposite bank.

Our clothes soon dried as we continued our joyful pedalling down coconut-tree-lined Playa Coyote. Along the way, we admired the graceful flight of several magnificent frigatebirds (*Fregata magnificens*). With their lithe black bodies, 1.8-m (6-foot) wingspans, and long forked tails, these are the elegant pirates of the airways. Their feathers are not waterproof, precluding diving for fish, so instead they launch aerial attacks on smaller birds that are carrying prey in the hope that they can force these birds to drop their catches.

Coconuts and crocodiles

At the very swollen Río Coyote our wading fortunes changed and Matt was forced to concede defeat. Like a true leader, however, he swam across the river to hire a small boat to ferry us across. While we waited, Goldie cracked open some fallen coconuts and we gulped down the refreshing, clear milk. From the tiny village of Puerto Coyote, we headed inland on a mainly flat track through lush pastures. With the temperature rising, it was a big relief to arrive at a small shop that sold ice-cold soft drinks. We relaxed under a thatched shelter and questioned the shop owner about crossing the Río Bongo. He thought it would be impossible owing to the rains, but he knew a man with a boat. His overstated insistence made us wonder if the boat owner was his brother, and when he also warned us that big crocodiles lived in the river we thought it would be better to go and see for ourselves.

At first sight, we wondered if the shopkeeper was right. The river was very swollen and coffee-brown. It was impossible to know how deep it was without trying it and, if there were any crocodiles, we had no chance of seeing them. Matt was convinced we could cross though. In front of a small gathering of locals on the lookout for a "crazy gringo" story, Matt and Goldie waded in. The current was the strongest encountered so far and required slow and sure foot movement. After the thumbs-up from Matt, we shouldered our bikes and followed them in. Facing upstream to prevent the flow from buckling our knees, John, Julie, and I edged across. For a short time the water rose as high as our chests, but we soon reached the respite of a shallow sandbar in the middle, and from there it was relatively easy to reach the muddy bank opposite. We all grinned at our success in conquering the "impossible" Bongo.

Primate confrontation

As we entered a forest at the Río Arco crossing, the last of the trip, we heard the unmistakable roar of mantled howler monkeys (*Alouatta palliata*). Incredibly, they were right next to the road, and after wading across the shallow river we stood right below the tree they were in. Goldie let out a big roar and the large, black howlers responded in kind, cautiously making their way down the branches so that they could get a closer look at us. Their incredible sound, which can be heard over a half a mile away, is made as air is forced through a special hollow bone in the throat. It is used to warn off intruders in the monkey's feeding area. We had no intention of stealing food from them, but they were not happy until we were well clear.

The dirt track continued through a pretty forest right next to the beachhead. A couple of rideable watersplashes added to the fun, before the track faded and we returned to the partially rocky beach for the final run towards **Malpaís**. It was Sunday and everyone in the village was dressed to impress, so when we arrived all mud-splattered and grimy we felt distinctly out of place. However, seeing Marvin in the Coast to Coast Adventures support bus at the end of the main street was like reaching the finishing line in a marathon: everything seemed to go into slow motion as our penultimate burst of energy pushed us home. Exhausted but elated after completing such an enthralling and, at times, challenging trip, we saved our final burst of energy for downing a celebratory drink…another thirst-quenching lemonade. The Nicoya Peninsula is indeed remote and we had discovered its wildest parts under our own steam; there can be no better, more satisfying way.

GOING IT ALONE

INTERNAL TRAVEL

Daily buses from San José serve the main town, Nicoya (two buses a day), and beach resorts, including Sámara (one bus a day, run by Empresa Alfaro, which takes 6 hours). Both Sansa and Travelair offer a daily flight from San José to Carrillo Airport, which is only a short distance from Sámara. Independent travellers should hire a four-wheel-drive vehicle to explore the peninsula thoroughly as public transport within the region is infrequent or non-existent.

PLANNING

Due to the remote nature of the region, it is far easier to visit it on an organized tour. There are no local facilities for hiring mountain bikes or kayaks to do a point-to-point tour. The Guanamar Hotel in Carrillo and a few private places in Sámara hire surf kayaks and mountain bikes by the hour to explore the local area on day trips or to do a multi-day round trip. Only Coast to Coast Adventures, based in San José, regularly runs the combination of kayaking and biking in its Paddles and Pedals package (this also includes a two-day rafting trip on the Río Pacuare; see page 214). Other operators may be able to tailor-make a trip.

WHEN TO GO

For the physical adventures it is probably best to avoid the dry season (December–April), when temperatures are high and the landscape is parched. December is the prime tourist month.

TRAVELLERS' TIPS

- ❑ Do not apply sunblock to your forehead when kayaking or biking as the water and sweat will make it run into your eyes, causing irritation.
- ❑ Take it easy when kayaking. Progress can seem slow, as only the distant coastline gives any indication of movement, but consistent paddle strokes are better than short bursts of high action.
- ❑ If you feel a little queasy on the ocean, it is better to keep moving; the rolling effect of the swell is far worse when you stop.
- ❑ If you have a favourite pair of bike shorts, shoes, or gloves take them with you. Try not to wear shorts with raised seams on the inside leg as they will rub.
- ❑ Even if it is cloudy, wear your sunglasses when biking as they stop mud and flies from getting in your eyes.
- ❑ The best route to take when cycling on sandy beaches is normally nearer the water where the sand is firmer.

WHAT TO TAKE

- ❑ Your own cycling clothing, shoes (although not if they have special cleat fittings), and helmet (basic helmets are provided if you don't take one).
- ❑ Plenty of sunblock.
- ❑ Torch for the camping stop.
- ❑ Sunglasses with retaining head strap.
- ❑ Brimmed or peaked sun hat.
- ❑ Insect repellent.

HEALTH

While the risk of malaria is low in Nicoya, it is recommended that you seek medical advice for up-to-date information. During kayaking it is important to apply sunblock to all exposed skin, including under your chin and nose, as the sun's rays are reflected off the water. Also take a brimmed sun hat and something to protect the back of your neck against the strong sun. Drink plenty of fluids, preferably water, throughout the day when kayaking and biking to ward off dehydration, and try to eat something salty, such as peanuts or potato crisps.

BEACH SAFETY

Whilst many of the beaches on the Nicoya Peninsula—including Playa Sámara—are safe for swimming, strong rip tides affect some and can quickly drag you far out to sea. If you are unlucky enough to get caught in one, do not attempt to swim directly back to the beach as the current will be too strong and you will soon exhaust yourself. As rip tides work in narrow channels at 90 degrees to the coastline, you should instead swim parallel to the beach to emerge from the side of the rip channel before attempting to swim back to shore.

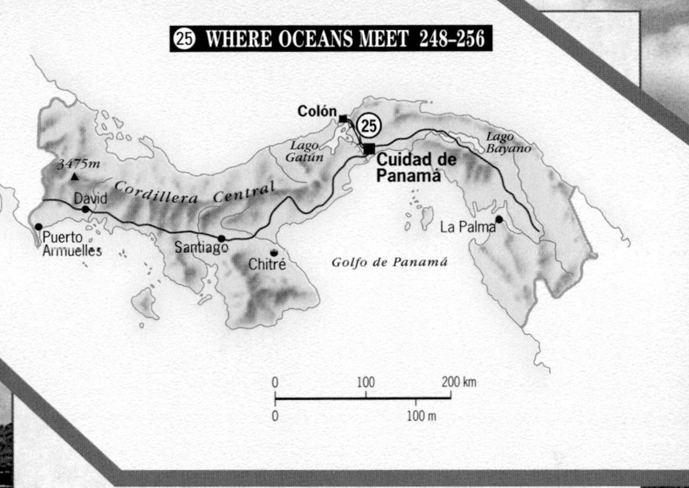

PANAMA

The mere mention of Panama immediately conjures up images of straw hats, giant cigars, and, of course, the canal. Beyond that, most people's imagination grinds to a halt. The country's immaculate rain forests (which easily match those of Costa Rica), spectacular coastlines, and distinct indigenous populations have somehow managed to escape the notice of most travellers' worldwide search for new, untouched destinations. Well, it won't remain hidden for much longer. Panama is, unsurprisingly, tipped to be one of the major growth destinations over the next decade. In addition, the imminent end of U.S. control over the canal (January 1, 2000) sees Panama moving into a new, exciting era of complete independence.

The canal is definitely the thing that inspires most travellers to come to Panama in the first place, but for those who bother to spend a little time visiting the rest of the country, it becomes just one of many highlights. For those looking to explore, Panama offers perhaps the only chance in Central America where a real feeling of discovery is still possible...just don't leave it too late.

The Madden Dam on the Río Chagres, Panama

Where Oceans Meet

by Steve Watkins

Panama is the most underrated destination in Central America, with natural and historic attractions to rival those of any country in the region. I took a fascinating voyage through the Panama Canal, visited the unique tropical island of Barro Colorado, and explored Portobelo, once a centre of colonial world trade.

No other waterway has had such a substantial and sustained impact on global trade as the 80-km (50-mile) long Panama Canal. Sitting in the Balboa Yacht Club bar, a slightly dilapidated, atmospheric watering-hole where bearded old sea dogs and expat Americans take refuge, I gazed out over this oceanic world crossroads. When it was constructed (the majority of it in the ten years between 1904 and 1914), the canal was one of the greatest engineering achievements of mankind, and it still attracts worldwide attention. Every year, around 300,000 tourists, the vast majority of whom see it from the bows of luxury cruise ships, transit the canal. I had come not only to sail on the canal's waters, albeit in a more modest vessel, but was also hoping to get a more balanced view of Panama by exploring the seldom-visited, diverse area that surrounds the canal.

1 The activities on and around the Panama Canal are open to people of all levels of fitness and are suitable for families. The hikes on Isla Barro Colorado and up to the lighthouse on Isla Grande require the most energy, but can be taken slowly.

★ Apart from a few hours' hiking with the mosquitoes in the rain forest of Barro Colorado Island and the optional 15-minute climb to the Isla Grande lighthouse, this adventure is very easy going. Accommodation can be arranged to suit all budget levels.

Hiking boots or training shoes are needed for the island hikes.

Understandably, the canal dominates most peoples' image of Panama, but there is far more to it than that. There are ecological parks and reserves to match those found in neighbouring Costa Rica, an abundance of idyllic islands, and several well-preserved historic towns, all within easy reach of the capital, Panama City. Within the canal itself, Barro Colorado Island, owned by the Smithsonian Institute, is home to a renowned rainforest ecosystem that attracts eminent scientists from around the globe. On the Pacific coast, Isla Grande is an island haven for sun and watersports lovers, while near by, the old colonial trading town of Portobelo still retains its forts

PANAMA CANAL MUSEUM

This recently opened musuem has an informative exhibition on the history of the canal, including graphics, artefacts, rare photographs, and movie footage relating the story of trade across the isthmus and the building of the waterway. It is definitely worth a visit, preferably before you journey on the canal itself. The museum (closed Mondays) is near the cathedral on the Plaza de la Independencia. Note that although this district (San Felipe) may have charm, it is very poor and crime is a problem. Take a taxi to and from the museum and don't walk around the backstreets, especially at night.

FIVE CANAL FACTS

- Grain is by far the most popular commodity shipped through the canal, mainly heading from the United States Gulf Coast region to Asia.
- The material removed during the canal's construction would be sufficient to build a Great Wall of China 4,000km (2,500 miles) long—1,600km (1,000 miles) longer than the real wall.
- Over 15,000 ships use the canal every year, averaging 42 per day.
- The average length of stay per vessel in the canal area, including queuing and transit time, is 24 hours.
- The canal operates 24 hours a day, every day of the year.

and charm from the heady bygone days of pirates, gold, and tall ships.

From the modern skyscrapers and neon signs of downtown Panama City, where at times it is difficult to remember that you are in Central America and not the United States, it is just a 15-minute taxi ride to the canal. For those with plenty of time to wait for a boat, it is possible to secure work as a line handler on a yacht going through the canal. However, most sailors drop anchor during the hurricane season, so despite asking around at the yacht club I had found it impossible to secure a passage in this way. Instead, Argo Tours, the only year-round operator on the canal, offered the sole opportunity to get onto the water and through the locks. The company runs a monthly full-transit tour and weekly partial transits that go through the Miraflores locks. The surprising lack of canal-tour options is due to the fact that the canal is primarily used as a commercial waterway and that the vast majority of visitors go through on cruise ships. Demand from independent travellers is consequently relatively small.

BRIDGES AND BIG SHIPS

At Pier 18 in **Porto Balboa**, the *Islamorada*, a freshly painted ferryboat, waited for our mixed group to board for a partial transit. As we chugged out into Bahía Panama (the Bay of Panama), we saw the most visually stunning piece of engineering on the canal, the wireframe **Bridge of the Americas** which carries the Pan-American Highway. Built in 1962, its wide arch symbolically marks the Pacific entrance to the canal (the dredged area actually continues 8km, or 5 miles, further out to sea). Our boat slipped quietly under it as *Happiness*, a Panamanian-registered cargo ship, passed us on its way to the Atlantic. The canal is so crucial to world shipping that a special size of container ship has developed to fit through it. Dubbed "Panamax," such vessels are of the maximum size that can squeeze through the locks. Around a quarter of all transits involve these mammoth ships, which measure 294m (964 feet) long and 32m (105 feet) wide. Guiding these vessels into the canal is very skilled work and is undertaken by up to four of the specially trained Panama Canal pilots.

Happiness was a relatively bite-sized boat compared to the Panamax vessels, and it was going to be our passport through the **Miraflores locks**. To avoid delaying commercial trade and to conserve water, the tour boats share their passage with such ships. As we turned back under the bridge to follow in *Happiness*'s wake, our guide emphasized how important the canal is for world trade. A boat sailing through the canal from Ecuador to Europe cuts around 8,000km (5,000 miles) off the shortest alternative route via Cape Horn in South America. That route could cost up to ten times more than the average charge levied on ships using the canal, which is $29,700. Charges depend on the net tonnage of the vessel. The highest fee levied to date was in 1997, when the luxury cruise liner *Rhapsody of the Seas* paid $153,622.66 for her passage. The lowest fee of 36¢ was charged to Richard Halliburton, who took seven days to swim through in 1928 (before you rush off to pack your swimsuit, this is no longer allowed).

Happiness edged slowly towards the first of two chambers at Miraflores. A couple of line catchers rowed out below it in a ridiculously tiny orange dinghy. They ensure that the steel cables that link the boat to the lock's electric locomotives, known as mules, are properly secured. The mules, which run on a cogged rail track along the lock edge, have two winches that can each exert 16 tonnes (35,000 pounds) of pulling strength to help position the boat in the lock. For the *Happiness*, four mules were needed, though up to eight can be used on larger vessels. As soon as the tanker was settled, we manoeuvred in behind her, like a baby elephant following its mother into a cage. Due to the large tidal range of 5.8m (19 feet) on the Pacific side, the Miraflores gates are the largest in the canal system. It felt quite sinister as the thick, black gates closed behind us to leave us bobbing at the bottom of a gigantic stone tub.

Water loss

The lock's powerful new pump system fired up, forcing water through a hundred holes in the chamber floor and causing mini-whirlpools to swirl around the boat. We began to rise quickly. The emergence above the stone wall of tourists' faces peering from the Miraflores viewing platform caused a few smiles on board. It certainly felt good to be watching them from the boat rather than vice versa. During each transit of a vessel through the 80-km (50-mile) long canal (a journey of eight to ten hours through six locks), 235 million litres (52 million gallons) of fresh water is used through a gravity-fed system of pipes and culverts emanating from Lago Gatún. The water is then lost to the oceans, so water management is a major priority for the Panama Canal Commission. Once the first chamber was full, the *Islamorada* sailed into the second chamber, where the raising process was repeated until we proudly sat 16m (54 feet) above the Pacific Ocean. Released from the lock, we continued the short distance across Lago Miraflores to the Pedro Miguel lock, where we watched *Happiness* go through the single-stage raise to reach Lake Gatún at the entry to the **Gaillard Cut**.

The success story of the building of the canal is tinged with the blood of the 22,000 workers who died during its construction—around one for every 3m (10 feet) of completed canal. No section proved more difficult to overcome than the Gaillard Cut. At the time, in the first decade of the 20th century, it was the greatest earth-moving project ever

attempted. It cost $90 million to excavate this 14-km (9-mile) channel, 100m (300 feet) deep in parts, through the rock and shale of the Continental Divide. Over 200 trains a day were needed to remove the 1.5 million cu m (2 million cubic yards) of material dug out. Frequent landslides claimed the lives of many diggers, to add to the toll from disease and illness.

Once through the cut, our voyage along the canal was over, and we returned via Miraflores to Balboa Port.

AN ISLAND HAVEN

With the canal being so commercially oriented, it was a surprise to learn that there is a biological reserve on Lake Gatún. **Barro Colorado Island** is the Smithsonian Institute's main centre for tropical research. The centre not only provides the strictly limited numbers of visitors with an opportunity to learn about the ecosystems of tropical rain forests, but it also involves another hour-long boat trip on a different, more scenic part of the canal. As the sun was rising, I took a 50-minute taxi ride from the city out to Porto Gamboa, to catch the Smithsonian boat.

Gamboa is located at the mouth of the Río Chagres, near the Atlantic end of the Gaillard Cut. During colonial times, the river formed part of an arduous route

The 14-km (9-mile) long Gaillard Cut proved the most difficult—and costly—section of the canal to complete

CANAL CONCEPT

Increasing trade in the 1850s from the Californian gold-rush saw interest in the canal idea gather pace, and in 1879 a French company signed a contract with Colombia (which controlled Panama at the time) to build it. Over 15,000 workers were recruited, and Ferdinand de Lesseps, construction director of Egypt's Suez Canal, oversaw the project. However, technical difficulties with the design, landslides, and rampant disease amongst the workforce slowed work until, in 1888, the company went bankrupt. Following the 1898 Spanish-American War, the United States renewed its interest in the project, but Colombia rejected a deal that gave the U.S. ownership of the canal. This led to Panama's move towards independence in 1903. Later that year, Phillipe Bunau Varilla, a Frenchman authorized to act for Panama in canal negotiations, signed the Hay-Bunau Varilla Treaty and ironically gave away far more land and control than the Americans even asked for. It took ten years for the canal to be completed, and on August 15, 1914, the steamer *Ancon* became the first ship to sail through the locks from ocean to ocean.

used by traders to transfer goods between the oceans. It was more difficult than the land-only route from Portobelo to Panama due to the more rugged terrain, but as it only cost half as much its popularity was ensured. As our boat manoeuvred out into the Chagres Crossing, a Singaporean Panamax ship, the *Humboldt Express*, eased towards the Atlantic with her cargo of bright orange containers.

Lake Gatún was formed by the construction of Gatún Dam in 1912; at the time, it was the largest earth dam ever built. Indeed, until the Hoover Dam was constructed in Nevada in 1936 to create Lake Mead, Lake Gatún was the largest man-made body of water on the planet. It is hard to imagine that all the verdant, rainforest-clad islands we passed on the way to Barro Colorado were once just the tops of significant hills.

A cool breeze kept the temperatures down and I soaked up the sunshine on the upper deck as we turned the sharp corner around Punto Caño Quebrado to reach the wide Tabernilla Reach channel. Soon after, at Punto Colorado, we pulled into the aptly named Laboratory Cove, home of the Smithsonian research centre.

A QUEEN'S PARADE

In 1923, Barro Colorado Island (named after a nearby valley town that was lost after the creation of Lake Gatún) was declared a biological reserve by the Panamanian government, and in 1946 the Smithsonian Institute became its administrator. Since then, numerous scientific studies have led to a much-improved understanding of tropical rainforest ecosystems and to some notable achievements. One researcher, Catherine Milton, developed a methodology for studying the island's monkeys that later inspired the author of *Gorillas in the Mist*, Diane Fossey, in her research techniques with the Rwandan gorillas. And in 1997, a German researcher became the first person in the world to observe soldier leaf-cutter ants (*Atta colombica*) carrying their queen to a new nest. In an impressive procession they paraded their leader right past the centre's main building. On Barro Colorado, you barely have to turn your head to see exotic wildlife.

Although the island is crisscrossed by walking trails, guided visitors are taken on one of two. I joined a Panamanian school group to hike the gentle, 2½- to 3-hour Donato Loop. It is only a short distance over mainly easy terrain, but there are so many interesting things along the way that it takes a few hours to see it all. As it was the rainy season, when the ticks are less active, we didn't need to tuck our trousers into our socks as protection against them. A quick spray of mosquito repellent was called for, though, before we crossed a small stream to the trail-head. Climbing a small bank, our guide signalled for us to slow down and keep quiet. A rustling sound was coming from behind a fallen branch, and we all crouched down and peered between the bushes. The rustling stopped and a long-snouted, brown-furred coatimundi (*Nasua narica*), which resembles a slim racoon, appeared. It had been searching in the ground leaf matter for insects, but had sensed our presence and ambled off down the slope.

Jungle guides often suggest that hikers don't clutch at trees to steady themselves, as many species have in-built defence mechanisms. It was probably after someone grabbed a tronador, or sandbox tree (*Hura crepitans*), that this cautious approach was adopted. The large trunk of the tree, which is sometimes used for making dugout canoes, is covered in strong, tiny spikes that would leave your hand looking like a pin cushion if you leant on it. If that wasn't off-putting enough, both the sap and seeds are poisonous to humans (the sap makes your teeth fall out within a month of being applied). Needless to say, we didn't pause too long near this exotic plant.

MONKEY BUSINESS

It was the mantled howler monkeys (*Alouatta palliata*) that we were all hoping to spot, and on a short detour to see a giant ceiba tree (*Ceiba pentandra*) we could clearly hear their blood-curdling roar. It is usually the sight of falling fruit or moving branches that guides you towards monkeys, and sure enough the howlers were dashing around, causing a stir high up in the canopy. Looking up through broad leaves and lianas, the rope-like plants that Tarzan swings around on, we spotted them. Over 1,200 mantled howlers live in roughly 65 troops on the island. Their unmistakable roar, which can be heard more than half a mile away, is made as air passes through a special hollow bone in the throat, and is used at dawn and dusk and to warn off intruders from new feeding sites. We were the intruders that had set off the alarm bells this time, and the monkeys continued to roar until we were completely clear of their territory.

Soon after, a small red brocket deer (*Mazama americana*) was briefly seen grazing just off the trail before it heard our approach and skipped away. It is definitely beneficial to be in small groups for spotting wildlife. Our monkey luck was holding, though. A troop of white-faced capuchin monkeys (*Cebus capuchinus*) appeared right above and around us. Some of them were even on the forest floor rummaging for fallen fruits and insects. Their expressive, pale pink faces, off-white upper body hair, and curled tail

CANAL HANDOVER

Midnight on December 31, 1999, marks the end of an era. After 96 controversial yet successful years at the helm, the United States hands back the canal to Panama. The Hay-Bunau Varilla Treaty of 1903 gave the United States almost limitless, perpetual power and rights of ownership on the canal itself and in the "canal zone," which includes everything within 16km (10 miles) of the waterway. This biased agreement led to decades of conflict between the two countries and resulted in the signing of a new treaty in 1977. This set out a timetable for a complete handover of the canal's control and operations to Panama by the turn of the century. Intermediate plans have been implemented since the treaty was signed to ensure the smooth continuation of the canal's operation, but feelings about the handover are still mixed. There is much pride among Panamanians that they will finally be able to call the canal their own, but it is mixed with concerns over the economic impact U.S. withdrawal will have on the country.

GOING IT ALONE

Planning

Argo Tours runs monthly full transits and weekly partial transits on the canal. All are one-day tours and leave on Saturday. Full transits normally depart at 7:30am and return around 5pm, while partial transits leave at 7:30am and return around 12:30pm. Prices include a buffet lunch. Most tour agencies in Panama City offer canal transits, but they are just booking spaces on the Argo Tours' boats, charging more than if you book direct.

If you want to work as a line handler on a private yacht hang out either at the Balboa Yacht Club or the Colón Yacht Club and talk to as many people as possible. You may need to wait days or even weeks before you find a ride. Some yacht owners pay line handlers while others just give a free trip. It is also possible to pick up on-board work to more distant locations.

To visit Barro Colorado Island, contact the Smithsonian Tropical Research Institute headquarters in Panama City as far in advance as possible as only 45 visitors are allowed on each week. On booking, you will be provided with bus timetables to get you to Gamboa (taxis are quite expensive) and information on what to take. It is essential to take your actual passport to gain entry to Gamboa Port. Tour agencies offer trips to the Barro Colorado National Monument, but this is not the same as the Smithsonian tour, though still very interesting.

To get to Portobelo and Isla Grande by bus, take one of the frequent buses from Calle P. (near Calle 26) and Avenida Central, Panama City, towards Colón. Get off at Sabanitas and pick up one of the hourly Colón to Portobelo buses. The total trip will take 3 to 3½ hours depending on connections. Several agencies run organized day tours to Portobelo. To reach La Guaira (for Isla Grande) from Portobelo it may be quicker to hitch than to wait for a bus. Nobody I spoke to seemed to know when buses ran there from Portobelo, though apparently there is a service. It is far easier and more interesting—though also more expensive—to hire a car in Panama City as I did and drive to Portobelo, which takes 2–2½ hours.

When to Go

Panama's dry season runs from mid-December to mid-April and is the best time to visit the country. Days are sunny and quite hot, and as the humidity is lower at this time, rainforest visits are more comfortable. Although it is quieter during the wet season and prices are lower, Panama is not crowded at any time of the year.

Travellers' Tips

- ❑ Shop around if you are hiring a car: competition is fierce and prices can vary substantially. There are no obvious give-way rules at junctions in Panama City, so be brave and edge into the traffic flow or you may wait all day. Look out for partially concealed stop signs at police posts on the highways. You do have to stop at them.
- ❑ Taxi rides in Panama City cost from $1.50 to $3, depending on distance. Taxis do not have meters, so fix a price before getting in.
- ❑ At La Guaira, the village where boats to Isla Grande depart, local children will offer to guard your car for $1. The family in the house nearest the water actually owns the parking land and sells "official" parking tickets, also for $1.

What to Take

- ❑ Mosquito repellent and long trousers for the hike around Barro Colorado Island.
- ❑ Hiking boots or sturdy shoes.
- ❑ Sunblock for the boat trips.
- ❑ Binoculars for wildlife spotting.

Health

Precautions against malaria should be taken before visiting Panama; consult your doctor or pharmacy for the latest recommendations. It is hot and humid in the rain forest, so drink plenty of fluids while hiking.

FURTHER READING

- ❑ McCullough, David, *Path Between the Seas: the Creation of the Panama Canal, 1870–1914* (Simon & Schuster, 1978). A gripping account of the project, from concept to completion.

INTRODUCTION

Contained in the first section of these "Blue Pages" are lists of selected contacts relevant to the 25 adventures related on pages 18–256. Because the adventures are personal accounts, the information provided here will reflect each author's own experience, and therefore details will vary accordingly. Remember also that some of the contacts are in remote places, so be sure to call or write in advance before setting out. None of the places in the Contacts or the A-Z have been vetted in any way by the publishers and, although some of the companies were used by our writers, this is no guarantee that they will still be run by the same people or to the same standard of proficiency. The Contacts section gives details of companies used by our authors and complements the Activities A–Z in the second part of these "Blue Pages." Below is some general information to help you plan your own adventures.

INTERNATIONAL DIALLING CODES

The telephone and fax numbers given in the "Blue Pages" begin with the area code. When dialling from outside the country, prefix this number with the international network access code of the country you are in, followed by the country code.

International Network Access Codes

For calls from the U.K. 00
For calls from the U.S. 011

Country Codes

Mexico 52
Guatemala 502
Belize 501
Honduras 504
Nicaragua 505
Costa Rica 506
Panama 507

EMBASSIES

British Embassies

Mexico
Calle Río Lerma 71
Mexico City
☎ (5) 207 2593

Panama
Calle 53
Edificio Swissbank (4th floor)
Marbella District
Panama City
☎/**Fax:** 269 0866

Guatemala
7a Ave. 5-10
Zona 4
Edificio Centro Financiero
Torre II (7th floor)
Guatemala City
☎ (2) 332 1601
Fax: (2) 334 1904

Belize
British High Commission
34–6 Half Moon Ave.
Roseapple St.
Belmopan
☎ (8) 22146 **Fax:** (8) 22761

Honduras
Colonia Palmira
Edificio Palmira
3rd Floor
Tegucigalpa
☎ 32 0612 **Fax:** 32 5480

Nicaragua
Entrada Principal de la
Primera Etapa
Los Robles
Managua
☎ (2) 780014

Costa Rica
Paseo Colón
Calles 38 & 40
Edificio Centro Colón
San José
☎ 221 5566 **Fax:** 233 9938

American Embassies

Mexico
Reforma 305
Col. Cuauhtémoc
Mexico City
☎ (5) 211 0042
Fax: (5) 511 9980

Guatemala
Ave. La Reforma 7-01
Zona 10
Guatemala City
☎ (2) 331 1541

Belize
29 Gabourel Lane
Belize City
☎ (2) 77161 **Fax:** (2) 30802

Honduras
Edificio Embajada Americana
Ave. La Paz
Tegucigalpa
☎ 36 9320 **Fax:** 36 9037

Nicaragua
Km 4½ Carretera Sur
Managua
☎ (2) 666010

Costa Rica
Carretera Pavas frente de
Centro Commercial
San José
☎ 220 3939 **Fax:** 220 2305

Panama
Ave. Balboa & Calle 40
Panama City
☎ 227 1777

GETTING THERE

From the U.K.

Mexico
British Airways (from London)

Guatemala
KLM (from Amsterdam) via Mexico City; or British Airways, Virgin Atlantic, American Airlines, Continental, or Delta (from London) to Miami, then Aviateca or American Airlines to Guatemala

Belize
British Airways (from London)

Honduras
British Airways, Virgin Atlantic, American Airlines, Continental, or Delta (from London) to Miami, then American Airlines or Grupo TACA to Honduras; or KLM to Guatemala then American Airlines or Grupo TACA to Honduras

Nicaragua
British Airways, Virgin Atlantic, American Airlines, Continental, or Delta (from London) to Miami, then American Airlines, Nica, Lacsa, or Iberia to Nicaragua

Costa Rica
British Airways, Virgin Atlantic, American Airlines, Continental, or Delta (from London) to Miami, then American, L.T.U., Lacsa, or Iberia to Costa Rica

Panama
British Airways, Virgin Atlantic, American Airlines, Continental, or Delta (from London) to Miami, then American Airlines or Copa to Panama

From the U.S.A.

Mexico
American Airlines, Aero México, Delta, Continental, United, Northwest, Taesa, and America West (from Atlanta, Austin, Boston, Chicago, Dallas, Denver, Detroit, Houston, Laredo, Las Vegas, Los Angeles, McAllen, Miami, Oakland, Orlando, Philadelphia, Phoenix, Portland, Salt Lake City, San Antonio, San Diego, San Francisco, San José, and Washington D.C.)

Guatemala
American Airlines (from Miami, New York, and Raleigh), Continental (Houston), Aviateca (Dallas, Houston, and Miami), Delta (Atlanta), United (Chicago, Los Angeles, New York, and San Francisco), Lacsa (San Francisco), Taca (Dallas, Los Angeles, New Orleans, New York, and Washington D.C.)

Belize
American Airlines (Miami and New York), Continental (Houston), Taca (Miami, Houston, Los Angeles, and New Orleans)

Honduras
American Airlines (New York, Chicago, Miami), Lacsa (Miami), Continental (Dallas and Houston)

Nicaragua
American Airlines (Miami and Nashville), Continental (Houston), Taca (Los Angeles; via San Salvador), Nica (Miami), Lacsa (Miami), Iberia (Miami)

Costa Rica
American Airlines (Dallas, Miami, New York, and Washington D.C.), Continental (Houston), Delta (Atlanta and New York), United (Los Angeles, New York, San Francisco, and Washington D.C.), Lacsa (Dallas, Los Angeles, Miami, New Orleans, New York, and Orlando), Taca (Houston), L.T.U. (Miami), Iberia (Miami)

Panama
Continental (New York and Houston), Eva Airway (Los Angeles), Taca (Houston), Copa (Miami)

GETTING AROUND

Grupo TACA

Head office:
Altos Edificio Caribe
2 Piso Nivel
San Salvador
El Salvador
☎ 298 5055
Fax: 279 4345
website:
www.grupotaca.com
U.K. contact details:
☎ (01293) 553330
Fax: (01293) 553321
email: taca@fltdir.com
U.S. contact details:
☎ toll-free 1-800/535-8780 or 1-800/327-9832
An alliance of five airlines that provides extensive coverage throughout Central, South, and North America. There is an airpass system for travellers who plan to visit several countries.

ACCOMMODATION PRICES

Hotels listed in the Contacts and A-Z sections have been split into three price categories. Some parts of the world are generally cheaper than others but a rough guide is as follows:

Expensive = over $85
Moderate = $40–$85
Budget = under $40

Into the Desert
Pages 20–27

Operators

Baja Expeditions
2625 Garnet Ave.
San Diego
CA 92109
U.S.A.
☎ 619/581-3311
Fax: 619/581-6542
email: travel@bajaex.com
website: www.bajaex.com
This established U.S.-based company operates upmarket diving, snorkelling, and whale-watching tours. It has its own luxury dive boats and adventure camps.

Baja Outdoor Adventures
P.O. Box 792
Centro
La Paz
☎ (112) 55636
email: boa@cibnor.mx
website: www.kayactivities.com
This operator arranges well-organized sea-kayaking, whale-watching, and fly-fishing tours in southern Baja. The group trips or customized tours suit a range of budgets. It is owned by a Welsh canoe coach and his Baja Californian wife.

Ecoturismo Kuyima
San Ignacio
☎ (115) 40026
Fax: (115) 40070
Eduardo Sedano and José de Jésus run this whale-watching and mule-trekking agency, based in San Ignacio.

Malarrimo Eco-Tours
Blvd. Emiliano Zapata
Guerrero Negro
☎ (115) 70100 or (115) 70250
email: malarimo@telnor.net
The young owner of this company, Enrique Achoy, organizes mule tours and whale-watching trips from his family's hotel in Guerrero Negro.

Information

Coordinacion General de Turismo
5.5 Carretera Transpeninsular
Fracc. Fidepaz
La Paz
☎ (112) 40100 or (112) 40199
Fax: (112) 40722
This is the main office of the Baja California Sur state tourist service, but is inconveniently located out of town; there is a small branch office (Officina de Turismo) on the *malecón* (promenade) at Paseo Alvaro Obregón 2130.

Accommodation

Hotel Los Arcos $$
Ave. Alvaro Obregón 498
La Paz
☎ (112) 22744
Fax: (112) 54313
The best hotel in central La Paz, with 190 air-conditioned rooms and cabanas on the *malecón* (promenade). Bar and restaurant. Pool. Fishing trips arranged.

Hotel La Pinta $$
San Ignacio
☎/Fax: (115) 40300
A 28-room hotel on the main road, with air-conditioning, pool, and restaurant.

Hotel Posada San Ignacio $
Ave. Venustiano Carranza 2
San Ignacio
☎/Fax: (115) 40313
This family-owned budget hotel has basic but adequate rooms. Mule treks can be arranged with the owner.

Hotel Yeneka $
Francisco 1
Madero no. 1520
Col. Centro
La Paz
☎/Fax: (112) 54688
A highly eccentric, personalized hotel popular with budget travellers. Spacious, comfortable rooms, courtyard restaurant, and countless odd antiquities.

Food and Drink

El Moro
Carretera Pichilingue, Km 2.5
La Paz
☎ (112) 27010
A beachfront restaurant on the road that skirts the peninsula. Wide choice of seafood dishes and salads at reasonable prices.

Palapa Adriana
Ave. Alvaro Obregón/5 de Mayo
La Paz
☎ (112) 28329
A relaxed and reasonably priced beach restaurant. Mexican dishes, seafood, and steaks.

The Railway in the Wilds

Pages 28–37

Operators

Expediciones Umarike
Apartado Postal 61
Creel
☎/Fax: (145) 60212
email: arturog@online.com.mx
This agency offers mountain-bike day tours from Creel, plus rock climbing for beginners and guiding for experts. It is run by Arturo Gutierrez and his Welsh wife, Audrey Hill. Basic mountain-bike and tent rental is also available.

Nuevo Horizonte Internacional
Ave. López Mateos
Creel
☎ (145) 60111 **Fax:** (145) 60311
View the canyons on a 15–30-minute helicopter tour. Prices are $90–150 per person, with a maximum of three.

Pantera Excursiones
Durango
☎ (18) 250682
email: pantera@omanet.com.mx
website: www.aventurapantera.com.mx
One of the pioneering adventure companies operating in northern Mexico. Arranges 4-day mountain-bike expeditions on a little-known route from Basaseachic to Divisadero. Strong environmental consciousness whether biking, hiking, or just camping in the desert.

Remarkable Journeys
Box 31855
Houston
TX 77231-1855
U.S.A.
☎ 713/721-2517 or toll-free 1-800/856-1993
Fax: 713/728-8334
email: cooltrips@remjourneys.com
A U.S.-based company that organizes hiking and camping trips for small groups (7–13 people) from Creel to Batopilas and in the surrounding area.

Señora Eva
Rarajipa 20
Creel
Señora Eva arranges 2–3-hour horse treks. Alternatively, try the local dentist (further south along the railway track), who is more expensive but has better horses.

S&S Tours
3366 E. Trevino Dr.
Sierra Vista
AZ 85650
U.S.A.
☎ toll-free 1-800/499-5685
Fax: 520/803-1355
email: ss@ss-tours.com
This U.S.-based operator arranges tours in the region.

Trips Worldwide
9 Byron Place
Clifton
Bristol BS8 1JT
U.K.
☎ (0117) 987 2626
Fax: (0117) 987 2627
email: post@trips.demon.co.uk
website: www. trips.demon.co.uk
U.K.-based specialists in tailor-made trips to Central America. The enthusiastic and knowledgeable staff can organize trips to suit most budgets. Also represents other adventure operators.

Getting There

Chihuahua Railway Station
☎ (14) 157756
Fax: (14) 109059

Estrella Blanca Railway Station
☎ (14) 104987

Information

Coordinacion General de Turismo
Edificio Agustín Melgar
31000 Centro
Chihuahua

☎ (14) 162106 or (14) 159124
Fax: (14) 160032

Accommodation

Hotel Korachi $
Ave. Francisco Villa 116
Creel
☎ (145) 60207
A comfortable cabin-style hotel with no frills, virtually opposite the railway station.

Hotel Margarita $$
Calle Chapultepec
Creel
☎/Fax: (145) 60245
This modern, 26-room hotel consitutes one element in Maragarita's Creel empire; the other is her eccentric old guest-house (Casa Margarita, Ave. López Mateos, Creel; ☎ (145) 60045), which somehow squeezes in over 40 backpackers. The wide price range suits all budgets. A third hotel will open in Batopilas in 1999.

Hotel Parador de la Montaña $$
Ave. López Mateos 44
Creel
☎ (145) 60075 **Fax:** (145) 60085
A well-appointed ranch-style hotel on the main street, with a bar, restaurant, and safe parking. Excursions are organized.

Hotel Mary $
Calle Juárez 11
Batopilas
Fax: (14) 146167
This popular hotel has a large courtyard and air-conditioned rooms, plus an excellent adjoining restaurant.From $15.

Riverside Lodge $$$
Batopilas
☎ (14) 158214
Bookings are made c/o Copper Canyon Lodges:
2741 Paldan Dr.
Auburn Hills
MI 48326
U.S.A.
☎ toll-free 1-800/776-3942
Fax: 810/340-7212
This has to be the most astronomically priced accommodation in Mexico. The immaculately restored turn-of-the-century mansion charges $250 per person per night in double rooms, including meals, drinks, and tours.

Food and Drink

There are no particularly recommendable restaurants in Creel. Vegetarians should be wary as most dishes are meat-based. In Batopilas the atmospheric Swinging Bridge Restaurant (by the bridge leading to the Satevo trail) serves excellent food, but you need to get in before the groups; if you can't, book in advance at the private house of Doña Micha on Plaza Constitución.

Ruined Lands of Oaxaca

Pages 38–45

Operators

San Felipe Riding Club
Apartado 252 Oaxaca
Oaxaca
Mexico 68000
☎ (955) 56864
email: french@antequera.com
A friendly American operator, who provides half- and full-day rides into the Sierra Madre mountains surrounding Oaxaca, and a 2-day ride to Monte Albán. Prices start from around $20 for a half-day ride, which includes hotel pick-up, experienced guide, light snacks, and samples of the owner's distinctive brand of mescal liquor.

Trips Worldwide
See page 260.

Information

SECTUR
Presidente Mazaryk 172
Bosque de Chapultepec
11587 Mexico DF
☎ (5) 250 0123 or (5) 250 0027, or U.S. toll-free 1-800/903-9200 or 1-800/482-9832
website: mexico-travel.com/sectur.htm
This office of the Mexico tourist information service provides general travel information on the country, plus useful literature and maps.

Car Hire

All the major car-hire firms have offices in Oaxaca. Prices start from around $35 per day; shop around as competition is intense and special offers are often available (check in local newspapers for the latest deals). Cars can also be booked ahead with these companies through any national office in Europe or the U.S.

Accommodation

Hotel Las Golondrinas $
Tinoco y Palacios 411
Allende
☎ (951) 68726
A lovely old colonial hotel with spacious, comfortable rooms set around a plant-filled courtyard.

Sea and Sierra Pages 46–53

Operators

Ecotours de Mexico
Ignacio L. Vallarta 243
Puerto Vallarta
☎/Fax: (322) 26606
email: 74174.2424@compuserve.com
A husband and wife team offering good though pricey tours and activities: diving, snorkelling, whale-watching, sea-kayaking, trekking, and bird-watching.

Expediciones Cielo Abierto (Open-Air Expeditions)
Guerrero 339
Puerto Vallarta
☎ (322) 23310
Fax: (322) 32407
email: openair@vivamexico.com
website: www.vivamexico.com
This well-organized eco-tourism agency offers whale-watching, snorkelling, bird-watching, hiking, and sea-kayaking.

Rancho Ojo de Agua
Cerrada del Cardenal 227
Fraccionamiento Aralias
Puerto Vallarta
☎ (322) 40607
Daily horse-trekking (10am–1pm, or 3–6pm) through farms and forest to the village of Playa Grande. Longer treks are also available.

Terra Noble
Information/booking address:
Centro para las Artes
Miramar 276
Puerto Vallarta
☎ (322) 30308
Fax: (322) 24058
email: terra@zonavirtual.com.mx
website: www.terranoble.com.mx
The centre lies high up in the hills directly north of McDonald's on the *malecón* (promenade)—most taxis know it. In addition to the *temazcal* and massages, Terra Noble arranges pottery and painting workshops.

Dive Operators

Chico's Dive Shop
Díaz Ordáz 722
Puerto Vallarta
☎ (322) 21895 or (322) 25439
Fax: (322) 21897
email: chicoss@acnet.net
website: www.chicos-diveshop.com
A well-established dive shop offering daily trips to Los Arcos, Las Marietas, and El Morro, plus snorkelling and scuba-diving lessons (PADI). It also runs Pathfinders ATV routes, which skirt the bay 9–12am and 1–4pm.

Information

Officina de Turismo
Municipal Offices
Calle Morelos
Puerto Vallarta
☎ (322) 20242/3
The policewomen in white pith helmets are Vallarta's special tourist police, so call on them if you need assistance.

Cycle Hire

Bobby's Bikes
Miramar 399, corner of Iturbide
Puerto Vallarta
☎/Fax: (322) 30008 or (322) 23848
Mountain-bike rentals and tours.

Accommodation

Hotel Encino $
Juárez 122
Puerto Vallarta
☎ (322) 20280
Fax: (322) 22573
The Encino has reasonable, air-conditioned rooms, some with balconies

and fine views to the sierra. Avoid the noisy rooms fronting the street. Facilities include a small pool and a restaurant.

Hotel Molino de Agua $$
Ignacio L. Vallarta 130
Puerto Vallarta
☎ (322) 21907
Fax: (322) 24601
Comfortable cottage accommodation in lush grounds in a central location beside Isla del Cuale and the beach. The ocean-view suites are more costly.

Hotel Rosita $
Paseo Díaz Ordáz 901
Col. Centro
Puerto Vallarta
☎ (322) 21351
Fax: (322) 21033
This is Vallarta's oldest hotel (opened 1948) and is still going strong. It has a central beachfront position, and basic but adequate and clean rooms. Good value.

Vallarta Sun Suites $
169 Rodolfo Gomez
Puerto Vallarta
☎/Fax: (322) 21626
These are pleasantly furnished self-catering suites in a small, centrally located block behind Playa de los Muertos. All have kitchens and balconies, and there is a communal pool.

Food and Drink

Adobe Café
Basilio Badillo 252
Puerto Vallarta
☎ (322) 31925 or (322) 26720
An upmarket air-conditioned restaurant in one of old Vallarta's most popular streets. Try the excellent beef *fajitas* followed by a rich chocolate mousse.

Archie's Wok
Francisca Rodriguez 130
Puerto Vallarta
☎ (322) 20411
A long-established restaurant near the Playa de los Muertos jetty, serving exquisite Asian cuisine. The restaurant founder, Archie, was once John Houston's personal chef.

Chez Elena
Matamoros 520
Puerto Vallarta
☎ (322) 20161
email: fourwinds@zonavirtual.co.mx
Open for dinner only. Delicious international and Mexican dishes are served in this intimate hotel-garden restaurant. Lovely views.

Rafting in Veracruz

Pages 54–61

Operators

Intercontinental Adventures
Homero 526
Officina 801
Mexico City
☎/Fax: (5) 255 4400 or (5) 255 4465
email: adventur@mpsnet.com.mx
website: www.rafting-mexico.com.mx
This Mexico City agency represents the country's longest-established rafting company, Expediciones Mexico Verde, and can arrange your trip to Veracruz. It also specializes in adventure activities within easy reach of the capital, such as mountain biking around Cuernavaca, ballooning in Guanajuato and Malinalco, para-gliding in Ixtapa, kayaking lessons in Cuernavaca, sea-kayaking in Veracruz, and mountain climbing on Iztaccihuatl volcano.

Río y Montaña
Prado Norte 450
Colonia Lomas de Chapultepec
Mexico City
☎/Fax: (5) 520 2041
Fax: (5) 540 7870
email: rioymontana@compuserve.com.mx
Adventure activities on offer include mountain climbing and whitewater rafting in Veracruz.

Veraventuras
Santos Degollado 81–8
Xalapa
☎ (28) 189579 or (28) 189779
Fax: (28) 189680
email: veraventuras@yahoo.com
A small rafting company operating on the Pescados, Antigua, and Actopan rivers.

It also offers camping facilities and scuba-diving. English is spoken.

Information

Secretaría de Desarollo Económico
Blvd. Cristóbal Colón 5
Torre Las Animas
Fracc. Las Animas
Xalapa
☎ (28) 127345 or (28) 128500
Fax: (28) 125439
There is also a tourist information office (Officina de Turismo) at the Palacio Municipal on the main square in Veracruz.

Car Hire

Autos Villa Rica
Miguel Lerdo 245
Veracruz
☎ (29) 327100, (29) 318329, or toll-free 01-800 7130071
Fax: (29) 327092
A local company, with cars ranging from V.W. Beetles to Chevy Monzas.

Dollar Rent-a-Car
Víctimas del 5 y 6 julio 883
Veracruz
☎ (29) 353377 or (29) 355231

Accommodation

Calinda Veracruz $$
Ave. Independencia, corner of Lerdo
Veracruz
☎ (29) 312233 or (29) 311991
Fax: (29) 315134
A well-appointed hotel overlooking the main square. The air-conditioned rooms plus a bar and restaurant.

Hotel Imperial $$
Miguel Lerdo 153
Veracruz
☎ (29) 321204 or (29) 328788
Fax: (29) 316565
The Imperial is well placed right on the main square, so is convenient for evening entertainment. It is a renovated turn-of-the-century building, with pool and parking facilities.

Hotel Mocambo $$
Calzada Ruiz Cortines 4000
Boca del Río
☎ (29) 220200/1
Fax: (29) 220212
email: hmocambo@infosel.net.mx
A revamped Veracruz institution dating from the 1930s, about 8km (5 miles) from the centre of Veracruz at Boca del Río, the town beach. Excellent amenities; good service.

Hotel San Agustín $
Heroes de Tlapacoyan 201
Tlapacoyan
☎ (231) 50023
A comfortable yet simple hotel in the centre of an attractive market town.

Mesón del Alfarez $$
Zaragoza, corner of Sebastián Camacho
Xalapa
☎ (28) 186351
Fax: (28) 149665
This charmingly converted 18th-century townhouse has tasteful decoration and a good restaurant. Cosseted comfort.

Food and Drink

Café de la Parroquia
Ave. Gomza Farias 34
Veracruz
☎ (29) 323584
This huge, ever-expanding café and snack bar moved to this modern site near the *malecón* (promenade) from a historic setting on the main square. It is just as popular since the move, and is a real Veracruz institution for power breakfasts.

For seafood, go to the breezy seafront at Boca del Río, where rival restaurants dish up *ceviche* (fish "cooked" in lime juice) and fresh grilled fish.

Art in the Jungle
Pages 62–73

Operators

Maya-Sol
Ave. Juárez 191
Palenque
☎ (934) 51006
Fax: (934) 50282
email: mayasol@hotmail.com
Chiapas' most dynamic adventure tourism agency (ATC in San Cristóbal) is

now linking its activities in Palenque and Flores (Guatemala). The fast-developing range of tours and activities includes combined treks and whitewater rafting on the Chacamax, Shumulja, and Raxilha rivers; all-day treks around Agua Azul; and one-day tours of the Piedra Negras ruins.

Viajes Shivalva
Calle Merle Green 1
Palenque
☎ (934) 50822 or (934) 50411
Fax: (934) 50392
email: shivalva@mail.ciberpal.com.mx
Arranges air reservations and confirmations, as well as tours to Yaxchilán/ Bonampak and Misol-Há/Agua Azul. The prices are higher than those of other agencies, but the transport is generally more comfortable. The office is centrally located next to the tourist office on the corner of Abasolo and Juárez.

Viajes Toniná
Ave. Juárez 105
Palenque
☎/Fax: (934) 50209
A popular travel agency with two offices, offering typical tours of the region at rock-bottom prices: waterfalls of Misol-Há and Agua Azul (often in a packed van); Yaxchilán and Bonampak; and Flores (Guatemala) via Bethel. Well organized.

Information

SEDETUR
Plaza de las Artesanías
Ave. Juárez and Abasolo
Palenque
☎ (934) 50356
email: sedetur@montebello.unach.mx
A helpful tourist office, although it offers little more information than local travel agents.

Accommodation

La Aldea del Halach Uinic $
Km 2.7 from Palenque ruins
☎ (934) 50309 or (934) 50297
email: aldea@mexico.com
These recently built budget tourist cabins are situated on a peaceful hillside above the main road. They are nicely designed, with thatched roofs, solar panels, and hammocks on the terrace. Priced by the cabin, very cheaply. Facilities include a restaurant and a small pool, and the staff arrange tours.

Centro Turístico Chan-Kah $$
Carretera Arqueológica Km 3
☎ (934) 51134
Fax: (934) 50820
Bungalow accommodation in large, beautiful grounds. There is a river-water swimming pool and an open-air restaurant.

Escudo Jaguar $
Frontera Corozal
☎ (961) 29020 or contact the SEDETUR office in Palenque (see Information above)
Near Río Usumacinta and Yaxchilán. Two thatched bungalows, each sleeping eight, plus one bungalow with two double beds. There is a large restaurant.

Hotel La Cañada $
Ave. Hidalgo
La Cañada
Palenque
☎/Fax: (934) 50102
This is a friendly, family-owned hotel in a tropical-garden setting at the edge of town. The now rather ageing cottages were originally built for the site's archaeologists.

Hotel Chan-Kah Centro $
Ave. Juárez 2
Palenque
☎ (934) 50318
Fax: (934) 50489
A good option right in the town centre, although rooms on the lower floors can be noisy. There are wonderful views from the top floor. The rooms are air-conditioned and have balconies. Facilities include a mediocre restaurant and a bar.

Food and Drink

Restaurant Maya
Calle Independencia 5
Palenque
☎ (934) 50042 or (934) 50216
Fax: (934) 51096
This large, friendly restaurant on the main square has been a budget fixture in Palenque since 1958. Avoid the cheap set

menus and stick to the à la carte selection instead. Good margaritas.

La Selva
Calle Hidalgo
Palenque
☎ (934) 50363
An upmarket tropical restaurant at the start of the road to the ruins. The waiters wear traditional dress and the décor reflects the nearby jungle. International and regional cuisine; good *fajitas*.

Between the Volcanoes

Pages 76–83

Operators

Los Caballos
Jim and Nancy Matison
Finca San Santiago
Santiago Atitlán
☎ (201) 5527
This ranch was established in 1995 and now has 11 horses. In the high season there is a choice of four horse rides, including either breakfast, lunch, cocktails, or dinner. Accompanied hikes can also be arranged.

Servicio Turísticos Atitlán
Hotel Regis
See Accommodation below.
☎ (762) 2075
Fax: (762) 2246
email: mayanet@guate.net
website: www.atitlan.com
Para-gliding, hiking tours, volcano climbs, and tourist shuttlebuses to Antigua, Chichicastenango, Guatemela City, Río Dulce, and La Mesilla. Flights to Central American destinations.

Tecun Uman
7a Ave. Norte no. 18
Antigua
☎ (832) 6632
Tourist buses between Guatemala City, Panajachel, Antigua, and Chichicastenango. Special buses to Copan (Honduras) and Tapachula (Mexico). Tours to Pacaya Volcano. Weekend sailing in Río Dulce.

Transportes Turísticos Atitrans
Edificio Rincon Sai
Calle Santander
Panajachel
☎ (762) 0146
Fax: (762) 2336
Tourist shuttlebuses to Antigua, Guatemala City, and Chichicastenango.

Information

INGUAT
Centro Commercial Panajachel
Calle Santander
Panajachel
☎ (762) 1392
The helpfulness of this office depends on who is manning the desk. There are lots of leaflets on activities, plus boat and bus timetables.

Accommodation

Hotel Bambu $
Santiago Atitlán
☎ (201) 8913
The Spanish-owned Bambu has new bungalows and hotel rooms in delightful a garden overlooking Santiago's ferry jetty. The restaurant serves a mix of international cuisine.

Hotel Regis $$
Calle Santander
Panajachel
☎ (762) 1152
A long-standing favourite with travellers. Apartments or rooms are available, both with hot showers sourced from underground thermal springs. It is a modern building on the main street, in the heart of the action, and is also home to the Servicio Turísticos Atitlán travel agency (see Operators above).

Hotel Utz-Jay $
Calle 15 de febrero
Panajachel
☎/Fax: (762) 1358 or (262) 0226
A family-run hotel in a large garden at the centre of Panajachel. The hotel is set two streets back from the lake. Rooms have either shared or private bathrooms, and there are also two self-contained cottages to sleep groups. Hiking trips can be arranged.

The Mayan Inn $$$
8a Calle and 3a Ave.
Chichicastenango
☎ (756) 1176
Fax: (756) 1212
A beautifully designed luxury colonial-style hotel surrounding a flowery courtyard. Even if you don't stay here, try to book lunch at the inn on a market day—the waiters wear traditional Quiché costume.

Posada de Santiago $
Santiago Atitlán
☎/Fax: (721) 7167 or cellular phone (702) 8462
email: posdesantiago@guate.net
These spacious stone-built cottages are set in a large hillside garden of avocados and coffee bushes overlooking the lake and volcanoes in a peaceful location outside the village. The American owners are friendly and helpful, there is ample reading matter, and the cuisine is imaginative and fresh. Very good value.

Rancho Grande Inn $
Calle Rancho Grande
Panajachel
☎ (762) 2255 or (762) 1554
Fax: (762) 2247
Comfortable, individually decorated bungalows set around a manicured garden in a quiet though central spot. The part-German owner owns a coffee *finca* in the hills, soon to open to guests.

Food and Drink

Circus Bar
Ave. Los Arboles
Panajachel
A popular restaurant and pizzeria. There is live music during weekend evenings, plus a much-frequented bar. German/French owners.

La Laguna
Calle Principal
Panajachel
Eat indoors near a log-fire or outdoors. This is the place to try Guatemala's national dish, *pepian*, which is a spicy chicken stew.

Mayan Heritage
Pages 84–91

Operators

Avinsa
Calle Principal
Santa Elen
☎ (926) 0808
Fax: (926) 0807
email: avinsa@guate.net
website: www.avinsa.com
Offers a wide selection of adventure trips and tours in the Petén. Follow the Scarlet Macaw Trail, take a 5-day trek to El Mirador (overnight stops at local *chiclero* camps), head overland to Palenque by road and boat, or try white-water rafting or horse riding. Avinsa also arranges trips to Río Dulce, Belize, and Yucatán. English, German, and French spoken; Swiss management.

Ecomaya
Calle 30 de junio
Flores
☎/Fax: (926) 1363
email: ecomaya@guate.net
Organizes 2- to 6-day adventure tours along the Scarlet Macaw Trail, to El Mirador, or to Tikal; fairly rudimentary comforts (you sleep in hammocks). The company also runs a Spanish-language school in San Andrés and organizes volunteer work in community projects.

Martsam Travel Agency
Flores
☎ (926) 0493
Fax: (926) 0624
email: martsam@guate.net
One of many local travel agencies offering bus- and plane-ticketing, plus car and mountain-bike rental. Arranges a day tour by bicycle and on horseback, returning by boat.

Monkey Eco Tours
Ni'Tun Ecolodge
See also Accommodation below.
Exceptionally well-organized camping tours and treks to lesser-known Mayan sites in the Petén and Chiapas (Mexico). Excellent food, comfortable tents, and even portable showers! Run by the

knowledgeable Bernie Mittlestaedt, a Guatemalan of part-German descent. Low-impact tailor-made tours in English or German.

Information

INGUAT
Parque Central
Flores
☎/**Fax:** (926) 0669
A very helpful tourist information office; located opposite the church on the main square. The staff will put you in touch with a local guides' association for accompanied treks: ask for Otto or Abel.

Accommodation

La Casona de la Isla ($/$$)
Flores
☎ (926) 0523 or ☎/**Fax:** (926) 0593
email: lacasona@gua.net
A large, colourfully decorated hotel beside the lake. The rooms are decent, and have air-conditioning and balconies. Facilities include a small pool and a restaurant. Rates are per room for 1–3 people. There are also good kayaks for rent by the hour.

Hotel Casazul ($/$$)
Calle Union
Flores
☎ (926) 1138
email: lacasona@gua.net
A friendly, small-scale hotel in a quiet location at the rear of the island. It has spacious air-conditioned rooms and terraces overlooking the lake. Rates are per room for 1–3 people.

Hotel Villa del Lago $
Flores
☎ (926) 0508
Fax: (926) 0629
email: villadelago@guate.net
A quiet, lakeside hotel not far from the causeway. It offers a wide range of clean, comfortable rooms with shared or private bathroom, air-conditioning or fan, and cable T.V. There is an open-air restaurant and sun terrace.

Ni'tun Ecolodge $$
San Andrés
☎ (201) 0759 or (201) 2028
Fax: (926) 0807
email: avinsa@guate.net
A wonderfully conceived eco-lodge in an isolated jungle setting overlooking Lago Petén Itza. There are four large thatched cabins, each sleeping up to three people, with good bathrooms and terraces. In addition, there is a spectacular open-air restaurant and bar area, home to Murphy the bat and Silvio the parrot. Lore and Bernie, the Guatemalan owners, are passionate about environmental issues.

Tikal Inn $$
Tikal
Fax: (926) 0065
In the heart of the Tikal National Park, conveniently close to the site entrance. There are comfortable double rooms beside a large swimming pool, or standard rooms in the main building. The generator functions only 6–9pm, so it's early to bed and mealtimes at set hours. Large, wild grounds complement the jungle atmosphere.

CRUISING AROUND RÍO DULCE
PAGES 92–101

Operators

Aventuras Vacacionales
Captain John Clark
1a Ave. Sur 11B
Antigua
☎/**Fax:** (832) 3352
email: sailing@guate.net.gt
The 4-day catamaran trips on offer (August–April) leave regularly on Fridays from Río Dulce; some people find conditions on the 14m (46ft) boat cramped, but the prices are low and the captain is reliable. Snorkelling trips out to a Belize reef are also offered.

Bruno's
Fronteras
Río Dulce
☎ (902) 0610 or (206) 9611
email: rio@guate.net
This open-air bar and restaurant is a useful meeting place for yachtsmen and those in search of them. Charter cruises can be arranged.

Happy Fish Travel
Calle Principal
Lívingston
☎/**Fax:** (947) 0271
Organizes a wide range of treks and tours, to Punta Manabique, Playa Blanca, Siete Altares, and Río Dulce.

Syrinx
email: sailingcharter@hotmail.com
George Hertzberg offers his comfortable yacht for charter from Río Dulce to the Belize cays or Honduras's Bay Islands. A minimum of four people (sleeps six maximum) and 4 days. Fresh yacht-baked bread is included!

INFORMATION

INGUAT
7 Ave. 1-17
Zona 4
Centro Civico
Aptdo. Postal 1020-A
Guatemala City
☎ (2) 331 1333
Fax: (2) 331 8893
email: inguat@guate.net
website: www.guatemala.travel.com.gt
There is no local tourist information office in Río Dulce; for help contact the main INGUAT office in Guatemala City, which also has maps of the Río Dulce region.

ACCOMMODATION

Hacienda Tijax $$
Fronteras
Río Dulce
☎ (902) 7825
email: rio@guate.net
Hacienda Tijax has basic rooms, cabins on stilts, or thatched, self-catering bungalows in an atmospheric jungle lagoon opposite Fronteras. It is accessible only by boat (negotiate hard for a 5-quetzal crossing). Horse riding is available on the extensive farmland behind the resort. There is a bar and restaurant, and a lively atmosphere generated by the friendly Guatemalan/American owners. The bungalows sleep four.

Hotel La Casa Rosada $
Lívingston
☎ (947) 0303
Fax: (947) 0304
email: junglestudy@earthlink.net
An American-owned waterfront hotel set in a small garden and with its own private jetty. The surroundings are charming and relaxed, with plenty of hammocks. The restaurant is also good. There are ten thatched cabins with shared facilities.

Hotel Cayos del Diablo $$
Aldea Las Pavas
Santo Tomás de Castilla
☎ (948) 2361
Fax: (948) 2364
Located 8km (5 miles) northwest of Santo Tomás, accessible only by motorboat from there or from Puerto Barrios. A Best Western hotel has air-conditioned bungalows in a waterfront setting. Good watersports, hiking, and biking.

Hotel Tucán Dugú $$
Lívingston
☎ (334) 7813 or (334) 5064
Fax: (334) 5242
An imaginatively designed hotel in lush tropical grounds overlooking the sea. It has comfortable fan-cooled rooms or bungalows fronting a garden, and there is a large pool. The excellent restaurant (El Tiburon) serves lobster and other fresh seafood, and has panoramic views from under its soaring *palapa* (palm-thatched) roof. Helpful staff.

Punta de Manabique Fishermen's Association
☎ (948) 2331 or (948) 2851
Contact the association to arrange accommodation in thatched beach huts at Punta de Manabique, an hour's boat trip from Lívingston or Puerto Barrios.

FOOD AND DRINK

Restaurant Margoth
Calle del Iglesia
Lívingston
A large, canteen-style, open-fronted restaurant, popular with locals. Excellent, inexpensive Garifuna seafood—try the *tapado* (seafood soup) or just plain grilled fish. The service is more efficient here than in most places.

El Tiburón Gato
Calle Principal
Lívingston

This open-fronted veranda restaurant is in a central location on the main street. It is clean, attractively decorated, and friendly, although the service can be slow. Good *ceviche* (fish "cooked" in lime juice) and grilled fish.

WATERWORLD PAGES 104–113

OPERATORS

Belize Land Air Sea Tours Ltd.
5 Eyre St.
Belize City
☎/Fax: (2) 73897 or mobile phone (1) 48777
Captain Nicholás Sánchez leads very enjoyable 2-hour tours of Belize City daily in his specially adapted coach.

Ellen McRae, Marine Biologist
47 Caye Caulker
☎ (22) 2178
email: sbf@btl.net
Tours of the Caye Caulker Marine Reserve, with prices ranging from about $40 to $100 per person.

DIVE OPERATORS

Blue Hole Dive Centre
Ambergris Caye
☎ (26) 2982
email: bluehole@btl.net
Arranges 2-day tours to the Turneffe Islands, Lighthouse Reef, and the Blue Hole; accommodation is on board or in tents. Prices are about $250 per diver, and about $175 per snorkeller.

Coral Beach Hotel and Dive Club
Ambergris Caye
☎ (26) 2817 or (26) 2013
Fax: (26) 2864
email: forman@btl.net
Offers trips to the atoll reefs lasting 1, 2, and 3 nights on the live-aboard *Offshore Express* dive boat. Prices range from about $250 for 2 full days' diving to $450 for 4 full days (includes all meals and drinks, plus accommodation and diving).

Fantasea
P.O. Box 32
San Pedro
Ambergris Caye
☎/Fax: (26) 2576
email: fantasea@btl.net
website: www.ambergriscaye.com/fantasea/index.html
Two-tank local barrier reef dives, single-tank dives, and single-tank night dives. Also PADI Open Water Certification ($400) and open water referral ($250).

Gaz Cooper's Dive Belize
Sunbreeze Beachfront
San Pedro
Ambergris Caye
☎ (26) 3202
fax (U.S. office): 954/351-9740
email: gaz@btl.net
website: www.divebelize.com
Two-tank local barrier reef dives, single-tank dives, and single-tank night dives. Dives cost around $50 Also day trips to the Blue Hole (about $130) and to Turneffe (about $150).

Larry Parker's Reef Divers Ltd.
6D Royal Palm Villas
San Pedro
Ambergris Caye
☎ (26) 3134
Fax: (26) 2943
email: larry@reefdivers.com
website: www.reefdivers.com
Reef Divers has had more than 19 years' experience of diving the waters of Belize, and as such has earned the title "The best and most professional dive shop" in the country. There are both NAUI Nitrox- and PADI-trained instructors, and Larry Parker, the owner and operator, is a world-class NAUI Instructor Trainer. Snorkelling at Hol Chan and Shark-Ray Alley costs about $30 per person, while a one-tank dive is slightly more. Full 4-day, all-inclusive certificate courses costs about $400.

INFORMATION

Belize Tourist Board
P.O. Box 325
2nd level
New Central Bank Building
Belize City
☎ (2) 31913
Fax: (2) 31943
email: btbb@btl.net
website: www.travelbelize.org

Getting There

Belize Marine Terminal

Belize City

☎ (2) 31969

There are three independent boat services that travel to Caye Caulker and Ambergris Caye from Belize City, as well as numerous other boats that belong to the Caye Caulker Water Taxi Association (CCWTA) and take turns in transporting people to the cays. Only boats from the CCWTA leave the Marine Terminal, departing about three times a day to San Pedro on Ambergris Caye and six times a day to Caye Caulker.

Maya Island Air

P.O. Box 458
Municipal Airport
Belize City

☎ (2) 31348 or U.S. toll-free 1-800/521-1247

Fax: (2) 30585

email: mayair@btl.net

website: mayaairways.com

Maya Island Air is renowned for its reliable service. It runs flights between Belize City, San Pedro, Caye Caulker, Corozal, Dangriga, Placencia, Punta Gorda, and Tikal. Charters are available.

Tropic Air

☎ (26) 2012 or U.S. toll-free 1-800/422-3435

Fax: (2) 62338

Flights to a number of destinations in the region.

Accommodation

Fort Street Restaurant and Guest House $$

4 Fort St.
P.O. Box 3
Belize City

☎ (2) 30116

Fax: (2) 78808

email: fortst@btl.net

website: www.belizenet.com/fortst.html

The guest house is good and the restaurant excellent. It is located in the Fort George area, only a few hundred yards from the Caribbean Sea. Food is served on the restaurant's veranda or in its air-conditioned interior. Rates quoted vary depending on the season, including breakfast but not the 7 per cent hotel tax or 10 per cent service charge. Expect to pay about $35 for two in the restaurant.

Radisson Fort George Hotel $$$

2 Marine Parade
P.O. Box 321
Belize City

☎ (2) 33333 or U.S. toll-free 1-800/333-3333

Fax: (2) 73820

email: radexec@btl.net

website: www.radissonbelize.com

This colonial-style resort has 102 rooms, all with air-conditioning, cable television, minibar, and the usual amenities. There is a swimming pool, fitness centre, a restaurant, and a bar. The hotel is located in the Fort George area of Belize City, overlooking the cays and Caribbean Sea, in a relatively safe district that is close to the markets, downtown and business areas, and the foreign consulates. Rates vary considerably for a double room from the low season to the high season.

Morgan's Inn $$

P.O. Box 47
Caye Caulker

☎ (22) 2178

email: sbf@btl.net

These are spacious beachfront cabins, some with hot and cold running water.

Rainbow Hotel $

Front St.
Caye Caulker

☎ (22) 2123

Fax: (22) 2172

This is a cemented, rectangular building with views out over the sea. It is basic, with hot showers. Some rooms have televisions.

Royal Palm Inn Ltd. $$$

P.O. Box 18
San Pedro
Ambergris Caye

☎ (26) 2244

Fax: (26) 2329

email: royalpalm@btl.net

website: www.belize.com/royalpm.html

The Royal Palm Beach's spacious seaside condominiums are set in tropical landscaped poolside gardens. There is a good restaurant, and a range of daily excursions is on offer. The properties received the Resort Condominiums International "Gold Resort Award," the first in Belize to do so. Room rates vary with the season. The resort is a 5-minute taxi ride from the centre of San Pedro.

Stuck on the South
Pages 114–121

Operators

MayaLand Tours and Travel
P.O. Box 137
Belize City
☎ (2) 30515 or (2) 32810
Fax: (2) 32242 or (2) 31784
email: mayaland@btl.net
website: www.mayalandbelize.com
The largest wholly Belizean-owned travel operator in the country. It offers tours throughout Belize, and specializes in archaeology and bird-watching.

Information

Belize Tourist Board
See page 270.

Car Hire

Budget
Phillip Goldson International Airport
Belize City
☎ (2) 32435 or U.S. toll-free 1-800/BUDGET7
email: jmagroup@btl.net

Crystal Auto Rental Ltd.
International Airport
Belize City
☎ (2) 31600
Fax: (2) 31900
email: crystal@btl.net
Crystal has a good range of vehicles at reasonable prices.

Thrifty Car Rental
Central American Blvd. and Fabers Rd.
Belize City
☎ (2) 71271 or U.S. and Canada toll-free 1-800/FOR-CARS
Fax: (2) 71421
email: tourbelize@btl.net

Getting There

Maya Island Air
See page 271.

Tropic Air
See page 271.

Accommodation

The Monkey House $$$
Monkey River Village
Toledo
☎ (6) 12032
email: watch@btl.net
The Monkey House is one of Monkey River's newest resorts, and is on the north side of the river, adjacent to the village. It is owned by Martha and Sam Scott, originally from Beaumont, Texas. They have two beachside cabanas, with plans for two more. Both are equipped with hot water and electricity. It is a very private resort with very clean and luxurious cabanas, certainly the best in the area. The owners can also arrange a number of tours.

Sunset Inn $$
Monkey River Village
Toledo
☎ (6) 12028
This nine-bedroomed hotel is owned by Clive Garbutt, who is also a very knowledgeable guide. The rooms are basic and clean, with hot running water. Rates are $50 per night. Clive leads bird-watching, fishing, snorkelling, and camping tours; the Monkey River tour costs about $25 per person.

Bob's Paradise $$$
Monkey River
Toledo
☎ (6) 12024
email: bobsparadise@webtv.net
website: www.bobsparadise.com
This place really is away from it all. It is 1½km (1 mile) north of Monkey River village and is accessible only by boat. If you're coming from Placencia, Bob will pick you up free of charge; if you reach Monkey River village by road, get one of the guides to take you on the last leg in one of their boats (this will cost you a couple of dollars). There is not much to do at Bob's apart from relax, although tours can be arranged. There are three private cabins, each with hot water and electricity.

Nautical Inn $$$
Placencia Peninsula
Stann Creek
☎ (6) 23595 or U.S. toll-free 1-800/688-0377
Fax: (6) 23594
email: nautical@btl.net
website: www.belizenet.com/nautical.html
This luxury resort is not far from Seine Bight Garifuna village. The owners, Ben and Janie Ruoti, have 12 rooms, all on the beach and equipped with either air-conditioning or fans. There is a bar, and ask to be shown how to play coconut bowling! They can also arrange several different tours. The meal plan is about $40 per person per day.

Singing Sands Inn $$/$$$
Maya Beach
Placencia Peninsula
Stann Creek
☎/Fax: (6) 22243
email: ssi@btl.net
website: www.belizenet.com/singsand.html
The staff at Singing Sands are truly marvellous, and go out of their way to make sure you have an enjoyable stay. But it isn't hard to do that here. There is a long beach a few yards from the six private thatched cabanas, each of which has its own patio, ceiling fans, and hot running water. There is also a separate house suitable for a family or for those seeking more seclusion. There is a good range of tours to keep you busy for at least a week, and there is also a resident diver who can take certified divers (bring your card) to several sites. The owners are Eldon Ebel and Marty Cottrell, but the onsite managers are Kathy and Hank Hays. Room rates are about $80 per night for a double room June 1–November 15, and over $100 for the same room November 16–May 31. Allow $40 per person per day for food.

Trade Winds Hotel $
Placencia
Stann Creek
☎ (6) 23122
Fax: (6) 23201
email: trdewndpla@btl.net
Owned by Janice Romero Leslie, who also own the Byrds Bar at Placencia port. There are five basic rooms.

Under the Spell of the Maya Pages 122–129

Operators

Belize Land Air Sea Tours Ltd.
See page 270.

Caves Branch
See Accommodation below.
There are four 1-day cave expeditions on offer, plus other adventures such as an overnight caving tour, jungle treks, and a gruelling 4-day/3-night jungle survival course where you leave the lodge armed only with a machete and your guide (certificates are awarded to those who complete the course). The 1-day trips cost between $70 and $80 per person. The 13-day Maya Mountain Expedition (part of the owner's "Bad Ass" expedition) costs over $2,000 per person.

Eva's Restaurant
22 Burns Ave.
San Ignacio
Cayo District
☎ (92) 2267
email: evas@btl.net
website: www.webspawner.com/users/evasonline/home.htm
See Food and Drink below for further information.

Ix Chel Farm
San Ignacio
Cayo District
☎ (92) 3870
Fax: (93) 3165
email: ixchel@btl.net
This is the home of the rainforest medicinal trail, where many of Belize's medicinal plants can be seen in their natural habitat. Tours and seminars are available, but contact the farm first. It is not possible to eat here, nor is there any accommodation, but you can stay at the nearby Cha Creek resort (see Accommodation below). Rainforest remedies are on sale in the shop and by

mail order, ranging from "Belly Be Good" to "Flu Away," "Nerve Tonic," "Strong Back," and "Traveller's Tonic." Costs are between $10 and $15, plus 15 per cent for shipping and handling. There is a minimum order of three items and delivery takes about 4 weeks.

Information

Belize Tourist Board

See page 270.

Car Hire

See page 272.

Accommodation

Caves Branch Jungle Lodge $/$$$

Mile 41½, Hummingbird Highway
Mailing address:
P.O. Box 356
Belmopan
☎/**Fax:** (8) 22800
email: caves@pobox.com

The lodge is located on a privately owned 23,500-ha (58,000-acre) estate in the heart of the Belizean jungle. It overlooks the Caves Branch River and is shaded by a 30-m (100-foot) high rainforest canopy. The lodge holds 35 people split between four cabana suites, six jungle cabanas, and an eight-bed bunkhouse. Packed lunches can be arranged.

Cha Creek Cottages $$$

P.O. Box 53
San Ignacio
Cayo District
☎ (92) 2037
Fax: (92) 2501
email: chaacreek@btl.net
website: www.belizenet.com/chaacreek.html

At Cha Creek there are 20 thatched rooms set along the riverside on a 120-ha (300-acre) private reserve in the foothills of the Maya Mountains. Guests can interact with nature, follow walking trails, canoe, horse ride, mountain bike, and join a range of tours to Xunantunich, Mountain Pine Ridge, Vaca Falls, or Caracol. Prices vary depending on the season, but range from about $100 to $175 for the luxury jacuzzi suite in peak season (November 1 to May 31). There is also a range of all-inclusive packages (minimum 3 nights). Prices exclude breakfast and 15 per cent VAT. There is also accommodation for backpackers or travellers on a limited budget at the Macal River Camp, in elevated safari tents with large, covered verandas. There are communal hot and cold showers here, and food is served in a central thatch-roofed restaurant. Prices are per person, including breakfast, dinner, and government taxes.

DuPlooy's Jungle Lodge $$/$$$

Box 180
San Ignacio
Cayo District
☎ (92) 3101
Fax: (92) 3301
email: duplooys@btl.net
website: www.duplooys.com

This luxury jungle lodge is not far from Cha Creek. It offers similar accommodation but has the added advantage of a wonderful boarded walkway set on stilts that winds its way through the jungle and ends at a tremendous viewpoint overlooking the Macal River. There is also a restaurant.

San Ignacio Resort Hotel $$$

P.O. Box 33
San Ignacio
Cayo District
☎ (92) 2034 or (92) 2125
Fax: (92) 2134
email: sanighot@btl.net
website: www.belizenet.com/sanighot.html

This is not just a hotel, but also a sanctuary for the threatened green iguana. Under the direction of the manager, Mariam Roberson, the Green Iguana Conservation Project raises young iguanas in a protected enclosure for two years until they are ready to be released on to the terraces alongside the Macal River. Visitors can come here to see what is being done to help this endangered species. Daily tours are available; call in advance. The hotel also has the only air-conditioned bar and grill in town.

Food and Drink

Eva's Restaurant

22 Burns Ave.
San Ignacio

Cayo District
☎ (92) 2267
email: evas@btl.net
website: www.webspawner.com/users/evasonline/home.htm
This gift shop, restaurant, bar, and tourist information office all in one is owned by Englishman Bob Jones and his wife, Nestora.So if you want to book accommodation or any tours in the area, Bob will help you out.

ESCAPE TO THE WILD SIDE
PAGES 132–139

OPERATORS

AFE/COHDEFOR

La Ceiba
Honduras
☎ (441) 0800 or (441) 1833
Fax: (441) 1832
email: prodebol@hondutel.hn
Ths is the organization in charge of the Parque Nacional Pico Bonito. Contact them for more information and for park entry permits.

Fundación Cuero y Salado (FUCSA)

Apartado Postal 674
La Ceiba
☎/Fax: 443 0329
FUCSA is situated in Edificio Ferrocarril Nacional, Zona Mazapan, in La Ceiba, and runs the Cuero y Salado park; reservations to visit the park must be made with them unless you go with a recognized tour operator. The friendly and helpful staff have information on bus times to La Unión (open Mon–Fri 8–11:30am and 1:30–4:30pm; Sat 8–11:30am). To reserve the *motocarro*, it is necessary to ring the Standard Fruit Company direct on 443 0511, ext. 2171 or 2184.

MC Tours

Col. Trejo
10 Calle 18 Ave. S.O. #235
2 cuadras arriba de la Cámara de Comercio e Industrias de Cortés
San Pedro Sula
☎ 552 4455
Fax: 557 3076
email: mctours@netsys.hn
website: www.netsys.hn/~mctours
One of Honduras's leading operators, specializing in more upmarket tours. Cuero y Salado is included as part of the 6-day Green and Blue Adventure Tour, and the company also operates a whole range of other tours to all parts of the country.

La Moskitia Ecoaventuras

Ave. 14 de Julio
Casa #125
P.O. Box 890
La Ceiba
☎ 221 0404
Fax: 442 0104
email: moskitia@tropicohn.com
A friendly, professional company run by Jorge Salaveri, who speaks fluent English. Highly recommended. It organizes tours to Cuero y Salado and Pico Bonito, and whitewater rafting on the superb Río Cangrejal, as well as trips to other destinations in Honduras. The company can tailor-make tours for most destinations—contact them for prices.

GETTING THERE

Aerolineas SOSA

Edif. ROMAN
8 Ave. 1y 2 Calle
San Pedro Sula
☎ 550 6545, La Ceiba 443 1399, Roatán 445 1154, Guanaja 453 4359, Utila 425 3161
email: aerososa@caribe.hn
A small regional airline that offers flights to La Ceiba, Roatán, Guanaja, Utila, San Pedro Sula, and Palacios. It is generally reliable in terms of schedules, and as it is popular you should book ahead.

Grupo TACA

See page 258.
Operates several flights daily to Tegucigalpa and San Pedro Sula from points throughout its network, and flights to La Ceiba, Roatán, and Palacios, Mosquitia, some in conjunction with the subsidiary Isleña Airlines (see below).

Isleña Airlines

Ave. San Isidro
Frente al Parque Central
La Ceiba

☎ 443 0179 or 443 0883
Roatán office 445 1088
San Pedro Sula office 552 8322, San Pedro Sula Airport 668 2218
Tegucigalpa office 237 3370, Tegucigalpa Airport 233 1130 or 233 9813
Fax: 443 2632, La Ceiba Airport 443 2693
email: islena@caribe.hn
A subsidiary of Grupo TACA, offering flights around the country between Tegucigalpa, San Pedro Sula, La Ceiba, Roatán, Guanaja, and La Mosquitia. Also operates two international services to Managua in Nicaragua and to Grand Cayman.

Information

Instituto Hondureño de Turismo (IHT)

Col. San Carlos
Edificio Europa
Apartado Postal No. 3261
Tegucigalpa
☎ 222 2124
Fax: 238 2102
email: ihturism@hondutel.hn
website: www.hondurasinfo.com
An increasingly active tourist board that has a range of very useful and colourful promotional material, including the full-colour magazine *Destination Honduras*. Very helpful, bilingual staff.

IHT International Office, U.S.A.

2100 Ponce de León Blvd.
Suite 1175
Coral Gables
FL 33134
U.S.A.
☎ toll-free 1-800/410-9608
Fax: 305/461-0602
Offers the same services as the main Honduran office.

Honduran Consulate, London

115 Gloucester Place
London W1H 3PJ
U.K.
☎ (020) 8486 4880
Fax: (020) 8486 4550
Offers the same promotional material and advice on travel in Honduras as the IHT.

Honduras Tips

Edificio Rivera y Cía
Piso 7
Oficina 705
3 Calle
6 Ave.
Apartado Postal 2699
Tegucigalpa
☎ 552 5860
Fax: 552 9557
email: hondurastips@globalnet.hn
Honduras Tips is a superb comprehensive guide to tourism in Honduras, packed with information on the different regions, hotels, restaurants, nightlife, and tours. It is available free of charge in the country, or via the tourist board offices abroad. Invaluable details for planning a trip.

Accommodation

Honduras Maya $$/$$$

3 Calle
Ave. República de Chile
Col. Palmira
Tegucigalpa
☎ 220 5000
Fax: 220 6000
email: reserve@hondurasmaya.hn or hmayager@gbm.hn
website: www.hondurashotels.com/hondurasmaya
One of the capital's top hotels, situated in the upmarket Palmira district. It offers all modern conveniences, including cable T.V., swimming pool, casino, bar, and restaurant, plus a number of shops, a hairdresser, and a newsagent. Rooms range from small studios (about $70 for a double) and apartments (about $120) to the luxurious Royal Suite ($400 for two people).

Paseo Miramontes $$

Calle Paseo Miramontes
Col. Miramontes
Frente a Bodegas de Larach #3
Tegucigalpa
☎ 239 1855
Fax: 232 8179
A pleasant new hotel in a quiet district of the city. The 20 rooms are well-equipped, with cable T.V. and direct-dial telephone, though they are quite small. Guest parking is available at the front. It is closer to the airport than most hotels, so is useful for brief stays in the city or if you have an early morning flight. Rates include a continental breakfast.

Grand Hotel La Ceiba $

Ave. San Isidro
5ta. Calle
La Ceiba
☎ 443 2747 or 443 0876
Fax: 443 2737
This centrally located hotel is very good value, and has 40 large, comfortable rooms that offer cable T.V., air-conditioning, telephone, minibar, and private bathroom. It also has a reasonable restaurant/bar downstairs.

Hotel Plaza Flamingo $

1ra Calle
al Final de Ave. 14 de Julio
La Ceiba
☎ 443 3149 or ☎**/Fax:** 443 2738
A modern hotel on the beachfront. It has very clean and comfortable rooms with cable T.V., air-conditioning, telephone, and security box. There is access from the rooms to a communal balcony area. The nearby disco can be quite loud.

Hotel Saint Anthony $$$

3a Ave.
Calle 13
P.O. Box 2291
San Pedro Sula
☎ 558 0744
Fax: 558 1019
This is one of San Pedro Sula's better hotels, despite its ageing appearance. It has a swimming pool/jacuzzi, gym, cable T.V., restaurant, bar, and pool table. Rates include breakfast and a newspaper.

TREASURE ISLANDS PAGES 140–149

OPERATORS

Captain Van's Rentals

Situated on the seafront in West End opposite the Evangelist church
email message service: online@globalnet.hn (write "Captain Van" in the subject line)
A small, friendly rental company run by Van and Gabriel. Daily rental rates are about: mountain bikes $10; mopeds $25 including petrol; motorbikes $30–35; and water rafts $5. They can suggest good routes around the island.

MC Tours

See page 275.

DIVE OPERATORS

Sueño del Mar Dive Center

West End
Roatán
Islas de la Bahía
☎**/Fax:** 445 1717 or U.S. toll-free 1-800/298-9009
email: suenodelmar@globalnet.hn
One of the most popular dive operators on the island, and spectacularly situated at the end of a jetty in West End (below the bar). The company runs three dives a day to numerous locations including the *El Aguila* wreck, returning to base between dives, so it is possible to join for just the second or third dive. The instructors are all qualified professionals and the dive boats are well equipped. It also has a good dive shop selling equipment and souvenirs. Single dives with all equipment cost about $30, five-dive packages cost about $130, and there is a deal on ten dives. PADI Open Water Certification courses cost about $180. Other courses are also available. Sueño del Mar also rents out sea kayaks, and snorkel gear—mask, fins, and snorkel. The company can arrange accommodation (see below), with generous discounts for those who book dive/accommodation packages.

West Bay Dive Resort

West Bay
Roatán
Islas de la Bahía
Fax: 445 1925
email: westbaylodge@globalnet.hn
website: www.stic.net/roatan/westbaylodge
The ideal location for mixing an adventurous diving holiday with a relaxing vacation. Situated overlooking the idyllic West Bay Beach, with fantastic snorkelling opportunities, this dive resort offers a personal and friendly service. It is owned by Maren and Reinhard Gnielka, who run PADI Certification courses and offer accommodation (see below). Single dives cost about $30 with all equipment, fand ten dives cost about $230. Six-night PADI Open Water Course and accommodation packages cost about $600 for two (sharing a cabin). Seven nights' accom-

modation, ten boat dives, and one night dive costs about $450/$650. Package rates include breakfast but exclude tax. Maren is a professional masseur, too, if you fancy the ultimate relaxing break. (Note that at the time of writing there is no phone and the email address is a message service, so it may take 2–3 days to get a response.)

Information

See page 276.

Getting There

Aerolineas Sosa

See page 275.
Daily flights to Guanaja and Roatán.

Isleña Airlines

See page 275.
Daily flights to Guanaja and Roatán.

Safeways

Municipal Dock
La Ceiba
☎ for reservations 445 1795
Operates the *Galaxy II* and *Tropical* ferry services to the Islas de la Bahía. Daily to Utila and Roatán, and twice-weekly to Guanaja (8am on Wednesday and Sunday at the time of writing). Prices are not much cheaper than flying, but it is quite a pleasant journey.

SeaWays

Municipal Dock
La Ceiba
☎ for reservations 445 5519
Runs the *Nautica* ferry services to Roatán, Gunaja, and Utila. Prices and schedules change frequently, so it is best to check on arrival in La Ceiba for the latest information. At time of writing, there were sailings from La Ceiba to Roatán Sun–Fri at 2:30pm, returning at 7:30am; La Ceiba to Guanaja sailings were on Wednesdays and Sundays only at 2:30pm, with boats returning on Mondays and Thursdays at 5am, both going via Roatán.

Accommodation

For accommodation in Tegucigalpa, see page 276.

Bayman Bay Club $$$

All reservations and enquiries are dealt with by Terra Firma Adventures:
7481 W. Oakland Park Blvd.
Ste. 308
Fort Lauderdale
FL 33319
U.S.A.
☎ 954/572-1902 or toll-free 1-800/524-1823
Fax: 954/572-1907
email: reservations@baymanbayclub.com
website: www.baymanbayclub.com
A superbly located dive resort on the north side of Guanaja. It offers accommodation in very comfortable rustic bungalows set high above the ocean, each with a private deck and breathtaking views that make waking up an event in itself. The spacious bungalows have private bathrooms, fans, and natural air-conditioning—wooden slats over the windows control how much sea breeze gets in! There is a lovely bar/restaurant with a pool table and reading area upstairs. All-inclusive dive/accommodation packages cost $1,080, including taxes, per person per week in the high season, based on double occupancy. Low-season rates start from around $650.

Posada Arco Iris $

Half Moon Bay
West End
Roatán
Islas de la Bahía
☎**/Fax:** 445 1264
email: roberto@hondutel.hn
One of the nicest hotels on the island, and very reasonably priced. It was recently built and designed by the friendly Argentinian owners, Andres and Valeria, and is situated right on the beachfront at the idyllic and peaceful Half Moon Bay in West End. The spacious, clean rooms are tastefully decorated, and have private bathrooms (with constant hot water), balconies, and hammocks. There is also a same-day laundry service for guests. There is larger apartment-style accommodation available for groups. Low-season discounts are available.

Sueño del Mar $/$$

See Dive Operators above.
This West End dive centre also offers a range of accommodation in the area, including the Sea Breeze Inn ($$), South

Winds ($), and, believe it or not, Fawlty Towers (very inexpensive). Discounts are available for divers and long stays.

West Bay Lodge $
See Dive Operators above.
This rustic wooden lodge, situated on a hillside within a couple of minutes' walk of the superb West Bay Beach, is owned and run by the welcoming Maren and Reinhard Gnielka, who speak English, Spanish, and German. They have three simple but comfortable double cabins with queen-size bed, private bathroom, hot water, and balcony. Rates include-breakfast, with delicious homemade bread Off-season and long-stay rates are available. West Bay Lodge is also a PADI dive centre.

A Life in Ruins Pages 150–157

Operators

MC Tours
See page 275
MC Tours arranges visits to Copán separately or as part of several itineraries, including Maya Adventure. The company's owners also run the wonderful Hotel Marina Copán (see Accommodation below). Trips include transfers from San Pedro Sula Airport in air-conditioned vehicles, professional bilingual guides, accommodation in the family's hotel, and relevant meals. Several interesting side-trips around the Copán area can be added on.

Information

See page 276.

Accommodation

Hotel Los Gemelos $
Copán Ruinas
☎ 651 4077
Fax: 651 4315
email: maricela@hondutel.hn
A very popular backpackers' hotel situated near the old town bridge. It has 13 basic rooms set around a courtyard, with communal showers (cold) and toilets. It also has Internet access, fax and international phone services, and a snack shop that sells imported chocolate bars and other foreign goodies.

Hotel Marina Copán $$
Central Plaza
Copán Ruinas
☎ 651 4070, 651 4071, or 651 4072
Fax: 651 4477
email: hmarinac@netsys.hn
website: www.netsys.hn/~hmarinac
The Marina Copán, located right in the centre of town, is one of the most charming hotels in the whole country. It has been run by one family for over 50 years, is in a delightful colonial style, and has a plant-filled courtyard at its centre. It has been the hotel of choice for many of the archaeologists who have, over the years, uncovered Copán's secrets. The 40 spacious rooms are tastefully decorated and offer all the modern conveniences, including cable T.V., private bathroom (with huge shower), air-conditioning. and telephone. There is a swimming pool, a very good restaurant, a gym, and a souvenir shop within the hotel. A real treat, and reasonably priced too.

Rivers of Time Pages 158–175

Operators

Adventure Expeditions
1020 Altos de la Hoya
Tegucigalpa
☎/Fax: 237 4793
email: cyber-place@hotmail.com
Adventure Expeditions specializes in trips to Mosquitia, and can tailor-make tours to all parts of the region.

MC Tours
See page 275.
This operator runs 5- and 6-day trips to Mosquitia, with professional bilingual guides.

La Moskitia EcoAventuras
See page 275.
Specialists in tours to Mosquitia. There are several possible itineraries to the region, including an epic 10–12-day rafting/jungle-trekking trip on the Río Plátano for serious adventurers; the company can also

tailor-make tours—contact them direct re prices. The 5-day tour our author took cost $850, including flights.

Information

See page 276.

Getting There

Aerolineas Sosa
See page 275.
Daily flights from Palacios to La Ceiba.

Isleña Airlines
See page 275.
Daily flights from Palacios to La Ceiba.

Accommodation

The villages in Mosquitia are contactable only via radio, so you will have to arrange accommodation from Palacios. For accommodation in Tegucigalpa and La Ceiba, see page 276.

Utopia in the Forest Pages 168–175

Operators

Careli Tours
Calle Principal Colonial Los Robles
Aptdo. Postal C-134
Managua
☎ (2) 782572
Fax: (2) 782574
email: info@carelitours.com
website: www.carelitours.com
This well-respected and reliable company runs tours all over Nicaragua. The packages are reasonably priced and the service excellent.

ORO Travel
P.O. Box 69
Granada
☎ (55) 24568
Fax: (55) 26512
email: orotravl@tmx.com.ni
ORO offers city tours of Granada, Managua, and León, plus trips to the Mombacho and Santiago volcanoes and to the Isla de Ometepe. It also runs trips to the Archipiélago de Solentiname and along the Río San Juan, and trekking tours to the Cerro Kilambe and within the Mosquitia region.

Sol Tours
Los Pipitos ½ cuadra al oeste
Managua
☎ (2) 663913 or (2) 663914
Fax: (2) 661591
email: soltours@tmx.com.ni
A local operator recommended by the Nicaragua Tourist Office.

Tours Nicaragua
Del Hotel International
2 cuadras al sur, ½ cuadra abajo
Edificio Bolívar
Bolonia
Managua
☎/Fax: 266 2663 or cellular phone 884 1712
email: nicatour@nic.gbm.net
website: www.nvmundo.com/toursnicaragua
Can arrange tours throughout Nicaragua, including to the Indio Maiz Biosphere Reserve and Los Guatusos, and boating along the Río San Juan and in the Solentiname Archipelgo. The company specializes in surfing trips with a guide.

Trips Worldwide
See page 260.

Information

Instituto Nicaraguense de Turismo
Del Hotel Intercontinental
1 cuadra al sur y 1 cuadra abajo
Apartado Postal A-122
Managua
☎ (2) 223333 or (2) 222962
Fax: (2) 226618
email: promo@nicanet.com.ni
website: www.intur.gob.ni
There is a variety of leaflets here, and some staff speak good English. The centre also stocks maps, but expect to pay for the better-quality ones.

Accommodation

Hotel Ideal $
Repuestos Brenes
1 cuadra al oeste
Matagalpa
☎ (61) 22483
Of the few hotels in Matagalpa, this is the best. It is not far from the cathedral, and has single and double rooms with private bathrooms.

Intercontinental Hotel $$$
Ave. Bolivar Sur
Frente al Banco de Finanzas
Managua
☎ (2) 283530
Fax: (2) 283087
This is one of the few luxury hotels in Managua, with very high prices even by Western standards. There is an outdoor pool, a fitness centre, a sauna, a conference centre, car-hire offices in reception, a bar, and a couple of restaurants. All rooms have T.V., phone, private bath, mini-bar, and air-conditioning.

Selva Negra Mountain Resort $$$
Eddy and Mausi Kühl
P.O. Box 126
Km 140 Carretera a Jinotega
Highway Matagalpa
☎/Fax: (61) 23883 or U.S. reservations 305/883-1021
email: selvanegra@sgc.com.ni or information@selvanegra.com
There are 24 lodges dotted over the resort. The large chalets have five bedrooms and cost $100–150 per night; the smaller bungalows (1–3 beds) are $50–100 per night; the hotel-style rooms cost between $30 and $70; and the cheapest option is the youth hostel, at about $10 per night. All the lodges have a private living room, an open fireplace, and en suite bathroom(s) (the number of bathrooms in a lodge corresponds to the number of rooms). Each lodge also has its own private porch, overlooking either the forest, lake, or coffee-processing mill.

Sollentuna Hem $
Batazo 1 cuadra al Norte
Jinotega
☎ (63) 22334
Popular with travellers on a budget—very low room rate.

Food and Drink

El Royal Bar
Chevron 2 cuadras al oeste
Matagalpa
☎ (61) 22487
Fax: (61) 22545

Selva Negra
See also Accommodation above.
There is only one restaurant at Selva Negra. An average breakfast costs about $2–$5, and lunch or dinner about $5–$15. The food is expensive by Nicaraguan standards, but it is good. Some of the cabins have refrigerators, but as there isn't a shop on site remember to take whatever you need with you. When you reach the entrance to the resort the guard will charge you a 20-cordoba entrance fee, which can be used towards payment for food and lodging.

Into the Volcano
Pages 176–185

Operators

For operators offering tours throughout Nicaragua, see page 280.

Accommodation

During the writing of this guidebook a number of deluxe hotels were under construction in Managua; as a result of the extra competition it is expected that prices for rooms in luxury hotels across the city will be slightly reduced.

Hotel Alhambra $$$
Costado oeste del Parque Central
Granada
☎ (55) 24486
Fax: (55) 22035
email: hotalam@ns.tmx.com.ni
This is one of the best hotels in Granada. It faces the pretty central park and is only a short walk from Lake Nicaragua. There are 60 air-conditioned rooms with cable T.V., telephone, and hot water. It also has a swimming pool, Internet service, free safe-deposit boxes, and an excellent restaurant. The hotel acts as a tourist information centre and arranges a number of different tours, including regular trips up Mombacho Volcano, just 15 minutes away.

Hotel Cailagua $
Km 29.5 Carretera Masaya–Granada
Masaya
☎ (52) 24435
Fax: (55) 24435
Located on the Granada highway. It has a reasonable restaurant.

Hotel Casa Blanca $$
del Hotel Estralla
½ cuadra norte
San Juan del Sur
☎/**Fax:** (045) 82135
Friendly staff.

Hotel El Pirata $
Rotonda del puerto
3 cuadras al este
Moyogalpa
Isla de Ometepe
☎/**Fax:** (045) 94262
This is a good though basic hotel. It has a pleasant flower-filled courtyard with hammocks suspended from the supports of the sheltered terrace. There is also a small bar and a restaurant that serves some excellent local food (ask for the specialities of the day). The two other hotels in Moyogalpa are the Hotel Santo Domingo, which is by the beach, and the Ometepetl, which is very close to the port.

Intercontinental Hotel $$$
See page 281.

Food and Drink

El Filete
Km 26 Carretera Managua
Masaya
☎ (52) 23525

The Historic Río San Juan Pages 186–193

Operators

ORO Travel
See page 280.

For fishing tours of Lake Nicaragua and the Río San Juan, contact Careli Tours or Sol Tours in Managua(see page 280), or one of the following:

Munditour
Km 4 Carretera a Masaya
Mangua
☎ (2) 670047
Fax: (2) 785167

No Frills Fishing Adventures
San José
Costa Rica
☎ 228 4812
A Costa Rican company established in 1988 to offer hardy anglers the adventure of a lifetime.

Getting There

La Costena
☎ Managua (2) 631281 or (2) 631228, San Carlos (2) 830271
Flights to San Carlos depart Augusto Sandino Airport in Managua daily at 6:30am and 12:30pm; return flights depart San Carlos daily at 7:30am and 1:30pm. Tickets cost about $100.

Information

Tourist Information Centre
See page280.

Accommodation

Although there are basic hotels in San Carlos, it is much better to stay in El Castillo if you can find a boat to take you there before nightfall. The three hotels in El Castillo are all quite basic, but they are clean and friendly, and they serve excellent local food—if you like fish you won't be disappointed.

Hotel El Castillo $
Muelle 1 cuadra al sur
El Castillo
☎ (2) 492508
Fax: (2) 703617
This is a comfortable, spacious hotel very close to the harbour. The rooms are pleasant, and they connect to a communal balcony (with hammocks) that overlooks the river. The restaurant is large and serves very good food: ask for the freshwater shrimp/crayfish. There is also a lounge area for relaxing and chatting with other guests.

Refugio Bartola Hotel $
No address; 20 minutes by boat from El Castillo, on the left-hand side of the river
☎ (2) 897924
Fax: (2) 894154
This hotel is an undiscovered gem. It is in one of the most beautiful locations along the river next to the Indio Maiz nature

reserve. Although the rooms are basic, the restaurant is fantastic: it is situated beneath a huge grass canopy, and is an ideal spot for eating, drinking, watching the river go by, or simply lazing in one of the numerous hammocks.

Cabinas Leyco $
Policia 1.5 cuadra al oeste
San Carlos
☎ (2) 830354
Rooms with shared or private bathroom.

Hotel Azul $
Frente a Plaza Malecon
San Carlos
☎ (2) 830282
Basic, with shared bathroom.

Hotel Mancarrón $/$$
Isla Mancarrón
Archipiélago de Solentiname
☎ (2) 603345 or (55) 22059
The only large building on the island. There are 15 rooms. It is possible to organize tours of Mancarrón from here.

Northern Exposure Pages 196–205

Operators

Aguas Bravas Fortuna
Costado Sur de la Plaza de Deportes
La Fortuna
☎ 479 9484
Runs rafting, horseriding, biking, and canopy tours.

Aventuras Arenal
La Fortuna
☎ 479 9133
Fax: 479 9295
Runs a number of adventure trips around the Fortuna region, including to Venado Caves and rafting trips on the Río Sarapiquí. Well established and competitively priced.

Camino Travel
Ave. Central & 1
Calle 1
San José
☎ 257 0107
Fax: 234 2350
A very friendly and efficient agency based in downtown San José that organizes a range of tours throughout the country.

Sunset Tours
La Fortuna
☎ 479 9199
Fax: 479 9415
Fortuna's largest tour agency, with trips throughout the region, including to Volcán Arenal, Venado Caves, and Laguna Arenal. Prices for local tours are very reasonable.

Getting There

Travelair
Based at:
Tobías Bolaños Airport
San José
☎ 220 3054
Fax: 220 0413
email: travelair@centralamerica.com
website: www.centralamerica.com/cr/tran/travlair.htm
A domestic airline that runs fast and efficient services around the country in small- to medium-sized aircraft.

Information

Instituto Costarricense de Turismo (ICT)
Apartado 777-1000
San José
☎ 222 1090
Fax: 223 5452
email: info@tourism-costarica.com
website: www.tourism-costarica.com
The very helpful main branch of the Costa Rican tourist information service, located temporarily in the main head office building on Ave. 4, Calle 5 & 7. There is another office at the international airport.

Car Hire

Hertz
Paseo Colon & Calle 38
San José
☎ 221 1818
Fax: 233 7254
email: hertzcr@sol.racsa.co.cr
website: www.mercadonet.com/hertz.html
There are also branches in the Hotel Irazú, Hotel Balmoral, and Hotel Corobici,

and at the international airport. Cars can be picked up in the city and dropped off at the airport. Daily rates start from around about $55 for basic cars and about $70 for four-wheel-drive vehicles.

Mapuche Rent a Car
Apartado 2060-1002
San José
☎ 286 0404
Fax: 286 0211
email: mapuche@sol.racsa.co.cr
website: www.crdirect.com/mapuche
Situated on the roundabout between Highways 34 and 214, near San Sebastian church. The company offers a 24-hour service, hotel pick-up and drop-off, and tourist information. Daily/weekly rates are from about $45/$200 for a standard car and $60/$360 for a four-wheel drive. Prices go up slightly in the high season.

Accommodation

San José acts as a central base for all the Costa Rica tours in this book; recommended hotels in the capital are listed below:

Gran Hotel Costa Rica $$$
Apartado 527-1000
Ave. Central
Calle 3
San José
☎ 221 4000
Fax: 221 3501
email: gran@centralamerica
website: www.centralamerica.com/cr/hotel/gran.htm
Located right next to the National Theatre in the heart of the city centre. Built in the 1930s, the Gran Hotel has all modern facilities yet retains a certain charm, despite having a 24-hour casino and big-screen television in the lobby.

Hotel Balmoral $$
Apartado 3344-1000
Ave. Central
Calle 7 & 9
San José
☎ 222 5022 or for U.S. reservations toll-free 1-800/691-4865
Fax: 221 1919
email: balmoral@sol.racsa.co.cr
A modern hotel located close to the National Theatre. Friendly staff and good-sized, quiet rooms with cable T.V., Internet connections, and air-conditioning. There is a good restaurant on the ground floor, and a Hertz car-hire office. Doubles start at $75.

Hotel Fleur de Lys $$
Apartado 10736-1000
Ave. 2 & 6
Calle 13
San José
☎ 257 2621
Fax: 257 3637
A beautiful, refurbished old building with wooden floors and ceilings, and tastefully decorated communal areas. The well-fitted rooms have bathtubs and all other modern facilities, and there is a tour agency in the lobby. Central location. Double rooms cost from $60, including a simple breakfast.

Hotel Galilea $
Ave. Central
Calle 11 & 13
San José
☎ 233 6925
Fax: 223 1689
A pleasant hotel with clean rooms and private bathrooms. Central location. Doubles from $30.

Local accommodation includes the following:

Arenal Observatory Lodge $$
At the base of Arenal Volcano
☎ 257 9489
Fax: 257 4220
email: observatory@centralamerica.com
website: www.centralamerica.com/cr/hotel/aobserve.htm
Also used by Smithsonian Institute researchers: this is as close to the volcano as you can get without burning yourself. A spectacular location. Offers 24 rooms in four categories ranging from rustic with bunk beds to very comfortable with private bathrooms. Prices for doubles range from $35 to $85 in the low season, and $42 to $97 in the high season. Meals are extra. Also operates tours to nearby attractions.

Balneario Tabacón and Tabacón Lodge $$$
11km (9 miles) west of La Fortuna
☎ 256 8412
Fax: 256 7373
email: tabacon@centralamerica.com
website: www.centralamerica.com/cr/hotel/tabacon.
This hot springs/hotel complex is a good place to relax after your adventures and is an attractive place to stay. Entry to the springs is $14 per person for the day, with optional massage ($26) and mud facials ($10). An excellent restaurant serves a good-value buffet meal. The lodge is just up the road from the springs and has very comfortable modern rooms with two double beds or one king-size bed, T.V., and air-conditioning. Doubles cost around $95 in the low season and $110 in the high season, including breakfast and unlimited access to the hot springs.

Cabinas La Amistad $
Calle Principal
La Fortuna
☎ 479 9342 or ☎**/Fax:** 479 9364
Reasonable double, triple, and family rooms with hot water and fans. Double rooms cost $20 in the high season and $16 in the low. There is also a laundry service. William Bogarin, a recommended guide, runs tours from here: trips to the Venado Caves cost $25 per person, horse rides to the Fortuna waterfall are $15, rafting on the Rio Peñas Blancas is $55, and a night walk to Volcán Arenal combined with a visit to the hot springs is $25.

La Garza $$$
Mailing address:
Apartado 100
Tres Ríos 2250
☎ 475 5222
Fax: 475 5015 or U.S.A. toll-free 1-888/782-4293
email: information@hotel-lagarza-arenal.com
website: www.hotel-lagarza-arenal.com
This working hacienda on the banks of the Río Platanar is situated just 25 minutes from Arenal Volcano on the road to Platanar. All the luxury bungalows have balconies with views over the plains to the volcano. La Garza runs a number of tours in the area, including to the volcano and Venado Caves, and also offers horseriding tours to its private forest reserve and around the farm's plantations. Rates do not include breakfast and tours are also extra.

Hotel Don Beto $
On the corner of the plaza next to the church in Zarcero
☎ 506 463 3137
A well-decorated, friendly hotel with some very economical double rooms with a shared bathroom.

WHERE WILD THINGS GO PAGES 206–213

OPERATORS

Camino Travel
See page 283.

Trips Worldwide
See page 260.
A U.K.-based company that specializes in tailor-made itineraries to Central America. Offers a range of tours to suit a variety of budgets to the Osa Peninsula and Corcovado National Park.

GETTING THERE

Travelair
See page 283

INFORMATION

Instituto Costarricense de Turismo (ICT)
See page 283.

ACCOMMODATION

See page 284 for recommended San José accommodation. Local accommodation includes the following:

Casa Corcovado Jungle Lodge $$$
Mailing address:
Apartado 1482-1250
Escazú
U.S. mailing address:
Casa Corcovado
Interlink #253

P.O. Box 526770
Miami
FL 33152
U.S.A.
☎ 256 3181 or U.S. toll-free 1-888/896-6097
Fax: 256 7409
email: corcovdo@sol.racsa.co.cr
website: www.ticonet.co.cr/beto/tests/corcovado
This lodge is built right on the northern edge of the national park, and offers very comfortable rooms and a good restaurant with views of the surrounding forest. They offer the same tours as Marenco (see below), with packages starting from around $650 for a 3-day/2-night package.

Marenco Lodge $$$
Mailing address:
Apartado 4025-1000
San José
☎ 221 1594
Fax: 255 1346
email: marenco@sol.racsa.co.cr
website: www.marencolodge.com
This ex-research station, wonderfully situated at the southern end of Bahía Drake, has rustic but comfortable bungalows and cabins with balconies offering superb views of the Pacific Ocean. It has landscaped gardens, a network of trails through the extensive rainforest grounds, and an open-sided restaurant. They offer tours to Caño Island, Corcovado National Park, and Río Claro as part of multi-day, all-inclusive packages. Prices per person start from around $400 for a 3-night/2-tour package and $500 for a 4-night/3-tour package in the low season.

JUNGLE PADDLERS PAGES 214–223

OPERATORS

Coast to Coast Adventures
P.O. Box 2135-1002
San José
☎ 225 6055
Fax: 225 7806
email: info@ctocadventures.com
website: www.ctocadventures.com/travel.htm
Arranges 1- and 2-day rafting trips on the Pacuare, with overnight stays at the beautiful, and remot, Nido del Tigre river camp. Friendly, knowledgeable guides and small group numbers make these wilderness trips both intimate and fun. Prices are around $100 for 1-day rafting trips and $250 for 2-day trips (this includes all local transport, food, accommodation, guides, and specialist equipment). The Paddles & Pedals tour combines rafting on the Pacuare with kayaking and biking in the Nicoya Peninsula (see page 000).

Costa Sol Rafting
Apartado 8-4390-1000
San José
☎ 293 2150 or U.S.A. and Canada toll-free 1-800/245-8420
Fax: 293 2155
A small but fun company that runs rafting trips on many of Costa Rica's rivers, including the Pacuare. Prices are similar to those of Coast to Coast.

Journey Latin America
12–13 Heathfield Terrace
London W4 4JE
U.K.
☎ (0181) 747 8315
Fax: (0181) 742 1312
email: sales@journeylatinamerica.com
website: www.journeylatinamerica.co.uk
The U.K. agent for Coast to Coast Adventures, and can arrange the Paddles & Pedals trip.

Ríos Tropicales
Ave. 2
Calle 32
San José
☎ 233 6455
Fax: 255 4354
email: info@riostro.com
website: www.riostro.com
The biggest rafting company in the country, running 1- and 2-day trips on all the major rivers. Their Pacuare trips are large affairs with many boats, lots of travellers and overnight stays in the company's own river camp. Prices are similar to those charged by Coast to Coast.

Getting There
Travelair
See page 283.

Information
Instituto Costarricense de Turismo (ICT)
See page 283.

Accommodation
See pages 284 for recommended San José accommodation.

Trail of the Turtle Catchers Pages 224–233

Operators
Camino Travel
See page 283.

Coast to Coast Adventures
See page 286.
The only company that runs kayaking trips into Tortuguero. Its 2-day tours cost around $250, and include all local transport, accommodation, food, guides, and equipment.

Costa Rica Expeditions
Apartado 6941-1000
Ave. 3
Calle Central
San José
☎ 257 0766
Fax: 257 1655
email: costaric@expeditions.co.cr
website: www.crexped.co.cr
Specializes in natural history tours, particularly to Tortuguero. Travel is by motorized launch in the company of a wildlife expert.

Trips Worldwide
See page 260.
Trips Worldwide organizes trips all over Central America as well as a variety of tours to Tortuguero National Park.

Getting There
Travelair
See page 283.

Information
Instituto Costarricense de Turismo (ICT)
See page 283.

Accommodation
See page 284 for recommended San José accommodation.

A Nicoyan Odyssey Pages 234–245

Operators
Coast to Coast Adventures
See page 286.
The Paddles & Pedals trip combines four days of kayaking and biking in Nicoya with two days' rafting on the Pacuare (see page 286). There are regular group depatures throughout the year, with prices around $1,400 for eight nights, including local transport, accommodation in good hotels or comfortable camps, specialist equipment, and guides.

Journey Latin America
See page 286.
Acts as U.K. agent for Coast to Coast Adventures, and can arrange the Paddles & Pedals trip.

Getting There
Travelair
See page 283.

Information
Instituto Costarricense de Turismo (ICT)
See page 283.

Accommodation
See pages 284 for recommended San José accommodation. Local accommodation includes the following:

Condominios Fénix $$
Apartado 31-5235
Playa Sámara
Guanacaste
☎ 656 0158

Fax: 656 0162
email: confenix@sol.racsa.co.cr
A small, pleasant hotel with a beachfront setting. The units have full kitchen facilities and hot water. Outside are tropical gardens and a small swimming pool.

Hotel El Sueño Tropical $$
Playa Carrillo
Guanacaste
☎ 656 0151
Fax: 656 0152
website: www.novanet.co.cr/tropical
A lovely hotel owned by an Italian family, set in landscaped gardens just a few minutes inland from the beach. There are 12 spacious, well-appointed rooms with air-conditioning. There is a thatch-roofed restaurant that serves superb food, plus a swimming pool.

WHERE OCEANS MEET PAGES 248–256

OPERATORS

Ancon Expeditions of Panama
Calle Elvira Mendez
Edificio El Dorado
Panama City
☎ 269 9414 or 269 9415, or U.S.A. toll-free 1-888/999-4106
Fax: 264 3713
email: travel@ecopanama.com
website: www.ecopanama.com
Ancon has an excellent reputation, and is committed to the conservation of Panama's biodiversity and cultural heritage. Tours range from half-day trips of Panama City (about $30) to the 14-day Trans-Darien Expedition (about $2,500).

Argo Tours
Based on the pier at Balboa Port
☎ 228 6069
Fax: 228 1234
website: www.big-ditch.com
The only boat-tour company that operates year round. Partial transits through the Miraflores Locks run every Saturday, leaving at 7:30am, and cost about $60. Full transits through the whole canal run once a month, and cost about $100 ($45 for children). The prices include basic snacks and drinks.

Panama Jones Tours
Based opposite the Marriot Hotel between Via España and Calle 50 off Ave. Federico Boyd
☎ 265 4551
Fax: 265 4553
email: pdtpanam@sinfo.net
website: www.panamacanal.com.
In the U.S.:
☎ toll-free 1-888/PANAMA-1 ext 11
Fax: 580/428-3499
email: pdt@iamerica.net
A popular agency with a wide range of tours throughout the country, including day trips to Portobelo on Wednesdays (about $80) and an eco-canal tour on Tuesdays (about $70), and also books places for the Argo Tours canal transits.

Smithsonian Institute
Visitor's Office
Tupper Building
Ave. Roosevelt
Panama City
☎ 227 6022 ext 2271
Fax: 232 5978
email: arosemo@tivoli.si.edu
The only way to get onto the Smithsonian-run Isla Barro Colorado is to book yourself on one of the institute's tours. Spaces are strictly limited, so sign up as far in advance as possible. Tours leave from Gamboa Port twice a week at 8am. Included in the ticket is a buffet lunch on the island and a guided tour around the rain forest. Passports must be taken to gain access to the port.

Trips Worldwide
See page 260.
U.K.-based specialists in Central America; they can tailor-make an itinerary to Panama, including trips on the canal and to Portobelo.

INFORMATION

Instituto Panameño de Turismo (IPAT)
Atlapa Convention Centre
Via Israel
Panama City
☎ 226 7000 ext 112
Fax: 226 6856
email: infotur@ns.ipat.gob.pa
website: www.ipat.gob.pa/index

The main Panama Tourism Office, with useful free information books, maps, and a hotel-booking service. There is a sub-office at the international airport with the same services. The website is excellent for accessing information on the country's regions and attractions.

Accommodation

Bananas Village Resort, Isla Grande $$

Mailing address:
Ave. Federico Boyd
Edificio Parque Urraca
Panama City
☎ 263 9510
Fax: 264 7556
email: gram@sinfo.net
A wonderfully located hotel on the far side of Isla Grande. All the bungalows offer sea views, and diving and snorkelling trips can be organized from the resort.

Hotel Las Vegas $$

Ave. 2a Norte
Calle 55 Oeste
El Cangrejo
Apartado 'D'
Panama City
☎ 269 0722
Fax: 223 0047
email: lasvegas@pan.gbm.net
website: www.hotelvegas.com
An apartment and hotel complex, offering large, well-fitted suites with lounge and kitchen areas, and views over the city.

INTRODUCTION

This book has, we hope, whetted your appetite for adventure, and the Activities A–Z is intended to supply a useful, if not comprehensive, list of as many adventurous activities as the authors could discover within an area.

The activities vary from volunteer work, cultural, and language opportunities to really intrepid sports. Most of the experiences call for interaction with local people and many are directly connected to ecotourism—where strict controls are applied to guarantee the benefits to the environment and to minimize the damage caused by the impact of increasing numbers of visitors to sensitive areas.

We have supplied the names and addresses of organizations that can help the traveller to achieve these challenging pastimes, but they have not been inspected or vetted by us in any way. Even where the authors have used a company to organize their own trip, this is no guarantee that any company is still run by the same people or to the same degree of efficiency.

Bear in mind that many of the regions covered can be volatile both climatically and politically. Weigh up all the factors first, get a feel for your chosen destination, and let us guide you towards the outfits that can help.

BIRD-WATCHING

Exotic birds such as hummingbirds, scarlet macaws (*Ara macao*), and quetzals (*Pharomachrus mocinno*) abound throughout the region, attracting ornithologists from all over the world. Costa Rica alone has about the same number of species as exist in the whole of North America. Generally speaking, the dry season (usually November–April) is ideal for bird-watching, with dawn and dusk the best times of day. If possible, take binoculars and a camera with a telephoto lens, and try to hire a guide who is an ornithologist. Check on facilities as they may vary greatly. Bird-watching trips are often combined with trekking and wildlife-watching.

BirdLife International
Wellbrook Court
Girton Rd.
Cambridge CB3 ONA
U.K.
☎ (01223) 277318
Fax: (01223) 277200
email: birdlife@birdlife.org.uk
Birdlife International is a global partnership of conservation organizations and is the leading authority on the status of the world's birds. It can provide details of birding associations worldwide.

Tikal, Guatemala

This jungle region, dotted with Mayan sites, has a variety of rainforest birds and mammals, including six species of parrot, crested guans (*Penelope purpurascens*), and the peacock-like ocellated turkey (*Agriocharis ocellata*). The national park has comfortable, lodge-style accommodation.

Field Guides Incorporated
P.O. Box 160723
Austin
TX 78716-0723
U.S.A.
☎ 512/327-4953 or toll-free 1-800/728-4953
Fax: 512/327-9231
email: fgileaden@aol.com
Arranges 6-day trips from Belize City in the care of experienced guides who specialize in bird-watching tours.

Chan Chich Lodge, Belize

Mailing address:
P.O. Box 37
Belize City
Gallon Jug
Belize
☎ (2) 75634 **Fax:** (2) 76961
email: info@chanchich.com
In Orange Walk district in the north of Belize is this jungle lodge, surrounded by 100,000ha (250,000 acres) of privately owned forest with Mayan ruins. More than 300 species of birds have been recorded, including great and slaty-breasted tinamous (*Tinamus major* and *Crypturellus boucardi*), bare-throated tiger herons (*Tigrisoma mexicanum*), and great curassows (*Crax rubra*). Spider monkeys (*Ateles geoffroyi*),

jaguars (*Panthera onca*), and tapirs (*Tapiris* spp.) may also be seen. Visits are possible only during the dry season (February–May).

Field Guides Incorporated
See above.
The company runs a 9-day package to Chan Chich Lodge. It also offers individual guide-led trips for clubs and private groups, with snorkelling and wildlife-watching options

Monteverde Cloud Forest Reserve Costa Rica

This private reserve 10,500-ha (26,000-acre) in the country's northwest, owned by the non-profit research and education Tropical Science Centre, has over 400 species of birds, including the quetzal and the bare-necked umbrella bird (*Cephalopterus glabricollis*). There is also a Hummingbird Gallery, plus over 100 species of mammals and around 2,000 species of plants. The best time to visit is during the dry season (January–May). Numbers of visitors are restricted, so arrive by 7am, especially in the high season, or book ahead with the reserve. See also Conservation Tours, page 297.

Albergue Reserva Biológica de Monteverde
Monteverde Cloud Forest Reserve
Monteverde
Costa Rica
☎ 661 2655
Can arrange full board dormitory accommodation at the Monteverde reserve.

Gary Diller
Apartado 10165
1000 San José
Monteverde
Costa Rica
☎ 645 5045
A knowledgable guide who specializes in birds, and who can be hired by the day.

Pipeline Road, Panama

In Soberanía National Park near Panama City, in a country with over 900 recorded bird species, is the 17-km (10-mile) long Pipeline Road, popular with bird-watchers.

Eco Tours de Panamá
Calle Ricardo Arias 7
Apartado 465
Panama 9A
Panama
☎ 263 3077 **Fax:** 263 3089
email: ecotours@pty.com
Eco Tours specializes in nature and cultural tours in Panama, including hiking and diving options.

BOAT TRIPS

A variety of craft, from tiny wooden fishing boats to luxury cruise liners, is available for exploring inland waterways, long stretches of coastline, and Central America's numerous islands. Speed, cost, and comfort are equally variable. Check what is included in the price, and make sure that canned soft drinks are available on board as the water is usually undrinkable (it is a good idea to take supplementary supplies of your own anyway). Wind on the water can dramatically increase the risk of sunburn, so cover up or use a sunblock.

Glover's Reef Atoll, Belize

This pristine marine reserve, 70km (45 miles) east of Sittee River village, is reached after a 4-hour sailboat trip. There is no electricity or running water on the atoll, so it can provide a near desert island experience, with diving and fishing.

Manta Reef Resort
Mailing address:
P.O. Box 215
3 Eyre St.
Belize City
Belize
☎ (2) 31895 or (2) 32767
Fax: (2) 32764
One-week packages in cabins on Glover's Reef are organized, with facilities including fishing and snorkelling at all levels of instruction.

Río Dulce, Guatemala

The Río Dulce spills into the Caribbean Sea, and is a favoured shelter for yachtspeople during the hurricane season in late summer. Boating opportunities include exploring the Río Dulce and surrounding inland waterways, or heading to the reefs of Belize to the north or the Bay Islands of Honduras to the east.

Aventuras Vacacionales
Captain John Clark
1a Ave. Sur 11B
Antigua
Guatemala
☎/**Fax:** (832) 3352
email: sailing@guate.net.gt
Four-day catamaran trips (August–April) leave regularly on Fridays from Río Dulce; some people find conditions on the 14m (46ft) boat cramped, but prices are low and the captain is reliable. He also offers snorkelling trips out to a Belize reef.

Syrinx
email: sailingcharter@hotmail.com
George Hertzberg offers his comfortable yacht for charter from Río Dulce to the Belize cays or Honduras's Bay Islands. A minimum of four people (sleeps six maximum) and 4 days. Fresh yacht-baked bread is included!

Managua, Nicaragua

Sandwiched between the vast lakes of Managua and Nicaragua on the west coast, the capital is surrounded by rivers and a chain of volcanoes. The shores of the lakes are home to recreational facilities, and there are also snorkelling, fishing, and swimming opportunities.

Explore Worldwide
1 Frederick St.
Aldershot
Hampshire GU11 1LQ
U.K.
☎ (01252) 319448
Fax: (01252) 343170
email: info@explore.co.uk
A 17-day boat and road trip from Managua, exploring volcanoes, islands, jungle towns, plantations, and wildlife.

Indo Maiz Biosphere Reserve, Nicaragua

This rainforest reserve is accessed via boat from the town of El Castillo on the Río San Juan, which borders Costa Rica. There is comfortable accommodation with the chance to fish, ride, and relax.

Ecotourism International de Nicaragua S.A.
1 Apartado Postal: LC93
Managua
Nicaragua
☎ (2) 76082
email: info@eco-nica.com
Runs conservation and wildlife tours throughout the country.

Tours Nicaragua
Del Hotel International
2 cuadras al sur, ½ cuadra abajo
Edificio Bolívar
Bolonia
Managua
Nicaragua
☎/**Fax:** 266 6663 or cellular phone 884 1712
email: nicatour@nic.gbm.net
website: www.nvmundo.com/toursnicaragua
Arranges tours to the Indio Maiz Biosphere Reserve and Los Guatusos, boating along the Río San Juan and in the Solentiname Archipelago, and surfing trips with guide (see page 306).

Highlights, Costa Rica

A regularly scheduled departure combines the Monteverde Cloud Forest Reserve, the Arenal Volcano, and beaches on a voyage along the remote Pacific coast. This trip is suitable for families, and offers activities such as bird-watching, hiking, and rafting.

Wildland Adventures
3546 NE 155th St.
Seattle
WA 98155
U.S.A.
☎ toll-free 1-800/345-4453
Fax: 206/363-6615
email: info@wildland.com
website: www. ecoventures.com
Arranges a 4-day trip with expedition cruising; yacht and hotel accommodation. Also other voyages and overland trips throughout Central America.

Panama Canal, Panama

The 80-km (50-mile) long Panama Canal was one of the greatest engineering achievements of mankind, and it still attracts worldwide attention today—

especially as control of the waterway passes from U.S. to Panamanian hands on January 1, 2000.

Argo Tours
Based on the pier at Balboa Port
Panama
☎ 228 6069 **Fax:** 228 1234
website: www.big-ditch.com
The only boat-tour company that operates year round. Partial transits through the Miraflores Locks run every Saturday, leaving at 7:30am, and cost $55. Full transits through the whole canal run once a month, and cost $99 ($45 for children). The prices include basic snacks and drinks.

Panama Jones Tours
Based opposite the Marriot Hotel between Via España and Calle 50 off Ave. Federico Boyd
Panama City
Panama
☎ 265 4551**Fax:** 265 4553
email: pdtpanam@sinfo.net
website: www.panamacanal.com
In the U.S.:
☎ toll-free 1-888/PANAMA-1 ext 11
Fax: 580/428-3499
email: pdt@iamerica.net
A popular agency that runs a wide range of tours throughout the country, including day trips to Portobelo on Wednesdays ($75) and an eco-canal tour on Tuesdays ($65), and also books places for the Argo Tours canal transits.

CANOEING/KAYAKING

A canoeing trip can be anything from a serene river tour for observing wildlife to an exhilarating battle against white water. Experience is needed if you are canoeing independently, and it is generally advisable to go with at least two other people. Whitewater canoeing demands that you have some experience and have mastered an Eskimo roll, and there may be fitness requirements. The International River Grade indicates the difficulty of the water, ranging from Grade I to Grade VI (see box on page 220); the frequency of rapids is another factor to consider. The thrill of whitewater canoeing is usually possible only during the rainy season, and requires a helmet.

British Canoe Union
John Dudderidge House
Adbolton Lane
West Bridgford
Nottingham NG2 5AS
U.K.
☎ (0115) 982 1100
Fax: (0115) 982 1797
Provides advice on destinations worldwide, and a list of B.C.U. clubs nationwide.

International Canoe Federation
Dózsa György út 1-3
1143 Budapest
Hungary
☎ (1) 363 4832
Fax: (1) 221 4130
email: icf_hq_budapest@mail.datanet.hu
website: www. datanet.hu/icf_hq
An umbrella organization providing information on national bodies worldwide, plus safety and destination advice.

Cayo District, Belize

The area offers inland adventures on Class IV rapids along the Macal River in kayaks and paddle boats, plus an underground river trip through a series of caves.

Ceiba Adventures
P.O. Box 2274
Flagstaff
AZ 86003
U.S.A.
☎ 520/527-0171 or toll-free 1-800/217-1060
Fax: 520/527-8127
email: ceiba@primenet.com
website: www.gorp.com/ceiba
This specialist operator offers a week of sea-kayaking, whitewater rafting, and caving, combined with other activities such as biking, hiking, fishing, snorkelling, and archaeological sightseeing.

Refugio Punta Izopo, Honduras

Tela, on Honduras's Caribbean coast, is the starting point for kayaking trips down this network of canals, surrounded by mangroves. Wildlife such as crocodiles, numerous birds, and monkeys can be seen.

Garifuna Tours
Parque Central
Tela
Honduras
☎ 448 1069 **Fax:** 448 2904
email: garifuna@hondutel.hn
Bilingual guides lead afternoon kayaking trips, as well as bird-watching tours and diving. Windsurf boards can also be rented for use off Tela's white-sand beaches.

Río Lempa, El Salvador

Class III and IV whitewater canoeing and rafting May–October. Trips last 1–4 days. Sea-kayaking is available at other times of the year.

Ríos Tropicales
Calle Mirador 4620
Colonia Escalon
San Salvador
El Salvador
☎ 223 9480
Runs canoeing trips down the Río Lempa and other rivers in El Salvador. Two-week advance booking is necessary.

Lower Sarapiquí and Pejibaye, Costa Rica

These rivers offer easy boating for beginners between August and December, with a chance to relax on nearby beaches.

Nantahala Outdoor Center
13077 Hwy. 19
West Bryson City
NC 28713-9114
U.S.A.
☎ 828/488-2175 or toll-free 888/662-1662
email: adtrav@noc.com
website: www.nocweb.com
Three-day canoeing tour with 2 days on the beach. Intermediate and advanced options on other rivers are available.

Tortuguero, Costa Rica

The "Turtle Catcher's" National Park covers 19,000ha (46,000 acres) of dense jungle, sweeping coastline, and wilderness rivers. As there are no roads in the region, access is only along waterways, so it is ideally suited to touring by kayak.

Coast to Coast Adventures
P.O. Box 2135-1002
San José
Costa Rica
☎ 225 6055
Fax: 225 7806
email: info@ctocadventures.com
website: www.ctocadventures.com/travel.htm
The only company that runs kayaking trips into Tortuguero. Two-day tours cost around $250, and include all local transport, accommodation, food, guides, and equipment.

CLIMBING

Many of the volcanoes dotted throughout Central America can easily be climbed, even when active. As is the case with the mountains in the region, they are often given national park status and provide sweeping views from their summits. Organized tours include all the necessary equipment and can advise on fitness requirements. If embarking on a trip independently, you may want to hire a porter or mule to carry equipment. Check on climbing seasons and likely weather conditions as these can change rapidly. It is essential to allow enough time to acclimatize; altitude sickness can kill. Climbing clubs at home can advise on short courses that will instruct you in the basic techniques before you go.

South American Explorers' Club
Ave. Portugal 146
Lima
Peru
☎ (1) 425 0142
email: montague@amauta.rep.net.pe
This non-profit-making organization provides maps, travel information and route planning for members ($40 fee). The club is one of the most comprehensive sources of information to Central and South America.

International Mountaineering and Climbing Federation (UIAA)
Monbijoustrasse 61

Postfach
3000 Bern 23
Switzerland
☎ (31) 370 1828 **Fax:** (31) 370 1838
email: uiaa@compuserve.com
website: www.mountaineering.org
Contact your member association direct for information (addresses of UIAA members can be found in the organization's website under the heading "National Federations").

Pico de Orizaba, Mexico

The highest mountain in Mexico (5,760m, or 18,898 feet), near Mexico City, is a moderate 2-day climb, but acclimatization is important. There are good views from the summit.

Raimand Alvaro Torres
Calle Sure 10 574
Orizaba
Mexico
☎ (272) 61940
An experienced mountaineering guide who can arrange equipment hire.

Antigua's volcanoes, Guatemala

Be aware that violent robberies are not uncommon here, especially on Pacaya, the active volcano that attracts most tourists. Make sure your guide is reputable, check with the embassy before you go, and take a torch as mists can descend quickly.

Servicios Turísticos Atitlán
6a Ave. Sur 7
Antigua
Guatemala
☎ (832) 0648
Climbing tours to nearby volcanoes, plus other activity-based trips such as trekking and rafting.

Volcán Barú National Park, Panama

The volcano, which soars to 3,475m (11,400 feet), can be climbed comfortably in 2 days from Boquete, giving spectacular views of both coasts. There are walking and climbing opportunities, with well-marked trails and lots of interesting birdlife and wildlife. Camping is possible near the summit, but there is no water.

Pension Marilos
Ave. a Este y Calle 6 Sur
Boquete
Panama
☎ 720 1380
Can arrange reliable guides, such as Gonzalo Miranda, for trekking.

CONSERVATION TOURS

Activities ranging from tracking forest animals to unearthing pre-Columbian relics may be included as part of a conservation project. This type of trip is very different from an ecotour, offering you the chance to carry out educational and scientific research. Participants act as volunteers, but nevertheless pay a fee to cover costs. This usually works out more expensive than a standard holiday, but may be tax deductable. Usually, no specific skills are required, although you must be prepared for hard work. Organizers should provide you with detailed descriptions of expected tasks. Food and accommodation can vary from makeshift tents with communal cooking to comfortable hotel accommodation with restaurant meals. Programmes change from year to year.

Chamela, Mexico

An 11-day programme in one of the last remaining areas of tropical dry forest. The work involves tracking and examining forest carnivores such as ocelots (*Felis pardalis*), jaguarundis (*F. yaguarondi*), and coyotes (*Canis latrans*) in order to understand this threatened ecosystem. Accommodation is in comfortable rooms in a field station near the beach resorts of the Pacific coast.

Earthwatch Institute
680 Mt. Auburn St.
P.O. Box 9104
Watertown
MA 02272 9104
U.S.A.
☎ 617/926-8200 **Fax:** 617/926-8532
email: info@earthwatch.org
This international organization offers a wide range of voluntary conservation programmes worldwide.

Earthwatch Europe
57 Woodstock Rd.
Oxford OX2 6HJ
U.K.
☎ (01865) 311600
Fax: (01865) 311383

Lamanai, Belize

A project studying howler monkeys (*Alouatta palliata*), based at an archaeological site in the north of the country. Work involves gathering information on social habits and distribution. There are also exploration and bird-watching possiblities.

Reef and Rainforest Tours
1 The Plains
Totnes
Devon TQ9 5DR
U.K.
☎ (01803) 866965
email: reefrain@btinternet.com
This company, in operation since 1989, specializes in small-scale, natural history-oriented tourism in Belize, Honduras, and Costa Rica, supporting local conservation initiatives. The trip to Lamanai is an 8-day tour from Miami.

Monteverde Cloud Forest, Costa Rica

See Bird-watching, page 291.

Monteverde Conservation League
Polly Morrison
Apartado 10165
1000 San José
Monteverde
Costa Rica
☎ 661 2953
Opportunities include practical work on the reserve, specialist research, and education in local schools.

Tortuguero National Park, Costa Rica

The 1-week programme involves educating and interviewing locals, and monitoring manatees and other marine life using dugout canoes. Accommodation is in a rainforest-backed hotel.

CULTURAL TOURS

In pre-Columbian times Central America was peopled by a number of fascinating civilizations, most notably the Aztecs and Mayas. The ancient powerhouse of Teotichuacan, the long-lasting influence of the Spanish, and the colourful Indian markets can all be experienced as living history. If you are visiting remote archaeological sites, don't travel alone and consider hiring a guide, who will be aware of particular dangers presented by potential thieves or bandits. When encountering local peoples, do not intrude, and avoid giving money.

Mayan Cities, Mexico

Most trips start from Merida, exploring historical cities along with the numerous important archaelogical sites. Many trips incorporate visits to Caribbean beaches.

Journey Latin America
12–13 Heathfield Terrace
London W4 4JE
U.K.
☎ (020) 8747 8315 **Fax:** (020) 8742 1312
email: tours@journeylatinamerica.com
website: www.journeylatinamerica.co.uk
A 7-day trip combines the ceremonial city of Uxmal with the ruins of Chichén Itzá and the cliff-top Tulum in Cancún. A 16-day Aztecs and Mayas tour of Mexico is also available.

Mila
100 S. Greenleaf
Gurnee
IL 60031
U.S.A.
☎ 847/249-2111 or toll-free 1-800/367-7378
Fax: 847/249-2772
email: milalatin@aol.com
A 8-day trip combining the archaeological areas of Uxmal and Chichén Itzá with a tour of Izamal and its Mayan pyramid. Bilingual guides are used, and accommodation is in high-standard hotels. The company offers heritage and cultural tours throughout Central America.

Mayan Sites, Guatemala/Belize

This trip explores ancient and contemporary Mayan sites in the interior of Belize, including Caracol, Xunantunich, and Cahal Pech, and Tikal in Guatemala. There are wildlife-viewing and other activity options.

Journeys International
107 Aprill Dr. Ste. 3
Ann Arbor
MI 48103
U.S.A.
☎ toll-free 1-800/255-8735
Fax: 734/665 2945
email: resources@journeys-intl.com
An 8-day trip is on offer between December and May. The company has been operating for 20 years, offering family trips with English-speaking guides.

El Mirador, Guatemala

El Mirador, near the Mexican border, is the largest Mayan site in Guatemala, with two additional sites of El Tintal and Nakbé near by. Mules, horses, and guides can be hired for the minimum recommended trip of 4 days from Carmelita, 36km (22 miles) away.

Far Horizons
Richard Hansen
P.O. Box 91900
Albuquerque
NM 87199-1900
U.S.A.
☎ 505/343-9400
email: journey@farhorizon.com
Archaeologist-led trips that include private lectures are run by this company, founded by a Mayan archaeologist. The emphasis on education.Local conservation projectsare given any donations.

Colonial and Modern Cities, Guatemala

This tour of Guatemala City and the country's former capital, Antigua, explores the country's churches, monasteries, and many other colonial monuments.

Tread Lightly
37 Juniper Meadow Rd.
Washington Depot
CT 06794
U.S.A.
☎ toll-free 1-800/643-0060
A 3-day trip with bilingual guide also a Mayan cities tour of Guatemala.

CYCLING

Whether you are cycling across country or off road, mountain biking, or taking a tour around a town, travelling by bike is a good way to enjoy the landscape and to encounter local people without polluting the environment. Most people can cycle 80km (50 miles) a day, four times the average distance that can be covered by walkers. If you go as part of a group, there is the advantage of prearranged accommodation and a vehicle is usually provided to carry your luggage. In places popular with tourists, bicycle-hire shops normally have a daily or hourly rate, but only for fixed-centre hire. If you want to take your bike with you, check that your airline doesn't charge extra; most don't as long are you are within your luggage allowance. Remember also to take a complete repair kit that includes tyres and spokes.

Cycling Touring Club
Cotterell House
69 Meadrow
Godalming
Surrey GU7 3HS
U.K.
☎ (01483) 417217
Fax: (01483) 426994
email: cycling@ctc.org.uk
website: www.ctc.org.uk
Provides members (£25 per annum; various discounts available) with information sheets for independent travel in specific countries, plus trip reports with detailed practical information. It also has details of cycling-holiday operators worldwide, and can answer other queries.

Copper Canyon, Mexico

The grandiose mountains and canyons of the Sierra Tarahumara, which surrounds the Copper Canyon, offer the perfect terrain for mountain biking, understandably a popular local activity.

Expediciones Umarike
Apartado Postal 61
Creel
Mexico
☎**/Fax:** (145) 60212
email: arturog@online.com.mx
Arranges mountain-bike day tours from Creel, plus rock climbing for beginners

and guiding for experts. The company is run by Arturo Gutierrez and his Welsh wife, Audrey Hill. Basic mountain-bike and tent rental is also available.

Pantera Excursiones
Durango
Mexico
☎ (18) 250682
email: pantera@omanet.com.mx
website: www.aventurapantera.com.mx
One of the pioneering adventure companies operating in northern Mexico. It organizes 4-day mountain-bike expeditions on a little-known route from Basaseachi to Divisadero. The company has a strong environmental consciousness whether its clients are biking, hiking, or just camping in the desert.

Sierra Madre, Mexico

A trip that crosses the most important mountain complex in the country, taking in huge cactus forests, ancient sites, the colonial city of Oaxaca, and a beach resort. As the tour follows dirt and gravel roads, it is best suited to experienced off-road riders, while the long climbs require above-average levels of fitness.

Exodus
9 Weir Rd.
London SW12 OLT
U.K.
☎ (020) 8675 5550
Fax: (020) 8673 0779
email: sales@exodustravels.co.uk
website: www.exodustravels.co.uk
A 12-night trip with hotel accommodation and camping, and with English-speaking Mexican guides.

Trujillo, Honduras

The country's former capital, Trujillo, is an attractive coastal town in the north. There are good beaches and a national park near by.

Turtle Tours
Hotel Villa Brinkley
Trujillo
Honduras
☎/Fax: 434 4431
email: ttours@hondutel.hn
In the U.S.:
Rd. 3
Parker
PA 16049
U.S.A.
☎ 412/791-2273
Day rental of bikes, along with week-long motorbike tours to Río Plátano, a jungle area with wildlife and archaeological sites.

Lake Arenal and Nicoya Peninsula, Costa Rica

From the volcano and hot springs at Lake Arenal, this trip takes you through rain forest to the hummingbirds and orchids of the Monteverde Cloud Forest Reserve and the banks of the Tempisque River, before ending at the beaches of the Nicoya Peninsula.

Backroads
801 Cedar St.
Berkeley
CA 94710
U.S.A.
☎ 510/527-1555 or toll-free 1-800/462-2848
An 8-day trip from San José, with some riding on dirt roads. The company was founded in 1979, and all tours offered (which include snorkelling, riding, and rafting options) carry a difficulty rating.

Coast to Coast Adventures
See page 294.
The Paddles & Pedals trip combines 4 days of kayaking and biking in Nicoya with 2 days' rafting on the Pacuare (see page 309). Regular group depatures throughout the year, with prices around $1,400 for 8 nights, including local transport, good hotels or comfortable camps, specialist equipment, and guides.

DIVING

With two long coastlines, the world's second largest reef system, and some of the cheapest diving to be had anywhere, the region is rated highly by divers. If you have never dived before it is a good idea to take a basic certification course at a sub-aqua club before you leave home, taking evidence of certification with you. However, most operators offer a certification course at the dive site. Bear in mind that diving presents particular dangers if you are inexperienced, and that the cheapest operator is not necessarily the safest. Large groups and badly maintained equipment may be features of cost-cutting outfits. Always check equipment before embarking on a dive, look at the instructor's dive book to confirm his or her experience, and make sure he or she has a valid instructor's card. If you are a novice, or have children, you may want to consider snorkelling instead.

British Sub Aqua Club (BSAC)

Telford Quay
Ellesmere Port
South Wirral
Cheshire L65 4FY
U.K.
☎ (0151) 350 6200 **Fax:** (0151) 350 6215
website: www.bsac.com
Offers information about diving abroad, and runs dive courses in the U.K.

National Association of Underwater Instructors (NAUI)

NAUI Worldwide
9942 Currie Davis Dr., Ste. H
Tampa
FL 33619-2667
U.S.A.
☎ 813/628-6284 or toll-free 1-800/553-6284
Fax: 813/628-8253
website: www.naui.org
Provides training and certification to high standards.

Professional Association of Diving Instructors (PADI)

PADI International Ltd.
Unit 7
St. Philips Central
Albert Rd.
St. Philips
Bristol BS2 0PD
U.K.
☎ (0117) 300 7234 **Fax:** (0117) 971 0400
website: www.padi.com
PADI certifies 55 per cent of all divers worldwide, and is recognized for its promotion of safety and training supervision.

Baja California, Mexico

The exceptional marine life found in abundance around the unspoiled islands of the Gulf of California makes Baja northern Mexico's best site for diving and snorkelling.

Baja Expeditions

2625 Garnet Ave.
San Diego
CA 92109
U.S.A.
☎ 619/581-3311 **Fax:** 619/581-6542
email: travel@bajaex.com
website: www.bajaex.com
This established U.S.-based company operates upmarket diving, snorkelling, and whale-watching tours. It has its own luxury dive boats and adventure camps.

Puerto Vallarta, Mexico

The Islas Marietas, at the northern end of the Bahía de Banderas, are much favoured by scuba-divers for their vertiginous drop-offs. The bay offers exceptional underwater life and a national marine park at Los Arcos, which, along with other spectacular formations, attract divers and snorkellers alike.

Chico's Dive Shop

Díaz Ordáz 722
Puerto Vallarta
Mexico
☎ (322) 21895 or (322) 25439
Fax: (322) 21897
email: chicoss@acnet.net
website: www.chicos-diveshop.com
A well-established dive shop offering daily trips to Los Arcos, Las Marietas, and El Morro, plus snorkelling and scuba-diving lessons (PADI).

Cozumel, Mexico

The island of Cozumel, on the Yucatán Peninsula, has a variety of drift (where there is a current) diving spots. There are certified resort courses, and a number of dive packages is available.

Ecotour Caraibe

C 1 Sur, between Aves. 5 and 10
Cozumel
Mexico
Small groups are led by reputable guides on diving tours that vary in length.

Belize Cays, Belize

Over 200 cays are sprinkled along 250km (155 miles) of Belize's waters in a natural wonder that rivals Australia's Barrier Reef. Many easily accessible sites can be dived on half- or full-day excursions, or you can head out to the atoll reefs to the east of the barrier reef (Turneffe, Glover's, and Lighthouse) for 2- or 3-day trips that involve sleeping on board the dive boat or camping on the atolls.

Blue Crab Resort

Seine Bight village
Placenica Peninsula
Belize
☎ (6) 23544 **Fax:** (6) 23543
email: kerry@btl.net
This local specialist offers diving trips from Placencia out to the barrier reef lasting 1–4 days, with hotel, cabana, or camping accommodation. Snorkelling options are also available.

Blue Hole Dive Centre

Ambergris Caye
Belize
☎ (26) 2982
email: bluehole@btl.net
Two-day tours to Turneffe Islands, Lighthouse Reef, and the Blue Hole; accommodation on board or in tents.

Coral Beach Hotel and Dive Club

Ambergris Caye
Belize
☎ (26) 2817 or (26) 2013
Fax: (26) 2864
email: forman@btl.net
Arranges trips to the atoll reefs lasting 1, 2, and 3 nights on the live-aboard *Offshore Express* dive boat. Prices are from about $250 for 2 full days' diving, up to $500 for 4 full days (includes all meals, drinks,and accommodation and diving).

Fantasea

P.O. Box 32
San Pedro
Ambergris Caye
Belize
☎/**Fax:** (26) 2576
email: fantasea@btl.net
website: www.ambergriscaye.com/fantasea/index.html
Two-tank local barrier reef dives, single-tank dives, and single-tank night dives . Also PADI Open Water Certification and open water referral.

Gaz Cooper's Dive Belize

Sunbreeze Beachfront
San Pedro
Ambergris Caye
Belize
☎ (26) 3202
fax (U.S. office): 954/351-9740
email: gaz@btl.net
website: www.divebelize.com
Two-tank local barrier reef dives, single-tank dives , and single-tank night dives . Also day trips to the Blue Hole (about $130) and to Turneffe (about $150).

Larry Parker's Reef Divers Ltd.

6D Royal Palm Villas
San Pedro
Ambergris Caye
Belize
☎ (26) 3134 **Fax:** (26) 2943
email: larry@reefdivers.com
website: www.reefdivers.com
Reef Divers has had more than 19 years' experience of diving the waters of Belize, and as such has earned the title "The best and most professional dive shop" in the country. There are both NAUI Nitrox- and PADI-trained instructors, and Larry Parker, the owner and operator, is a world-class NAUI Instructor Trainer. Snorkelling at Hol Chan and Shark-Ray Alley. Full 4-day, all-inclusive certificate courses costs about $400.

Bay Islands, Honduras

The Bay Islands, a 20-minute flight from Honduras's north-coast town of La Ceiba, are a continuation of the Belize barrier reef. Their rich underwater environment, with stunning coral formations, caves, and caverns, combined with excellent visibility, attracts divers and snorkellers from around the world.

Sueño del Mar Dive Center

West End
Roatán
Islas de la Bahía
Honduras
☎/**Fax:** 445 1717 or U.S. toll-free 1-800/298-9009
email: suenodelmar@globalnet.hn

One of the most popular dive operators on the island, spectacularly situated at the end of a jetty in West End (below the bar). Runs three dives a day to numerous locations including the *El Aguila* wreck, returning to base between dives, so it is possible to join for just the second or third dive. The instructors are all professionals and the dive boats well equipped, and there is a good dive shop selling equipment and souvenirs. Single dives with all equipment cost about $30 wuth special deals for up to ten dives. PADI Open Water Certification courses cost about $180. Other courses are also available. Sueño del Mar also rents out sea kayaks, and snorkel gear—mask, fins, and snorkel. It can arrange accommodation, with generous discounts for those who book dive/accommodation packages.

West Bay Dive Resort
West Bay
Roatán
Islas de la Bahía
Honduras
Fax: 445 1925
email: westbaylodge@globalnet.hn
website: www.stic.net/roatan/westbaylodge
The ideal location for mixing an adventurous diving holiday with a relaxing vacation. Situated overlooking the idyllic West Bay Beach, with fantastic snorkelling opportunities, this dive resort offers a personal and friendly service. It is owned by Maren and Reinhard Gnielka, who run PADI Certification courses and offer accommodation. Single dives cost $30 with all equipment and special deals for ten dives. Six-night PADI Open Water Course and accommodation packages cost about $400 for one person or $600 for two (sharing a cabin). Seven nights' accommodation, ten boat dives, and one night dive costs about $450/$650. Package rates include breakfast but exclude tax. Maren is a professional masseur, too, if you fancy the ultimate relaxing break. (Note that at the time of writing there is no phone and the email address is a message service, so it may take 2–3 days to get a response.)

Osa Peninsula, Costa Rica

Diving is possible from either resorts or lodges on the Osa Peninsula and nearby Nicoya Peninsula. For the experienced, hammerhead sharks can be observed offshore near the Pacific island of Coco.

Reef and Rainforest Tours
See page 296.

Bocas del Toro, Panama

Bocas del Toro, in the southeast of Isla Colón (off Panama'a northwest coast) is also the name of the archipelago. It has a lovely bay with good diving and snorkelling. Trips can be combined with jungle walks and sailing excursions.

Mangrove Inn Eco Dive Resort
Mangrove Roots Shop
Calle 3
Bocas del Toro
Panama
☎/Fax: 757 9594
email: manginn@usa.net
website: www.bocas.com
Tank diving is offered, and snorkelling and diving equipment is available for hire.

FISHING

The northern Caribbean is known for its tarpon and snook, while the Pacific coast is famous for record-breaking catches of sailfish, marlin, dorado, and tuna. The Costa Rican government strongly believes in the preservation of its fishing resources, and encourages the release of all billfish and non-edible fish. Belize has restrictions on fishing for lobster, shrimp, and conch according to season. Make sure you are aware of any such restricions and seasonal variations. Check what tackle is provided on organized trips; you may want to take your own equipment or a travel rod. When travelling outside an organized group, ensure that you have a valid licence—information on requirements can normally be obtained from tourist offices. You can arrange to have your catch sent home with you.

Cozumel, Mexico

Light-tackle enthusiasts can fish this island off the Yucatán for a variety of inshore and offshore species, such as bonefish, sailfish, and marlin. There is also excellent diving and wildlife-watching, plus numerous archaeological sites to visit.

Cutting Loose Expeditions
P.O. Box 447
Winter Park
FL 32790-0447
U.S.A.
☎ 407/629-4700 **Fax:** 407/740-7816
email: ucutloos@aol.com
Tailor-made, specialist fishing trips are offered throughout Central America.

Belize Cays, Belize

The flats offer fishing for bonefish, while the sea is full of gamefish such as sailfish and barracuda. There is permit and tarpon fishing throughout the cays.

Quest Global Angling Adventures
3595 Canton Hwy.
Suite C-11 Marietta
GA 30066
U.S.A.
☎ 770/971-8586 or toll-free 1-888/891-3474
Fax: 770/977-3095
email: questhook@aol.com
This specialist runs an 8-day trip with accommodation on Turneffe Atoll, plus other fishing trips worldwide.

Sea Masters Company Ltd.
P.O. Box 59
Belize City
Belize
☎ (2) 33185 **Fax:** (2) 62028
Specializes in fishing trips, and also runs diving trips in Belize.

Arenal, Costa Rica

An attractive artifically created lake lies in the shadow of the Arenal Volcano, which has three active craters. In the northwest, both the volcano and lake form a large national park, where there is good walking, horse riding, and superb bird-watching.

Rainbow Bass Fishing Safaris
P.O. Box 7758 1000
San José
Costa Rica
☎ 229 2550 **Fax:** 235 7662
Arranges day trips and fishing licences.

Río Chico, Costa Rica

This rainforest area offers the opportunity for lake, river, and ocean fishing. Tarpon, trophy snook, and rainbow bass are just some of the possible catches, and you have a houseboat as your base and accommodation.

Quest Global Angling Adventures
See above.
This specialist runs a 5-day trip with houseboat accommodation on Río Chico.

Coiba, Panama

This island off Panama's Pacific coast forms a national park and provides good year-round angling for black marlin, tuna, sailfish, wahoo, and roosterfish.

Trek International Safaris
1503 The Greens Way
Jacksonville
FL 32250
U.S.A.
☎ 904/273-7800 or toll-free 1-800/654-9915
Fax: 904/273-0096
email: trek@treksafaris.com
website: treksafaris.com
The company has been operating in Central America for over 20 years. Accommodation is in a floating lodge, and the use of an 8m (26ft) boat can be arranged on Coiba.

HORSE RIDING

Travelling on horseback allows full appreciation of the region's varied landscape, and means that up to 30km (20 miles) can be covered each day. You may choose a trip based at a centre, returning to the accommodation each night. If you decide to set off for a week or more, accommodation is usually in comfortable ranches, or in tents where you eat and socialize around a campfire. For the overnight trips previous experience may be required, but many operators are happy to take novices and children. Be prepared for saddles that differ in shape from those at home, and horses that are a little on the wild side. Wear shoes or boots with a 5cm (2in) heel as this will stop your foot slipping out of the stirrup.

Oaxaca, Mexico

Escape the traffic and pollution of Oaxaca City by taking a trek in the Sierra Madre mountains or to the Zapotec city of Monte Albán.

San Felipe Riding Club
Apartado 252 Oaxaca
Oaxaca
Mexico 68000
☎ (955) 56864
email: french@antequera.com
This friendly American operator provides half- and full-day rides into the Sierra Madre mountains surrounding Oaxaca, and a 2-day ride to Monte Albán. Prices start from around $20 for a half-day ride, which includes hotel pick-up, experienced guide, light snacks, and samples of the owner's distinctive brand of mescal liquor.

San Cristóbal de Las Casas, Mexico

Day trips are possible from this attractive mountain town along forest trails or to the beautiful church in the village of Chamula. (Check on safety before visiting nearby villages as assaults on tourists have occurred in the past.)

Bar La Galería
Hidalgo 3
San Cristóbal de Las Casas
Mexico
☎ (8) 81547
Daily horse rental, with English-speaking guides, can be arranged.

Mayan Jungle, Belize

This tour passes through a region of Mennonite farmland, rain forest, and river valleys, and takes you to waterfalls, the Mayan ruins of Xunantunich and Cahal Pech, and spectacular caves with limestone formations.

Equitour
P.O. Box 807
Dubois
WY 82513
U.S.A.
☎ 307/455-3363 or toll-free 1-800/545-0019
Fax: 307/455-2354
website: www.ridingtours.com
A 6-day trip from Belize City, open to riders of all abilities. Riding tours throughout the world are also available.

Atitlán, Guatemala

From the head of the lake inlet on which sits the town of Santiago Atitlán, a lush cloud forest rises up to a *mirador*, or lookout point, with views to the Pacific.

Los Caballos
Jim and Nancy Matison
Finca San Santiago
Santiago Atitlán
Guatemala
☎ (201) 5527
This ranch was established in 1995 and now has 11 horses. In the high season there is a choice of four horse rides, including either breakfast, lunch, cocktails, or dinner. Accompanied hikes can also be arranged.

Chacocente Wildlife Refuge, Nicaragua

The turtle sanctuary along the Río Escalante contains the largest tract of unspoiled dry tropical forest in Nicaragua. Access is possible only via four-wheel drive or on horseback.

Ecotourism International de Nicaragua S.A.
See page 292.
Environmentally sensitive nature and wildlife tours are available throughout the country.

Guanacaste, Costa Rica

A trail along the Pacific coast through this sparsely populated province follows a mountain range, taking you across beaches and through a wildlife-filled landscape.

Cross Country International
P.O. Box 1170
Millbrook
NY 12545
U.S.A.
☎ toll-free 1-800/828-8768
Fax: 914/677-6077
A 5-day trip (November–May) open to non-riders, with guides who have a good knowledge of the local area.

OVERLAND TOURS

The contemporary equivalent of the Grand Tour allows you to take in highlights from several countries in a limited amount of time. Areas that are often otherwise inaccessible can be explored using four-wheel-drive vehicles. Any number of forms of transport may be used, but accommodation is usually in fairly comfortable hotels. Packages, which often involve a complex itinerary, can usually be tailor-made to suit your requirements. A bilingual guide will accompany the group at all times. Before committing yourself, check the number of particpants (many trips can be taken with just two people), the standard of accommodation, and what is included in the price in terms of food, entry fees, and internal flights.

Mexico, Belize, and Guatemala

From the Yucatán's resort of Cancun down to Belize's offshore cays, this tour takes in Caribbean beaches, varied rainforest wildlife, and the ancient site of Tikal before reaching Guatemala City.

The Imaginative Traveller
14 Barley Mow Passage
Chiswick
London W4 4PH
U.K.
☎ (020) 8742 8612 **Fax:** (020) 8742 3045
email: info@imaginative-traveller.com
website: www.imaginative-traveller.com
A 9-day trip with hotel accommodation can be arranged, along with tailor-made options and overland trips through Central America.

Cancun, Mexico, to San José, Costa Rica

This tour travels through six Central American countries, with scenery ranging from Caribbean beaches to dense jungle, and includes visits to ancient sites and wildlife reserves.

Guerba Expeditions
Wessex House
40 Station Rd.
Westbury
Wiltshire BA13 3JN
U.K.
☎ (01373) 826611 **Fax:** (01373) 858351
A 29-day trip with hotel accommodation, and using buses and local flights. Hiking, rafting, and horseriding options.

Darién Gap, Panama

The jungle between Panama and Colombia is one of the world's great wilderness areas, with no roads and rugged terrain. This can be a gruelling trip, and is only possible in the dry season (January–April). If you travel here independently, check which danger areas to avoid before you set off, hire a reputable Indian guide, and go with at least one other travelling companion. It is also vital that you get an entry stamp for Colombia in advance.

Wildland Adventures
See page 292.
A 14-day trip tracing the footsteps of the Spanish conquistadors, with three guides who reflect the cultures of the area. A variety of tours in Central America, including most activities, is also available.

PARAGLIDING

Atitlán, Guatemala

Tandem glides are offered with a trained para-glider. There are no glides during the rainy season, but otherwise they are arranged every morning in time to exploit the first winds as they pick up.

Servicious Turísticos de Atitlán
See page 295.
Rates for half-hour and full-hour glides included transport to the cliff edge above Santa Catarina Palopó.

SURFING

The Pacific coast offers surfing on long point breaks, river mouths, and beach breaks from March to November. Serious surfers hit the Atlantic coast between December and March, where deepwater waves break over the shallow reef in an imitation of Hawaiian surf. It is possible to hire boards at certain sites, but as few places have wetsuits you may want to take your own. Familiarize yourself with any local hazards, such as stong currents and undertows. There may be local restictions on surfing at swimming beaches, nature reserves, and on waters used by ships and smaller craft.

Surfer Publications
P.O. Box 1028
Dana Point
CA 92629
U.S.A.
☎ 714/496-5922
Fax: 714/496-7849
Publishes the *Journal of International Surfing Destinations*. A list of destinations is available on request, and trip reports of interest can be ordered for a fee.

Zunzal, El Salvador

Zunzal beach, south of San Salvador, is the site of international professional surfing competitions. The season runs from November to April, but be aware of dangerous currents and the threat of sharks. The neighbouring resort of La Libertad also has excellent surfing.

Amphibious
Centro Comercial Plaza San Benito
Calle La Reforma 114
Local 1-16, San Salvador
El Salvador
☎/Fax: 335 3261
Surfboards can be rented on a daily basis. Kayak rental and windsurf lessons can also be arranged.

San Juan del Sur, Nicaragua

The tranquil half-moon bay of San Juan del Sur on the Pacific coast has consistent waves and well-known breaks such as San Martín and Poypoyo.

Tours Nicaragua
See page 292.
Organizes a 6-day trip with guide and boat to take you to the biggest breaks. Also arranges other tours in Nicaragua.

Jacó, Costa Rica

This is a popular beach resort on the central Pacific coast, with good facilities for renting boards. To the south, at Playa Hermosa, there is an annual professional surfing competition. Hotels may offer a discount to surfers.

Playa de Jacó
Puntarenas CR
Apartado #43
Jacó Garabito
Costa Rica
☎/Fax: 643 3328
email: chuck@surfoutfitters.com
website: chucks@sol.racsa.co.cr
A local company specializing in surfing holidays; also offers tailor-made tours with other activities, such as fishing and walking.

Guanacaste, Costa Rica

This region, in the northwest corner of Costa Rica, has prime surf spots such as Tamarindo and Playa Nosara, both of which have excellent breaks, as well as swimming and snorkelling opportunities. Playa Naranjo also offers good tube rides.

Worldwide Adventures
1301 S. Patrick Dr., Ste. 67
Satellite Beach
FL 32937
U.S.A.
☎ 407/773-4878 or toll-free 1-800/796-9110
Fax: 407/773-4214
email: surfer@surfingadventures.com
website: www.worldwideadventures.com
"Follow the surf" programmes in Costa Rica and El Salvador, with a choice of hotels on the beaches with the best breaks. Also organizes diving, fishing, and eco-tours, and arranges surfing and diving packages specifically tailored for families.

TREKKING

Central America's scenic trails, national parks, and remote wilderness areas provide almost limitless hiking opportunities through varied landscapes. However, mountain regions in particular are susceptible to extreme weather changes, and you will need to be prepared for both sunburn and frostbite. Remote areas present other dangers in the form of thefts and attacks. Volcanoes are particularly risky areas, making group travel with a guide a sensible option. If you are embarking on an independent trekking trip, make sure you have accurate, up-to-date maps. The South America

Explorers' Club (see Climbing on page 295) can provide maps, lists of guides, and travel planning information, and tourist offices can usually help with information for shorter walks.

Sierra Madre, Mexico

A trek from the highlands down to the southern section of one of the most impressive sierras in the country, passing through remote villages and jungle before arriving at the Pacific Ocean. Climbs of up to 1,000m (3,300 feet) are involved.

Explore Worldwide

See page 292.
A 14-day trip from Mexico City. The company specializes in small group exploratory holidays, including a rainforest adventure in Costa Rica, and a "Beneath the Volcanoes" tour of Nicaragua.

Petén, Guatemala

The dense forest of the Petén is famous for its Mayan ruins and for the variety of its birdlife. The Scarlet Macaw Trail is a 5-day trip through the macaw's main breeding area from Centro Campesino to Laguna del Tigre National Park.

Avinsa

Calle Principal
Santa Elen
Guatemala
☎ (926) 0808
Fax: (926) 0807
email: avinsa@guate.net
website: www.avinsa.com
Follow the Scarlet Macaw Trail, take a 5-day trek to El Mirador (overnight stops at local *chiclero* camps), head overland to Palenque by road and boat, or try whitewater rafting or horse riding. English, German, and French spoken.

Ecomaya

Calle 30 de junio
Flores
Guatemala
☎/Fax: (926) 1363
email: ecomaya@guate.net
Offers 2- to 6-day adventure tours along the Scarlet Macaw Trail, to El Mirador, or to Tikal; fairly rudimentary comforts (you sleep in hammocks).

Monkey Eco Tours

Ni'tun Ecolodge
San Andrés
Guatemala
☎ (201) 0759 or (201) 2028
Fax: (926) 0807
email: avinsa@guate.net
Exceptionally well-organized camping tours and treks to lesser-known Mayan sites in the Petén and Chiapas (Mexico). Excellent food, comfortable tents, and even portable showers!

Mosquitia, Honduras

The remote Mosquitia region of northeast Honduras is characterized by an almost complete lack of roads. Even with the increase in interest in adventure travel, the area remains little visited.

Adventure Expeditions

1020 Altos de la Hoya
Tegucigalpa
Honduras
☎/Fax: 237 4793
email: cyber-place@hotmail.com
Adventure Expeditions specializes in trips to Mosquitia, and can tailor-make tours to all parts of the region.

MC Tours

Col. Trejo
10 Calle 18 Ave. S.O. #235
2 cuadras arriba de la Cámara de Comercio e Industrias de Cortés
San Pedro Sula
Honduras
☎ 552 4455 **Fax:** 557 3076
email: mctours@netsys.hn
website: www.netsys.hn/~mctours
One of Honduras's leading operators, specializing in more upmarket tours. Runs 5- and 6-day trips to Mosquitia, with professional bilingual guides.

La Moskitia Ecoaventuras

Ave. 14 de Julio
Casa #125
P.O. Box 890
La Ceiba
Honduras
☎ 221 0404 **Fax:** 442 0104
email: moskitia@tropicohn.com
A friendly, professional company run by Jorge Salavari, who speaks fluent English. Highly recommended specialists

in tours to Mosquitia. There are several itineraries to the region, including an epic 10–12-day rafting/jungle-trekking trip on the Río Plátano for serious adventurers; the company can also tailor-make tours.

Talamanca Mountains to Osa Peninsula, Costa Rica

Travel from the central mountains of Talamanca to the tropical jungle of the Osa Peninsula by car and boat. Half-day hikes are scheduled alongside wildlife-watching and visits to nature reserves and beaches.

Roads Less Traveled
2840 Wilderness Place
#F Boulder
CO 80301
U.S.A.
☎ 303/413-0938 or toll-free 1-800/488-8483
Fax: 303/413-0926
email: fun@roadslesstraveled.com
An 8-day trip from San José. Multi-activity tours that include biking, hiking, and rafting in off-road locations in Belize are open to all ages. Speciality trips such as women-only, singles, and teens are also available.

Volcán Barú, Panama

See page 295.

WHITEWATER RAFTING

River rafting offers the enjoyment of white water without any need for experience or knowledge of techniques, unlike canoeing (see page 293). It is an exhilarating activity that can take you through remote scenic river areas, but is possibly only during the rainy season. Trips may include paddle rafting, where all members of the group use their paddles to steer, or oar boating, when the guide directs the raft alone. Rivers are graded internationally from I (slow-moving current) to VI (the fastest white water, suitable only for professionals); see box on page 220. Check if there are any fitness requirements for tours, and take waterproofs (helmets and safety equipment will normally be provided by any reputable company).

Veracruz, Mexico

There are five raftable rivers in Veracruz, graded from Class II to Class V; the season depends on the river you choose (see box on page 56).

Intercontinental Adventures
Homero 526
Officina 801
Mexico City
Mexico
☎/Fax: (5) 255 4400 or (5) 255 446
email: adventur@mpsnet.com.mx
website: www.rafting-mexico.com.mx
This Mexico City agency represents the country's longest-established rafting company, Expediciones Mexico Verde, and can arrange your trip to Veracruz. It also specializes in adventure activities within easy reach of the capital, such as mountain biking around Cuernavaca, ballooning in Guanajuato and Malinalco, para-gliding in Ixtapa, kayaking lessons in Cuernavaca, sea-kayaking in Veracruz, and climbing on Iztaccihuatl volcano.

Río y Montaña
Prado Norte 450
Colonia Lomas de Chapultepec
Mexico City
Mexico
☎/Fax: (5) 520 2041 **Fax:** (5) 540 7870
email: rioymontana@compuserve.com.mx
Activities on offer include whitewater rafting and mountain climbing.

Veraventuras
Santos Degollado 81–8
Xalapa
Mexico
☎ (28) 189579 or (28) 189779
Fax: (28) 189680
email: veraventuras@yahoo.com
A small rafting company that operates on the Pescados, Antigua, and Actopan rivers. It also offers camping facilities and scuba-diving. English is spoken.

Piedras Negras, Guatemala

This important Mayan site, on a cliff overlooking the river, is accessible only on a rafting tour, which includes presentations by archaeologists. Although the waters are generally calm, there are some sections of rapids.

Maya Expeditions
C 15 1-91
Zona 10
Oficina 104
Guatemala City
Guatemala
☎ (2) 363 4955 **Fax:** (2) 337 4666
email: mayaexp@guate.net
This official operator for the site can arrange a 2-week expedition (advance booking is essential).

Río Cangrejal, Honduras

This attractive river, in the north of the country, has Class III and IV rapids and passes through woodland. There are also fishing opportunities.

EuroHonduras Tours
Edif. Hospital Euro Honduras
Maternidad Centro Médico
Primera Calle
La Ceiba
Honduras
☎/Fax: 443 0933
email: eurohonduras@caribe.hn
English, Spanish, German, and French are spoken at this family-run business, which offers city and other tours in Honduras in small groups.

Río Pacuare, Costa Rica

San José, the country's capital and located at its centre, is the starting point for a number of whitewater rafting trips. Río Pacuare is particularly attractive.

Coast to Coast Adventures
See page 294.
Arranges 1- and 2-day rafting trips on the Pacuare, with overnight stays at the beautiful Nido del Tigre river camp. Friendly, knowledgeable guides and small group numbers make the wilderness trips both intimate and fun. Prices are around $100 for 1-day rafting trips and $250 for 2-day trips (this includes all local transport, food, accommodation, guides, and specialist equipment). The Paddles & Pedals tour combines Pacuare rafting with kayaking and biking in the Nicoya Peninsula (see page 298).

Costa Rica White Water
P.O. Box 6941-1000
San José
Costa Rica
☎ 257 0766 **Fax:** 257 1665
email: crexped@sol.racsa.co.cr
website: crexped.co.cr
Specialist rafting company, offering a 1-day trip on the Río Pacuare and other rivers in the area.

Costa Sol Rafting
Apartado 8-4390-1000
San José
Costa Rica
☎ 293 2150 or U.S.A. and Canada toll-free 1-800/245-8420
Fax: 293 2155
A small but fun company that runs rafting trips on many of Costa Rica's rivers, including the Pacuare. Prices are similar to those of Coast to Coast.

Ríos Tropicales
Ave. 2
Calle 32
San José
Costa Rica
☎ 233 6455
Fax: 255 4354
email: info@riostro.com
website: www.riostro.com
The biggest rafting company in the country, running 1- and 2-day trips on all the major rivers. Their Pacuare trips are large affairs with many boats and overnight stays in the company's own river camp. Prices are similar to those of Coast to Coast Adventures (see above).

Río Chiriqui, Panama

Whitewater rafting trips on the Río Chiriqui in a rural area known as "El Interior" start from Caldera, near Boquete.

Chiriqui River Rafting
Entrega General
Boquete-Chiriquí
Panama
☎ 720 1505 **Fax:** 720 1506
email: rafting@panama-rafting.com
website: www.panama-rafting.com
A family-run company with bilingual guides who lead half-day rafting trips on rapids that range from Class II to "serious" Class IV. Some sections are run only during the rainy season (May–mid-December).

WILDLIFE SAFARIS

With creatures ranging from white-faced monkeys to green sea turtles, and the world's only jaguar reserve, biologically diverse Central America supports a huge range of wildlife. You may be lucky enough to get sightings of animals as you travel around, but a specialist tour lasting a minimum of three days is usually suggested. During the dry season creatures are more visible as they come out to look for water; the other advantage is that there are fewer insects at this time. Wildlife reserves and national parks may have conservation programmes to encourage population growth and to protect local fauna, but local awareness is not always as it should be. Do not interfere directly with wildlife, do not leave litter, and do not participate in any tour that includes hunting.

Baja California, Mexico

Between January and March grey whales (*Eschrichtius robustus*) congregate off Baja to mate. They can be seen in particular at Laguna San Ignacio, Laguna Ojo de Liebre (Scammon's Lagoon), and Bahía Magdalena.

Baja Expeditions
See page 299.
This established U.S.-based company runs upmarket whale-watching tours, plus diving and snorkelling. It has its own luxury dive boats and adventure camps.

Baja Outdoor Adventures
P.O. Box 792
Centro
La Paz
Mexico
☎ (112) 55636
email: boa@cibnor.mx
website: www.kayactivities.com
Well-organized whale-watching tours in southern Baja. The group departures or customized tours suit a range of budgets. The company is owned by a Welsh canoe coach and his Baja Californian wife. Also sea-kayaking and fly-fishing tours.

Ecoturismo Kuyima
San Ignacio
Mexico
☎ (115) 40026
Fax: (115) 40070
Eduardo Sedano and José de Jésus run this whale-watching agency, based in San Ignacio. They also organize mule treks.

Malarrimo Eco-Tours
Blvd. Emiliano Zapata
Guerrero Negro
Mexico
☎ (115) 70100 or (115) 70250
email: malarimo@telnor.net
The owner of this company, Enrique Achoy, organizes whale-watching trips from his family's hotel in Guerrero Negro. Mule treks can also be arranged.

Puerto Vallarta, Mexico

The Puerto Vallarta hinterland, the sierra beyond, and the waterways of La Tovara around San Blas to the north are home to numerous unusual bird species. Offshore, Bahía de Banderas is a breeding ground and seasonal haunt (November–April) for numerous dolphins and whales.

Expediciones Cielo Abierto (Open-Air Expeditions)
Guerrero 339
Puerto Vallarta
Mexico
☎ (322) 23310
Fax: (322) 32407
email: openair@vivamexico.com
website: www.vivamexico.com
A well-organized eco-tourism agency offering whale-watching, bird-watching, snorkelling, hiking, and sea-kayaking.

Anganguero, Mexico

Swarms of brightly coloured monarch butterflies (*Danaus plexippus*) can be seen near Morelia from mid-November to mid-March before they migrate north.

Union-Castle Travel
86/87 Campden St.
London W8 7EN
U.K.
☎ (0171) 229 1411
Fax: (0171) 229 1511
email: u-ct@u-ct.co.uk
Tailor-made tours are available, as well as turtle-watching at Puerto Vallata and whale-watching on the Baja Peninsula from July to March.

Sian Ka'an Biosphere Reserve, Mexico

This reserve south of Cancún covers 526,000ha (1.3 million acres), and has tropical forest, mangrove swamp, and Caribbean barrier reef habitats that support pumas, jaguars, monkeys, and manatees.

Journey Latin America
See page 296.
Day trips are arranged to the reserve from Cancún. Accommodation can be booked in nearby cabanas. Tours can also be arranged throughout Central and South America.

San Buenaventura de Atitlán Nature Reserve, Guatemala

A 160-ha (400-acre) wildlife refuge with ½- to 1-hour self-guided nature trails (English and Spanish), as well as a butterfly sanctuary with over 500 specimens. Particularly suitable for families.

Hotel San Buenaventura
Panajachel
Guatemala
☎/**Fax:** (762) 2059
Provides information on the San Buenaventura de Atitlán Nature Reserve.

Cockscomb Basin Wildlife Sanctuary, Belize

Also known as the Jaguar Reserve, this sanctuary in the southern tropics covers 40,000ha (100,000 acres) and has jaguars, tapirs, pumas, ocelots, and 300 species of birds. There are walking trails and camping facilities.

Discovery Expeditions
126 Freetown Rd.
P.O. Box 1217
Belize City
Belize
☎ (2) 30748, (2) 30749, or (2) 31063
Fax: (2) 30750 or (2) 30263
email: info@discoverybelize.com
Daily return flights from Belize City or San Pedro (on Ambergris Caye) to the wildlife sanctuary with a guide can be booked, as can tours throughout the country.

Mila
See page 296.
Mila organizes a 9-day trip from Dangriga, including a day tour of the Cockscomb reserve, snorkelling in South Water Caye, a tour of Belize City Zoo, and a day's hiking around the Jaguar Paw resort. Also on offer are wildlife and cultural tours throughout Central America.

Cuero y Salado Wildlife Reserve, Honduras

This reserve on Honduras's north coast covers 13,225ha (32,680 acres), and is home to anteaters, boa constrictors, manatees, and a variety of birdlife. Most of the sights can be seen in a day, but overnight accommodation is available. Independent travel is possible, or you can take a 1-day tour from La Ceiba. Boat and canoe hire is available on arrival.

Fundación Cuero y Salado (FUCSA)
Apartado 674
La Ceiba
Honduras
☎/**Fax:** 443 0329
Group tours and boat reservations can be arranged, and reserve information (including accommodation) is offered.

MC Tours
See page 307.
One of Honduras's leading operators, specializing in more upmarket tours. Cuero y Salado is included as part of the 6-day Green and Blue Adventure Tour, and the company also operates a whole range of other tours to all parts of the country.

La Moskitia Ecoaventuras
See page 307.
A friendly, professional company run by Jorge Salaveri, who speaks fluent English. Highly recommended. It arranges tours to Cuero y Salado and Pico Bonito, and whitewater rafting on the superb Río Cangrejal, as well as trips to other destinations in Honduras. The company can tailor-make tours for most destinations—contact them re prices.

La Flor Wildlife Refuge, Nicaragua

This half-moon bay near the southern tip of Nicaragua is a key nesting site for the olive ridley turtle (*Lepidochelys olivacea*). As many as 5,000 turtles a night have been recorded on this beach during the egg-laying season (July–December).

Ecotourism International de Nicaragua S.A.
See page 292.

WINDSURFING

The region's huge stretch of coast and many islands make for varied windsurfing, sometimes referred to as sailboarding. Ideal conditions are strong, steady winds combined with calm water. If you are a novice, take windsurfing lessons before you go or at your destination as it can take a while to master. You may want to take a wetsuit with you to protect you from strong winds and cold water. Always wear a lifejacket, don't go out alone if possible, and make sure someone knows of your whereabouts.

International Board Sailing Association
The Race Office
P.O. Box 1439
Kings Norton
Birmingham B38 9AU
U.K.
☎/**Fax:** (0121) 628 5137
email: jim@bsa.demon.co.uk
The IBSA can advise on windsurfing courses and organizations worldwide.

Punta San Carlos, Mexico

This beach on the Baja Peninsula is a quiet spot, and offers great opportunities for wavesailing (riding the waves like a surfer, but using a windsurfer).

Solo Sports
One Technology
Ste. E305
Irvine
CA 92618
U.S.A.
☎ 949/453-1950 **Fax:** 949/453 8082
email: baja@solosports.net
website: www.solosports.net
An 8-day trip from San Diego in the company's "Baja Assault Vehicle," with accommodation in a beachfront campsite. Gear is provided or you can take your own. Also mountain-biking, surfing, fishing, snorkelling, and kayaking trips.

San Pedro, Belize

Ambergris Caye in the northern cays, with its nearby barrier reef and marine park, is primarily a diving destination but is also very popular for windsurfing. The town of San Pedro has a large number of hotels and tour operators.

Victoria House
P.O. Box 22
San Pedro
Ambergris Caye
Belize
☎ (26) 2067 or (26) 2240
Fax: (26) 2429
Good windsurfing equipment is available for hire. There is also a dive shop, and accommodation can be booked.

Tela, Honduras

A relaxing Caribbean town in the north of Honduras, with relatively uncrowded white-sand beaches. Around the town's saint day (June 13), holidaymakers flood in for a week-long party, when hotel accommodation is expensive and available only with advance booking.

Garifuna Tours
See page 294.

Lake Arenal, Costa Rica

This lake in the north of the country has consistent strong winds and warm water between May and December. Good equipment is available, although it is not cheap. There is bump and jump sailing, plus activities for non-windsurfers.

Tilawa Windsurfing Centre
Lake Arenal
Costa Rica
The centre is on the west side of the lake, which is the best side for windsurfing. There is good equipment for hire.

General Index

Gazetteer

ACKNOWLEDGEMENTS

Steve Watkins would like to thank the following for their support and advice during his work for this book:

General—Coralia Dreyfus and Ian Lord at Grupo TACA, British Airways

In Belize—Thanks to the Belize Audabon Society for supplying Latin names for the species mentioned. Thanks to Jon Hill for supplying additional text for the Waterworld chapter.

In Costa Rica—Mike Lapcevic at Coast to Coast Adventures, Instituto Costarricense de Turismo, Marenco Lodge, Hotel La Garza (La Fortuna), Gustavo Quesada, Gran Hotel, Hotel Balmoral and The Fleur de Lys Hotel (San José)
Steve Watkins explored the Nicoya Peninsula with San José-based operator Coast to Coast Adventures and flew to Costa Rica, via Mexico, with TACA Group Airlines and British Airways: rafted on the Pacuare River with San José-based operator Coast to Coast Adventure: kayaked in Tortuguero with San José-based operator Coast to Coast Adventures and flew to Costa Rica, via Mexico, with TACA Group Airlines and British Airways.

In Honduras—Kenia Lima de Zapata, Joáquin and Vince Murphy at the Instituto Hondurêo Turismo, Bayman Bay Club, Fundacion Cuero y Salado, MC Tours (SanPedro Sula), Copán Marina Hotel, Professor Oscar Cruz (Director of Copán Ruins), Hotel Honduras Maya (Tegucigalpa), Hotel Saint Anthony (San Pedro Sula) and Roberto Marin at La Moskitia Ecoaventuras (La Ceiba)
Steve Watkins flew to Honduras with Grupo TACA.He travelled to Copán with San Pedro Sula-based operator MC Tours and the Copán Marina Hotel, Copán Ruinas; travelled to Mosquitia with La Ceiba-based operator La Moskitia Eco-Adventures.

In Panama—Abilio Menédez. Steve Watkins flew to Panama with TACA Group Airlines and British Airway

---

Abbreviations for terms appearing below: (t) top; (b) bottom; (l) left; (r) right; (c) centre.

Cover acknowledgements
Front cover (t): Guy Marks
Front cover main picture: Tony Stone Images
Front cover (b): AA Photo Library/Clive Sawyer Spine: Guy Marks
Back cover (t): Image Bank
Back cover (ct) Steve Watkins
Back cover (cb): Robert Harding Picture LibraryBack cover (br): Guy Marks
All inside flap pictures: AA Photo Library/Steve Watkins

The Automobile Association wishes to thank the following photographers and libraries for their assistance in the preparation of this book.

Jan Baldwin 8 (tl); **Bruce Coleman Collection** 14(t), 15(c), 15(b), 99, 102/3, 103, 110, 195, 207, 231; **Robert Harding Picture Library** 182/3; **Pictures Colour Library** 250/1

The remaining photographs are held in the Association's own photo library (AA PHOTO LIBRARY) and were taken by the following photographers:

Fiona Dunlop 2/3, 3, 6/7, 14/5, 15(t), 18/9, 22, 22/3, 26(t), 26(b), 27, 30(t), 30(b), 30/1, 34, 35(t), 35(b), 46/7, 50/1, 54/5, 55, 58/9, 62/3, 63(t), 63(b), 66(t), 66(b), 67, 70/1, 74/5, 75, 78, 79, 82(t), 82(b), 87, 90, 91, 94, 94/5, 98; **Carl Pendle** 106/7, 107(t), 107(b), 110/1, 115, 118, 118/9, 122, 123(t), 123(b), 126(t), 126(b), 127, 166/7, 170/1, 171, 174, 175, 179, 182, 186/7, 187, 190; **Clive Sawyer** 19, 227(b); **Rick Strange** 51; **Steve Watkins** 7, 14(t), 39, 42, 43(t), 43(b), 130/1, 134(t), 134(b), 135, 139(t), 139(c), 139(b), 142/3, 142, 146, 151, 154(t), 154(b), 155, 158/9, 159(t), 159(b), 162/3, 162, 194/5, 198, 199, 202/3, 203, 206/7, 210, 211, 214, 215, 218/9, 219, 222, 223, 226/7, 227(t), 230/1, 234/5, 235, 238/9, 239, 242(t), 242(b), 243, 246/7, 254, 255.

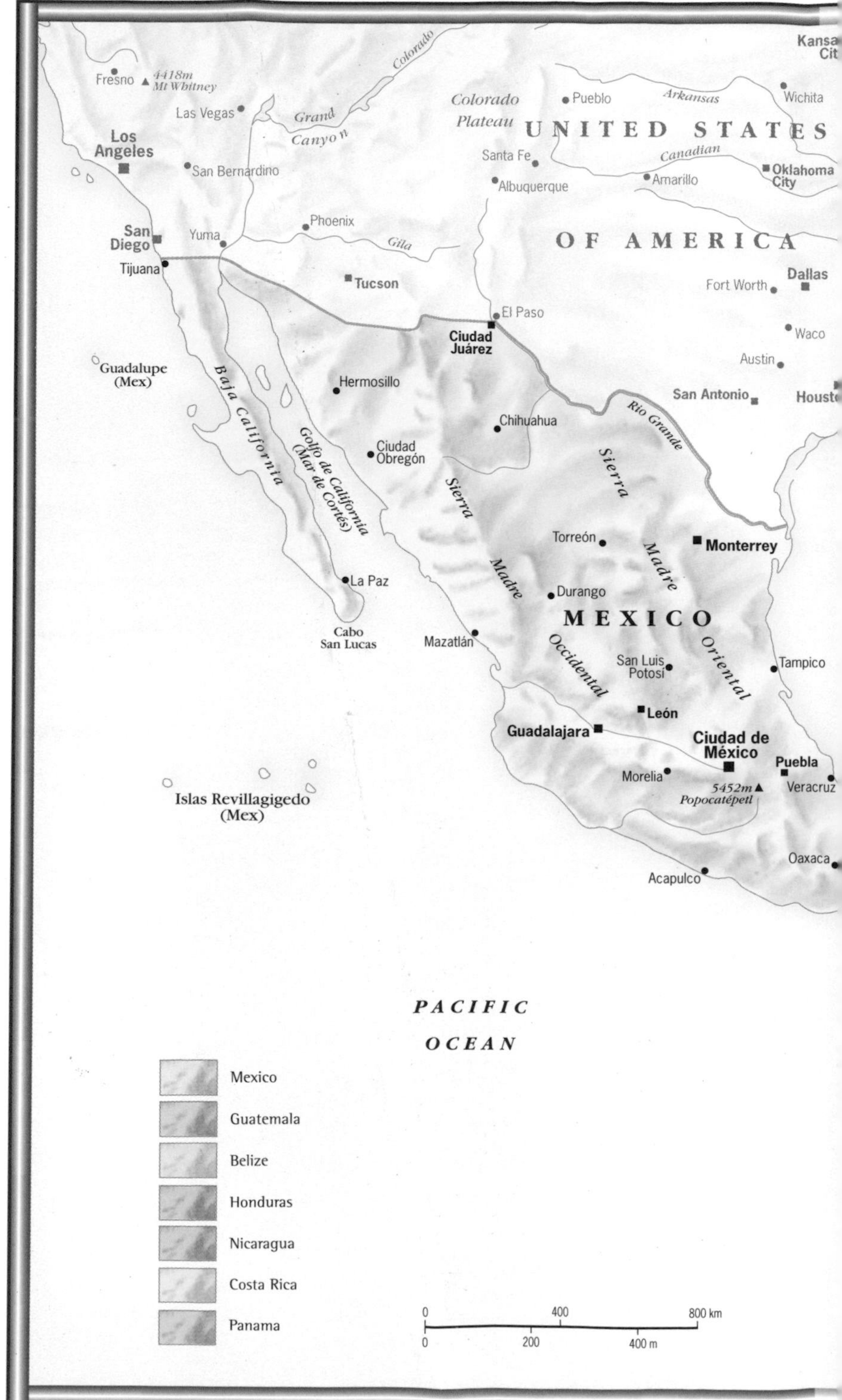
Fresno
4418m
Mt Whitney
Las Vegas
Los Angeles
San Bernardino
San Diego
Yuma
Tijuana
Colorado
Grand Canyon
Phoenix
Gila
Tucson
Colorado Plateau
Pueblo
Arkansas
Wichita
Kansas City
UNITED STATES
OF AMERICA
Santa Fe
Albuquerque
Canadian
Amarillo
Oklahoma City
Fort Worth
Dallas
El Paso
Ciudad Juárez
Waco
Austin
San Antonio
Rio Grande
Guadalupe (Mex)
Baja California
Golfo de California (Mar de Cortés)
Hermosillo
Chihuahua
Ciudad Obregón
Sierra Madre Occidental
Sierra Madre Oriental
Torreón
Monterrey
La Paz
Durango
MEXICO
Cabo San Lucas
Mazatlán
San Luis Potosí
Tampico
León
Guadalajara
Ciudad de México
Puebla
Morelia
5452m
Popocatépetl
Veracruz
Islas Revillagigedo (Mex)
Oaxaca
Acapulco
PACIFIC OCEAN
Mexico
Guatemala
Belize
Honduras
Nicaragua
Costa Rica
Panama
0
400
800 km
0
200
400 m